THROUGH OUR FATHERS EYES

Saladin Shabazz-Allah

authorHOUSE®

AuthorHouse™
1663 Liberty Drive
Bloomington, IN 47403
www.authorhouse.com
Phone: 833-262-8899

Published by AuthorHouse   07/31/2020

ISBN: 978-1-7283-6860-3 (sc)
ISBN: 978-1-7283-6859-7 (e)

Library of Congress Control Number: 2020913816

Print information available on the last page.

Black men have been completely cut out of this American Society with very little hope, of ever becoming viable. For us to regain our self-respect we must separate ourselves from everything that's in, opposition to our rise as people also as Black men.

This society, government also people have failed black men as well as black people completely. This society, government also people will continue to fail black men as well as black people. We have been going about things wrong black people; we have been looking at things through the eyes of open enemies. We have been using the methods also approach that our enemies set up for us, knowing that this will only bring about the complete destruction of black men, as well as black people.

Look throughout America my brothers look at your fate for looking, also approaching your life, through the eyes of the enemies that work day also night, in destroying us all. Examine how you have accomplished absolutely nothing in regaining your heritage thus you aren't able to provide a haven for our women our children as well as our seniors amongst us. Look my brothers everywhere throughout America black men young as well as old are being murdered or imprisoned, by our enemies. Look my brothers everywhere throughout America black men families are being ripped away from them; in many cases children don't know their fathers, in many cases they have no love for their fathers.

We must take a completely new as well as different approach my brothers as well as black people. We must begin to turn back to our fathers; not the enemies of our fathers. Through Our Fathers Eyes we must search for how we can best accomplish this task as we weld ourselves together, as one people. I pray that Allah our Holy Savior in the person of Master Fard Muhammad, to whom all holy praises are due forever; guide me through this undertaking. I thank Allah for raising up from amongst us His last also greatest Messenger the Most Honorable Elijah Muhammad/Muhammad RasulAllah.

INTRODUCTION

Once again, I must let everyone know that I couldn't do this work without the help also input of my brothers also sister. This is a great task in which many things must be covered this is such a great feat here in America no one person can do this by his or herself. I'm thankful to Allah to have my brothers at my side always in these undertakings. My brothers also sister have been my constant companions always bring to me wise advisement, information, technical skills as well as just company. Their presence is worth its weight in platinum. I forever extend my thanks also appreciation to them all they believed in what I began doing from the very beginning to the very end.

The world around us is being destroy there is absolutely nothing anyone can do to stop or advert this most deadly destruction, that is here. You read about these deadly plagues that will overtake this world my people, well these plagues are here. All the insanity that is taking place in America as well as throughout the world are the plagues sent upon this world also society, by Allah Almighty Himself. One Hundred Percent Dissatisfaction rules today times; one hundred percent insanity rules today's times. President Trump is totally insane and a pure insane Nazi thus a complete change is taking place so my people, we must look at things differently. We must have a different view of everything happening around us. We can no longer afford to walk around blindly not knowing or understanding what's really happening.

The enemies have absolutely no answers to what's happening they will only lie to us, as they all have done as well as continue to do. Our enemies my people it matters not what our enemies call themselves or what religion they may ascribe to; they are all here to support Americas along with her allies; their new version of White Supremacy as well as White Nationalism. Don't be fool my people by President Trumps Speech he is a liar, they have absolutely no solution, also they can't win any war ever again; their time is up. The reason why they have no solution is due to their time being up. In the Holy Quran and the Sura entitle By the Time. The question we should be asking ourselves What Time, is the Holy Quran speaking about; the Time of the Judgement, in which we are now living in my people. The time of the Destruction, in which we are now living in. We are living the time of the destruction of Yakub's Civilization, as well as the world he had made.

My people; there isn't any mystery god by any name has the power to stop what's happening. There isn't any religion that will not face this destruction due to the lies about Allah; they all teach black people, too keep us under their cruel also evil spells. When you examine these interlopers all of them they all mean black people, no good at all. All these interlopers are here to support advocate also spread America's brand of White Supremacy as well as America's brand of White Nationalism. They have embraced Americas plan to destroy black people; to keep black people disenfranchise as well as keep black people a prisoner, at the bottom of the well. None of these people are the friends of black people they are all our open enemies, my people.

People are always sending me pictures or some other correspondence without any solutions just problems. The problems are known how about working on solutions instead of focusing on the problems. These problems began once we boarded these slave ships. These problems have continued as well as escalated since the Jamestown landing in 1555, aboard the Slave Ship Jesus also Grace as well as other slave ships. Time has shown me that these cowards aren't going to do anything at all as they walk around in suits, bowties as well as phony newspaper, calling it Muhammad Speaks; when in truth it's no one speaks; even bean pies without any ingredients on the pie or label. They are even afraid to come out of the devil name so when they are in the black communities they have righteous names; when they are at work on all their government papers, these phonies use their slave masters name. You must keep your eyes on these as well they offer no tangible solution reason being is that they are concentrating on sucking your hard earn money, from you, this is their primary goal. Them projecting themselves as false ministers or leaders my people this is exactly what they are, false so-called ministers as well as false leader, that have absolutely no solution for black or Indian people.

We need results physical results nothing else is acceptable by anyone at all. My people we have allow all type of charlatans to come amongst us to do nothing more than rob us, as they cast us deeper into Americas bottomless pit of despair. We have for the past 450 plus years have been looking at things through the eyes of our many, open enemies. They our open enemies smile in our face, they pretend to like us, they our open enemies pretend to care for us, they are very skillful at deceiving black people, since they all have been doing this for the past 6,000 years. We my brothers along with our women also children have been deceived be everyone including this Orthodox so-called Islam. We must trust only ourselves; we must do for ourselves as we keep our enemies, from coming amongst us. We don't need anyone coming amongst us making suggestions reason being is that their suggestions are evil in firm resolutions meaning they are very convincing, to mislead us all away from our salvation.

All our lives my black also Indian people since the Caucasian Race landed on the shores of the Northern part of the Western Hemisphere, we have endured nothing but absolute hell, even from black people from the Motherland, calling themselves Africans as well. We my people must look to ourselves there is no one else that is going to help us, we must turn to ourselves there is no other people for us to rely on, cause none of them care about us black people in America; who was kidnapped made a slave, our language stolen from us; our god also heritage stolen from us, since 1555. We are fools to continue this path, of death for us all. There will be nothing of good ever to come to us trusting these other people, they love America the Accursed Devil. Check out how the Arab women are now dressing they have on the head piece, but they are no longer in Hajji. The Arab women are flaunting as much behinds as every other disbelieving Christian or Zionist woman, in America.

We my people must not trust or have any belief in such people they all came to America to die it's written in the history. In fact; my people they all deserve to die women also children included. The scout planes aboard the Mother Plain are already releasing their deadly bombs, upon America. There is no amount of prayers from anyone that can stop or prevent the awesome destruction, that's happening right now. Your Agreement with Hell Will Not Stand. I'm speaking about all the immigrants that has come to America also that believes, in America; there is a very high price you must pay, for the goods that you all have purchase. You all have come here not to put an end to evil but to help evil flourish as well as to help also aid America, in murdering as many black people as you can.

You cowards how disgraceful you all are instead of building up your own countries as you help to benefit everyone in your countries, no you cowards would rather run here as you steal from others who have been sacrificing their lives for over 450 years. You all deserve to die with America, your families included. I have absolutely no sympathy or empathy for any of you disgraceful cowards I don't care what your religion maybe; you are all disgraceful cowards may Allah punish you all harshly also without any mercy; none of you deserve any mercy at all. You come to America bring your brand of evil as well then you all partnered up with America to make a bigger even greater evil against Black also Indian People. You aren't Muslims you are all nothing but devils trying to disguise yourselves as Muslims. I wouldn't give anyone of you two cents, for what you have to say or what you worship. None of you immigrants are on the side of the true also living god whose proper name is Allah in the person of Master Fard Muhammad. None of you immigrants are on the side of Allah's last also greatest Messenger the Most Honorable Elijah Muhammad/Muhammad RasulAllah. How can I possible call or consider any of you my Brother or Sister, when all of you are the open enemies of Allah as well as His Holy Messenger. My people we must all be careful these are our enemies I pray for the death of our enemies; I have no love for our enemies they have absolutely no love for us. We my people must stop being so merciful also caring for our enemies they are only trying to blood suck your knowledge, then turn on you this is what they all do to black people. While these immigrants are amongst Caucasian people they confess their hatred of us, the ex-slave of America who has given more to America than anyone else.

We my people must come to grips with the truth of the times in which we are living in. We must come to grips with the reality that these immigrants as well as American people are our open as well as secret enemies. America the Accursed Devil has given these cowards all sorts of benefits, housing, food -stamps, Medicaid jobs, as they place us black people in concentration camps all throughout America. As you sit back still praying to this devil, you are silly enough to call Jesus. Christianity as well as Sunnah so called Islam are the very enemies, of Black as well as Indian people, here in America. We can't trust any of them my people Sunnah so-called Islam is just as poisonous to black people as Christianity. We will always be slaves of a mental death also power following either one of these doctrines, none of this will save black people.

These so-called African people are just as hateful to the ex-slave of America as well. These so-called Africans demonstrate a complete hatred for

Black as well as Indian people. Those that have come to America have more love for the devil, than they do their own people in which they themselves have sold into slavery. They also are getting food stamps, wick, medicate rent being paid as they don't care that black people are being placed into concentration camps. The foolish Negroes that are married to them are also disgusting cowards as they shut their eyes, to the evil that these so-called Africans are doing to black people here in America. If these traitors feel they are getting over to hell with us all, they allow these so-called Africans to rob us.

We my people must turn to ourselves rely upon ourselves stop patronizing these people you are only making them rich, as they spit on black people here in America. When I say Through Our Father's Eyes I'm not speaking about these disgusting cowards; we have absolutely no use of them either. Through Our Father Eyes I will reveal to everyone who I am speaking about; I will tell you this I'm not speaking about any of these cowardly traitors as well or their Negro lackeys.

There is something I must say also acknowledge my ex-wife Juliana Ruth Anderson she has been there for me even after our divorce. We have a son together name Ibn-Saladin Shabazz-Allah more important is her devotion towards helping me. I am forever grateful for her help always as well as thank her for everything she has done.

Black also Indian People must wake up in order that they may see exactly what is happening also taking place here, in America. America stole our [Black People} language, our heritage our way of life; we want it all back in fact we demand that you America give it all back, to the descendants of our fathers in which you stole, it all from. We my people must have back that which will solidified us once again as a people this is our language, my people. Since we are no longer speaking our language; since we no longer serve our heritage; since we no longer practice our way of life; we are just like the moon absent of water; dead also lifeless. For ever having to reflect the light of someone else this describe black people perfectly calling themselves Americans; as they live this filthy American way of life; always at the mercy of everyone who hates us; always at the beck also whim of our open enemies.

DEDICATION

I Saladin Shabazz-Allah contribute this manuscript to all the fallen soldiers who have fought for the freedom, of our people. This has been a long very hard-fought battle with many causalities on our behalf. These fallen soldiers' male also female America has tried to write them off as criminals my people none of them are criminals. These fallen soldiers were fighting against the criminals this Zionist/Christian/Arab/Asian American Government, of Global Terrorist.

So many; of our people were murdered by this American CIA, FBI. Local Gestapo Police so-called departments throughout America from the twenties, this is when America murdered our beautiful brother Noble Drew Ali. Our beautiful brother Marcus Mosiah Garvey they were destroyed for coming to help his brothers also sisters, by our enemies. We must remember my people the American Government along with the American people had instituted the Jim Crow Laws that were enforced, by this American Zionist/Christian Government of Global Terrorist.

We my people have absolutely nothing to be proud of by calling ourselves Americans or African Americans. We do ourselves a great injustice by calling ourselves by this disgraceful terminology African American. This is another method of our former slave masters clamming black people as their personnel property. We are the personal prosperity of Allah in the person of Master Fard Muhammad, to whom praises are due forever. We my people must begin to understand that we have absolutely no time for fighting amongst ourselves, especially on these enemy controlled social media. This is just plain stupidity that our enemies are watching also monitoring, as they laugh at your unimaginable foolishness.

Through these false also grafted teachings by these magicians of Pharaoh/America our enemies have been able to keep black people destabilized, as well as disenfranchised. In fact, my people this is the 21st Century modified version, of Jim Crow Laws against we the ex-slave of America. The tentacles of America/Satan the Accursed Devil have penetrated deep into the very moral fabric of black people due to these false teachings, of America's Magicians; misleading you away from the only teachings that will lead us all, into heaven at once. We must examine my people any doctrine that can't take us into a physical heaven while we live; any doctrine no matter what it maybe label that can't produce an immediate change in our conditions, then it isn't worth having at all.

The fallen soldiers did not sacrifice their lives also freedom for us to be fools or to still be second class citizens, in as well as to America. Here we are still trapped by these religious pimps' insane teachings taking us all further and further away, from what any intelligent people should be doing for themselves as well are doing for themselves. We can't rise with all these different conflicting doctrines also concepts that are plaguing black people, while none of these doctrines or concepts produces anything positive, for black people. Just a bunch of want to be Rosters, walking around with their chest sticking out believing they are doing something when in truth they are doing absolutely nothing tangible, for black people only feeding their own self inflated egos. This is fine with this Zionist/Christian/Arab/Asian American Government of Global Terrorist; the Wizards of this American government understand the necessity of these foolish traders, so they even aid these fools. Now if these foolish so-called leaders; don't try to lead black people across the River Jordan; in which these fools have absolutely no intentions on doing nor do they know how to cross the River Jordan anyway.

This is the reason why we must look Through Our Father's Eyes as we stop looking through our enemy's eyes. We must stop embracing what our enemies have to say or think. We must look towards ourselves my people we must examine our own beyond rich lustrous history that reaches all the way to eternity. This work in which I am venturing on is to bring some understanding to you my people, how also why we must change our direction, methods as well as objectives. The path that we are following will as well as has led us to absolute destruction, mentally as well as physical. We owe it to our fallen brothers also sisters that sacrificed their lives as well as freedom, so that we may achieve also enjoy real freedom, justice as well as equality.

The list is endless my people of the many black lives that were lost as well as we still are losing black lives, till this very day. We must my people not allow ourselves to become involved with America's insanity they have started, with North Korea. We black people as well as Indian People have absolutely nothing to do with America's insanity as well as America's Insane President Donald Trump; he President Trump is totally insane drunk with power, as he leads America to destruction. We my Black as well as Indian People have absolutely nothing to do with this insanity as well as we have absolutely nothing to gain from America's insanity. We aren't Americans we are the victims of America as well as American People. Let those who are benefitting from being an American fight also die for America we Black also Indian People shouldn't lift a finger to help protect America ever again; no, my people we should only lift our fingers to protect also help ourselves also our kind.

We must take a stand my people we must not ever lift our hands to aid America in her quest of continuing, to be the Global Terrorist America is. Fight for ourselves my people let other than ourselves fight for themselves, we are no longer aiding our enemies in anything they do domestically or globally. Through Our Fathers Eyes not through the eyes of our open enemies ever again it is time we demonstrate Black Pride; it is time we demonstrate Black Intelligent; it is time we demonstrate Black Ingenuity; it is time we stand up to do something for ourselves; it is time we weld ourselves together as a nation of people, in order that we may prevent any more looting, raping, murdering, injustices amongst us as well as from any of these interlopers, called immigrants in which they are now calling themselves Americans.

You my brothers you my sisters that are living in these concentration camps/shelters all throughout America I dedicate these writings to you reason being, is that you are all the fallen. You my brothers also sisters locked away in these American Prisons I dedicate these writings to you, reason being, is that you are the fallen. I dedicate these writings to all my people that suffered from as well as under the diabolically cruel hands, policies, laws of America/Satan the Accurse Devil.

My people the time has come for us to end the arguing; the bickering, the distrust; the lack of corporation; and the self-hate; all of this must come to an end right now my people. My Indian People I am of you as well I bring to you as our Holy Messenger of Allah taught me to bring to all people, the truth. I revealed in my previous writings the truth of who Grand Father is. If you didn't see it then I will say it again Master Fard Muhammad is the Almighty that the world has been waiting for, for the past 2,000 thousand years. My Indian People you have been waiting for over 16,000 years, for this Mighty One. Prayer is better than sleep, as the Holy Quran states; nevertheless, the Remembrance of Allah is the Greatest Force the Holy Quran states this also. I remember who Allah is and I also remember His name, his name is Master Fard Muhammad Allah Almighty Himself. I'm forever grateful to Allah for raising up from amongst us; the nineteen million original people, in North America; His last also greatest Messenger the Most Honorable Elijah Muhammad/Muhammad RasulAllah.

Let us my brothers also sisters let us look Through Our Fathers Eyes let us see the great over whelming greatness, in comparison, to the history of our open enemies; to the absolute lies of our open enemies; to the despair that we all have suffered through also from our open enemies; let us my people take a different look opposite of what all our enemies, have presented to us they are all liars. They our open enemies have always worked together for their common goal my people; all of these interlopers have been working together, here in America to steal from black also Indian people; they do this with smiles; as they follow their maker Yakub rules, regulations as well as all laws, of destroying the original people; called Birth Control; we have never been included in or apart of Yakub's plan; We are the target of Yakub's designated plan, to kill the original people at birth. We are living in the day of decision my people I hope you make the right decision As-Salaam Alaikum.

CHAPTER 1

ALPHA

We can't put a beginning to our beginning due to the very fact that the very first one, who created Himself from the Atom of Life, wasn't able to record his beginning; as Allah Almighty Himself taught His last also greatest Messenger the Most Honorable Elijah Muhammad/Muhammad RasulAllah. You can read chapter 11 in Our Savior Has Arrived "THE KNOWLEDGE OF GOD HIMSELF" This speech was delivered on Savior's Day 1969 by the Holy Apostle Himself. So, when we say Through Our Father's Eyes we are speaking infinity my people this is what has been stolen from you/us. Our history is so vast that in every Caucasian Museums throughout the world are filled with our stolen heritage also legacy. Stolen by these Caucasian Grave Robbers they called themselves Archeologist in which they have robbed many of our Ancestors tombs; claimed their coffins as well as all the riches these Great Kings, Emperors Sultans. If you don't understand this, then you can never see Through Our Fathers Eyes; thus, forever being trapped, looking through the eyes of our open as well as secret enemies, never giving yourself a chance, to know or understand yourself, or how truly great you are.

Our open enemies have convinced you black woman that a black young male is dangerous, to us all. Young black men imitating their mothers is a sin where as young black men looking like their mothers; walking like their mothers; talking like their mothers; dressing like their mothers; even acting like their mothers; What a shame. Instead of looking through their father eyes, these young lost black souls are looking through the eyes of the evilest people ever birth, on our planet. Young Black Men are lost due to them not knowing or having love for their fathers or themselves for over 450 years. Black people here in America have absolutely no love for themselves at all, you measure love by the material, you have may obtained. This isn't love this isn't even respect this is following the ways also actions, of our enemies.

We are still living as well as searching through the eyes also mind set of our enemies who have absolutely no love or concern, for any of us. Yet you my people fashion also conduct yourselves just like our enemies. By you conducting yourself like your enemies you are giving them the power, over you, your women also children as well. You are under the belief that you are an American also you believe that you are entitled, to full rights that Americans have. You aren't included in these American rights due to the fact, that you aren't an American. These are the lies that our enemies have been feeding us for many, many years as these enemies of ours, are flooding America getting more rights than we, black people, have ever had. Why is this happening? It's happening due to you believing also trusting our enemies. This is continuing due you are believing in America; this is happening due your total ignorance of the times in which you are living in.

You believe that being a great basketball player, a football player, baseball player, tennis player or on these Wizards other Blood Sports that you are in engaged in, make you an American. No, it doesn't my people it just makes you property of these enemies who own these professional teams. We don't any of these teams, so you are going to tell me about Michael Jordan or Magic Johnson owning professional teams, these are only front men, for our enemies helping to keep them rich. None of them Michael Jordan or Magic Johnson are concerned about how many jobs are distributed to black people in fact they don't even care if black people, have any work at all. All the jobs are going to other people other than black people. Other people are enjoying the fruits of America everyone except black as well as Indian people. People who have done far less than black people also Indian people are living the American dream while Black also Indian people are living the American Nightmare.

Why is this happening my people? It's happening due to you believing also looking through the eyes, of our enemies. This insane concept of loving everyone is from our enemies, which is designed for our destruction as well as the destruction of black women as well as children. This destruction has been going on since 1555 which has intensified especially into today's times. Our enemies and we have many enemies my people all working to up hold the American lies, as they engage in the destruction of Black as well as Indian people. Black people aren't helping themselves young men want to live at home with their mothers, as they do nothing acting more like little girls than men. These cowards love to shoot of with their mouths until things get thick, then they want to run to the police; why do they run to the police? Is because they are nothing but cowards. This is what's happening amongst black people all of this is due to black people, looking at things also believing that they are Americans. Before these cowards fight our enemies, they will rather talk tuff to their mothers also fathers, then call our enemies. What good are these cowards to the rise of black people. These cowards living with their mothers are liars just like their Caucasian Masers cowards. They would rather live also think like black people enemies they haven't the courage to look Through Their Fathers Eyes.

Only by looking through our father's eyes can we then begin to unravel this snake mentality, that we have been Raped up in, for over 450 years. Black children haven't a clue as to what's happening or what's going on they don't even care about their heritage they are only concerned about going to hell with their enemies. These foolish children care nothing about being black they care more about being a filthy cowardly American. They the young people promote more American Evil than any generation has ever done before. They have no love for themselves this is the reason why, homosexuality has flourish amongst them due to them, not doing anything to prevent or stop it. They my people don't even realize that they are being pushed out of main stream America, as they sit back playing computer games, blogging, texting all about nothing. While the enemies sit back laughing at them reasoning being is that our enemies know, these fools are going to end up in one of their concentrations camps, due to them looking through the eyes also perception, of our enemies.

Black young also elder men are looking through our enemy eyes. Black young women also elderly black women are looking through the eyes of our enemies. Look at the condition of black people today the majority, of black people, are living in concentration camps, with absolutely no hope of ever getting out. Young black men walking around doing nothing as they allow our enemies to walk around getting away with these diabolical crimes, they have been committing for over 450 years. You will not step up to regain your proper heritage as well as origin in this world. Through Our Fathers Eyes is the only solution to our problem my people. When you search the history my betrayed and misled people that since, we fell under the diabolical control of our enemies, we have never been the same. We are talking about nearly 500 years of pure hell. All most 500 years of being deprived until many of our people believe this is the natural order of things. Many of our people believe that black people are supposed to suffered as they live day to day. My people this is a lie we aren't supposed to be suffering in fact no human being are supposed to suffer or be deny the basic things, that every human being, is entitled to have. The fact every life forms my people are entitle to food, clothing also shelters.

By us not looking through our father's eyes we have been convinced that we must conduct as well as operate, as our fathers enemies dictate to us. We can't begin to interpret right from wrong as this society continue to present us with absolute wrong then tell us to except their insanity peacefully. We are taught by our enemies to suffer peacefully. We are taught by our enemies that America is the best place, for us to be. We are taught by our enemies not to do something for ourselves but take whatever crumbs our enemies decide to give us. If we my people continue to trust our enemies, decisions on us we are domed. We must understand these people that are in power a no friends of ours; the deck is stacked against us as well as has been stacked against us, since 1555. In fact, things have been decided for us by our enemies and the deck has been stacked against us since 1492.The life style our enemies have made for us, is nothing but a life of endless hell. A revolving door of despair as well as miseries; a revolving door of hatred for self; a revolving door pain also suffering; a revolving door of false religions that never bring the mass of black people, any relief only suffering; a revolving door of lies also false promises and then death; a revolving door without any mercy or relief, from the enemies of our fathers as well as ourselves.

Every one of our enemies, are telling us to be patience, have faith you will then go to heaven, once you die. Our enemies know full well that you aren't going to any heaven because you didn't create a heaven for yourself, while you were living. Our enemies have been able to keep you in a slumber due to you, looking through our enemy's eyes. My people our enemies don't want you to ever know the truth. Our enemies never want anyone telling or waking you up to the truth. Our enemy's only desire is that we remain a subservient mindless fool always depending, waiting at the beck also call, of our open enemies. Our children haven't any chance overcoming these atrocities due to them not knowing anything, about themselves or their fathers. Every other people on this planet are allowed, to enjoy their heritage except we the descendants of the slaves of America. Why should we sit back and take this evil from anyone? Why should we have to take this filthy society ways of life, as our own. We didn't come from this filth. We didn't come from such evil. This has absolutely nothing to do with our fathers at all. No, the time has come that we cast down our enemies' way of life as well as their politics.

We are an independent people we want nothing to do with American evils, lies also false promises. We demand that America let us go. We have anymore desire to play basketball, football, baseball, tennis or any other, of America's blood sports. We created scientist, educators, inventors, mathematicians' builders of great civilizations, with the absent of Caucasian People. Why do we need them now? I can't find any reason why we do. I'm not impressed by anything from their world it's all lies as well as deceit. It has never amount to any good for black or Indian people. We have been suffering so cruelly from America as well as American Caucasian People. In fact, every immigrant that comes to America it doesn't matter where they come from, are helped also aided by America in making sure they have housing, food stamps, jobs, medical, cars everything to make them comfortable; in fact, their children even get better education also play grounds also parks, than the so-called ex-slave of America. Why are we still looking at things through the eyes of our open enemies? Why are you still calling yourself an American when absolutely no good have ever came to us, from America or American People.

We are an independent people we don't belong to anyone except ourselves absolutely no one has the right to tell us, what to do. Absolutely no one has the right to dictate to us policies also procedures, on how we black people should conduct our lives. We have been living under their suggestions and black people have been always living in misery. We have been living under these hateful people for hundreds of years all we have received is misery, misery, misery from America as well as American People. This treatment hasn't stop my people look at your communities throughout America; the people who is responsible for building also defending America are the ones who have nothing in America. So, you say I got a job my people you aren't saying anything at all, except that I am still the property of America. I say we aren't America's property any longer. Let us go for ourselves then every black man as well as woman would have employment, with the absent of our open enemies. There is no freedom the way we are going about things; just because you are allowing to participate in this American Foolishness, does not make everything alright. You are still in the position of servant you still don't own the business. You are still at the mercy of another person or persons. The time has come that we as a people must become more enterprising; more aggressive in doing for self; we must become more involved in the higher levels, of management; we must become more involved in planning also designing huge projects, such as building homes for thousands of people; such as building bridges; such as how to bring life support systems, to these buildings as well as areas; such as learning how to use heavy duty equipment such as Crane Operators all the different heavy duty equipment necessary, in building something for ourselves. Through Our Father's Eyes my people not through our enslaver's eyes which have led us straight to hell that we have been living in, for the past 450 plus years.

This destructive path of going to school then getting a job is another form of slavery when you should be thinking about starting your own business. You should be establishing your own international contacts as well as contracts, my people. We must understand the necessity of fishing for a mass of people is a science that every intelligent people must know, as well as have. The knowledge of agriculture also agronomy is essential to the survival, of any as well as all Nations of People. Through Our Father's Eyes my people are where we must look my people through Our Father's Eyes. The answers to problems have been explained to us the solution has already been given to us, as well. We must act on that which we have already received our unity is the key as well as necessary, for us to change our present conditions. This world in which we are now living is about to explode death also destruction is on the way, this can't be stop, prevented or averted. This is the destiny of Yakub's world the world in which we are now living in.

By you my people not taking what is serious you aren't preparing yourselves for the catastrophes that are surely coming, upon America as well as the American People. The Holy Messenger taught us that there is a high price, that you must pay for the goods that you have purchase. This is referring to the immigrants as well as everyone else that is, as well as has bought, into this American Nightmare. There are so much my people you should be doing to improve your condition; nothing is coming down to you from the American Government. You should be searching in a different direction for a solution to our problems. We will never change or stop the decay that has eroded away our moral fabric as well as sense of right also wrong. We are trapped in this vicious cycle of despair, misery also no hope or prospects. This is a very, very bad position to be in my people. We must prepare our children to entered schools like MIT, Harvard, Yale, there are many other schools of great importance, that black children must prepare themselves for, instead of acting like clowns on the subways of New York City.

The mass of Black Children is not motivated or idea as what life is about other than making a CD as they walk around, with their pants hanging below their behinds; this is a total disgrace as well as total ignorance. What civilize people would take anyone seriously when they are walking around with their pants, hanging below their behind? Who will want any such person around them bringing nothing but total ignorance? Here is a question my people that you should ask yourself; what kind of political religious leader, would allow their young people to walk around looking so disgraceful as well as unintelligent. Look at what your young black daughters look like in the eyes of civilize people or people trying to be civilize? This behavior is disgraceful will only produce disgracefulness. Where there are no wise intelligent women, there can be no wise as well as intelligent children. So where does this leave us my people we have no concern or love for ourselves, until you ignore this desperate behavior from your children, trying to create an identity for themselves; different from their open enemies. The children aren't wrong in wanting to create a different identity for themselves; the problem is that they not having proper knowledge of themselves or anyone else as well as, the serious times in which they are living in.

Black children are being breaded to be clowns, court jesters to further enhance the master/America diabolical plan, of White Supremacy as well as White Nationalism. My people singing, dancing, basketball, football, hockey, tennis soccer there are others as well; are all blood sports that the Wizards use to profit off as well as keep control of everyone, under their rule. Singing also dancing are other avenues that these Wizards use, to control also direct the mass, of people in the direction in which they want them to go in; as they profit off these entertainers; as they rob the mass of people; they call them Court Jesters in American history also European history as well. My people I'm just telling you the truth about your condition as well as how to get out of this pitiful condition. Look at what other people are doing as well as how they do it, my people. They are successful due to their unity as a people in which you my people don't have. Leave it to our enemies you will never have.

My people ever since we crossed the Atlantic we have been forcing to except also look through the eyes of our enemies, as we have been cast into a bottomless pit of hell, with no sign of relief at all. You my people have been made as well as taught to believe that there is nothing that you can do. You have been taught that this is the way things are. You have been taught that this is your life also be happy purchasing all our enemy's goods, as you better keep your mouths shut. This Zionist/Christian/Arab/Asian American Government of Murdering, Thieving Global Terrorist, has not the right to tell us anything. We should no longer disgrace ourselves following such evil as well as evil people. We my people are too trusting this we must stop we are the only ones being hurt also destroyed, by this diabolical government. Every other people are benefitting also prospering, while we our children also wives are suffering. There is something very wrong in this equation my people look around you will see how the so-called American Negro, is suffering like no other people here in America. The shame in everything is that you don't know it in fact the Zionist controlled music industry condoned your so-called gangster rap, because they knew this will be another weapon that our enemies could use, against us, in which they did. Now the Zionist controlled music industry has turned it over to the Homosexual community, while they push you out.

They our enemies have been as well as still are stealing our music practicing trying to sound like black people, with a homosexual twist. Look at how many homosexual sites out there with black men being penetrated by white boys, as these worthless Negro fools scream how much they love it. This Zionist controlled music also motions picture industry projects these disgraceful of black homosexual men being penetrated, by white men. The same is being done to black women as well; white women penetrating black women in the anus as well as every part of her, while she is screaming how good this feel. This is absolute as well as total insanity my people therefore this civilization is being wiped off the earth forever. Even all of these you tube shows, blog Shows talking about nothing of important; nothing of value for black people. The only thing that's this is producing as well as strengthening, is our enemy's White Supremacy as well as their White Nationalism.

Through Our Father's Eyes my people in which we must connect with. It is Through Our Father's Eyes where the answers lye. Looking also operating from the eyes also thoughts of our enemies, will only keep us in the position of servant. We must my people understand my people America Europe as well is being as I speak, wiped off our planet. It doesn't matter if you believe or except my people you will be wise to except; yet if you don't except your god whose proper name is Allah who visited us in the person of Master Fard Muhammad to whom all holy praises, are due forever; your life is doomed there is nothing that can save you, once you disbelieve in Allah and His Holy Messenger the Most Honorable Elijah Muhammad/Muhammad RasulAllah.

You have no beginning or ending my people the only way to tap into this unlimited power of ours, we must look Through Our Fathers Eyes. We can't swim or will be able to return home which is back to ourselves also called the 9,000 miles, continuing this path of death also destruction. You have been convinced into believing that our enemies are right due to them apparently holding all the cards; my people our enemies are holding only one card, that card is the card of death, for themselves; if you continue to follow the enemies of Allah as well as yourself, my people. The historical truth is absolute that can't be denied or refuted by anyone. If you continue to rebel as well as not submit to the over whelming truth, then you my people are responsible for your own destruction; in which you don't deserve any mercy at all.

The church with this crazy Christianity religion cannot help or save you at all in fact the church is your greatest enemy as well; the church is working with the enemies of Allah as well as our ancestors. Examine the mentality of the young males they have a female mentality they like to mouth off not all of them but most them do; then when things get heated these young cowards run to the police, if they aren't running to the police they just don't know what to do. Puerto Rico has been completely devastated these Puerto Ricans are looking to come here to America; they are coming here to take from your black people, whatever you may have left. They will be successful due to your own ignorance as well as not protecting yourself; this is also due to our lack of unity as well as wanting to be, an African American.

They as well as everyone else don't care anything about you, your wives also children; in fact, they don't care about your parents or grandparents or where will they live; or what will our people have to eat; or sleep; or do they have medical provisions. Why would you be concerned about anyone who in truth doesn't care a damn thing about you, your families, your parents or your grandparents, when they don't care anything at all, about black or Indian People at all. My people you are in a very bad position more enemies are on the way they don't mean black people any good at all. Our enemies are looking through their father's eyes why won't you look through your father's eyes, my people. No, we aren't, or should we black as well as Indian people, make any more concessions to anyone, or for anyone. We sacrificed to much already also we have nothing else to give anyone; we must get wise very quickly things have already gotten extremely ruff, my people things are going to get much, much more terrible. Black also Indian people must fly to Allah our Holy Most Merciful Savior Allah in the person of Master Fard Muhammad to whom all holy praises are due forever. My people we must follow Allah's last also greatest Messenger, the Most Honorable Elijah Muhammad.

You must understand my people this is another method of America's complete annihilation of black as well as Indian people. I'm not speaking hatred for the people in Puerto Rico I'm speaking self-preservation for Black also Indian people first. Through Our Father's Eyes my people not anyone else eyes, we must protect also make sure we are secure also safe, before we be concern about anyone else. A young black man with children living in a shelter as his children wife also another young woman is involved in this most vicious cycle; are also in shelters. The young man has nothing absolutely to give or offer his children, although he loves them. How can we afford to let anyone come amongst us taking from black people, as we sit by doing nothing to protect, whatever we may have left? Through Our Father's Eyes my people we must stand as we hold our grounds, also as we advance our course. Every other people that came here have sucked the very blood out of black people, we haven't any more blood to give to anyone.

Young black men born with a female mentality trying to bully their mothers yet when it comes to dealing with people in the street, they don't have any heart or mouth then. Also, when these cowards get themselves in any situation they call the police or want to be snitch. These cowards are the ones attacking also killing their parents as well as the ones attacking the elders; in many cases raping elderly woman. Who eyes are they looking through my people? I can most defiantly say they aren't looking Through Their Fathers Eyes; so, they must be looking through the eyes of our open enemies.

Alfa means beginning we are in a new beginning not a new resurrection there is no new or second resurrection; it is only the resurrection. We are no longer living in the resurrection we are now fully living in the judgment, of Allah. The beginning for us began in 1914; the awaking began in 1914; Lazarus rising out of his shadow grave began in 1914; the truth of God and the Devil began in 1914; The knowledge of self also kind began in 1914; it was in 1914 when the knowledge of the original man began, after being lost for 379 years, from their own people also kind. It was in 1914 when Allah our Holy Most Merciful Savior gave us 50-year extinction; it was in 1914 when Allah our Holy Savior began raising up black people, from the grave. The first 25,000 raised or first born did not know that Allah was amongst them due to them, not being able to recognize Allah Almighty.

My people you don't realize that July 4 is not a celebration of America's Independence, for Black as well as Indian People; July 4, 1914 is the coming of Allah Almighty to us; also, the beginning of the resurrection, of us; as well as the beginning of the judgment of Yakub's civilization as well as Yakub's making. You must understand these infidels' holidays are just that, holidays of the infidels; none of these holidays Christmas, Easter, Thanksgiving as well as all the rest, are holidays of the enemies of our fathers, as well as ourselves. So why the hell are you still worshipping these days my people? These are the holidays of the enemies of Allah as well as Allah's Holy Messenger; don't you know or realize the suffering we endured our forefathers also foremothers endured, for hundreds of years, day as well as night. Through Our Fathers Eyes my people is the only chance we must save ourselves, women our children included. We must instruct as well as teach our children president day is about praising your slave masters; how insane you must be to make or force your children to honor these devils; it doesn't matter what the devil name may be, he or she are the devil in the flesh.

You must understand my people we haven't recorded our history in hundreds of years so the enemies of our people, have writing history as they chose to. This has caused Black also Indian People children to be colonized thus kept in mental slavery, for over 400 years. So, history has been fabricated by our enemies on all levels the things we must remember is that they are mostly lies. Yes, our enemies put some truth in their lies in order that they may better conceal their lies, from black people. The enemy stealing our language from us made it easily for them to break us or divide us, as a people. We aren't speaking the language of our fathers which makes it impossible for us to connect, with our fathers. You can't praise your father due you are speaking the language of the enemies, of your fathers. This my people are what's holding you under the spell of our enemies as I said before, we have a great deal of enemies that all are taking a bite out of us.

It doesn't matter who the people might be their language is not the language of our fathers, so we are looking through the eyes of the enemies of our fathers, as well as ourselves. We must use a complete different approach to solve, our problems my people, we have a great deal of problems. Everything of bad that is happening amongst is due to us following or looking through the eyes, of our enemies. Many people may not like the term our enemies then tell me what they are, if they aren't our enemies? Examine the diabolical hell also conditions mental as well as physical, we have suffered under as well as still, suffering under. We can't advance ourselves as a people is due to us not having our father's language, my people. We my people the descendants of the ex-slave of America are the only people that don't, have their own language as a people. What does this tell us my people it tells me this we must gather together all our Lindquist personnel amongst us so that we, may re-create our language, as we give our enemies back their evil filthy language.

History proves that we had our own language long before any of these strangers ever came into existence, now we are deprived by America as well as American people, of us having the language of our fathers. The language that the Arabs speak is not the original Arabic they are speaking a dialect especially the Quran-an. The Qu-an is written in the dialect of the Outrush tribe in which Prophet Muhammad peace and blessings be upon him; received his revelations. He Prophet Muhammad did not speak the same language of Ibrahim, Muza, Esa, or any of the Prophets before him may Peace also Blessings of Allah be upon, them all. So, explain to me why are we speaking the enemy's language? The stealing of our language is seriously important my people this was by designed to prevent us from ever returning home again, so our enemies thought. Our enemies back in 1555 never ever wanted us to be able to return to our original selves.

Look at all these different people coming to America speaking in their language so that we black people can't understand, what they are saying, also when they are plotting against us. Yet everyone knows what we are saying even doing, even while we are amongst ourselves; as the American Gestapo law Enforcement bug our homes, offices, meeting places, Temples of worshipped as well. Why is this so my people? It's done to prevent us from rising out of the grave of ignorance; to prevent us from rising out of the grave of despair; to prevent us from enfranchising ourselves; to prevent us my people from rising from the bottom of the well, in which the traitors amongst us along with our many enemies, cast us into. While they our enemies along with their families, enjoy the good life, here in America. We my people are living exactly how our enemies want us to in which they designed for us also; an eternal prison my people, in which we have been living in since 1555.

Through Our Fathers Eyes is where we must begin to examine all things as well as well as through the language, of our fathers. This is the reason why we must have back our Muhammad Universities of Islam so that we can, begin to teach our people especially our children, their fathers language. English is not our first language my people English is the language of the slave masters/devils; English is also a bastard language, in which we should abandon post haste. Latin, French, German, Russian, Portuguese, Spanish which derives from Latin, the Arabs dialect of Arabic, Polish, Albanian all these grafted languages, do not belong to black people as well as are not the languages of our fathers, or our people. This is keeping you a prisoner my people to this Zionist/Christian/Arab/Asian American Government of Global Murdering Terrorist. These lies against our fathers by our enemies are keeping you from returning home; these lies by our enemies have been keeping you away from your salvation from our Holy Savior Allah Almighty Himself in the person of Master Fard Muhammad, to whom all holy praises are due forever; as well as Allah's last also greatest Messenger the Most Honorable Elijah Muhammad; these are the lies that are keeping us all in the bottom of the well of civilization; these are the lies as well as the liars that robbing us of our atmosphere.

We are purposely being led away from what we must for ourselves as a people to enjoy heaven while we live, not believing these make-believe stories of heaven after you die, by our enemies. Remember my people it was our Prince Hall who brought Islam to America in the 1700 hundreds not some Arab, Sunnah or Persians/Sufi. It's Through Our Fathers Eyes my people we must look through for us, to see as well as understand, the time in which we are living in as well as what we must do, protect also elevate ourselves, from this grave of ignorance. We must stop acting like silly ignorant fools allowing others to reap the rewards, that none of them deserve. Alfa my people means the beginning of the hell that we fell into in 1555, as we have been living as well been living for over 450 years. We can never free ourselves by using the enemies, way of doing things; our enemies have one objective that is to keep us wallowing in filth as their eternal slaves. Look throughout America the American government has shut down every boxing club in black people's communities; they have reduced the martial arts schools in black people's community; they have shut down the football fields in every black community; they have shut down every baseball field in black communities. Why has this been done Saladin? This has been done my people to prevent black people from ever coming together, as a unit. In every other community the people are allowing to assemble as a people choose up teams, as they participate in these American as well as European sports, such as soccer; except the descendants of the once slaves, of America. These other people coming into America are allowing to operate as a people even have uniforms, except you also I my people. This another American policy to keep us separated as a people while others, are allowing to conduct themselves as a people, speaking in their language.

Double Dutch goes back to slavery along with quilting also hair braiding amongst the black women I can remember my mother grandmother, aunts, cousins, friends, neighbors, would all come together for these gatherings, or church, birthdays weddings. There was a time we black people were denied a church wedding, so we had this method, of jumping over the broom together. The history of the weddings as well as birth of children, were recorded, in the family bible. This is how America treated us then my people we aren't treated any better today. The men would be playing baseball, fishing, drinking, chasing the women, as the children would engage themselves in children activities, even spying on the adults, activities. We must never forget the degradation that we had to suffer under, at the hands of our enemies. How can you call these people your friends? How can you yourself an American? How can you be so happy wallowing in America's filth? How can you my people accept this American hypocrisy, of still treating Black also Indian people as second-class citizens? How can you sit back while other immigrants come here take whatever job that you help created, as America give these jobs to these immigrants, that are spitting on you, as you have no home; but the immigrants do; while you have no food but the immigrants do; while you are begging also pleading for equality from the enemies of our fathers; while the immigrants are living well having pick nicks, driving fine cars, living in decent apartments; their children are getting better education than your children. You are still putting America first, while America is still putting you last. What has been a so-called African American has gotten any of us? The Answer is absolutely nothing.

It's Through Our Fathers Eyes my people not the eyes of our enemies which we must look through, not through the eyes of our lying American enemies. Young black men are being programmed to submit to this feminist mentality, that many so-called African American are poisoning them with. Many of these young black men are confused as they work very hard, in destroying themselves; the worst of it is that they have no love for themselves; yet all the love for their enemies. This is the reason also method how this American Government of Global Terrorist, can circulate also promote their Homosexuality, amongst also through every black community, throughout America. This is a filthy disease my people deadlier than America's implementation of Aids, amongst black people. This isn't looking through our fathers, eyes my people!!! This is looking through the eyes of the enemies of our father. Julius Caesar, Nero, Alexander, Plato, Starling, Peter the so-called great, Sacristies, Aristotle none as well as all this condemned Yakub's Society; so-called Scholars, including King James, his 50 to 60 scribes; George Washington, Abraham Lincoln, Eisenhower, Franklin D. Roosevelt, John F. Kennedy, as well as all the rest; are the enemies, of our fathers.

Examine the history my people it will reveal the truth also explain why you are kept in the position, of servants, here in America. We must change the course of us predetermine course by our enemies, instead of us determining the course we dictate, for ourselves. This is historical facts that we have been misled by our enemies not to believe in our fathers but believe in the enemies of our fathers. With the help of these religious also political so-called leaders who are aiding, our fathers' enemies, to keep us believing in our fathers' enemies; as they these Negro political also religious leaders, walking around trying to imitate our fathers' enemies. History clearly refutes also proves that the history being taught in school to black children, is nothing but lies designed to produce retardation amongst black children. Also, to keep black males imprisoned to this evil matriarchic rule designed by these wicked evil feminists starting from Eleanor Roosevelt to the filthy evil feminist movement, of the sixties. The devils targeted the black woman their objective was to separate black man from black woman; then move in destroy the black baby at birth; as the foolish ignorant Negro women, agreed to help the enemies of our fathers, as well as ourselves also themselves.

The Alfa I'm speaking about is the beginning of the absolute most diabolical hell began, in 1492 and 1555, that we as well as our Indian brothers also sisters, had to endure as well as survived. It was in these years that our destruction was planned as well as carried out, against our fathers' mothers as well. The children of today are so lost also confused they believe they are smart as our enemies laugh at then. The reason the enemies are laughing at them is due, to them not knowing what to do; as they these young fools believe they can defeat the many enemies, using the enemy's rules. These lost miss-guided children are doomed these ignorant young children don't even realize that they are a disgrace, in the eyes of their fathers; as they happily embrace their enemies; also, as they breathe life in our dying enemies; the young amongst us are allowing these Caucasian Vampires, to suck the blood out of them; thus, prolonging the enemy's worthless life; as they put an end to their own lives; very rapidly.

The shame in the whole matter is that young black men care absolutely nothing about their fathers which means they care nothing about themselves; so, they go through life with this evil feminine mentality, empowering Caucasian Woman superiority as they promote their total ignorance. These young fools don't even know that they were breaded by ignorant Negro women, to be servants of the Caucasian people life style, thus sub-servant to Caucasian People. The beginning of a hell my people in which we are still suffering you don't believe me, then answer me this what self-respecting black man will wear these faggot jeans/skinny jeans or clothes? This shows the female mentality that rules the younger black generation thus forever keeping you a slave. Absolutely no woman can make a black man a black man; no, she can only make a weak man; a colored man, nothing else my brothers.

The more you examine this lost generation they are always marveling after this Jackal of a woman, as if she is all that, in which she isn't. They have more love for this Jackal of a woman then they have, for their own black woman; even after they have impregnated these black women; many them aren't doing anything to support or protect their own. Through Our Fathers Eyes there isn't any way you could love, desire or marvel, after this Jackal of a woman. It matters not what she claims what religion she is my people; she represents White Supremacy as well as White Nationalism. Gay Rights is nothing more than White Supremacy as well as White Nationalism. Gay rights being spread amongst as well as throughout black communities in America, is the death of the righteous Black Mind as well black conscious; better way of saying this is putting the blinders, on young black people minds, where as they will never be able to connect to their fathers; this is an outright shame my people. You my brothers will also sisters will surrender your fathers also mothers up, for the admiration of these Jackals of a man also woman. Through Our Fathers Eyes my people is where we must begin to look through. We are still mental slaves; which is keeping black people physical slaves, to the whims also wishes of America/Satan the Accursed devil. Since you have bought into the many things that America has allow you to have which is nothing more, than pacification. You believe you are free when in truth you are nothing more than 21st century mental slaves. The only threat you represent is to your ignorant self and no one else.

For us to be a people we must drop everything of the enemies if not you are all dead, with our enemies. My people our enemies are going to die this can't be stopped; this isn't going to go away; this can't be changed; this can't be defeated by such primitive people such as our open enemies; their religions aren't going to stop the destruction; their prayers aren't heard by Allah; They will as well as are paying a very high price, for the goods they have purchased. What are the goods they have purchased Saladin? Citizenship my people these are the goods these fools have purchased, from America/Satan the Accursed Devil. Black women have gotten fight as well fill of sickness as they continue to eat poison physical foods, as well as mental foods. What does this mean Saladin? This means my people you are only birthing Negro slaves, for American Caucasian people as well as all their allies; which are our enemies. Once again, the Alfa I'm speaking about is the absolute destruction of us as a people which began in 1492 then intensified in 1555. If you haven't the courage to face also deal with this, you your women as well as your children, are doomed.

CHAPTER 2

OMEGA

The end my people what we must consider whose end is it, it certainly isn't our end then whose end is it also why is this end here. The end my people is the end of Yakub's civilization as well as Yakub's making. This end has absolutely nothing to do with the original people at all, unless these fools continue to believe as well as follow Yakub's making, these will be destroyed with this present civilization. This Civilization in which we are presently living in is dying as well as being destroyed, Allah Almighty Himself; this civilization own people are destroying their world themselves. We have nothing to do with this world or civilization, my people. It's written in scriptures about this destruction it's now upon them. We must understand this has nothing to do with black people at all therefore we must work very seriously, towards us building our own civilization or world. All of those who believe in Yakub's world will be destroyed as well as people who don't want, to do something for themselves. You must understand my people our enemies have a recorded beginning not us. Their beginning began 6,660 years ago around the year 8,400 ago this has absolutely nothing, to do with original people especially Black people.

You can investigate the vastness of space my people the signs of our everlasting presence are everywhere. If you look the many oceans in fact all body of waters, our darkness is eternal, there is no beginning or ending, to the Blackness or Black man, anywhere in the universe. There is no Omega for Black people Omega exist for the enemies of Allah; it doesn't matter what you look like or wearing, Allah know all His enemies; Allah know all of those who disbelieve in Him as well as His Holy Messenger. This is Omega my people the end of the disbelievers as well as the hypocrites that claim to believe, then turn their backs as they proclaim to the enemies, of their fathers that they never believed; in Allah who visited us in the persons of Master Fard Muhammad, to whom all holy praises, are due forever; also, they didn't believe in Muhammad RasulAllah the Most Honorable Elijah Muhammad. It is only Through Our Fathers Eyes and no other eyes should we even dare, to look through, my people. History even today's events show us that nothing that these other strangers are trying to convince us black people, to believe will ever take us out of want as well as physical, economical despair; educational despair; scientific despair; construction despair; agriculture despair; self-help despair; no unity despair; the no fishing for self-despair; the none participating in raising our own animals, for food also hides for clothing despair; not being represented in a corrupt political system equality despair; Forever by our enemies which are the enemies of Allah the Best Knower Of All Things; to deceive us as they helped America, keep us black people, in the filthy endless well of despair.

Only Through Our Fathers Eyes can we begin to understand the necessity of having our own banking system, as well as a Central Bank. Only Through Our Fathers Eyes can we built an accounting system that is equitable to us all, as well as beneficial to us all. Only Through Our Fathers Eyes will be able to build a righteous political system to govern us all; fact our father also creator Allah Almighty Himself; have given us our Declaration of Independence as well as our own Constitution for The Once Lost Now Found Members of The Tribe of Shabazz, who are Members of The Nation of Islam; through His Holy Messenger the Most Honorable Elijah Muhammad/Muhammad RasulAllah. Only Through Our Fathers Eyes will be able to build a hospital for ourselves, to attend to our sick also needy; as prepare our children to become once again, the skill medical professionals, they once were. Only Through Our Fathers Eyes will we be able to build for ourselves a heaven that all of us, may enjoy while we live. The Omega my people is for all the enemies of our fathers none of them are going to escape the reasoning being they are all on the side, of America/ Satan The Accursed Devil, not the side of Allah our Creator. Allah didn't create these grafted people no matter what they call themselves, like weeds my people they showed up amongst us in 1300, 1400, 1500 now the weeds filled, our homeland, belong to them. Look into North so-called Africa the people that are there are not the original owners; they stole the land from the black original owners, through murder also rape. These are historical facts, my people. So, I ask you my people, what kind of so-called Islam is this? How could you possibly trust anyone who murdered your fathers, then raped your mothers, sisters, aunts, daughters, grandmothers, then stole our land, from u, in North so-called Africa.

Everyone of Yakub's making is purposely doing everything in their power to lead us away, from our fathers. They do everything to prevent us black people from looking Through Our Fathers Eyes; so that we can look through their make eyes. They know absolutely nothing about Islam at all my people, we had Islam for trillions, trillions, trillions of years, before their maker was born; how can they tell us anything about Islam when he had Islam before their maker, was even made a man; as well as before they were ever grafted at out, of the original black man 6,600 years ago.

Today October 5, 1817 is the birthday of our father also Liberator the Honorable Frederick Douglass 200th birthday, nothing has been mentioned from any of these Negro Organizations or any other so-called black organization, about this great black man; who fought all his life, to free his people from Chattel Slavery. None of these; phony Negro Organization has done anything to commemorate the birthday of this great black giant, who sacrifice his life, for his people; this is the Honorable Frederick Douglass 200th birthday, while nothing is ever mention by these Negro Cowards, this includes everyone that forgot our Great, Great, Great Grand Father; what a damn shame. I say to our most beautiful father "May the Peace Also Blessings, Of Allah BE Upon Him Iman.

This is personnel note from myself, brothers also sister our brother C-Wisdom/Larry expired on December 10th, 1994 this is my third eldest brother, we were a year apart who encouraged me, to start writing forty plus years ago. We all say, "May the Peace, Also Blessings of Allah, Forever Be Upon Him Iman".

There are many fools believing that they are being righteous following unrighteous people, in which history prove, that these people aren't righteous at all. In fact, these so-called fools have entered the realm, of being a hypocrite. The sad part about it is that these fools don't even know that they have betrayed Allah, as well as Allah's Holy Messenger. Through Our fathers Eyes my people is our only priority this is where freedom, justice

21

also equality, are to be found. I have had so-called Sunnah so-called Muslims spying on me at work, for their Zionist partners; these are not our brothers my people. These are our enemies that work very hard on keeping us black people, in a submissive role to them. This is nothing but White Supremacy also White Nationalism in which so-called Sunnah has embraced. Why has this so-called Sunnah so-called Islam embraced this American White Nationalism as well as White Supremacy Saladin? They need America's help to try to set them these Sunnah infidels up as the leaders of Islam, in which they aren't my people. These infidels are part of the conspirators that murdered our brother Malcolm X, as they were as well as are, working with this American government of Murdering Global Terrorist.

None of these enemies of our fathers or ourselves ever want us to rise, out of their control. Many so-called negroes have fallen in the traps, of our enemies; it so sad to see our people go from slave master, to another slave master; one thing is for sure we black people will always be nothing but mental also physical slaves, to the enemies of our fathers. When you examine the writings of the so-called Quran-and it speaks about this Viceregent, my people. The question my people is, who is this viceregent? The viceregent is Yakub whose wisdom was to rule for 6,000 years. So Yakub stood in the place of the true also living god, as his wisdom ruled, for his makings. These Arabs also their so-called Sunnah are supported by Yakub not by Allah; their rituals are for them not for us. We my people have been given by Allah our own Islam; these infidels aren't part of this my people. This so-called Sunnah Islam is working hand in hand with America as they did back in 1555, to enslave black people; then murder of the Indians in the Western hemisphere, to establish White Supremacy also White Nationalism in the Western Hemisphere. The Sunnah so-called Islam is a part of this diminishment; my people not Prophet Muhammad but those to who took charge, after his death. These are the ones that said or made the choice, of what they consider what Prophet Muhammad said twenty-three years, after his death. Forty-six years after Prophet Muhammad, is when these same enemies of our fathers, produce this book called Hadith. I don't care if these infidels like me they aren't my or our father they are the enemy as well, my people. Therefore, we must look Through Our Fathers Eyes not our enemy's eyes. How can Yakub's making tell us about that in which they don't even know? If you support America, you support White Supremacy. If you want

American Citizenship you want to be part of American White Nationalism; all of this is coming to an end, my people. Let these silly Negro fools believe as these fools want to believe; it doesn't matter at all.

None of these interlopers are our friends as well as anything to us like family. Jumma is filled with nothing but our enemies as well as the enemies of our fathers, so why go there my people. You are looking for our enemies that murdered countless of black men as well as boys, as they raped black women also young girls, in north so-called Africa; we should trust these devils? These same devils are still raping black women also young girls, in the back of their stores; then go to Jumma. We are supposed to pray with our proven enemies, my people? My people these are the enemies of our fathers, so they are our enemies as well. Omega is about the ending also destruction of this diminishment that our enemies, believe they are getting away with; they all are on the side of America/Satan the Accursed Devil. I know our enemies as well as the fools who have been tricked by our enemies, don't like what I saying I don't care one bit. I look Through Our Fathers Eyes not the eyes of our fathers as well as our enemies.

We can't any longer consider anyone else my people but ourselves we aren't dealing with people that are concern about black people. In fact, my people they aren't even Muslims. These aren't the people that Ibrahim was talking about when Ibrahim said make them Muslims; we my people are the ones that Ibrahim said make them Muslims. Ibrahim is one of our many ancient fathers, whose eyes we must look through. What I'm about to reveal is what Allah's Holy Messenger revealed to us all. Yakub was given 6,000 years to rule. Not Yakub who took the 30% dissatisfied people with him to the island of Pelan. The wisdom of Yakub was given 6,000 to rule as he Yakub's wisdom stood as vicegerent or one who stands in the place, of Allah, but is not Allah; the one whose wisdom would rule for 6,000 years.

Let us examine something my people other people are always trying to ram their version of god as well as their version of a so-called holy book, which offers black people absolutely no independence for black people. Allah the true also living God visited us in the person of Master Fard Muhammad to whom all holy praises are due forever; taught his last also greatest Messenger the Most Honorable Elijah Muhammad Supreme Wisdom about the creation of Himself. He Allah also taught us the Holy Messenger about Yakub's history, in which only Allah could know. So, let us examine this history my people. In the year 8,400 Yakub was born he was born with the determine idea to make a man or people, other than the original people. His uncle told him if you make a people different from the original people, you will be making the devil. Yakub replied I know that which you know not.

This is all in the history of Yakub my people. After Yakub completed his studies at the University of Al-Alzar at the age of 18, he began his mission. When Yakub was in the prison in Mecca this is before these present dwellers were ever there; he wrestles with the Angle the Angle was our fathers who is Allah, gave Yakub everything that he would need to begin building his new civilization as well as people. Allah also gave Yakub as well as Yakub's wisdom 6,000 years to rule.

Now in the Quran-a Yakub is referred as the vicegerent one who stands, in the place of Allah reasoning being, is that Allah granted Yakub's wisdom to rule for 6,000 years. Not the physical presence but the wisdom of Yakub. Therefore, none of these other people know or are they able to see Allah Almighty. So Yakub wisdom has been ruling for the past 6,000 years; Yakub himself died at the age of 150 years old so his makings never saw nor, will they ever be able to see their Yakub/Israel/John the Revelator; then later called himself Allah. Understand my people Mr. Yakub understood Islam extremely well Mr. Yakub also knew his purpose, in the world. He set up a governing body that would carry out that which he was born to do, after he died physically. Yakub knew what his mission was when he was a little boy therefore he told his uncle, I know that which you know what. So, he Yakub the Vicegerent wisdom will rule for 6,000 years he Yakub making, also wisdom would have command over everything on land, in the waters, in the skies as well as the angles; who would be standing in the place of Allah, but he isn't Allah; he was only using the name also identity of Allah.

My question my people is this; according to what Allah Almighty revealed to His Holy Messenger the Most Honorable Elijah the Muhammad, of the Quran-an as well as the Elijah of the Bible; His supreme wisdom going back further than Quran or any other teachings on our planet, or in the universe. Our God My People Is Allah Almighty the True Also Living God Who Has Absolutely No Recorded History of His Beginning; Nor is there Any Recorded history of Allah's as well as Our Ending at all. We are living in Omega my people; Omega my people are the end of the of the Vicegerent rule who is Yakub; who is also father as well as maker of the devil; the Caucasian Race also Yakub's Grafted Mentality which is nothing but defilement.

My point is this Allah the Universal Lord also Master gave Yakub 6,000 years to rule; he Yakub had command over all things. The Question is this, my people; Muhammad of Arabia received his revelations from the Vicegerent, not from Allah Almighty. Muhammad Of Arabia never saw Allah nor did anyone of the so-called Sunnah world, ever saw Allah; Allah revealed himself after Yakub's rule of 6,000 years had concluded. Therefore, Allah Almighty Himself brought us a new Islam or the Original Islam, as a way of life. Therefore, we who are the followers also students of the Holy Messenger the Honorable Elijah Muhammad; study the Supreme Wisdom given to us by Allah through his Holy Messenger. This is for us my people it doesn't matter who disbelieve; it doesn't matter how many people stand against us; With Allah on our side none can defeat us. Through Our Fathers Eyes my people not through the eyes of the enemies of our Fathers.

There was a 6,000-year vacuum in this present 25,000-year History also called Holy Quran-an; as I pointed out to everyone the original black man, writes His History or Quran-every 25,000 years to equal his Home/Earth/Asa/Asia circumference. This has been going on trillions of years before the birth of Yakub, as well as Prophet Muhammad; peace and blessings of Allah, be upon him. I'm not being disrespectful towards the Prophet I'm just telling the truth as Allah revealed it to His Last also greatest Messenger, the Most Honorable Elijah Muhammad; the true Muhammad RasulAllah. Everyone believes that they are the best guide for black people when in truth they are the worst guides, for black people. We aren't looking Through Our Fathers Eyes we have been as well as still are looking through the eyes of our open enemies. This is the reason why we can't rise it's due to all these different interlopers, believing they can tell us what to do, as they are being supported by America/Satan the Accursed Devil.

Sunnah so-called Islam is not for black people it's for the enemies of black people as well. The Vicegerent/ Yakub, whose wisdom still had 1,400 years, to rule as he completed his favors on his makings. This is when the Vicegerent/Yakub perfected Islam as a religion for his makings; this has absolutely nothing to do with black people. Therefore, we are living in Omega the end of Yakub's wisdom as well as Yakub's makings. For the past 6,000 years we have been living under the rule of the Vicegerent not Allah the Universal Lord As well as Master. For the past 6,000 years we have been looking through the eyes of evil. When it comes to black people our enemies including Sunnah so-called Islam has purposely kept everything of substance, from black people; thus, keeping black people at their mercy while they get rich. These so-called Sunnah Muslims never employ any black people they only employ themselves; while the black people suffer. Why should we my people embrace something not from our creator Allah Almighty, but from the Vicegerent/Yakub; whose only objective was as well as still is, murder the black baby at birth.

Through Our Fathers Eyes my people who has no beginning, nor does he have an ending, older than the Sun, Moon also Star. This is who we should be honoring also listing to not anyone else my people. They our enemies have only one concern that is to keep black people, in the bottom of the well. If we continue to be listing to the enemies of our fathers, we are the only ones my people that will continue to suffer; your children will continue to suffer; your wives will continue to suffer; as the enemies of our fathers are prospering; their children are prospering; their wives are prospering; as they our fathers enemies partner up with the enemies, of Islam. Omega my people is the end of Yakub's rule as well as wisdom my people. We should reject everyone as well anyone that tried to convince us, to reject our fathers; then accept them our spiritual leaders; this is a disgrace these people aren't our fathers. In fact, these people that are trying to trick also fool us, into believing in them also what they believe in; what the enemies of our fathers believe in, will only produce suffering for black people while they prosper. Yes, you have many Negro fools that are servants to the enemies of our fathers; these fanatics are no different than the Christian Preachers. They don't eat pork nevertheless they eat a lot of bottom feeders, in which Allah Himself taught us through His Holy Greatest as well last Messenger the Most Honorable Elijah Muhammad, the true as well as only RasulAllah; not to eat certain foods such as bottom feeders, in the sea; as well as certain vegetables.

No one my people including Sunnah so-called Islam cared about us or did anything for us but help as well as aid America/Satan the Accursed Devil, to destroy black people in America as well as throughout the world. Through Our Fathers Eyes My People we must return home stop listing to the enemies, of our fathers. If you are the enemies of my father as history prove they all are; then you are my enemies as well. I love my father's I have absolutely no love for any of our enemies; I don't care one bit for their so-called Sunnah Islam; that Islam comes not from Allah it comes from the Vicegerent Yakub father also maker of the devil, as well as imperfection. Omega my people; is the end of our enemies' Sunnah so-called Islam as well included. These other people have absolutely no idea of who Allah is; the infidels that are on the Arabs payroll, are just that my people liars, thieves, hypocrites also disbelievers. Our enemies calling themselves Sunnah have partner up with America the Global Murdering Terrorist. Through our Fathers Eyes my people To Hell with absolutely everyone else. We are living in Omega my people the end of Yakub's Civilization as well as his most poison wisdom, for black people.

CHAPTER 3

THE DECEIVED

The questions my people are who has been deceived also, who are the deceivers. Let us examine this subject my people. This is an absolute fact black people have been deceived by everyone that has come to America as well as those that are coming to America, are no friends of black people. Why do I talk about black the reason being is that no one else will? Others want us to believe that these are interlopers are our brothers also sisters, in truth these so-called Sunni Muslims are our brothers my people these so-called Sunni Muslims have just as much hatred also contempt for black also Indian People, as any Confederate. The Enemies of our fathers claiming to be Muslims in truth they aren't, therefore the Vicegerent gave them these rituals, for them to follow. Since these interlopers came to America they have partner up with America, my people. They are getting the grants, for schools for their children, as well other businesses; they are getting the better housing; they are getting better food; they are getting everything better than you, my people. You have been deceived on all accounts as well as by everyone, my people. We aren't even allowing to have our own way of life we are being force, to except our fathers' enemies, as our teachers in Islam as well as our leaders.

Here is the sorrow my people these strangers don't even like you they pretend to like you; in truth my people they just like robbing you of your money. Why are we going to another people restaurant that may have decent food, instead of us having our own restaurant with great food, thus a place for us to meet. Why would you allow yourself to be placed in a subservient by people that aren't of you, or even like you my people; in fact, Sunnah so-called Islam has committed the exact same atrocities on black people as their Zionist, Christian Brothers. This is proof that you have been deceived my people, right in front of you are all the answers, that you need. My people you have been so completely fooled by our enemies until you aren't able to see, exactly what is happening to you; to your children; to your wives; as these strangers who can bailey speak the language, are being made your boss at work. My people you can't even get a job as a cab driver due to all these strangers, have been given the jobs. They are going to schools while this society purposely, mislead the mass of black people, into the very bottom of the civilized well.

This is your reward for giving up what Allah brought to you; this is your reward for denouncing Allah's last also greatest Messenger. Instead of building things for yourself, wives also children, you rather worship another version, of this mystery god; while our enemies get rich; as you become more disenfranchised. You have been completely deceived my people you who have been here for over 450 years have absolutely nothing, but maybe church or mosque, to go too and nothing else. Look around my people these are strangers controlling every aspect of your life. Every other people are producing for themselves that which they need to be a civilize people, except you so-called Negro the Ex-Slave of America. Whose eyes are you looking through my people it's a damn shame that you are grateful to the demons, that trapped you in this hellish nightmare; where you think detoxifying or the program, Methadone, AA or some other American made dope or program; design to destroy you, your families, children as well; you can't see how foolish you are, my people. We as a people are being wiped of the planet the reason this is happening, is due to your ignorance black people. Everything that you do is from the eyes also thoughts, of the enemies of our fathers, as well as ourselves, my people.

It is a shame my people that you allow yourself to be played out of pocket you have nothing while strangers, have everything. This American Government as well as the society they have your black people the bottom feeder, while other strangers as well as their families are doing well. You have absolutely nothing for yourself or your families. Every other people have traditions for themselves as a people while you have absolutely nothing, for yourself. Detoxifying in some drug program but won't detoxify yourselves from the deadliest of all their drugs is Christianity, you haven't detoxified yourselves my people from this slave making Christianity; so, anything other than detoxifying ourselves from this most deadly of our enemies drugs this slave making Christianity, amounts to nothing. We must stand up for ourselves my people we must create our own traditions, for ourselves. We already have our own, but you won't gravitate to them due to you my people, following also looking through the eyes of our enemies. Jesus doesn't save my people this fake, make believe so-called Jesus, only destroy. Look at yourself my people you are accomplishing nothing; you haven't accomplished anything except, presenting yourself as absolute fools, in the last 40 plus years, up till this present day also time.

Our enemies have stolen our music, stolen our history, stolen our heritage, stolen our language, stolen from us everything, it takes a civilize person as well as people, to be a civilize person also people. What could you possibly be waiting on or for, my people? Nothing is coming if you are not willing to stand up then do it for yourself, then you will only know hell, all your life. Your wives also children will only know hell, all their lives as well. Is this what you want my people a life of hell also damnation, while other people are enjoying themselves; in the land that history proves that you helped build as well defend also protect. Through Our Fathers Eyes my people is crucial that we all begin to look though; this is the only way we can achieve Freedom, Justice as well Equality. This is the deceit that we have been experiencing also suffering my people in America, as well throughout the world. We must realize that we can no longer allow this deceit to control our lives; we can no longer allow this deceit to dictate what cause of action, is best for us all. We have been suffering so terrible under this Government as well as people now this very same wicked American Government has brought as well as still bringing in more immigrants that are the enemies of Black as well as Indian people.

We have been so unmercifully deceived by our supposed to be own people as well as others we trusted, until we can no longer afford to trust anyone; it doesn't matter what they say their religion may be, we can't trust them; we will be even bigger fools to continue to trust any of them. We have been deceived my people as we have been suffering conditions, that would have wipe these other interlopers, completely out. America has projected to the world that you are nothing black people; that you should not be even taken seriously; that you aren't a danger to anyone only yourself; America/

Satan the Accursed Devil are as well as has allowed these interlopers to bring drugs into every black community, throughout America; poison black people as they murder black children. America/Satan the Accursed Devil has disarmed black people of the arms to prevent these interloping demons, from coming amongst us spreading these poisons throughout Black Communities, everywhere in America. These drugs dealing demons are no friends to or for black people; these drugs dealing demons are the enemies of black people as well as agents of America the Accursed Devil; whom they swore an oath, to help also aid America, in murdering Black men, women also black children. Where are these so-called political as well as religious leaders at my people, no were to be found, until you get angry then act; then every phony religious organization is there helping our oppressors to continue their unholy assault on black people; this includes Sunni so-called Islam as well; talking about a peaceful resolution. There can never be a peaceful resolution until all these murderers, are completely stopped; driven back into the caves in which they come from; or completely removed off our planet, my people. Then and only then will black people receive JUSTICE.

My experience my people tells me none of these interloping immigrants are ever going to help us, except drive the stake of deception, deeper as well as deeper into our hearts; to all black people in America, as well as all black people throughout the world. We have been greatly deceived my people as Allah revealed to us, through His holy Messenger the Most Honorable Elijah Muhammad/Muhammad RasulAllah. In America all Caucasian People are taught this anytime they see two or more black people together speaking with each other; if they black people aren't fighting with each other; all Caucasian people are taught to spy on us to find out what we are speaking about. It doesn't matter where these devils may come from they are all ready to spy on black people; especially those who dare call themselves Muslims. These are enemies my people to black people that do everything in their meager power, to gather information on what we black people are doing; then report back to their Zionist brothers, on what we are thinking or maybe planning. We can't trust anyone other than our black selves. Through Our Fathers Eyes my people not our enemies' eyes. Our enemies have the desire to keep us in hell, so these worthless peasant immigrants are working on the side, of our 6,000-year-old enemies; here in America.

We have absolutely no help coming from these immigrants coming to America they have pledge their legion to our open enemies, America the Accursed Devil. I'm watch all the time our enemies want to see what I'm doing what am I writing about; the lies that always being taught as well as being spread in America, is to destroy all black people in America, as well as throughout the world. Look at the President of America his own Attorney General said he is a moron, what does that tell you about American People. Through Our Fathers Eyes my people is where the truth lye not through the eyes of our enemies; looking through our enemies have only gotten black people in America as well as throughout the world, death, misery, suffering as well as heart break. The entire Caucasian World is the heart break hotel for black people all over the world. Why is this so Saladin? The reason being is all we have ever received is misery, suffering then death, from the lies also false promises that we have for over 450 years, my people. How much longer are we going to sit back waiting on their mystery god it doesn't matter what name they called this mystery god my people; whose proper name is Yakub. Suffering, slavery then death, is all we will receive nothing else my people.

We have been deceived by the enemies of our fathers for the last 500 years my people. We have been living under the cruel deceitful lies of the enemies, of our fathers. Their religions, their politics, their made up laws that benefit our enemies, not black people; the filth, indecent, the horrors, the lies, the suffering, the miseries; the false religions; the hatred; the false leadership; the hatred; by America as well as those who love America; the to destroy as well as keep black people, at the very bottom of the well, of civilization; forever savages in the pursuit of happiness; obtaining nothing at all; always being hunted by our enemies with their phony religions, all of our lives. You can't overcome our enemies when you can't see the enemies, standing in front of your face. Why can't our people see the many enemies black people have Saladin? They have been completely deceived, tricked also fool by the enemies, of our fathers; until black people believe the religious lies being forced upon them, by the enemies of our fathers as well as our selves. My people these religious murderers have murdering us as they ram their made up lies about Allah as well as Islam, upon us black people.

If you research the history you will discover these are liars, murderers, rapist, thieves of our fathers also ourselves. This is nothing but White Supremacy as well as White Nationalism in which we have been living also suffering under for more than 400 years. Our enemies have taught our people all over the world, to hate as well as not to trust black people, in America. So, the seed of hate for self has already been placed in the minds, our own people, to hate the innocent as they praise also worshipped our enemies as well their made-up religions. If you believe in our enemies lies that's all they are my people lies from our enemies. We should no longer listen to the enemies of our fathers; we should no longer embrace any of their false interpretation of any religion; it doesn't matter what name they place on it, they are all the enemies of fathers. We no longer allow ourselves to be deceived by the enemies of our fathers; we must examine the true history Through Our Fathers Eyes; not through the eyes of these lying murdering devils, calming to be a part of the human so-called race. No, my people these are the enemies trying to pass themselves as human beings, when they are nothing more than some sub- human species, that Yakub made in the laboratories on the Island of Pelan 6,600 years ago. We my people are the deceived by our enemies, taught by our enemies to hate ourselves. How much longer are you going to allow our enemies to deceive us, my people; in fact, you don't have any more time my people the destruction of the Vicegerent/Yakub World is being destroyed. This crazy Christianity religion is also being destroyed. In fact, every aspect of the Vicegerent/Yakub world is being destroyed along with all their interpretations of religions as well as Allah.

For us not to be deceived we must keep the deceivers from amongst us, they are always trying to get into our business, pretending to be our friends when in truth they are looking for other means, to destroy black people. These interlopers are always looking on how they can keep black people separated as well as hating, each other. Our 6,000-year-old enemies are always looking for efficient methods to destroy black families without any remorse my people; only gratification for their evil deeds, committed on Original People. You are the deceived my people what's really concerning is that you can't see it as you trust the Murderers, of you, us as well all black people, on our planet. This Christianity is not the religion of our fathers thus making it not our religion, as well. This so-called Sunni Islam is also not the religion of our fathers thus making it not our religion, as well. Allah Himself brought us back the way of life of our fathers, not the religion of our enemies.

Think about it my people until the wisdom of Yakub came into existence 6,600 years ago; the evils that has over run, our planet, never existed. We must return to our style of dress. We should burn; these garments that represents, everything of absolute evil, of our as well as from our 6,000 old enemies. We have built civilizations after civilizations after civilizations before these enemies have ever been grafted out of us then given form. What do we need from them they don't know what civilization is; they only knew how to murder then steal from us, who create civilizations. My people no matter what part of the planet you are living on, we are my people, the creators; we have been creating for ourselves for trillions, trillions, trillions, trillions of years, before the creation of the Sun; which was 78 trillion years ago, we have built civilizations, before our enemies also the maker of these the Vicegerent Yakub, was ever birth on our planet.

We are taught my people to be enemies to ourselves by the enemies, of our fathers as well as ourselves. Our enemies hide in the shadows of our ignorance of believing that Allah can't be seen, or touch. These are absolute lies by our enemies my people to convince you that there is something greater than you. There is absolutely nothing at all greater than our unified self, my people. Our enemies know this my people you don't know this. Our enemies work extra hard on trying to convince us of their maker who physically died, before his experiment was completed. In fact, their Maker our enemies' maker died 450 years before his experiment was completed. So, our enemies never saw their maker unlike us the Original People we see our creator every time we look at a black man, we are looking at the Universal Creator, so saith, Allah Almighty Himself. Let us examine all things especially for the past 6,000 years when our open enemies were given the power to rule. Nothing but death, destruction, rape, starvation, misery, suffering, wars a complete hell, my people especially for Original People. In fact, it has been hell unleashed on our planet, from this so-called mankind. Every living creature on the planet has suffered slaughter at unimaginable levels, never known on our planet. Why are you listening to these mass murderers of every life form, tell you about Allah? What could Yakub makings; know anything about Allah when they are a bunch of mass murderers. You are suffering my original people due to you listening, believing also following, the enemies of Allah as well as all of Allah's prophets; history verifies that what I'm saying is the truth that can always be proven the truth.

There are many servants of our enemies that will fight passionately defending their religious masters if they are able to feel important. These traitors care absolutely nothing about the deaths of their original people, if they are pleasing their now Arab masters. This is what's happening my people these traitors won't even look at the evils these people have committed as well are still committing; as they carve out their section of this American Nightmare, as they continue to mislead black people to an absolute destruction. Convincing black of this insane nonsense of a make-believe heaven after you die this total insanity my people. The Christians told us the same lies my people how many people have come back from the dead, to tell us about this insanity of their make-believe heaven; including all the Prophets; which one has come to tell us about this make-believe heaven? Which one my people there is no such insanity recorded cause it's all make believe. Heaven is while you live there is nothing after death my people these are the lies, of our enemies my people. I love my people I have absolutely no love for our enemies my people. All our enemies as well as their lies have only brought Original People Suffering, Slavery as well as death, to us all, examine the undistorted history you will see I'm right.

You are the deceived my people by all these different people that aren't of you as well as none of these interlopers, care anything about you my brothers; your wives my brothers; your children my brothers as well as your elders my brother. These partners of America care nothing about us at all it's time we care about ourselves, as we tell our enemies to get behind me Satan We are servants of Allah our Holy Savior also Deliverer in the person of Master Fard Muhammad to whom all holy praises, are due forever. Let our enemies take their religious also political hypocrisies for themselves my people; we don't want it in fact we don't need it at all. It hasn't done us my people any good at all, in fact their nonsense has only benefitted themselves, wives also children. You are the deceived my people the question is who have deceived us? Everyone coming into America has absolutely no love or concern for Black as well as Indian People. Then why my people are you making our enemies rich, by patronizing, their poison businesses all throughout America, my people? I say my people let our enemies keep their insane beliefs we have absolutely no use for their insanity; all that believe in them then go with them let us my people, do something for ourselves.

35

Stop patronizing the enemies' business my people in fact they should be removed from amongst us, let our enemies take their insanity amongst themselves we don't want it as well as we don't need it. We should no longer allow ourselves to be deceived by anyone, my people. We shouldn't allow our enemies to impose upon us their lies about religion no matter how enticing or romantic our enemies make it seem, it is poison to all black people everywhere on our planet. None of these immigrants especially this so-called Sunnah Islam ever come to the aid of black people, as this American Gestapo law Enforcement gun down black men as well as black children; you never see these cowards nor any of their paid lackeys. Black also Indian people being murdered all over America this so-called Sunnah Islam, has absolutely nothing to say. Black people being murdered all over the world as this so-called Sunnah Islam, has nothing to say, about these injustices, being committed on as well as against black people. It is these Arab's with their so -called Sunnah Islam that are murdering black original people in Serra Leone, who are Muslims. This further proof that these frauds are on the side of America when comes to murdering black people; robbing black people; raping black women, lying to black people; doing everything to aid America, in destroying black people, Indian people as well. Our enemies are robbing us; killing us; raping black girls as well as women, as they get with these crimes, only due to them being one of America's partners in Global Terrorism. Then these same enemies are going to tell us to read Quran-a like that's going to put a stop, to these atrocities. You are the deceived my people as you are still foolish enough to listen also trust the enemies of our fathers, as well as ourselves.

These cowards come to America to be disgusting Americans look at how their women have adopted the American style of dressings; not all of them but a great deal of them have, you can see them everywhere in the city visiting these filthy stores, of the enemies of Islam. My people in the Western Hemisphere we have been taught to hate each other by our enemies, we all came to the Western Hemisphere by the slave ships, of our enemies. We all my black brothers also sisters have suffered cruel atrocities, from our enemies; these same enemies have taught us to hate each other so that we never unify ourselves, to deal with the evils, of our many enemies in America as well as throughout the world. The truth must be told my people I once again am a follower also student of Muhammad RasulAllah, the Most Honorable Elijah Muhammad. See how the Arabs spread their version of Islam through black people throughout the Jungles of East Asia, now called Africa. Examine the brutality of these Arabs as well as their so-called Sunnah Islam, as they murdered black men as well as boys, elder men as well; then raped black woman also young black girls. How could this be the religion of Allah it is impossible my people. This is the religion of the Vicegerent claiming to be Allah, in truth he isn't Allah he is Yakub the father and maker of the devil.

This isn't coming from me this is from the Best Knower through the mouth of His Holy Messenger the Most Honorable Elijah Muhammad/ Muhammad RasulAllah. We are all black people not matter where we maybe we are all black people. We lived in harmony with each other for trillions of years, before the Yakub grafted the Caucasian Race out of us 6,600 years ago. Our enemies are safe if we continue fighting, hating also distrusting each other my people. We all must understand no matter where we maybe we are one people always have been always will be. Once we understand this then learn to reconnect with ourselves; have love for our black selves; have trust for ourselves; as we collectly stop allowing our enemies to deceive us all. We built civilizations for trillions of years before our enemies' maker, was even made a man himself. Through Our Fathers Eyes my people is the only eyes we should ever look through. It doesn't matter what our enemies have to say we don't care what anyone have to say we choose for ourselves, what we want for ourselves. Then and only then can we no longer be deceived by anyone

CHAPTER 4

BETRAYAL

This is a most distributing subject as well a painful my people no matter where you may be betrayal is a part of our lives, it's awful that our so-called leaders are this way, but this is what's happening to black people, everywhere. We must forever be vigilant my people we have enemies amongst us all over the world. Our political also religious so-called leaders have betrayed us all unilaterally without any concern of the overall most devastating destructiveness; their betrayal will have on black people universally. We my people are fighting against our 6,000-year-old most dangerous enemies that have a proven history, of murdering innocent women, children as well as our elders. These cowards amongst us have sold as well as are still selling us out globally not all of them, but many them, have done this; for the praise of our enemies. The devastation amongst black people worldwide is due to these cowards' betrayal of their people, thus aiding the enemies of their own people to destroy their people. I've been watching this all my life here in America this betrayal has been nothing but catastrophic, for the ex-slave of America. I have seen so much carnage from these political also religious so-called leaders' betrayals, to no civilize people want to deal with black people. This betrayal of black people has left black people incapacitate to do anything for themselves or for anyone to us seriously. The most devastating affect is that they don't even have the desire, to anything for themselves; reasoning being is that these enemies have convinced black people, to believe in a mystery god that has never answered any prayer, of black people in America. These so-called religions that have been force upon us by our proven enemies have done us absolutely nothing of good for the mass, of black people as well.

This betrayal of these religious also political so-called leaders; were heinous as well the effects were horrendous my people. These cowards are the puppets for our enemies, look at who they are watching out for; they surely aren't watching out for black people. If they were why are the descendants of those who made that most dreadful James Town Landing in 1555 as well as the second James Town Landing in 1619; are in such a wretched condition; the amazing thing my people is that our open enemies, as history proves them to be our enemies. You my people continue to believe in their lies, of god also religion; these lies have done absolutely nothing to improve the conditions, for the mass of black people. I'm lying! I'm wrong you want to tell me! Then why the hell are these descendants living in concentrations camps, all throughout America? Why the hell are these descendants being used as lab rats? After over 400 years of the most hellish treatment as well as service, entertainment as well; we are left without anything, we can call our own?

How is it possible that this American Gestapo call Law Enforcement can murder black men, women as well as children, as these Gestapo Criminals disguised as Law Enforcement, get away with these crimes; violating black as well as Indian People, Human Rights? This is nothing but planned executions, by this American Gestapo Government, my people; while these religious also political hypocrites do absolutely nothing at all, about these atrocities being committed, on their people. How can anyone explain why we the descendants of our fathers also mothers, that made this most horrifying James Towns Landings; beyond any sane person, imagination; should continue to take this from this Zionist/Christian/Arab/Asian American Government of Global Murdering Terrorist? This betrayal my people are of global proportions that we, the ancients of the ancients, of the ancients of all people; why must as well as why should we except this any longer, in America as well as throughout the world. Why do we whose creation is older than the Sun, Moon also Stars; who have been creating civilizations for trillions of years, in fact everything I am saying, is verified by history. History proves that black people existence transcends every other people on this planet. Then why should we sit back as these religious also political hypocrites betray the mass of black people, to make their Caucasian as well as their partners in genocide happy, at our expense?

My people no one has the right to tell us what we should be. None of these strangers have the right to tell us anything about Allah, Islam or

Allah's Holy Messenger. These strangers whom Islam was perfected by the Vicegerent for them, approximately 1,400 years ago; how can they tell us about something they know absolutely nothing about? These rituals of theirs are exactly that the rituals of the seed of the Vicegerent /Yakub; this has absolutely nothing to do with Original People. We aren't from the Vicegerent my people; our enemies are from the making of the Vicegerent/ Yakub. Zionism, Christianity, Arabism, as well as Hinduism are the seeds of the Vicegerent/Yakub; who was given 6,000 years to rule. The rule of the wisdom of the Vicegerent/Yakub has completed itself now only death also destruction of the Vicegerent /Yakub's making as well as his world, are being destroyed right before our eyes.

It is wrong that strangers supported by their American Partners have been sanction by America, to spread this so-called Sunnah Islam in America; while this very Sunnah so-called Islam never support anything that represent black people, advancing themselves as a people. Zionism has their version of the Vicegerent /Yakub Islam as well; they received Islam as a way of life from Muza a Prophet of Allah. The Vicegerent/Yakub along with his makings, were exiled into the Cave sides of the Caucasus Mountains, in West Asia now called Europe; for the next 2,000 years. This is when the devil was cast out of heaven down to hell or into hell; the hell is not being able to participate in society, as a civilize people. Hell, my people is being at the very, very, very bottom of any so-called civilization; in which you my people are living in this very present day also time.

The Original Turkish People are the Original Black People from Mecca, that by the government, who commissioned General Muk -Muk; to execute the punishment of us the righteous people; on those who didn't fall under the spells, of the Vicegerent/Yakub's makings, especially the Vicegerents females; marched them across the Hot Arabian desert, in tow. This is the absolute truth of the devil being cast down, out of the heavens; as Allah Almighty Himself in the person of Master Fard Muhammad; to whom all holy praises are due forever; taught His Rasul the Most Honorable Elijah Muhammad. As the Holy Messenger taught us all; that some of the Original People that were helping the Vicegerent's/Yakub Wisdom to be spread, amongst the Original People causing Original Black People in Mecca, to start fighting as well as killing each other; the black women to begin hiding, the devil under their skirts. This is the history my people as only Allah would know taught us through His Holy Messenger; this is the history that Allah's Holy Messenger the Most Honorable Elijah Muhammad taught us all.

The Original Turkish People are black people that were charged also proven to have been aiding the wisdom also plans, of the evils this Vicegerent /Yakub; wanted to be spread amongst black original people. So, by the mercy of Allah they realized their error, as they asked for forgiveness, from Allah as well as their people. Allah through His Great General Muk-Muk speared their lives of these fools, from Allah's waft. Yet the Great General Muk-Muk made these un-knowingly Advocates of the Vicegerent/Yakub, to be the Guardians, of the Gates of the Garinel. This happened 4,600 years before the mission of Prophet Ibn Abdullah Muhammad of Arabia, May peace also blessing of Allah, be upon him. This happened 2,000 years before the birth of Prophet Muza mission; May the peace also blessings of Allah, be upon him. This happened 4,000 years before the birth of Prophet Esa Ibn Yusuf /Jesus mission, May the Peace also blessings of Allah be upon him. Why would or should we my people believe or consider anyone else, or what they have to say or believe? Cause the enemies have some Negro flunky, advocating for them. A flunky is a flunky my people it doesn't what religion they claim to represent. They are only representing the Vicegerent/Yakub, not Allah the Universal Creator, it's written in their so-called Quran-an. Allah our Savior; our Deliverer in the person of Master Fard Muhammad; to whom all holy praises are due forever; the Best knower; the Best planner; told us something completely different, then what our proven enemies has told as well as shown, black people in America also black people throughout the world. The answers my people have already been given to us by Allah Almighty Himself, in the person of Master Fard Muhammad to whom all holy praises are due forever. He Allah my people Himself raised up one from amongst us to be the Rasul, the Seal of the Prophets. The True name of the Rasul is the Most Honorable Elijah Muhammad. Allah the Most Merciful the Most Kind, the Wisest, the Most Exalted, the Highest; Our Holy Savior also Deliver taught His holy Messenger what he had to do for us all, as well as how to do this biblical task, most monumental task. The answer is as follows. The Supreme Wisdom, The Many Imports including Metric Tons of Fish, The Muhammad Universities of Islam, The Many Temples all throughout the Country, The Many different Farms, The Many Different Produces, The Corp Programs; The Banking System also

Bank, The Three Year Economical Program, The FOI, The MGT GCC, The Unity Amongst Ourselves, The Muhammad Speaks Newspaper, The Housing as well as Different Developments For Self, The Shabazz Steak Houses, The Many Steak and Takes All throughout the Country, The Many different Heads of States, The Transportation System, The Sewing Classes throughout every Temple of Islam in America, The many Different Social Events that Drew Thousands of Black People including non-followers, The Many Lectures By The Holy Messenger Himself, The Many Ministers Raised Up From Amongst Ourselves, The Clothing, The Bean Pie, The Bean Soup, The Many Bakeries Throughout America, The International Trading, The Black Awareness as well as the creating an extremely great interest amongst Black People Learning About Ourselves, The Many Different Black Own Businesses Throughout America, A Brotherhood For Black men, A Sisterhood for Black women, The Greeting Of Peace also Paradise Amongst Black People, The Love For Black Self as well as Kind, Teaching Black People How To Be Civilize, The Putting Us Back On The Road of Being a Productive People, The Many Different Professions Amongst Black People, Our Own Declaration Of Independence, Our Own Constitution To Govern Ourselves By, The Meetings On Sunday, Wednesday, Friday as Well as Saturday, The FOI Drill Teams, The MGT GGC Drill Teams as well as more, my people. How To Eat To Live taking us away from that poison foods, the slave masters force black people to eat, that was cutting our lives short as well as causing mental Retardation, amongst Black People. Removing the many destructive vices amongst Black People such dope, alcohol, Prostitution, killing of ourselves, such as gambling. This is what was taken from replaced with another version of this mystery god as we once again end up with nothing as a people, as our enemies were given everything we built for ourselves, was gone due to BETRAYAL.

Never since crossing the Atlantic were we as Productive as a people. There were shades of our Greatness when we had Black Wall Street in which was destroyed by the American Government as well as the Caucasian People. Where towns were burned to the ground as well as the many murders these enemies committed also rapes, against a people who were only doing for self. This Betrayal my people was at Epic Proportion our enemies are now in possession of that which we built, for ourselves under the Leadership of the Holy Messenger of Allah the Most Honorable Elijah Muhammad. Our enemies for the past 6,000 years are trying to make you as well as I believe in their Vicegerent/Yakub. All one must do is examine the history, don't let the enemies tell you there lies about anything concerning Allah or Allah's prophets my people. What Allah Himself gave to us that have filled the 400 year of pure hellish absolute nightmare that only we black people, in America had to endure. We are that Seed of Ibrahim that Ibrahim Whom Ibrahim asked Allah to make them Muslims, this is you my people. This was before the Vicegerent/Yakub was born. This other so-called Orthodox Islam is not for us the Lost Found Members of The Tribe of Shabazz, who are members of the Nation of Islam; have been members for this so-called Sunnah Islam, ever came into existence. Islam as Allah taught us through His Holy Messenger; is older than the Sun, Moon as well as the Stars; Islam has no beginning, so something is very wrong with this so-called Sunnah; it doesn't belong to or for Black People that fore filled the Prophecy of Ibrahim Seed, this is only us my people. Can't you see how devastating this Betrayal has been for Black People these are strangers my people; they aren't of us as we aren't of them. They don't know their Maker the Vicegerent/Yakub; they never saw the Vicegerent/Yakub due to him being physically dead. We Know who Allah is cause He Himself visited us in person He Allah fashion us after Himself; He Allah taught His Holy Messenger face to face for 3 years also 4 months; Prophet Muhammad can never claim reason being, he Prophet Muhammad of Arabia never saw Allah, nor did he see any of the Angles/Scientist, of Allah the true also living God. The Betrayal my people you must understand these hypocrites also disbelievers were honeycomb throughout the members, of the Tribe of Shabazz, belonging to Islam here in the Wilderness of North America. This is the Betrayal my people not only from the Christians but also from the many, many Hypocrites inside as well as amongst, of ourselves. These are the Betrayers of you as well as myself, my people; these are nothing but traitors my people. Instead of learning their own language, they choose to learn the dialect of our enemies.

Just as the Christians gave black people their concepts of god, writings, traditions, holidays interpretation of bible also language; this so-called Sunnah has given black people their worthless values as well as they steal from us that which we worked for; as these traitors amongst us were aiding America to give everything we built under the Guidance of Allah; under the Leadership of Allah's Holy Messenger the Most Honorable Elijah, to our enemies of 6,000. My people don't miss understand me I'm not against anyone that's not against my people as well as myself. Since these strangers are on the side of America/Satan the Accursed Devil, then they are against Black People ever having anything for themselves, women as well as our children. If anyone think or believe that they can turn us away from our fathers, to except them as a foster father; I say to hell with them all as well to hell with whatever they have to say; or worship; these are the enemies of our fathers as well as the enemies of ourselves.

This is the betrayal of these traitors that were amongst us as well as the Holy Apostle; this is the betrayal of these Christians as well, this is also the betrayal of this so-called Orthodox so-called Sunnah Islam. We have been so unmercifully betrayed it is a sin in the eyes of Allah, by supposed to be our own people; now these traitors called themselves African Americans. America or one of America's partners own them, lock stock also the barrel. These traitors that were in the ranks of the FOI as well as the MGTGCC believed they could put out the light, of Allah; they deceived only themselves; Allah will punish them all for their treacheries, against His Chosen People. Our enemies are always trying to convince us their mystery god also of their false heaven that exist nowhere. If you believe in this falsehood my people you are doom as well as you will never be able to become an independent self-productive intelligent people ever.

My People you must wake up except the truth of what has happened as well as who participate in these crimes, that were committed against us. I want every true believer who has a temple or have a program, instituting the Teachings of Allah as He Allah taught His Holy Messenger, who taught us all; I'm not in any opposition against anyone of us. I'm not condemning or speaking against you. I'm speaking about the traitors that were amongst us that were a co-conspirator as well participant, in the evil crimes committed against black people, in 1975. If what I'm saying offends you then you must be of the guilty that aided the enemies of, Allah, His Holy Messenger as well as every Black Person in America, as well as throughout the world. Through Our Fathers Eyes my people we all must look my people not through any other eyes. Everyone else that we were foolish enough to trust has betrayed as well as robbed us, black people throughout America as well as the rest, of the world. Their days of false happiness are ending; their days of false prestige are now over; their days of robbing also deceiving black people are now over; their days of protecting the enemies of ours are now over; everyone that sold us out my people are going to face the chastisement of Allah. It's Through Our Fathers Eyes my people no matter what part of the planet you may be, or live on, it's through our Fathers Eyes and absolutely no other eyes will we dare look through. It doesn't matter that they are caring a Bible Or Quran-an, history proves these ones have been the deadliest, the most poisonous, the biggest liars, the biggest deceivers, the biggest thieves, the biggest murders, the biggest rapist, that come amongst black people, here in America as well as throughout the world. Here is what's truly as well as disgraceful, my people, is that these traitors learned, their Marital Arts Skills many of them, by being in the FOI. This is where self-defense began also you will find many, many black men were introduced, to Marital Arts by the Nation of Islam in the Western Hemisphere. There were many Grand Masters amongst us currently. There was a time when boxing was the main art amongst black people of self-defense as well as it should be; yet in the early sixties also mid-sixties the Martial Arts were introduce, to black people.

In New York we had Grand Master Musa Powell, Grand Master George Coalfield, Grand Master Ronald Duncan, Grand Master Lukman, Master La Puppet there are many, many more brothers that were teaching, us Marital Arts. Professor V; there were so many my people that were active in teaching black people how to defend ourselves, from this American Gestapo. Many of these so-called believers turned traitor as they sold their souls, to Satan the Accursed Devil; the shame is that these fools didn't or couldn't see that they were also have purchased, very sour goods; as they aided their fathers also mothers enemies; what a shame. I thank Allah that I'm not that foolish or silly to betray my fathers, for the enemies, of my fathers, as history clearly reveals that what I'm saying is the truth. This was the Betrayal of 1975 by Wallace as he revealed all the hypocrites as well as all the disbelievers, surrounding the Holy Apostle. I applaud the brothers also followers that are doing magnificent work, in upholding Allah's Teachings as Allah's holy Messenger taught us; as well as building temples to educate our people that's done an excellent job of upholding teachings as well as programs, of Allah as He Allah taught His Holy Messenger, the Most Honorable Elijah Muhammad; I salute this brothers also sisters for upholding Allah in the person of Master Fard Muhammad, to whom all holy praises are due forever;

as well as His Holy Messenger the Most Honorable Elijah Muhammad; I salute them all.

Through Our Fathers Eyes my people we must look through; every black person in the world must understand, that the Vicegerent/Yakub wisdom has come, to an end; this devil is out to murder as many original people that they can. I want the world to know that I'm not doing this to be recognize as some new Malcolm X, I put Malcolm picture there to be a reminder for us not to stray away from, Allah in the person of Master Fard Muhammad, to whom all holy praises are due forever; also, His Allah Holy Messenger the Most Honorable Elijah Muhammad. My brothers also sisters Jerusalem Must Be Taken Back, From the Devil. The Jerusalem my people is not the physical city, it is the New Islam That Allah Himself brought to us; taught His Holy Messenger; whom intern taught us all; Allah's Supreme Wisdom; the New Jerusalem; the Original Islam that is older than the Sun, Moon Also Stars; in which Allah created the entire universe. It was on this day 1,400 years ago or approximately 1,400 years ago that the Vicegerent/Yakub perfected Islam as a religion for his making; thus, completing his/Yakub favors upon them; not us my people; we are not the Vicegerent/Yakub making or experiment, our enemies are the making of the Vicegerent/Yakub.

I was told by a brother that I truly care about in words he doesn't approve of what I'm doing I was very surprise, at this conversation we had. It's very hard to believe that many of our people ability to reconstruct the period, of the time better yet the person that made them uncomfortable. I'm very surprise by these brothers' negative response. One brother even said to me I shouldn't do it; I listen to them which only strengthen my conviction to do what I'm doing. We must understand that the time is now that We Must Make America Know her Sins; It's time We Make The American People Know Their Sins; It's Time We Let The World Know That We Are Alive As Well As Standing Up For Ourselves; It's Time We Let America Also The World Know That We Are Now Looking Through Our Fathers Eyes, Not Through The Eyes Of Our 6,000-Year-Old Enemies. We must be preparing to fight as well as die defending that which is ours, instead of attacking or being displeased over a picture, before trying to gain understanding of why. We can't have this type of narrow minded thinking amongst us reason being is that this narrow-minded thinking, is destructive in the growth also development of black children worldwide.

We must be able to critically think as we analyze our history starting from 1555 till this present day as well as time. The Betrayal as well as everyone who participated in our Betrayal must be exposed to the world. Staying under the radar is nothing more than hiding how much longer are we to hide, from our enemies? How much longer are we my people supposed to conduct ourselves in the parameter that our enemies have set for us? How much longer are we supposed to set around waiting for something to drop out of the skies, before we realize that we must do this ourselves? When my people will we understand that we must create for ourselves, in every aspect of modern civilization as well as a people. When are we my people going to make these hypocrites be held accounted for the crimes, they have committed against their own people. How much longer are we going to sit back saying absolutely nothing, I say the time has arrived that we stand up for ourselves as we let the entire world, know of the Great Betrayal of 1964/1965 as well as 1975, as well as all those who participated in these Horrific Crimes against their people.

CHAPTER 5

OUT OF THE BOX

Allah to whom all Holy Praises are due Forever taught His Holy Messenger the Most Honorable Elijah Muhammad, who intern taught us all; the average man only speaks 400 words well; the Lion in his cage work back and forth; the Lion is searching for a way out of his cage. The Holy Messenger mission was to wake up us then put us back on the road of being independent. We had to be put back on the square where we can think out of the box. This means that we should be able to critically think as well as critically analyze every as well as all things that happened in the past. We must be able to examine the events that happened in our history that we must, put together ourselves. What happened in the past when we were children we must now critically analyze it all, to bring conclusion to our confusion, my people. Out of the box my people we must begin to think we been in the box since 1555 how much longer, are you going to remain inside the box? Master Fard Muhammad is Our Savior as well as our Deliverer; Master Fard Muhammad Is Allah Almighty to whom all holy praises, are due forever; not His Messenger the Most Honorable Elijah. I submit to Allah Himself; I follow the teachings that Allah gave to His Holy Messenger in which His Holy Messenger, taught us all. In fact, Allah told His Holy Messenger when it came to prayer, for us; Allah said stand them up Elijah they been on their knees to long; I Came To Make Them God. So, to be God, You Must Think As God; this means think out of the box. To think out of the box We Must Look Through Our Fathers Eyes.

As a people also as individuals we don't think outside the box that was made for us over 450 years ago. Till this very day many in fact I would say 90% of black people think inside the box, where they believe it is safe. Now due to them staying in the box under the radar they believe they have the right to voice their displeasures about something, or someone they disagree with; before asking or allowing said person to explain themselves. These are people that are narrow minded thinking also operating in their own corner of the box that they believe where they are safe. These people are always voicing their useless opinions on what someone else should do, when they don't really understand what is happening. So, it doesn't matter what they say reason being they don't understand, what's happening in this day also time; they don't think out of the box. The box is a prison my people that never allow you to see beyond what have been set up, for us. We must ever be able to convey an intelligent analogy of our over 450 years, in the most hellish, diabolical prisons the world has ever known. How can you have a civilize society without having scholars, to bring our children new ideas, new way of examining things also analyzing all things. How can we heal ourselves of the many diseases that are plaguing us, if we can't think out of the box, Through Our Fathers Eyes My people is our way out, not through the eyes of the box, that our open enemies have made for us?

Ignorant people voicing their silly opinions about a picture without any serious examination of the time, in which they are living in. They would rather condemn without even examining the absolute truth in the time, that this happening in. We are a doom people due to the moronic ignorance of our people not being able, to critically think as well as analyze anything. If you can't see beyond the scope of something that happened 50 years ago how can you believe that you are capable, of building a nation. Going to a temple or mosque is not building a nation this is only operating in a comfort zone, in which most black people do. I really don't care what anyone of them have to say as well as I most surely don't care, what any of them have to say; reason being they are all a worst hypocrite, then the ones they claim to be a hypocrite. These fools are the ones that can speak only 400 words as they will never get out of the cage, so they walk back and forth looking for a way out their cage. They don't even realize that the key to get open the rusty lock is in our own selves. Many believe that they aren't still in the box due to them having pre- conceived notions, of being awaken; yet they are still living pre-ordain perimeters, by our enemies. Through Our Fathers Eyes my people is our only way out the approximately 500-year-old box, in which we have been living in; as well as still living in.

Having a Temple, a Mosque or a Church we are only operating in the parameters in which our enemies have designed, to keep the Lion/Black People trapped in the cage. We must come out of thinking in the box this is the cause of us to remain caged up; we will never be able to build an independent Nation, for ourselves. The cage is specifically designed to keep us held in captivity forever at the mercy of our open enemies. Instead of supporting our own the first thing we do as a people is to criticize the brother or sister, that are seeking Freedom, Justice also Equality; before you even try to find out what or why, they are doing or have done what they may have done. It is very short sighted as well as un-intelligent to attack anyone before you gather understanding, this thinking Inside The Box; This juvenile thinking is the reason why our open as well as secret enemies, can keep us as a people in their cage of absolute ignorance; walking back as well as forth making absolutely no progress, in gaining our Independence as a Nation of Black People.

Through Our Fathers Eyes my people we must look through for us to correct the mistakes that we are continuing to commit, as well as have been committing. We are my people the Lion in the cage of ignorance, mistrust, hatred, envy, back biting self-importance, economic isolation, educational depression, political sterilization, religious castration. These are the circumstances that keep you my people the Lion in the cage, locked in the cage. The only way out is to think out of the box which means you must speak more than 400 words well, as we begin to think out of the box. Many self-appointed so-called ministers don't have the power or strength to think out of the box, so they these self-appointed so-called ministers keep black people in the cage, trapped just like a Lion walking back and forth looking for a way to free himself, from his 450 plus year prison. When we learn to think out of the box then we learn not to un-intelligently criticize a brother or sister work, before you examine the work they have performed. This childish behavior only aids our enemies to keep us the Lion, trapped in the cage that was built by our enemies.

Here is something else my people we also pay very close attention to is that these so-called Eastern Europeans embrace White Supremacy as well as White Nationalism, when they come to America. Even those from different parts of Russia can't wait to be inducted, into American White Nationalism as well as White Supremacy; even those who say they follow the Sunnah I'm telling you from personal experiences. We must be very, very, very, careful of who we allow around us as well as in our communities, they are only here to rob us as they call black people Dumb Niggards. As you think these devils are different from the other devils; my people they are all our enemies. The so-called Sunnah work hand in hand with Zionist to rob also keep black people trapped in the cage of complete hopelessness; We my people must begin to think out of the box to save ourselves, wives as well as our children.

You aren't paying attention my people how the planning commissions throughout every major city in America when it comes to black communities, all the baseball fields, football fields, boxing clubs even martial arts, have been removed from black communities throughout America; as our enemies replaced them with drugs, alcohol as well as black on black crimes. This is the box this filthy American Government of Murdering Global Terrorist, has designed also built for you as well as I, my people. Walking back and forth is nothing more than voting for the Democratic Party, the Republican Party or the Conservative Party, none of these devilish political parties will ever set you free. All these political parties as well as their different religions, this the cage that you are being held a prisoner; this is the more than 450-year box, that black people have been imprisoned in since 1555.We will never escape this prison if we allow our enemies to control what religion is best for us; what we should eat; what we should think or how we should think. This is what is keeping us all in this unmerciful made cage of hopelessness by our many enemies. Young black men sleeping on the streets of New York while absolutely no one cares; hungry, naked as well as out of doors; In desperate need of all type of assistance, as they get nothing from this ruthless unmerciful American Government. Yet we still won't think out this hellish box that we are confined in for the past 450 plus years.

If we don't begin to think as well as operate out of this cage there will be no tomorrow for any of us. Sign, dancing as well as none of these blood sports will ever get us out of this dreadful cage that we are living in, my people. These above mention activities are part of the box never will you ever build a nation for ourselves, participating these activities. Every athlete or entertainer that may have achieved some wealth, America will never allow them to use their wealth to aid their black people. If they are caught using their wealth to open the cage door for their people, they will be destroyed by these American Devils; as in the case of Bill Cosby also O.J. Simpson; lied on by disgusting Caucasian woman, or some ignorant Negro woman as in the case of our brothers Mike Tyson also Floyd Mayweather Jr. All these so-called political also religious so-called leaders never came to any of their aid. If we don't protect ourselves from this American Injustice, then who will? If we don't put a stop to this American Diminishment as well as American Terrorism; then tell me who will. Waiting around for some mystery god to help us is insane on our behalf. Believing this mystery god, no matter what name our enemies give this lie, is keeping trapped in the cage of hopelessness, despair, retardation for our children, homeless, naked as well as out of doors; beaten also killed by the ones that advocate this mystery god insanity. I don't care what name these enemies of black people in America as well as throughout the world; put on this made up so-called mystery god, of theirs my people. This is how they are keeping us locked up in the cage, my people.

What's really ridicules is that anyone thinking for a second they can tell me what to do or what I should do, as if they know what Allah has plan for me; I consider this a great insult to me, cause they don't like a picture on my book cover; I serve Allah in the person of Master Fard Muhammad to whom all holy praises are due forever; to hell with everyone else that didn't even read a word of the contents, then think they have something negative to say, like I care. This is thinking conduction as well oneself in the box I don't ever have to come around them or any silly fool who think like them. I embraced Islam as Our Holy Savior Allah Almighty taught His Holy Messenger the Most Honorable Elijah Muhammad; at the age of 12 years old. Allah Almighty taught His holy Messenger all you must do is except your own then be yourself, no one is putting me back into a cage. Out Of The Box my people we must think as well as conduct ourselves this is the only way, we can be totally free. You can't build a nation thinking that you know what's happening as you are staying under the radar; the Holy Messenger Of Allah didn't stay under the radar; I refuse to hide under the radar. I fear Allah and absolutely no one else; so, think what you want I will be happy to leave you alone, just leave me alone.

My people the Holy Messenger thought as well moved Out of the Box the majority of everyone that is claiming to be doing his work, in truth they aren't doing the real work. The Holy Messenger instructed us to Make America Know Her Sins, I don't see anyone doing this. For you to Make America know Her Sins you must come out of the Box. The Key to open the lock cage has already been given to us by Allah Almighty Himself through His Holy Messenger the Most Honorable Elijah Muhammad; who thought Out Of The Box My People Here is Where Your Salvation lye. Don't ever allow anyone to convince you into believing that there is something else, there isn't anything else. We must begin to create our own values not allow our enemies, to do this for us; or allow our enemies to super impose their corrupt evil values, upon us. This world as well as society is against us ever escaping from the cage that has been built by our enemies, for us. Black people can't escape the cage due to them having petty disagreements as well as having these strangers amongst us, that mean us absolutely any good at all; they are only trying to be a religious pimp, so they can live a life of luxury or ease at your expense; pretending to represent Allah and His Messenger, when in truth they represent only themselves. If you aren't one of us why are you coming around us? If you so call believe why don't they go to their own people then make them bare witness, to the truth? We don't need them amongst us they bring false also misleading information to us. We must run these frauds from amongst us as we did 6,000 years ago.

I was in the Bronx the other day when I saw a most disgusting sight a so-called black woman very dark black woman; she was wearing a micro mini skirt with blond hair, strutting up the street believing she was beautiful, desirable as she believed in her sick mind; believing that she is better than black people, as she is living in the very same drug infested neighborhood, as the black people living there. This was one of the most disgusting sights I ever seen this is a regular disgusting as well as evil sight, that these Negro Colored Women are presenting to young black men as well as their daughters. We have absolutely no chance of ever escaping our cage with such ignorant colored Negro women; we will never escape from the cage listening to ignorant men believing they, are special that they know what's happening; in truth they don't have a clue. For us to escape out of this cage that our enemies have setup for black people Indian People as well, we must stop listening to fools; trying to look like they are real, but their narrow minds will never allow them, out of the box; that our enemies made for us over 450 years ago. This mean my people they have not the power to teach us how to speak more than 400 years well, thus they can't free black people or Indian people from the cage of Hell. Why can't they free us Saladin from this approximately 500-year-old prison; Out of Box my people we must think for us to escape this cage of absolute unimaginable hell, that we have been suffering since 1555. Through Our Fathers Eyes my people is where we much look through no other people eyes, thoughts or religion, will ever free Black or Indian People, from this cage of total ignorance; non-productivity; self-hatred; believing in others than ourselves.

We must break out of this box that produces nothing but hell with these religious pimps as well as political pimps, working hand in hand with each other, to keep us all in our over 450-year-old cage. These are nothing but fools who in truth don't have any clue on how to free black people, from box that we have been trapped in since 1555.Look at what's happening all these fools are doing is perpetuating the image of that which our entrappers, have set for us hundreds of years ago; our enemies call this, position of prestige. These same fools are keeping black people in the cage reason being is that they don't know, acting like Sunday Come to Meeting Muslims, is accomplishing nothing; when you can't even produce unity amongst ourselves. These so-called Sunnah Muslims on Jerome and Kingsbridge are selling Italian Sausages, calling it Halal. All of this is proof that none of what these interlopers, their religion, thoughts, beliefs or practices, will ever free Black or Indian People from this hellish cage that our enemies put us in. It doesn't matter how Negro Servants they may have on their payroll, you are never to be allow out the cage. Everyone is very happy to live here in America living as Americans I am not American never have been, never will be. I will make America the American People as well as everyone of their filthy evil partners, Sins Be Known to the World. The only way you can do therefore you must think Out Of the Box my people, to build a real Nation for Ourselves as the Holy Messenger demonstrated to us all, how to do it Nationally as well as Internationally.

Freedom, Justice also Equality is only obtained by Thinking, Planning as well as Operating out of the 400 words. The Holy Messenger Yes this Is Who He Is The Holy Messenger Of Allah; his name as we refer to As the Most Honorable Elijah Muhammad. I am a student also follow of the Holy Messenger of Allah Almighty Himself; we my people must stand up to tell those that worshippers of this so-called Sunnah that our Holy Messenger the

Most Honorable Elijah Muhammad met Face To Face With Allah Almighty Himself; He is, Muhammad RasulAllah. If This Wasn't Out Of Box Then Please Someone, Tell Me What is Out Of The Box. He; The Holy Messenger Muhammad RasulAllah is the Lion Freed from the Cage By Allah Almighty Himself; in the Holiest Person Of Master Fard Muhammad To Whom All Holy Praises Are Due Forever. The mistake that is being made is that many are taking on the image of the Uniformed Code Of Dress as well as some of the conduct; yet they aren't thinking out the box for this reason the Holy Messenger Is A Black Nationalist; This is only Black Pride; This is only Black People Looking Out for Black People; The Holy Messenger wasn't about Black Supremacy; although one may think or believe so. These enemy sympathizers or just plain fools don't understand what Nationalism is, so they want to believe as their masters tell them, He was teaching Black Supremacy. No, my people The Holy Messenger taught as well as demonstrated what we can obtain, by having Black Nationalism. This is what we were doing under his guidance Building A Black Independent, Self Sufficient, Intelligent Nation; capable of doing trading with other world leaders also people, from Independent Nations throughout the world. You can only do or accomplish this feat, is by Thinking; Out Of The Box.

We are to promote the teachings of Allah in which He gave His Holy Messenger who intern taught us all. We are building a government also nation for ourselves is Black Nationalism this is the reason why no Black parades, are allow on 5th, 6th, or Madison Avenue; this will be demonstrating Black Nationalism as well as the New Islam, given to us all by Allah Almighty Himself; in the person of Master Fard Muhammad to whom all holy praises are due forever. This wicket American Government along with her partners in these genocidal crimes, the Zionist, the Christian, the Arabs, the Asian as well; against Black as well as Indian People; is to prevent us Black also Indian People from ever escaping the cage of despair; that has been created for us by White Nationalism as well as their White Supremacy.

How can America justify not allowing Black People to have their parades on 5th, 6th as well as Madison Avenue, when every other people are having their parades on these above mentioned avenues; This is to prevent us from ever becoming a recognized unified Nation of Black People; as America along with her partners in these horrific genocidal crimes against Black people; allow every other people on the planet who have done absolutely nothing, in comparison to us Black People, who have been serving this wicket American government since 1555; This is a matter of history my people that can be proven at any time. Black People who have served this evil, wicket American Government of Global Terrorist are not allowing to develop our own way of life, government, religion or politics, for ourselves. This filthy evil American Government along with the American people work extremely hard on convincing Black People that we, are all different; also, that we should hate each other; as they plant in everyone that they our open enemies are better for us all, rather than us unifying with our Black selves. This is White Nationalism as well as White Supremacy embraced by every immigrant, coming into America. The objective my people, is to keep the Lion Black People, forever locked into the cage our enemies built for us in 1555.

The only way we can think out of this box is that we must look Through Our Fathers Eyes we have been Through The Eyes of Our Fathers Enemies, as well as our enemies my people. They have no love for us Black People at all therefore they have been as well as still are doing everything, in their power to keep us divided as well as separated; warring also hating each other; while our enemies raped black communities throughout America, of the wealth. Promising us false hope through their made-up religion, trying to convince black people, to believe in them due to some made up nonsense, they want us black people to believe in the partners of America. Believing In any of America's Partners is nothing more than believing in America/ Satan the Accursed Devil. Through Our Fathers Eyes my people is our only way out of this approximately 500-year-old cage, we black people have been imprisoned in.

People may not like what I am saying but this is the absolute truth we don't need to study any other people or religion, it will not save black people; it hasn't saved black people it only allows the enemies of black people, to prosper while black wives also black children to suffer horribly. This was another plan that America implemented to keep black people in the cage; the Arabs better yet there made up interpretation they call Sunnah Islam; will only keep us Black people locked in the cage; we black people suffer while our enemies prosper this garbage my people we need to dump immediately, in order that we may have a chance to save ourselves, wives, children as well as our seniors. We can't do this by operating inside the box as a caged-up

Lion designed by our enemies, to imprison us forever; as they run around spreading their devilishment. If you don't submit to what they want or say, then comes their armies to murder also rape black woman as well as black young girls; this is what the Arabs are doing in the Sierra Leon murdering also raping black women. Where is this Allah these enemies of our fathers as well as ourselves, is at except protecting the enemies of Black People; no difference then the Christian with their so-called Jesus; no difference then the Zionist with their Jehovah; the one thing all these make-believe religions have in common, is to keep Black People in the cage of absolute hopeless. Look around my people the truth is right in front of your eyes, these people aren't any friends of Black People. Through Our Fathers Eyes we must look through my people not through our enemy's eyes; the eyes of our enemies are their religions; their politics; their customs; their beliefs; their lies; only mean the death of Black People in America, as well as throughout the world.

All these different people along with their religions also practices are designed to keep the Mighty Black Nation Forever Caged up, in the cage they designed for Black People, Indian People as well; the Cage of Absolute Despair, Hopelessness, Ignorance; absolute Hell. Don't be fooled my people these people no matter what they call themselves; no matter what they called their religions or what name they call their god, it will only keep black people the world over lock in this cage of Mental Slavery, to the enemies of our Fathers, as well as ourselves. This so-called Sunnah Islam was allowed in America by this wicket American Government to lead black people into believing in their Mystery God who has many different names; his identity is the Vicegerent who true name is Yakub; also known as Israel; also known as John the Revelator, in Revelations; father also maker of the Devil in the laboratories on the Island of Pelion/Patmos 6,600 years ago.

Yakub the father also maker of this physical devil designed this box for Black People as he was conducting his experiments, to bring a new also different life form, on our planet the Caucasian Race. This Box/Cage was part of Yakub's plan this why he taught his makings to question the Holy Black People on the reality, of Allah. He Yakub the Vicegerent knew already knew they couldn't answer; he Yakub the Vicegerent knew he had the power to rule, for next 6,000 years; as well as how to cage the Original People for the next 6,000 years. My people those 6,000 years are now over the cage is open all you have do, is walk out. Walking out means to get up and do something for yourself; you were given an Islam designed by Allah for the Original People not only in America but the Original People throughout the world. Out of the Box my People we must begin to think as well as operate then you and only then will you know also enjoy, true Freedom, Justice also Equality. Out of the Box my people as we Look Through Our Fathers Eyes, that span all 76 quintillion square miles, of the university, including the entire circumference, which is endless. Through Our Fathers Eyes my people there is no beginning or is there any ending, for us the Original People.

CHAPTER 6

THE PURSUIT OF HAPPINESS

The pursuit of happiness my people is another thing we must examine as well as how we go about obtaining this happiness, that have been eluding black people, ever since we crossed the Atlantic over those many centuries ago. Here in America where we have been reduced to nothing but livestock we had absolute no clue how to achieve happiness. Our enemies never told or taught us, what is happiness they gave us a false interpretation, of happiness as we went through life in America, conducting ourselves as complete savages, for hundreds of years. America as well as the American people never intended for Black People, to ever know true happiness. They our many enemies forced their concept of happiness on us, so we never knew what self-happiness was, since we boarded these dreadful slave ships. We have been wondering through life without a clue how to obtain happiness. This was plan by the American Government as well as American People to make absolute sure, that Black people never know anything about happiness; they meaning Black People are only to know suffering and misery, hunger, nakedness, homelessness diseases and nothing else. This is what we have been experiencing for over 450 years things aren't getting any better, for Black People. We have been condition by our enemies to except these hellish conditions as normal many Black People has excepted this lie; my people this isn't normal this is devilishment made for us by our open enemies my people.

This make Black People savages in the pursuit of happiness without any clue on what's really happening due to you not being taught the truth of what, is true happiness or how to achieve true happiness. Black People were never taught or trained by our enemies to achieve happiness only help them our enemies, to obtain happiness, in which they can't achieve themselves. They our enemies are haunted by the evils their ancestors have done as well as they are still doing, in this present day and time. My People you must be aware of what our enemies the American Government as well as the American People, have done to us. We must understand that these aren't our friends these strangers with their religions only want to aid America, in keeping black people in the cage. The pursuit of happiness my while you don't have a clue the enemies of black people, are pursuing their happiness in America. This Zionist/Christian/Arab/Asian American Government of Global Murdering Terrorist have purposely misled black people away from true happiness as well as how, to pursue it. They our enemies with their false religions also politics are doing everything to keep us from uniting to prevent us from intelligently, pursuing happiness.

By us allowing these many different strangers amongst us we are giving our enemies the very ammunition, to use against us. They come amongst us studying us then use our weaknesses to turn brothers also sisters, against each other. This is what their maker taught them to do when they are amongst us, cause trouble also to get us black people to fight and kill each other, in which we are doing in abundance. Our enemies put all these drugs into our communities my people to stop also prevent us black people, from building a nation for our own for us to intelligently engage ourselves, in the pursuit of happiness. This gentrifying of our neighborhoods is the destruction of black people you don't believe me, look at the different people living in our neighborhoods, that we lived in for generations. Now as black people we are being ushered in to these concentration camps all throughout America, called shelters my people. Under these conditions we have absolutely no chance of pursuing happiness, as a people for ourselves as every other people are doing.

We are kept in this cage by our enemies this so-called Sunnah Islam is an enemy to black people reason being is that it is, an intricate part of White Supremacy as well as White Nationalism. They the partners of America are allowing to do, something for themselves as they rob black people, every day then dare think they can tell us about Islam; when these cowards with their Negro lackeys keep black people locked into cage, walking back and forth searching for a way out. Through the help of these Negroes our enemies can keep us caged in as they all walk around feeling free; enjoying the riches also freedom of America, that we sacrificed our lives for not any of them. We have been given the real Islam that will unlock this prison, for all Original People in America and throughout the World. We don't need this so-called Sunnah Islam which is nothing more than another version, of Christianity as well as White Supremacy and White Nationalism. This so-called Sunnah Islam isn't from Allah it is from the Vicegerent Yakub, the enemy of Islam. Yakub the Vicegerent taught his making to lie to black people as the Vicegerent perfected his interpretation of Islam as a religion, to better deceive also keep black people, caged up in the prison, that he the Vicegerent/Yakub taught his making to build, for all Original People.

Look around my people look at who is not pursuing happiness we aren't pursuing happiness; we have excepted from our enemies to accept the hell they made for us, as happiness; as they our enemies are pursuing happiness in America that we help built, in which they did absolutely nothing. We must return to the teachings that Allah in the person of Master Fard Muhammad to whom all holy praises are due forever, taught His Holy Messenger the Rasul; the Most Honorable Elijah Muhammad. Everything is nothing, but weapons use to keep black people in the cage, not ever able to pursue happiness; thus, never enjoying Freedom Justice or Equality. We must beware of these phonies coming around claiming to represent Allah, but these fools are also representing the Vicegerent/Yakub also. There is no Supreme Minister the Messenger of Allah Himself said this. So where are these ignorant fools saying they are a represented of Supreme Minister John Muhammad. John Muhammad was never appointed to such a post as Supreme Minister by Allah or Allah's Holy Messenger. Also, my people these silly fools are not even representing the Allah or His Holy Messenger, they are representing only themselves; I wouldn't give two cents for these want to be pimps. You also my people will find out they aren't even one of us if these frauds believe so much, why don't they go and teach their people? We don't need them to teach us anything about Allah or His Messenger; Allah did not come from these interlopers because they aren't Allah's people, they are liars and nothing else my people. Trust absolutely no one that isn't one of us trying to each us about ourselves, when these want to be pimps don't even know about themselves. They are also in place to prevent our pursuit to happiness.

These frauds were able to steal our history due to ignorant want to be important people teaching also giving them our information also these frauds marring a so-called black woman. Ask them why you don't go and teach your people they will give you a lot of nonsense but the truth; the truth is that you are my people are easily led into wrong direction, by anyone that isn't of you thus making it easy, for these strangers to rob also kill black people. Don't be fool by these interlopers they none of us any good at all they are only trying to get rich, off your ignorant of trusting them. They have absolutely no interest in black people pursuing happiness due to them aren't one of us, my people they are only looking to rob black people, so they can live a life of luxury, as they feel important. They these frauds will stop black people pursuit to happiness helping our enemies, to keep black people in the cage forever looking for a way out.

We must take blame for what is being done to us my people we have absolutely any reason to trust anyone, that isn't of us. You will find these interlopers aren't from the Tribe Of Shabazz even throw they are trying to steal our name as well as heritage. In fact, you will that their ancestors are the murderers of black people as well as Indian People. These interlopers never spent any time at all, in slavery her in America. So, who the hell are these decedents of the murderers of Black also Indian People, as well as enslavers to come amongst us spreading more poison, as they're for fathers and mothers did. How foolish are we to have our enemies trying to teach us these people should be ran from amongst us, not letting them amongst us? Tell me where Allah came for these interlopers who are the descendants of the murderers, of our ancestors? This is preventing our pursuit of happiness reason being they don't want us black people to ever achieve happiness; their intentions are to make themselves rich from our labor. My people these are our enemies dressed in the sheep clothing they are deadlier that our enemies, dressed in short pants and sneakers. Ever since we allow these interlopers to come amongst us in the Motherland all we have experience is hell, the Spaniards included. They have sold black people out ever since the Zionist brought them here for cheap labor, in their factories in New York and elsewhere, in America. We must exile all these interlopers from trying to be our teacher thinking they can teach us about our Savior. They aren't created by Allah they are made by the Vicegerent Yakub and the lust of their maker they will do as well as have been doing, betraying Back People; This is our pursuit to happiness my people in America as well as black people throughout the world, we don't need these interlopers amongst us. If they believe in which they don't go teach your own kind, we don't need you.

Our history spans over seventy-six trillion years before their maker Yakub ever came into existence these interlopers come from Yakub, not from Allah. We must my people pursue our happiness as a unified people as we keep out everyone that isn't of us, it doesn't matter what they may call themselves; we don't need them amongst us. We must unite our people in America as well as throughout the world; if not for these interlopers' ancestors with their most diabolical evil intentions as well as actions, they would have never been amongst us and we shouldn't have them amongst us today. Our pursuit of happiness is ours not theirs my people examine the history of all these devils. Master Fard Muhammad Allah Almighty Himself proclaimed them to be, a race of devils. He included all of them including their descendants as well; they mean us black people any good at all never did and never will. We my people have suffered like no other people have suffered from the very enemies whom these interlopers are the descendent of. This is history then you got one of these interlopers saying he is a represented of Supreme Minister John Muhammad, this is a complete lie. Show me where Allah said John Muhammad was Supreme Minister you can't due to it Allah never did. Show me where the Holy Messenger appointed his younger brother John Muhammad as Supreme Minister; this never happen show me where it does not exist; this means this is nothing but A LIE; THERE IS NO TRUTH IN THIS STATEEMENT AT ALL; THIS MEANS WHOM EVER SAYING THIS IS A LIAR AND SHOULD NOT BE TRUSTED AT ALL. THIS PERSON IS A LIAR OR HAVE BEEN MIS- INFORMED, WHICH MAKES THESE PEOPLE EXTREMELY DANGEROUS TO BLACK PEOPLE PURSUIT OF HAPPINESS.

I'm not against any people doing for themselves I'm against these other people wanting to steal the food from out of black people mouths, including our children. I will fight them all no matter where they maybe black people are my people I will reveal the truth of everyone that are out to rob us, no matter how they pretend to be one of us they are lying my people. We are the only one that will bring ourselves Freedom Justice also Equality, so that we may pursue our march to happiness without any of these interlopers, interference. We don't need any of these interlopers help. We my people must turn to ourselves no other than ourselves for anything; we have been creating also building civilizations before Yakub grafted them out of us. Examine their history you will find they came from out of the cave sides of Europe so how the hell can anyone of them be of us; this is impossible my people. You would be wise to drive them from amongst us they will only cause trouble amongst black people, they have a history of doing this examine their history also remember you can't reform devil.

This is our Black People in America as well as throughout the world our pursuit of happiness not theirs they only come around us to prevent us from becoming an independent Black Universal Nation, as we were before Yakub grafted them all out of us. These people other than ourselves are very dangerous to us all; they mean us absolutely no good in our pursuit of happiness. Religion is use by our enemies to keep black people in check preventing us from ever rising, to once again become the greatest people that ever lived, on our planet. Our pursuit to happiness is always being interfered with by people that are trying to force their beliefs on us. These strangers are always seeking to keep black people cage up as if they know what's better for black people. None of these people or their ancestors spent 400 years in bondage; ask any of them you will find that they didn't. So, the question is this; what right; have any of them to come amongst us telling us black people, what is best for us? What right has any of these interlopers, to tell us black people, what religion we should have? What right; have any of these interlopers must interfere in our pursuit of happiness? What right has anyone that is not, of us to tell us anything, when they will not help us go for ourselves? What right does anyone has to come amongst us as they are deceiving also lying to black people, to make themselves rich as they are doing nothing more than robbing black people. What right has any of these interlopers must come amongst us as they molest young black girls as well as black women, while black men are supposed to do nothing? What right my people do you have to sit back and allow these atrocities to continue, as you sit back doing nothing; while our enemies bastardize our people through the black woman? What chance do we have my people in the pursuit when you are allowing these atrocities to continue?

We my people must reject every religion being brought to us by our enemies who are in partnership with America, to keep black people cage up into believing also trusting any of our 6,000-year-old enemies. Sunnah so-called Islam will as has destroyed black people it has done absolutely nothing to help or aid black people anywhere in the world, in our pursuit to happiness. If so then explain to me why the Arabs are, with this so-called Sunnah Islam murdering the Black Muslims in Serra Leone. We must never again embrace anything our enemies have to say in fact just run them, from amongst us. This is our pursuit of happiness my people these strangers are not here to help us Black People; these strangers come amongst us to help America keep black people in this cage of despair as well as ignorance. It doesn't matter how these strangers may dress or how they imitate us claiming to be of us; I can have assured you my people these are enemies, of our pursuit of happiness.

My people you are your own worst enemy you are allowing these strangers amongst you. You are the only people on this earth that allow anyone, to come amongst you; take your woman also little girls s you stand by and do nothing. You can't go into any of their communities and do this to them they will kill you out right. The American support these interlopers treating black people in this manner reason being you are the only people that believe in this insanity of Integration. Now you have every demented demon prowling black communities throughout America; these demented demons have targeted the concentration camps where black people are being warehouse; better yet where black people are being held prisoners. In fact, these demented demons are as well as have targeted the family concentration camps America call shelters, due to the fact in most cases there is no male protector. This insane religion Christianity teaches you not to resist these devils due to you buying into this madness, of loving everyone and forgive your enemies, no matter what they may do you. We all know the evils these Arabs so-called Sunnah Islam commit in black communities, throughout America and get away with them. This is by designed by the American Government of Global Murdering, Rapist Thieving, Global Terrorist, to all black people in America, as well as throughout the world.

All of this is designed to prevent black people from ever pursuing happiness as an independent self-governing people; who is wise enough to keep their enemies away from themselves wives also children. We have been given our own Islam from Allah Almighty Himself through His Holy Messenger the Most Honorable Elijah Muhammad we have absolutely no use, for anyone else telling us anything about Allah or His Messenger. We just must follow what Allah our Holy Savior and Deliverer in the person of Master Fard Muhammad to whom all holy praises, are due forever; taught His Holy Messenger the Most Honorable Elijah Muhammad who in fact is Muhammad RasulAllah; taught us all. We don't have to turn to any other people for guidance especially this so-called Sunnah Islam who conspired with this Zionist/Christian American Government, then murder our brother Minister Malcolm X; for the American Government to put the Heroin in Harlem back in 1965/1966. This was designed by the American Government with their partner Sunnah Islam, to prevent our pursuit of happiness. This is historical my people that we can prove at any time, examine the time line as you examine the history the absolute truth is there. This so-called Sunnah Islam are our enemies those that are here in America come here to be Americans, thus they are all in agreement with American Government to keep Black People in the cage. This so-called Sunnah Islam can be proven it didn't come from Allah it came from the Vicegerent who is Yakub; who was given the power to rule for 6,000 years as he pretended to be Allah, but the Vicegerent isn't Allah, only acting as Allah. Therefore, Prophet Muhammad never saw Allah due to the Vicegerent didn't want his makings to know, that he was from the Original Black People. We will never be able to achieve our march to happiness following anyone except our own Black selves. History bear me witness that ever since we allow the Vicegerent makings to come amongst us, all we Black people have experience is absolute hell from all of them.

The Pursuit of happiness my people we must expel everyone that isn't of us they can go and teach their own people, if they truly believe. My people they are not believers they are only trying to rob black people rather than pimp their own people; reason being is that you believe in this insane concept develop by our enemies, to love also to forgive our enemies; as well as except them amongst us. These so called black Imams are no different from the Christian preachers they are both representing the enemies, so-called religions; to prevent Black People from ever escaping from out of our cage; to pursuit our happiness without any interference from them, whom history reveal them to be enemies of Black People ever since the Vicegerent Yakub grafted their entire species out of Black People. Outside of our brother General Qurdafie, none of these other so-called Sunnah Islam cowards here in America have ever spoke up or help black people anywhere, on the planet only to murder, rape and steal from black people. These same murdering devil so-called Arabs murder the General in fact my people these so-called Arabs aren't even the Original Arab the Original Arabs are Black, not these Caucasians or their half breed children.

If we don't secure ourselves and expel or just exile all interlopers from amongst us how can we purse our happiness? By expelling also exiling all people that are not of us from amongst us then we will be able to pursue our happiness my people, without interference. Let them all go to their own people we don't need any of them nor do we need to listen to their lies, which is nothing more than con games. The pursuit of happiness is for us to do for ourselves without these interlopers they aren't one of us; we shouldn't let them amongst us calling themselves our teachers when history proves they only been on the planet 6,000 years. It doesn't what they call themselves they aren't one of us. Tell them all go teach your own people we don't need any of you to teach black People and we don't want your kind amongst us. I'm talking about us Black People Building our Nation Back I'm telling you we can only do this be exiling everyone that isn't of us, no matter how smooth they may sound or how much they may try to imitate the Original People, they aren't Original People. When you examine the history of their people as well as their ancestors, you will see they are nothing but devils also. Our pursuit is what I'm speaking about my people what has that to do with any other people? If you want to do trading with us that's fine but we don't need or want, you are living amongst us and we won't live amongst any of you. If you believe you know Islam, then go teach your people if you believe this; I know you truly don't know Islam nor do you believe in Islam. My people all these interlopers are White Nationalist as well as believe in White Supremacy, therefore they come amongst us trying to prove that we need them or that they are one of us; when in truth they aren't one of us. I don't care who feelings I may be hurting these outsiders don't care about our feelings in fact they enjoy seeing black people suffer, ever since Yakub grafted them out of us 6,000 years ago. What kind of idiot would say I am a representative of Supreme Minister John Muhammad when this is an absolute lie my people. This can be proven at any time John Muhammad was not, the Supreme Minister. The Fool didn't have enough respect to say that I'm a representative of the last and greatest Messenger of Allah. How stupid are we to listen to such a ridicules person? How stupid are we to have such a person amongst us, as we pursue our happiness? The history proves that this fool come from Yakub not Allah examine the history this is a complete fool, trying to rob black people, as they have been doing for the past 6,000 years.

The pursuit of happiness is something that every other people are doing except black people we are too busy, befriending everyone but ourselves; thus, neglecting our own wellbeing. The Islam that Allah taught His Holy Messenger the Most Honorable Elijah Muhammad, is the only Islam that will free Black People in America as well as Black People throughout the world. When you examine the front page of Muhammad Speaks Newspaper you will see the Black man in the Western Hemisphere end the Black man in East Asia extending their hands to each other as we did before the last 500, when we separated by our enemies; as we in the Northern Part of the Western Hemisphere spent 400 years in slavery, as our enemies destroyed also rape the Homeland of the resources; while the black people suffered. The treasures these devils stole from us belong to us they were as well as still are thieves. Everything is designed to prevent black people from our pursuit for happiness. Think about this my people before these makings of Yakub were ever made a man none of them lived amongst us. As soon as we allowed these interlopers amongst us they turned our homeland into a complete nightmare. So, if we are to regain that which was stolen from us we would be wise to keep every other people that aren't of us, from amongst us; then we can unite ourselves as Allah in the Master Fard Muhammad to whom all holy praises are due forever; taught His Last Holy and Greatest Messenger the Most Honorable Elijah Muhammad, who in turn taught us his people. Allah came for us my people not these interlopers.

CHAPTER 7

THE LOVE FOR SELF AND UNITY AMONGST OURSELVES

The love for self is important my people the Holy Messenger lecture us extensively on the importance of having this amongst ourselves. My people we are a people that have been taught by our enemies to hate ourselves as we love our enemies, including their children. We celebrate their holidays we never celebrate our holidays due to you my people not excepting Savior's Day also the 4th of July is the day when Allah, appeared in America in 1914. This represent the beginning of the end for Yakub's making as well as the world they have made, through murder, rape also thievery. Being under the absolute unmerciful control of these America Demons, we taught to hate ourselves. We must also remember this my people no one from this so-called Sunnah Islam ever came to help us, as they aren't helping any black people anywhere in the world. We were forced to except our enemy's religion this most deadly Christianity, that made sure we never love ourselves or re-build the unity amongst ourselves. The stealing of our language was designed so that we could never identify with our people across the oceans, thus always at the mercy of our enemies. In fact, they our enemies taught us that our people across the oceans weren't our people also that they were all savages. So, this self-hared was in bedded in black people over 450 years ago. Also, our enemies taught us to worship anyone that was of Yakub's making, that didn't look like us. Thus, preventing us from loving ourselves also uniting with ourselves, an extremely wicket also diabolical, by our enemies as our enemies enjoyed the fruits of this evil.

Our enemies stole from us our National as they force us to except their flag and taught us to serve their flag of untruth, without question. We have never received any good from or under this American flag but absolute pure hell; even up till this present day and time. The fact that our political also religious sold out the mass of black people, by them supporting White Supremacy as well as White Nationalism, for a little bit of crumbs of our enemies table; while the mass of black people starved as well as suffered; these traitors have been doing this for the past four and a half centuries. When these political also religious leaders sold out the mass of black people by excepting this dreadful Integration and Civil Rights, this open the door for all these different interlopers, to move into black communities a rape the black communities of the wealth, also the black woman. Look at who brought the Heroin into the black communities throughout America. Look at who brought the Cocaine in every black community throughout America, it wasn't black people it was our enemies. Look my people and see who have prospered from these evils it wasn't black people, our enemies prospered from these evils, my people. Look at how our enemies devastated black communities throughout America, as their communities thrived. Why would we want any of them amongst us my people when they our enemies, don't want us, amongst them.

All these interlopers amongst us are diluting our blood also our ability to unite ourselves, many of them are feeding lies to our people. These interlopers are bringing mix instruction to black people to keep us from uniting, as well as loving ourselves as a people. These interlopers my people this is what they are my people and they don't belong amongst us bastardizing our people, as we now must except their bastard children amongst us; our enemies have been doing this for the past 450 years. It matters not what they call themselves we don't need them amongst us, they will always spread lies also deceit amongst us. They don't want a united black people as well as they don't want us to love ourselves, as a people. I don't care what they say take it to your own people and stop trying to be our black teacher as well as leader. My people with these interlopers gone from amongst us we have a greater chance to unite ourselves also begin to re-build love for ourselves. Therefore, we ran them from amongst us 6,000 years ago for causing trouble amongst the Original People and they are still causing trouble amongst the Original people, with their lies; still spreading poison that we should

70

trust them, rather than unite with our people and begin once again to love ourselves. This filthy evil wicket America Government of Murdering Global Terrorist set this up to destroy any chance of black people loving themselves as we begin uniting ourselves globally, with the absents of Yakub's Making. You and I loving each other is extremely important; us uniting globally is extremely important. Examine these interlopers' history they aren't of the Original Family in fact history will prove these Vicegerent Makings, have always brought lies, confusion, hatred also murder amongst black people, as they have done since we let them amongst us at the Holy City Mecca, 6,000 years. Therefore, General Muk-Muk was commissioned to drive them out of the Holy City Mecca; these same Yakub makings are amongst us doing the same thing as they did 6,000 years ago, Keep Original People from loving ourselves and prevent us from building black unity amongst ourselves globally.

We must my people recognize the traps that keep black people trap in the cage of despair which allows the interlopers, to carry out their diabolical plans against black people with impunity. What are the plans of these interlopers Saladin? Their plans are to set themselves up as our leaders and teachers as they rob black people, of their wealth; this will allow them to live a life of luxury. This has been happening on a grand scale for the past 500 years, with impunity. Our enemies have adjusted with how they precede in implementing their plans amongst black people; they have learned some of our language from foolish black people and now they are looking to cash in on what they have learned, about black people. This is the same method that was used when they launch the Despicable Slave Trade as the Chinese referred to it. In fact, the same people that were involved back in the late 1400 and early 1500 hundreds are the same people trying to do it again, in the 21st century to black people. Why are these interlopers doing this Saladin? These interlopers never want us to love ourselves and unite with ourselves, so they do everything they can to prevent black people from achieving what we must do, for ourselves. These are the same people came amongst us to destroy our love for our black selves also our unity amongst ourselves. They sound like they are sincere but my people they are liars as well as deceivers and we must not fall their lies again. We my black people must rise above their lies also our enemies' deceit and they have had time, to perfect their lies also deceit amongst black people; everything is designed to prevent love for our black selves also unity amongst our black selves; thus, these enemies can continue to rob black people with impunity and don't have to worry.

We my people must concentrate on understanding the necessity of us loving ourselves for us, to unify ourselves as a people, once again before these enemies invaded our Homeland. These same enemies are in our black communities still spreading their poison amongst black people, trying to prevent our rise back to prominence, in which we originated from. They our enemies didn't come from the creation; our enemies came from the making. This most evil, diabolical American Government planet these interlopers amongst us to make sure we never establish love and unity amongst ourselves. I was looking at a statement made on face book by an unlearned person saying the Tribe Of Shabazz 50,000 years ago was in the making. This is so in correct until it is pitiful the Tribe Of Shabazz was not in the making 50,000 years ago, certain members of the Tribe of Shabazz were going under a change, when the leader of his family decided to go into the jungles of East Asia, now call Africa to make his family physically stronger. This wasn't the entire tribe my people it was a certain Scientist from the Tribe of Shabazz that took his family into the Jungles of East Asia, in which everyone calls Granddaddy Shabazz. What kind of fools are we to let others not of the Original Family tell us about ourselves, as they try to steal our heritage including our name Shabazz. Allah never told or said any of these interlopers that they were from or a part of the God Tribe Shabazz, my people. These are the descendants of our fathers' enemies yours as well as mines also; trust absolutely none of them no matter what they look like or what they may sound like, these are black people enemies always have been always will be.

When we examine other people here in America they are all pursuing happiness in their own way of choice, as a people. Yet when it comes to black people this Zionist/Christian/Arab/Asian American Government of Global Terrorist; always do everything in their power to prevent black people from choosing for themselves, what we black people need for ourselves. We have these other interlopers trying to tell us about religion how we should practice that which Allah gave to black people, through His Holy Messenger. Thus, all this interference is preventing us from building unity amongst black people in America as well as throughout the world. By these enemies always interfering with our approach to dealing with ourselves, this is preventing black people from rebuilding the love and trust amongst ourselves, due to black people are trying to please the enemies of our fathers and mothers. Instead of looking Through Our Fathers Eyes black people are through the eyes of our enemies. Black people can't accept the fact that Allah Himself visited us and He Allah raised up from amongst us, the rejected also the despised His last also greatest Messenger the Most Honorable Elijah Muhammad. This Holy Messenger taught us to love our black selves; this Holy Messenger taught black people to unite ourselves, as one Globally Black People. This Holy Messenger taught us the truth God also the Devil; this Holy Messenger gave us the Holy Flag of Islam given to him by Allah Himself; this Holy Messenger taught us to pool our little bit of resources together, so that we can build a Nation for ourselves; this Holy Messenger Met with Allah Himself in person; Through Our Fathers Eyes my people is where we must begin to look through, not the eyes and ways of our enemies.

This filthy evil Zionist/Christian/Arab/Asia America Government of Global Terrorist have allowed our enemies to invade every black community throughout America. This another one of the many plans of the American Government and the American people, to destroy black people; while these interlopers prosper leaving their bastard children behind, for black people to deal with. While the American Government implemented this Gentrification Program to further prevent black people, from ever loving ourselves as well as unifying ourselves. This American Gestapo are the ones protecting our enemies also has empowered our enemies, to do whatever evils, they choose to amongst black people with impunity. This so-called Sunnah Islam is just as poisonous as Christianity to black people reason being it only takes black people from one of America's partners in these evil crimes against black people, to another of America's partners in these evil crimes against black people; not only in America but throughout the world as well. This why we black people in America as well as throughout the world we all must the look Through Our Ancient Fathers Eyes who were trillions of Years before the birth of the Vicegerent/Yakub grafted these strange people out of the Original Black People, 6,600 years ago. Imagine my people the power we will have collectively just by excepting what Allah gave to us black people in America, for us to give to black people all over the world.

Love for ourselves my people as well as unity amongst ourselves worldwide, is the only way to defeat this White Supremacy, as well as White

Nationalism worldwide. Our Dear Holy Apostle taught us, or I should say Allah taught us, through His Dear Holy Apostle that our unity is the key my people in America as well as throughout the world. Through Our Fathers Eyes my people in America and throughout the world, we share the Ancient History; the same Ancient Heritage; the same Ancient Culture; the same Ancient Fathers also Mothers; the same Homeland; we are one people no matter where you see black people we are not only looking at ourselves as the Holy Messenger taught us; that whenever you look at a black man you are looking at Allah. It doesn't matter where we may be, Africa, America, Germany, France, England, Australia, the Netherlands, Russia, China, Japan, Korea, it doesn't matter where you see a black man, you are looking at Allah, the true and living God. My people the rule of the Vicegerent is over everything this Vicegerent has made, will be destroy, my people. We who have been held captive in America for the past 450 plus years, in the Caribbean, in South America, in Central America, we all got here via the slave ships. We were all kidnapped by the same enemies of these interlopers that are living amongst us in black communities throughout America, spreading lies, deceit also mix instruction; preventing black people from loving also uniting ourselves, as one people. This isn't by accident my people this is by designed by our enemies that have only one desire and that is to keep black people, in the cage of hopelessness, despair as well as disenfranchisement, in America as well as throughout the world.

My People all the atrocities that are happening in the world Yakub the Vicegerent made cannot be stop, or adverted this world is absolutely doomed; praise be to Allah the creator also the Supreme Administrator also protector of Universal Justice. The insanity that has creep into the brains also hearts of Yakub's making is only going to get much worst. The Dear Holy Apostle the Most Honorable Elijah Muhammad/Muhammad RasulAllah told us that 100% total insanity is all this world is going to receive, as well as they are already receiving. All these interlopers with their so-called religions are always telling us about prayer, my people Remembrance of Allah is greater than prayer; prayer is better than sleep amongst the guilty reason being they have absolutely no clue Who Allah is. We my people know who Allah Himself is due to him visiting us in Person; we know Allah by His name not just by His Title which is Allah; His name is Master Fard Muhammad to whom all holy praises are due forever; In the Quran-and He is called the

Great Mahdi; in the Bible he is called Christ the Crusher as well as the Son Of Man. This is Allah Almighty Himself in Person my people we don't have to wait on His coming He has already come my people, He Allah left His Holy Messengers His representative for us all my people.

We my people in America as well as throughout the world must have true love as well complete unity amongst ourselves, then we my people; globally together can build for our black selves, a Global Economy for our black selves, and our children. These interlopers living amongst us aren't welcome amongst us and we should drive them from amongst us, never to ever come amongst us again. We had civilizations before these strangers were ever made a man now these makings of the Vicegerent who is Yakub their maker also god, believe they can educate us Original People when we are created in the image of Allah Himself, while these strangers are made in the image of the Vicegerent Yakub, the maker of imperfection and an imperfect people. Their maker Yakub was mission by Allah to remove this germ from amongst the Original People and give it form. Therefore, the Vicegerent Yakub wisdom was given 6,000 years to rule but now his also his making time is up; the true also living god is now present bringing the Vicegerent to his complete destruction along with the Vicegerent making also all of those that believe and follow them.

We my people must understand if you come in the name of the enemies, then you are the property of our enemies. We must free ourselves from our enemies, names, religions, culture, practices, actions as well as their deeds. We don't need anything from any of them all we need is our unity globally there is nothing we can't accomplish, my people. Once we cast our enemies out from amongst us we will be able to set ourselves in heaven overnight. The love amongst self globally will cause our enemies to run and hide but there will be no place for our enemies to hide, from the Universal Justice from Allah. Don't look up in the sky for Allah this totally foolish my people; all we must do is look at our Black Original Selves we will see Allah 24 hours a day 7 day a week 365 day every year. All we need is love for ourselves as well as unity amongst ourselves globally. The Holy Messenger Of Allah the Most Honorable Elijah Muhammad taught us every time you look at black man, you are looking at Allah. The Holy Messenger of Allah isn't just for the Black man also Black woman in the Western Hemisphere; the Holy Messenger Of Allah is the Holy Messenger for all Black People

Globally. Allah my people came to your kidnapped brothers and sisters in America the Accursed Devil first devil, because we were the ones that were kidnapped over 450 years ago; brought to a strange land at the diabolical merciless people ever recorded in history. He is Allah my people his names are Master Fard Muhammad to whom all holy praises are due for ever. He is the one my people you and I have been waiting for, for the past 500 years that would reestablish our Mighty Black Nation as well as the Original Islam Himself. My people in America as well as throughout the world; this is our time to unify ourselves globally with love and trust, for ourselves. We don't have to fear our enemies my people anywhere fear our Holy Savior Allah Almighty the true and living Allah. Let our enemies keep what the Vicegerent their maker, whatever he gave them we don't need any of it. It hasn't done us black people globally any good at all just examine the last 500 years of their history. Ever since these Arabs came amongst us with their false religion they call Islam is nothing but another version of Christianity, designed to keep black people submissive to Caucasian People and the Arabs are of the Caucasian family.

It is our unity my Black Original People globally will give us the weapon to defeat this evil White Supremacy and their White Nationalism; along with all their made religions and their filthy politics. We will then my people be able to build us a global economy beneficial to all black people globally, with the absence also noninterference, of our enemies. We will also be able to build our own banking system globally that will also be beneficial, to all black people globally. We will also my people be able in control of printing our own currency with our heroes and ancient ancestors' pictures, on our own currency globally. We will be able my people globally to import as well as export also manufacture everything that we need, for ourselves globally. We my people once again be able to build schools also universities for ourselves globally. Everything that we did for trillions and trillions of years before the Vicegerent makings came amongst us; as they stole murdered also rape black women, young girls, also young boys. Love for ourselves my people globally is what we must have; unity amongst ourselves globally is also what we must have amongst ourselves, we can defeat everyone, of our enemies. Our Love also Unity my people we can defeat this Zionist/Christian/Arab/Asian American Government of Global Murdering, Thieving, Rapist of Global Terrorist, along with their European Allies.

I am your brother my people what I am saying is what my Leader Also Teacher the Holy Messenger of Allah instructed me to do. We must cast off all these false images of angles, Mary also Jesus In fact we must my people cast off every false image in this poison book that some of our enemies call Bible, that are used as weapons to keep black people globally mental slaves as well as dependent on them our enemies, for everything that we need also to prevent us from becoming an independent people globally. We should be building hospitals, research centers, medical centers, for our people who need our help, American society. It was the enemies of our fathers and mothers that invaded our homeland my people bringing death, murder, rape, destruction, diseases, suffering, taught us hatred for ourselves, false religions, complete hell my people. These people weren't friends my people these were the enemies of our ancestors and they are our enemies today my people globally. This so-called Orthodox Islam are part of these demons that brought death and destruction, to us all globally. These aren't our people my people these are the enemies made by the Vicegerent 6,600 years ago. Examine the history my people it is all there naming everyone, of these murdering, thieving, rapist devils and this includes this so-called Orthodox Islam with their so-called Sunnah. Here in America these so-called Sunnah or Sunni Muslims have embraced America's White Nationalism as well as White Supremacy.

These so called seven heavens are lies being taught to us by our enemies my people; there isn't any seven heavens my people at all. There are seven planets with life on them that is very much like our own my people; they all along with our selves are created by the Universal Creator. Our enemies are made by the Vicegerent 6,600 years ago on the Island of Pelan/Patmos; not by the Universal Creator. If they came from the Universal Creator they would look like us in which they do not; also, if they came from the Universal Creator they wouldn't be murderers, liars, thieves, rapist, enslavers, downright diabolically; also, my people they wouldn't have these false made up religions. Their maker the Vicegerent Yakub placed in them this evil the Vicegerent put in them through his grafting them out of us and then gave it form. It is their nature to be evil to the Original People Globally, my people. They use their made-up religions to keep black people globally submissive to White Supremacy and White Nationalism. The Vicegerent Yakub wisdom was given 6,000 years to rule, so the Vicegerent took on the title of Allah and it was the Vicegerent who perfected Islam as a religion, for his making my people. This has absolutely nothing to do with us the Original People Globally. These strangers my people are responsible for the destruction of black people globally along with their false religions that come from the Vicegerent their maker and not our Creator who is the Creator of the of the seven planets of life; in which the Vicegerent making call heaven and the seven heavens; this is believe by fools my people as well as embraced by traitors amongst us; they call themselves preachers, reverends, imams, priest they are all the enemies of Black People Globally; they all uphold White Supremacy as well as White Nationalism.

My people we didn't ask to be kidnapped then transported from our Homeland to this Allah forsaken Western Hemisphere, at the un-merciful most diabolical, most evil of the Vicegerent Makings; made slaves for 400 years amongst a strange people and strange land. The evils we have been suffering is beyond anyone imagination my people. We didn't ask to be kidnapped then transported to England, France, Germany, Russia, South America, the Caribbean, where we were made slaves by the enemies of our fathers also mothers as well as our open enemies today. Taught to hate ourselves as our enemies taught us to love and fear them. This so-called Orthodox Islam were part of this evilest of the evil crimes against the Universal Creator people. In fact, this so-called Sunnah Islam spread their made up so-called Islam amongst black people in our Homeland through murder, rape, pillage and thievery; the history verifies that what I am saying is the truth. Our enemies stole from us our language; our enemies stole from us our way of life; our enemies stole from us our heritage; our enemies stole from us the ability to love ourselves; our enemies taught us to hate ourselves; our enemies rape our mothers and daughters; our enemies murdered our leaders; our enemies even murdered the last Prophet sent to them Prophet Noble Drew Ali, who set up the Moorish Temples in Newark New Jersey in 1913. Through Our Fathers Eyes my people we must examine all things and recognize as we identify the enemies of our fathers as well as ourselves, in today times; these are the same enemies my people from 500 years ago.

These so- called black Imams are no different from the Christian so-called black Reverends they are both only leading black people to destruction, poverty, despair, hopelessness, disenfranchisement as well as self-hatred and love for our enemies. None of them are teaching you about Allah they are all teaching you about the Vicegerent Yakub our enemies maker. If you pay attention you will see our enemies are prospering while black people are suffering globally, due to these traitors amongst us teaching the lies, of our enemies to their people. We my people globally must unite ourselves for us to deal with our 6,000-year-old enemies and their false religions. We my people don't need anything regarding religions, traditions or anything else, from the murderers of our fathers and mothers as well as ourselves. Love for ourselves as well as unity globally my people we can defeat all the Vicegerent Makings and their false religions my people; history proves that all the Vicegerent making are nothing but murders, rapist, liars, thieves just pure evil, that we must at all cost keep them all away from us.

My people in America as well as globally the restorer of the real Islam as well as the Original Black Nation visit us in the person of Master Fard Muhammad Allah Almighty Himself, to whom all holy praises are due forever. He Allah raised up from amongst His last also greatest Messenger the Most Honorable Elijah Muhammad/Muhammad RasulAllah. We can tell the making of the Vicegerent to get behind me Satan we are no longer under your spell or any of your false religions; or any of your puppets. We serve the true and Living Allah not the Vicegerent who in truth is Yakub, the maker of devil. Allah the True and Living god through His holy Messenger taught black people to love ourselves and to unite ourselves globally and separate ourselves from the makings of the Vicegerent who name is Yakub. Yakub knew he was the Vicegerent whose wisdom would rule for 6,000 years; Yakub also knew that he could assume the title, of Allah until the real Allah make himself known 6,000 years later my people. The true and living Allah has made Himself known, in the 1930s. This so-called Orthodox Islam has been in partnership with their brothers and sisters Christians, during the Despicable Trans-Atlantic Slave Trade and history proves this to be true. We my people globally must love ourselves as we did before the Vicegerent Yakub making came amongst us after being exile from civilization, for 2,000 years; until the Vicegerent mission Muza to go to the caves of the Caucasus Mountains in West Asia now call Europe 4,000 years ago to teach them civilization. Prophet Muza spent over 300 years in this prison with the vilest creatures ever birth on our planet, the Caucasian Race in which all our enemies are members of; teaching them how to build homes for themselves also to try and conduct themselves somewhat like civilize creatures; therefore, the Vicegerent makings are known as mankind. Study the history my people globally you will see I am speaking the absolute truth, so help me Our Holy Savior Allah Almighty.

Through Our Fathers Eyes my people globally is where we will find the love for our black selves. Through Our Fathers Eyes my people globally is where we will discover how to unity ourselves. Through our fathers eyes my people globally is where will see how we can cast out this Satanic Race of Demons along with their false religions, as well as their corrupt politics, from amongst us. I have absolutely no love for the enemies of our fathers as well as the enemies of our elves. We have suffered enough from our enemies we should put an end to this suffering as we drive our enemies from amongst us, as we did 6,000 years ago, as our ancestor the Great General Muk –Muk did 6,000 years ago. My people these Arabs were amongst them at this time they weren't referred to as Arabs then; they are now referred to as Arabs today times, came thousands of years later.

As China during the rule of Chairman Mao leadership the Chinese People exile everyone from amongst themselves then they instituted the five-year economic program; where every Chinese person contributed to re-build the economy of China as well as their country. We my people globally should institute the same procedures as China did. In fact, this the procedure that the Holy Messenger of Allah instituted amongst us, so that we could build our economy here in America in which Wallace Mohammad and the hypocrites stole then turned these many resources, over to the Arabs and Asians; with the help also aid of the American Government, their partner in these unholy crimes. Therefore, my people globally we must unite ourselves against our 6,000-year-old enemies as we keep them from amongst us, this way we can re-build our world as their world is being destroy. America along with her partners are doing everything to prevent us my people from uniting, so that they our enemies can continue to rob black people globally, to prevent us from building our world together. We must my people globally come together as we did in 1955 at the Van Dome Conference, excluding all our enemies from amongst us; including all our enemies' religions, politics and all their practices. We must understand the history of the past 6,000 years in which our enemies are doing everything in their power, to keep hidden. My people our enemies have been revealed to us by Allah Almighty

Himself through the mouth of His Holy Messenger; our enemies are Satan the Accursed Devil.

Through Our Fathers Eyes my people globally it doesn't matter what part of the planet you are my brothers and sisters. It is time once again that we realize we are one people that share the same ancestry as we all came from the only Universal Creator, not made by the Vicegerent. We aren't mankind my people we are the Original People; our enemies are mankind therefore they have many different false religions as well as corrupt politics. For the past 500 years we black people have suffered from our enemies' immeasurable atrocities this includes this so-call Orthodox Islam, as well. Liars and thieves my people this is what all our enemies are, and history will support everything I'm saying to be the truth. Our enemies never want us to establish global love and unity amongst ourselves therefore our enemies have paid agents amongst us, to do whatever our enemies want done, to keep us from unity amongst ourselves including murders, then blame it on some of our own people. This is all planned by America the Accursed Devil and her allies in Europe, Asia, the Mid East, Far East Russia included, my people.

When you cast off our enemies' false values, religions, politics, language, beliefs also way of life, we will be able to establish a global unity amongst black people. Love for ourselves and unity amongst ourselves globally my people. The Wizards of the Vicegerent world also referred to as the dragon, that swiped down one third of the stars in heaven, is only talking about these so-called scholars that have partnered up with the dragon, to commit evil also keep black people in mental, economical, religious, political as well as mental slavery, for all eternity. We are living in a Matriarch society therefore we have this explosion of homosexuality, amongst black people. Our enemies don't want any strong black positive black men around so the extra hard, on trying to prevent this from happening Orthodox so-called Islam included. Our enemies are only concern that we love them and not ourselves. Our enemies want us to trust them to be our religious also political leaders; my people we have trusted these enemies for the past 450 years and we all know the hell that we have received from them all. Everything also every time we stand to do anything for ourselves our enemies are always against black people, doing everything they can to prevent black people from loving ourselves as well as uniting amongst ourselves globally.

Look at the American filthy political system now they openly have transgender in congress, the senate next thing they will be running for president. What kind of fool would want to come here and become an American citizen, these people can only be nothing but evil traitors to their own people. Then these political also religious traitors amongst us lie to all black people, that these transgenders are going to make things better for black people. The American political also religious system has riddle with these homosexuals since their beginning, now they are just coming out of the closet in full force. My people in America as well as globally these are our enemies absolutely in which we should never trust at all. These enemies of ours have done everything in their power to keep black people globally divided also separated as they our enemies, spread their poison amongst black people worldwide; to prevent black people from loving ourselves also uniting amongst ourselves, worldwide.

Through Our Fathers Eyes my people worldwide and not through the eyes of our enemies we will be able to defeat all our enemies their false religions as well as their false politics, have never done any good for black people ever. Our enemies only give black people globally certain perimeters for black people to operate within, keeping black people globally locked into this cage of despair and damnation forever; while they our enemies live a life of ease; this includes this so-called Orthodox Islam. My people our enemies' maker the Vicegerent Yakub is not our creator so our enemies worship that which is other, then ourselves. Our enemies spend much time trying to convince black people globally, to believe in their maker and not our creator. Our enemies are allowing to celebrate as they practice their way of life, but our enemies will do everything they can to prevent black people, from celebrating our way of life. My people it is time we begin demonstrating love and unity amongst ourselves; let our enemies believe as they choose we must make sure, that we stay as far away from everything our enemies believe in, as well as practice then we can save ourselves Through Our Fathers Eyes is where the answer lye for all black people globally.

CHAPTER 8

DESTRUCTION

The destruction my people must be examine extremely carefully as well as closely. We must not be like Samson as we destroy our enemies, we destroy ourselves as well. Remember Samson anger caused him to destroy himself we can't be or have such rage, till we make the same mistake as our father Samson. What drove him to this rage was him allowing himself to be deceived by his enemies and trusting Delilah a Caucasian Devil. The world that we have known is being destroyed right before our eyes and there is nothing that can stop this destruction. America must pay for her sins also her most hideous crimes against Black and Indian people. America's partners also must pay for partnering up with these American Criminals in fact their participation in the Despicable Trans-Atlantic Slave Trade, that this Zionist/ Christian/Arab/Asian American Government of Murdering, Thieving Global Terrorist, America in fact the entire Caucasian Race are trying to sweep it under the rug, as if it doesn't matter. It does matter my people these atrocities were done to us all globally; therefore, the destruction of this world is happening. The Vicegerent Yakub world was only given 6,000 years to rule these 6,000 years are up their religions, their politics, their educational system everything of this world, is being destroyed; we my people must make sure that we don't get caught in this destruction.

The world that we are living in today has gone completely insane nothing makes any sense at all. Homosexuality is running rampant tearing down what very little moral fabric that maybe left. Young people are beating robbing also murdering the elders without hesitation or any caring at all. Christianity along with this so-called Sunnah Islam, have failed black people completely and miserably. Thus, preventing you my people; from escaping the destruction as you worship these holidays, of unmerciful death also suffering, for black people, for hundreds of years. Diseases insanity is the order of the day as you my people are following our enemies to their well-deserved destruction. You are believing the lies that have been taught to you as well as still being taught to black people, by our enemies are keeping you blind to what is really happening. The religions of our enemies are more damaging than any other drug our, enemies have flooded black communities with, throughout America. Religious dope is more poisonous my people than anything this is how our enemies are keeping you held in mental also spiritual bondage, not allowing you to escape this destruction that is over taking Yakub's civilization and his making.

My people you must stop considering these strangers that America has flooded black communities with, as the government move black people into these concentration camps, called shelters. Where you have absolutely any chance of escape; as these interlopers live a much better life than the ones who were more intricate in building also helping America, to become the power she has become. You still love the devil my people although the devil gives you absolutely nothing. Black children; born still believing in the lives of our enemies, being taught to them mostly by black mothers thus making their black children as well as themselves, nothing but fuel for the fire. Black generations are being wiped out due to this ignorance of trusting our enemies while our enemies, sit back laughing at us all. Our enemies including this so-called Sunnah Islam is being supported by the American government; as the American government keep you my people disenfranchised living in absolute and total misery as well as despair; with absolute no relief, from our enemies' religions as well as their politics also our enemies way of life; that never benefits black people only benefitting our open enemies. The Destruction my people you are bringing it upon yourself by believing also trusting, our enemies; who are going to be destroyed with America because they are Americans; also, they are helping America to destroy black people not only in America, but globally my people. History proves these are all enemies of black people globally also by following their interpretations of religion, politics or anything else, is bringing about your destruction my people. We have been given our salvation we are destroying ourselves by considering others, who care absolutely nothing about black people, in

America as well as globally. When you examine all things my people you will see how our enemies are prospering while you are suffering, my people. These same enemies along with their interpretation of religion are keeping black people trapped in the cage of despair as well as hopelessness, with absolutely any hope of escape. My people in America as well as globally we have been trusting our enemies, for the past 500 years look at what we have received from all of them; this includes this so-called Sunnah or Orthodox so-called Islam; that was made up by the wisdom of the Vicegerent who is Yakub; the enemy of Allah our Creator as well as all black people globally.

The Destruction my people is happening, rather you like it or not it is happening right before your eyes, then you ask yourself what is going on. This is what's happening my people the world of the Caucasian Race, is being destroyed and it can't be stop or adverted. We must make sure that we aren't caught up in this Divine Destruction by turning away globally don't need it. Let our enemies keep what their maker the Vicegerent gave them, let us keep what Allah our Creator gave us through His Holy Messenger, the Most Honorable Elijah Muhammad/Muhammad RasulAllah. All we must do is follow the teachings as well as all the Holy Messenger's programs and we will be successful globally, for all black people; as we watch our enemies perish. We must be fast moving and fast thinking up to the modern day and time my people as Allah taught us all through His Holy Messenger. This means my people we can no longer think on the plain that our enemies, have designed for us which is nothing more than a cage, my people that was designed for us never to escape by our enemies.

Through Our Fathers Eyes is the only way we can escape the destruction that is over taking, the world in which we are living in. There is no hope for this world or society it has been condemned by Allah Almighty Himself; who visited us in the persons of Master Fard Muhammad to whom all holy praises are due forever. I am only revealing to you my people that you have absolutely no hope at all in this society. Never had and never will. All these different strangers also interlopers that the American Government have planet in black communities throughout America, don't care about black so-called Negroes. These strangers also interlopers have been deceiving us black people ever since they came to America. This why we my people in America and throughout the world must unite ourselves, so we can begin building a globally economy, for ourselves. We can't trust any of these other people to do anything for us my people we must do it ourselves, as we keep these strangers also interlopers from amongst us. These strangers coming here or that have come here with their so-called Sunnah Islam, are dying to become Americans, then turn around and spit on black people with distaste; even through black people have helped them. We can't continue such a destructive path my people whereas all these different people coming here, are enjoying themselves who did absolutely nothing towards the building also defending America; as we black people have done are the ones being deprived living in concentration camp all throughout America.

Tell me which one of these so-called Sunnah Muslims have ever come to the aid, of black people or any cause pertaining to black people. When this Gestapo Law Enforcement Agencies all throughout America murder black men, black women as well as black children; when have this or these so-called Sunni Muslims ever rally behind black people against these atrocities, being committed by the American Government against black people? The answer is never my people reason being is that they are America's partners in crime, against black people. Our enemies are very deceitful when dealing with black people in America as they laugh in our faces, as they stick the knives in our backs to show White Nationalist America, they are on their side. Our enemies only want to see black people destroyed as they were part of the Despicable Trans-Atlantic Slave Trade that placed us all globally, in so terrible condition. Destruction my people; of black people is due to us trusting these enemies and listening to their religious lies as well as their political lies. I wouldn't give any of them two cents for anything they have to say, at all. These are our enemies my people in America as well as globally who care absolutely nothing about black people, only themselves. We my people have been suffering in America for over 450 years which one of these strangers' care about what we as well as our ancestors had to endure; the answer is none of them. It is either our destruction my people or the destruction of our enemies I say the destruction of our enemies this includes, all of them my people.

Destruction of us my people is most desirable by all our enemies' Sunnah so-called Islam included this so-called Sunnah Islam isn't even real Islam my people and those who follow this, aren't real Muslims, they are Moslems Sons. You must understand my people their Maker the Vicegerent Yakub Ibn Lucifer came in the 6,600-year vacuum and his wisdom was given by

Allah, permission to rule for 6,000 years. It took this Vicegerent, 600 years to graft mankind out of us, the Original People. It matters not to me if one believes or not this is from Allah Almighty Himself the true and living Allah, in the person of Master Fard Muhammad to whom all holy praises are due forever. Our enemies including this so-called Sunnah Islam do not want black people in America as well as globally to ascribe to the truth that Allah Himself brought, to us all.

This so-called Sunnah Islam is just as poisonous to black people as Christianity has been and always will be. Why Saladin; are they black people enemies? Examine the history of these demons and what they have done to black people. Examine this so-called Sunnah Islam participation in the Despicable Trans-Atlantic Slave. Examine the history of What this so-called Sunnah Islam play or better yet did, in the destruction of the Black Civilization, in North now called Africa; nothing but murdering devils my people. It doesn't matter how many so- called black people calling themselves Imams, they are on the enemies pay role, just like the Christian preachers. Their job is to keep black forever locked into the cage of despair, depression, disenfranchisement, suffering, educational slavery, as well as disbelief in the Savior that came to save us all, from our enemies, who built this prison for black people in America as well as black people globally. These traitors amongst black people are in place to keep black people globally from preventing us from building a global economy that all black people, can prosper from. You will also find that these traitors have been taught by our enemies my people, to speak their language also their ways as well as practices; our enemies didn't return to these so-called black Imams or black people our own language, before they our Father's Enemies this includes this so-called Sunnah and their brother Christians, Diabolical Treachery in the Despicable Trans- Atlantic Slave Trade, as well as the Destruction of the Black Civilization in North Africa. Now these same enemies my people with the help of their partners in crimes, the American Government of White Nationalism are trying to institute our enemies' ideology, as the founders of Islam and every intelligent person knows this is an absolute as well as total lie; amongst black people globally, just as Christianity did with the Negro Preachers, spreading their lies about Allah. This is what is being done by these makings of the Vicegerent Yakub Ibn Lucifer, doing with this so-called Sunnah Islam today, amongst black people not only in America but globally as well my people.

I'm not speaking hatred my people I'm just telling the truth that history verifies as well as support, so don't call me a racist because I am revealing the truth about our enemies and their diabolical treachery. Through Our Fathers Eyes my people every enemy of ours will be revealed to us all. The diabolical treachery of these enemies must be made known to all black people due these diabolical treacheries were done to black people as well as still being done, to black people in America as well as globally. Following our enemies will only take us all to complete destruction, along with them. How can we trust these Arabs when it is absolute known fact that the government of Saudi Arabia has asked America to help them, to Attack their Muslim so-called brothers and sisters in Iran? Why would we want to make a pilgrimage to Mecca when the very government is corrupt and now they have brought their version of Supreme Evil, over here to black people in America in which we don't need at all.

This is what has brought about our destruction my people and following this so-called Sunnah is only helping to continue the destruction of black people, in America as well as black people throughout the world. We should be forever great full to our Holy Savior who is Allah Almighty in person; we should follow the teachings He Allah gave to His Last Holy and Greatest Messenger, the Most Honorable Elijah Muhammad. These are the only teachings that will save black people in America as well as globally. We are so trusting; of our enemies as we absolutely no trust amongst or for ourselves. History proves that these enemies when they come amongst black hell follow with them. It doesn't matter what their religion death, destruction, starvation, rape, diseases pure suffering my people and history proves this to be true. It is time my people that we reject everything they all have to say or what they believe in, as we return to what Allah brought here to this Wilderness of Sin, iniquity and Transgression call America, for black people; through His Holy Messenger. These are the only teachings that will free black people in America as well as globally; thus, bringing about an end to black people being locked up in this cage of despair and destruction. Then we my people once again can begin to weld ourselves back together as a people also a Nation, flying our own Flag that was given to us by Allah Almighty Himself.

CHAPTER 9

THE HEALING COMES FROM WITHIN OURSELVES MY PEOPLE

The Healing My People begin with ourselves as well as begins within. We had been so poisoned into hating ourselves, killing ourselves, selling drugs to ourselves this began over 450 years ago here in America. We have my people been taught by our enemies to love them and hate ourselves women also children. For centuries this self- hatred has been institutionalized amongst black people in America not by friends my people but by enemies. When you examine my people the history of our treatment towards ourselves this is the poison our enemies put in us and really nothing has change due to us still practicing the evils that our enemies, put in us those many centuries ago. Then to make sure that this self-hatred continues to build in us this wretched American Government and the American people, past the Jim Crow Law; preventing black people from participating in the times of the Industrial Revolution, that began in the 19th century and carried into the 20th century. This was placing black people back into the cage of despair that they believed, they had achieved by fighting in the Civil War as well as the Spanish American War, the service that the Buffalo Soldiers performed during the taking of the Western part of North America, from the Indians by murder also the spreading of diseases amongst them.

Every black man stood up against this evil was outright murdered in many cases horribly without any mercy at all. In fact, the American Government and people would have parties, orgies I should say, murdering black people that only demons could have invented and enjoyed. The atrocities that were committed against black people by the American Government and people can never be forgiven. The despair that continued to fall on black men and their families were to continue forever, as they are still being carried out in today's times. Black people couldn't even afford to by decent food for their families, decent clothes for their families, decent housing for their families, a good education for their children; as our enemies drove this self- hatred wedge between black men, black women and black children. I'm talking about the beginning of the 20th century my people where every Caucasian person in America, took part in denying black people, from making a decent living to provide for himself wife and children. This breaded self- hatred between black husbands, black wives and their black children. The Healing My People we have absolutely no choice but to reconcile with ourselves in order that we may have any chance, of healing ourselves of the poisons of 450-year-old devils the enemies of black people.

You must understand my people they didn't give our fathers a fair chance at putting food on the table for his family; he couldn't even by a new dress for his wife or shoes for his children. While every Caucasian person Zionist included took great pride in denigrating the black man, all throughout America. Laughing at our fathers, as they our enemies with the help of the American Government, along with the American Gestapo call Law Enforcement Agencies did everything in their power to prevent our fathers from proving, that they were men also able and ready to do for himself wives and children. Our enemies gave to our people a most evil as well as most dangerous religion Christianity they knew would keep us divided as well separated. As our enemies crucified our fathers, hanging him on the cross of lies deceit, treachery and just downright hatred, for their black selves. Where does the Healing begin my people? These cowardly Jews could come into black communities' rape black women as well as young black girls, in many cases young black boys. If any black man stood up against these Jewish, Italian, Irish, Polish, Russian, or German devils, they; our father's enemies called in the Gestapo to arrest or murder our fathers, and nothing was ever done about these many injustices. The courts painted them as criminals sentencing them to cruel and indecent punishment for absolutely nothing. Justice is supposed to be blind when it comes to race, creed or color except black people; then justice is no longer blind as she sees every black man, woman or child that comes before the bench; where they are always in most cases, found guilty especially black men in many, many cases never to see their wives and children ever again. The healing my people must begin you are in hell without Jacob's latter to help you climb out preventing you my people, from ever becoming a people again. An enemy sold out everything we had built for ourselves under the guidance of Allah's last and greatest Messenger the most Honorable Elijah Muhammad; then the American government gave it to their new partners as they allow our enemies America's new additional partners, to prosper as they spread their false teachings of Islam.

The healing my people can only happen when we return to Allah who visited us in the person of Master Fard Muhammad, to who all holy praises are due forever. This evil wicket most diabolical American Government Murdered the Prophet Noble Drew Ali for no other reason, then trying to unite his people. The Honorable Marcus Garvey was destroyed by our enemies thrown in jail for no other reason than him trying, to raise his people. The Honorable David Walker was murdered by our enemies for no other reason, then him trying to unite his people. The list or amount of murders the American Government has committed against black people, make Hitler, Stalin, Napoleon look like child's play. The murder of Malcolm X was done for no other reason than he wanted to help, unite his people. Adam Clayton Power Jr. was murder for only one reason he was trying to help, unite his people. Langston Huge was murder for no other reason than trying to help, unite his people. Meager Edwards was murdered for no other reason than trying to help, unite his people. The Black Panthers and every other Revolutionary Party were murdered also destroyed for no other reason than they were trying to help, unite as well as protect their people. This is an ongoing process by this American Government of Global Terrorist, to murder and keep black people, forever in this cage of despair. The Healing my people must begin now, or you are all domed.

Now America has partner up with the so-called Sunnah or Sunni so-called Muslims who are murdering as well as enslaving, black people in Serra Leone who are Muslims. This is another enemy of ours my people trusting them is nothing more than trusting this Cobra like Rattle Snake American Government and the American people. All of America's partners are working together my people to keep us in this cage of hopelessness and despair. All these people that are coming into America or have come to

Saladin Shabazz-Allah

America in the last 40 plus years are the enemies of our ancestors, as well as the enemies of ourselves, my people. Our enemies know we can never heal ourselves from the poisonous wounds we have suffered from them my people by listening to them, as well as trusting them. The murdering of black people anywhere on our planet is the murdering of all black people, everywhere on our planet. We can't heal our wounds by incorporating our enemy's religions, or ideology it won't work my people; never has it work and never will it ever work. To heal ourselves of the spiritual wounds inflicted, the mental wounds as well as the physical wounds, we must cast all our enemies out from amongst us. The Healing My People must come from within amongst ourselves not from our enemies who are responsible, for black people having these wounds for over 500 years globally.

Our enemies with the help of these cowardly traitors amongst us are working diligently in making sure that black people never heal themselves from the poisonous wounds that they are responsible for; this includes this so-called Sunnah/Sunni so-called Islam. Much lies have been told by our enemies my people and yes, they are our enemies my people history proves that they were 500 years ago, 6,000 years ago up till this present day and time. Being narrow minded also judge mental against your brother or sister, is only aiding our enemies cause as it prevents us from ever having a chance in healing ourselves, from the poisonous wounds inflicted upon us by our enemies. We must turn to ourselves to heal ourselves my people. Absolutely no one cares about black people the reason being is that we don't care about ourselves enough to selfheal ourselves. We have suffered my people atrocities that no other people have ever suffered before, in the history of our planet. The Healing my people comes from within ourselves not from outsiders; the outsiders regardless of what they say their religion may be are the ones that betrayed our fathers and mothers 6,000 years ago, 500 years ago and 42 years ago. We can never heal ourselves following these proven enemies of black people. These interlopers have been deceiving us for thousands of years and think nothing of it as you sit back loving also trusting our enemies. The Healing my people amongst is being prevented by these interlopers who are nothing but thieves and liars; that are working hand and hand with the Zionist and Christians, also the Asians. For what purpose Saladin are they doing this? My people our enemies are working together to keep us black people as economical slaves to them. Therefore, our enemies are controlling every aspect of black communities which is food, clothing, shelter, religion and politics; thus, leaving black people at the unmerciful hands of our 6,000-year-old enemies.

Thus, my people preventing us from ever healing ourselves from this deadly Cobra, Rattle Snake serpents that put this poison of self-hatred, into us all. Our enemies are working daily using their useless religions to keep us from ever healing ourselves of these most poisonous wounds, inflicted on us by our enemies, my people. If we continue to trust these enemies we will never be able to heal ourselves of this deadliest of all the poisons which, is SELF HATRED. Look at how the American Government support also aid to our enemies, to help them build schools for their children also Mosques for them; the American Government give aid also support to the Christians, Zionist, as well as the Asians, to build schools also places of worship, all for our enemies my people a nothing for black people except hell. Show me where the American Government ever did anything to aid or support to the Lost Found Members of the Tribe of Shabazz? When did the American Government; or any of their partners; gave aid or support to any Muhammad University of Islam? When did the American Government or any of their partners; gave aid or support to any of the Holy Messenger of Allah programs of self-help for black people this includes this so-called Sunnah Islam? When did this American Government or any of their partners; did anything when the NYC Gestapo police force stormed Temple # 7 in Harlem? When did the American Government or any of their partners in crime; gave any support to prevent this unfounded aggression against any of the temples or its members? When did the American Government or any of their evil partners; did anything for black people in America or anywhere else? When have the American Government or any of America's evil partners including so-called Sunnah Islam did anything for black people except keeping us divided, separated and disenfranchised? When my people will you wake up and see these are our open enemies and none of them will ever be our friends as well as want the best, for black people? We my people in America as well as globally are we turning to the enemies of our fathers as well as ourselves. THE HEALING COMES FROM WITHIN MY PEOPLE NOT FROM ANYWHERE ELSE OR ANYONE ELSE; BUT OURSELVES MY PEOPLE.

For the past 450 plus years, have been, a complete an endless nightmare, for black people not only in America but for black people, worldwide. This nightmare will not end until we end it my people in America as well as worldwide. We were one people before these enemies came amongst us my people for us to heal ourselves we must cast these enemies from amongst us globally. We must not allow them to come amongst us to set up trading post ever again, this is their platform to launch their evil poison amongst us; this includes all their so-called religions, politics and their way of life we don't need to any understand of It at all. Through Our Fathers Eyes is the only way we can heal ourselves my people our enemies you must understand my people, never want us to heal ourselves from their poisonous wounds, inflicted on black people by them, our enemies. The Healing Comes From Within Ourselves, My People this must be understood by all black people, in America as well as throughout the world.

We my people must establish a worldwide conference of black people, so we can build dialog amongst ourselves, this will begin the Healing process amongst black people globally. We must my people not only in America but all over the world must look Through Our Fathers Eyes then and only then can we cure ourselves, of the poisons of self-hatred and division of black people globally, that have engulfed us all, for the past 500 years, by our enemies. The Healing Must come From Within us my people I'm speaking to all black people worldwide we all must come together, as one universal Black Nation. We have no reason to love our enemies this is insane teachings my people in fact this is another weapon our enemies use against black people; we should love our enemies no matter how much they may hate us. This statement came from Martin Luther King Jr. how insane this statement is and all our enemies are using this as a weapon against all black people. They our enemies don't have any love for us, but we should love them. Another statement that is used against black people is that forgive them lord they know what they do. As Malcolm said they are experts at what they are doing. How did Brother Malcolm know that they were experts Saladin? Malcolm was student of the Holy Messenger of Allah, the Most Honorable Elijah Muhammad and Malcolm study our enemy's history and the enemy's history tell us all about the evils they all have done to black people this includes this phony so-called Sunnah Islam, given to them by the Vicegerent Yakub Ibn Lucifer.

The Healing my people comes from ourselves not from any outsider pretending they have our best interest at hand; these are nothing but lies my people. This includes this so-called Sunnah Islam also these other interlopers that aren't of us, pretending to be for us my people. These are the making of the Vicegerent Yakub Ibn Lucifer not Allah the Universal Creator, in which we are created from. History will prove conclusively that every time they come amongst us hell comes with them, for black people. They learn from silly fools amongst us who are silly enough to teach them, now these same enemies believe they can teach us the Original People. These people no matter what name they may call themselves aren't our people, no more than Jim Jones was of us and look at what that devil did to the foolish black people that believed in him; he stole their money then murdered them all as he walked away with their money and possessions. While this evil filthy American Government allowed this devil to commit mass murders and get away with it. This proves my people; that we shouldn't allow any of them amongst us most surely never allow them to teach us black people. If these children of the Vicegerent Yakub Ibn Lucifer and history will prove absolutely that they are, they are out to destroy the world of black people globally in which they all have participated in doing and history will verify this, as the absolute truth.

Every time for the past 6,000 years we allowed these makings of the Vicegerent Yakub Ibn Lucifer to come amongst us, they always spread lies, deceit, treachery, miss instructions amongst the Original People, causing us to fight and kill each other. These demons are very skillful at pretending to care about black people but in truth they are out to prevent black people from healing ourselves. The makings of the Vicegerent Yakub Ibn Lucifer are always coming around black people saying they believe in truth they don't believe; if they believe then why don't these liars teach their own people we don't need them around us, we are able to teach ourselves. Through Our Fathers Eyes my people not through the eyes of the Vicegerent Yakub Ibn Lucifer or any of his makings, or any of their false religions that have produce absolutely nothing for black people in America or any black people globally. The Healing my people can never happen with any of the Vicegerent Yakub Ibn Lucifer makings, involved in our business. Examine the history of these interlopers coming amongst us you will discover they aren't of us at all, which means we shouldn't listen or trust any of them they are our enemies, my people.

We must my people turn inward to ourselves for us to heal ourselves of these poisonous wounds physically, spiritually and mentally. This can only be accomplished by us looking Through Our Fathers Eyes I am of my father and to my father I trust and rely on. What was done to our fathers my people were done to us as well. The same Cobra like Rattle Snake makings of this Vicegerent Yakub Ibn Lucifer are always coming amongst us hiding behind the Allah and Allah's Holy Messenger the Most Honorable Elijah Muhammad teachings and black people buy into these demons lies, next thing before you know it black people are fighting amongst themselves killing each other, spreading the lies these strangers be spreading amongst us. Then the resurgent of the poisons from the Vicegerent Yakub Ibn Lucifer makings have again been injected amongst us, preventing black people from healing ourselves. These strangers are not our fathers' children or off spring as well. This devil plot to remove black people from our supposed to be communities called Gentrification, is another attack on black people to destabilize black people process of healing ourselves of their most deadly poisons, that have been injected into black people, by the Vicegerent Yakub Ibn Lucifer makings. They the Vicegerent makings can do this through their false teachings, religions, politics, food, clothing even shelter, my people. There is ample amount of proof that what I am saying is 100% right and exact; just examine the history that's all but you must examine the history Through Our Fathers Eyes my people and not through the eyes of our enemies who are the proven enemies of our fathers.

The Healing My People Comes From Within not from the sky not from any false religion or politics. The Healing My People Comes From Within not from people other than ourselves, it comes from ourselves. We my people everywhere on the planet black people are my people must turn to each other. The healing must begin with ourselves globally, my people. I'm not concern about our many enemies or their religions, families at all; I am concern about my people and those that are like me. I'm also not concern about narrow minded people as well they refuse to come out the cage they have been prison in, for the past 500 years. The Healing Comes From Within Ourselves My People! There are plenty of obstacles blocking our path these obstacles seem to be imposing but in truth they aren't, we have the True and Living Allah on our side or I should say backing us in the person of Master Fard Muhammad to whom all holy praises are due forever. We were blessed by Allah Almighty Himself He Allah raised up one from amongst us to be His Last also Greatest Messenger/Muhammad/RasulAllah, the Most Honorable Elijah Muhammad.

There isn't any use looking up into the sky there isn't anything up there that will come down to help us, these are the lies being told to black people by the Zionist, the Christians, the so-called Sunnah Islam and the Asians, as they gain control over the wealth of the society we are living in, everywhere on our planet. Through Our Fathers Eyes my people not through the eyes of our enemies' fathers who were also are nothing but thieving, lying, murdering devils, ever since Yakub grafted this make matters even worse, as the enemy's lies have always made things worse, for black people. If you listen also believe in the lies, of our enemies' things will continue to get progressively worse for black people as it, always have. Black people are always gravitating to the un-truth of our enemies believing in their evil. Our enemies have been stilling from black people and our culture for thousands of years and have gotten away with it. Now the Judgement is upon them all Sunnah So-called Islam included and they aren't going to escape. The Vicegerent Yakub Ibn Lucifer cannot save them from the destruction that Allah is bringing down upon them. If you believe in the lies of the Vicegerent Yakub Ibn Lucifer makings you are doomed. Look at how this so-called Sunnah Islam is being destroyed today as they are on the side of Supreme Evil America. This why you find these cowards running to America paying black people r any American $10,000 so they can become an American, as they sell whatever soul they may left, if any my people. How can these children or the makings of the Vicegerent Yakub Ibn Lucifer help black people the only thing they can do, is to take you to the destruction with them?

My people the history will tell you everyone that was involved and are still involved with the slaughtering, of over 600,000,000 black people; One Hundred Million never making it out of the Middle Passage and the count is still rising; how can we be so stupid to trust any of the Vicegerent Yakub Ibn Lucifer makings or better yet Grafted People. It doesn't matter what they may say or how they say it my people, examine the history you will see the actual truth of these people, that the Zionist/Christian Control America, Martin Luther King Jr. along with the Big 6, Integrated, black people in America into. My people The Devastation after this most deadly of the deadly plans the Integration implementation act is as evil as anything, that this Vicegerent Yakub Ibn Lucifer makings have ever done, this open the door of phase two of the integration act and that was to start a war in Viet Nam, so that the American CIA also Military; could smuggle Heroin down the Ho chi Mein trail into Harlem my people, in which they the Zionist / Christian American Government did. Now the partnership with this so-called Sunnah Islam was in the makings as well to help America put the black man back into the cage, that the Vicegerent Yakub Ibn Lucifer makings had them caged in. Enter Wallace D. Mohammad who was extremely eager also ready to aid our enemies, my people into our destruction. This traitor Wallace D. Mohammad was the Ambassador for this so-called Sunnah Islam as well as the Arabs coming into America and spreading their version of the poison of our enemies, this Mystery God they dare call Allah; when history reveals he is the Vicegerent Yakub Ibn Lucifer. The Zionist/Christian American Government then began the implementing of their genocidal plans, of the mass murdering of black people, throughout America. So that America could begin the insurgent, of their colored people also known as so-called African Americans better known as Negroes, to be the voice of black people, in which they aren't my people. This Zionist/Christian American Government knew these made colored people would never stand up against them because this is how our enemies made them, to be obedient and this includes this so-called Sunnah Islam as well.

Now these devils call it Gentrification where the Mass of Black People are being pushed out of the communities, where their great, great grandparents migrated to from the South where they believed things would be better. These elders were in error and they lived to see it also many regretted coming to these big cities, as they watch their children died from overdoses from the dope in which the damn CIA brought into America and dropped it smack dead into Harlem. This plan was executed under the orders of the White House by the Democratic Party whose President and Vice President were none other, then John F. Kennedy and Linden B. Johnson. Two un-merciless, notorious murdering devils especially when it came to black people, in America as well as throughout the world. Don't forget my people the FBI and the CIA were all involved in murdering black people by the millions, with their treachery here in America and the lies also the traitors, that were amongst us that sold us all out. Our Healing My people must come from ourselves this is something we have to work on. Look how the prison institutions are filled with young black men across the country, as America and her partners filter in these immigrants. People who can't even speak the language are being employed. While young black men are unemployed living in concentration camps all throughout America.

We are being very foolish following other people as these strangers are making themselves rich, from black people. We must understand my people we must begin to do something for ourselves and stop letting other than ourselves rob us. These are enemies my people not friends they pretend only to be our friends as they offer black people absolutely no help at all. Therefore, Sunni Ali change the way his people in Timbuktu practice Islam in which these so-called Sunnah Muslims didn't like Sunni Ali knew they were not the Original People. Sunni Ali also knew that these Arabs were trying to set themselves up as the chosen people, in Islam; just as the Jews try to set themselves up as god chosen people. Both are lying my people as they try very hard to set themselves up as benefactor, in which they aren't. We have all seen how these Arabs conduct themselves in black communities throughout America; we all have seen the evils they do in black communities throughout America; no Imam or any ranking official of so-called Sunnah ever came down or even investigated the evils, their people are committing and put a stop to it. Allah Himself revealed to us that the Holy Quran is written every 25,000 years to equal his home circumference, so how could this book that these so-called Sunnah Islam claim that their book is the Holy Quran when Prophet Muhammad [peace and blessings be upon him] was dead 23 years before their so-called Quran, was ever written. We must my people examine all these things that our enemies are trying to put over on black people. History will prove absolutely this so-called Sunnah Islam has as much horrible diabolical crimes against black people, as any of their brothers have done to black people, in the past 500 years even longer. Why would we lend an ear to any of these liars? Why should we believe in anything these liars have to say? Why should let these liars anywhere near us when they have demonstrated, their hatred for black people. We had Islam as a way of life trillions and trillions of years before these Arabs were ever made a kind of a man and history verifies what I'm saying is the truth. Why my people are we trusting our 6,000-year-old enemies with the last 500 years being a complete diabolical and evil nightmare, that is still happening today.

We can't heal ourselves my people by having the self- hatred for ourselves that our enemies have been put in us centuries ago. If you come from any other part of the Western Hemisphere your ancestors better yet I should say our ancestors came here on the many slave ships as well as part of the Despicable Trans- Atlantic Slave Trade, in which this so-called Sunnah Islam was a key player along with their Caucasian brothers all throughout Europe were part of this Supreme Evil, the Despicable Trans- Atlantic Slave Trade. It is so illogical for us to believe or trust any of them after what they all have done to our ancestors, as they continue to do to black people in this day and time, we all the evils this so-called Sunnah Islam are doing in black communities, throughout America. Rather you believe or except it my people Allah Almighty Himself visited us in the person of Master Fard Muhammad to whom all, holy praises are due forever. He Allah Himself raised up from amongst us His last and greatest Messenger, the Most Honorable Elijah Muhammad/Muhammad RasulAllah. He Allah gave to His Holy Messenger Supreme Wisdom which is greater than this book this so-called Sunnah or Orthodox so-called Islam, call Quran in which it isn't my people. The Holy Quran will not be renewed for another 9,000 plus years my people/ history/Bible /Quran. This is from Almighty Allah Himself my people not from the wisdom of the Vicegerent Yakub Ibn Lucifer, who only had 6,000 years to rule.

My people therefore the American Government partner up with the Arabs or this so-called Orthodox Islam as well as these treacherous Asian, they are all the makings of the Vicegerent Yakub Ibn Lucifer and we black people are from the Universal Creator, not our enemies. Keeping us locked my people in this cage of despair, hopelessness, disenfranchisement, in proper education and self-hatred; our enemies can then lie to themselves that Allah has blessed them. This is an absolute lie my people being told by our enemies the Zionist, the Christians, this so-called Orthodox Islam and these Asians, that are on the side of America the Accursed Devil; the East Indians from India are also included. They are all the makings from the Vicegerent Yakub Ibn Lucifer experiments on the Island of Pelan 6,600 years ago.

My people if you are silly enough to believe that Allah Almighty blessed these unworthy enemies of ours and not bless us, who have suffered such un-imaginable most evil, most diabolical horrors, from these enemies of ours;

you believe my people these demons have been given the right to guard the secrets of Allah's Creations; you are absolutely and totally wrong; therefore, our enemies don't have the Supreme Wisdom of Allah. This is also why Allah didn't reveal Himself to our enemies He Allah knew they weren't believers in Him; He Allah Almighty Knew they all believed in the Vicegerent Yakub Ibn Lucifer and they all weren't worthy of his Holy Presence or His Supreme Wisdom, my people He Allah Almighty Himself revealed Himself in the physical person of Master Fard Muhammad to whom all holy praises, are due forever; to one of us my people, the Holy Messenger the most Honorable Elijah Muhammad. Allah Almighty Himself in person, through the mouth of His last and greatest Messenger/Muhammad RasulAllah, the Most Honorable Elijah Muhammad taught us His Supreme Wisdom and the makings of this Vicegerent Yakub Ibn Lucifer, hate us all for this reason my people. So, the plot to murder black people in America at the whole sale level was being plotted by all our enemies collectively, my people. We must understand my people Allah Almighty Himself came to us in person it doesn't matter what the Vicegerent Yakub Ibn Lucifer makings think or anyone else think or believe. Allah did visit us in person Allah gave to us the greatest gift any people has ever received in fact Allah gave us two Supreme Gifts; one His Supreme Wisdom which goes back to when Allah created Himself, from the Atom of life; two Allah raised up from amongst us His last and greatest Messenger the Most Honorable Elijah Muhammad/ Muhammad RasulAllah. I don't care what anyone has to say I will defend this truth against anyone, anywhere in the world.

The healing comes from within ourselves my people we have already been given the remedies to heal ourselves, all we must do is apply them nothing else except stay away from our enemies and keep our enemies from amongst us. Any as well as everything else will prevent us from healing ourselves from becoming a people and a unified Nation of Black People, flying our flag given to us by Allah Almighty Himself. Through Our Fathers Eyes my people not through the eyes of our enemies in which we have been looking through, for the past 500 years. We my people must stop patronizing our enemies' businesses in our communities; we should be sending them the message, to get from amongst us as we build our unity as well as our economy, for black self. The Healing Comes From Within Our Selves my people following our enemies and their interpretation or their maker the Vicegerent Yakub Ibn Lucifer, will only keep black people for locked in this dreadful cage that we have been in, for the past 500 years. Remember my people the True and Living Allah visited us in the person of Master Fard Muhammad, to whom all holy praises are due forever. He Allah raised up from amongst us His last and greatest Messenger the Most Honorable Elijah Muhammad/Muhammad RasulAllah. Let absolutely no one turn you away from your salvation it doesn't matter whom it may be, or what they claim to be, or what they have to say. The Healing Comes From Within Ourselves My People.

CHAPTER 10

LOVE FOR SELF FIRST

My people this chapter is very important it is about black people understanding the necessity of love for self- first, before we even consider loving anyone else. For the past 500 years our enemies have taught black people to hate themselves and love our enemies. For the past 500 years our enemies taught us to believe in them and distrust ourselves. For the past 500 years so much poison from our enemies have been about instilling self- hatred for ourselves, as we love also feared our enemies. For the past 500 years our enemies have injected in us self-hatred for our black women who is the mother, of Allah Himself, which is ourselves, my people. For the past 500 years my people we have been fighting and killing each other for the pleasure of our enemies without even thinking about it. The poison injected in us by our Cobra Rattle Snake enemies approximately 500 years ago has kept black people divided and separated, from each other; always at war each other killing each other, at the pleasure of our enemies. For the past approximately 500 years we have been sacrificing our children for the pleasure of our Lucifer makings have taken bites out of black people, with impunity and they are still doing it today. Love for Self- First my people we are justified in doing so, my people.

My betrayed and lied to black people we once again must love ourselves above all other people reasoning being, is that none of these other people have absolutely any love for us at all. All these strange people with their religions, also world, once in the harder you fighter, is the quicker you will sink and have sunk into the Abyss, of the insanity of the Vicegerent Yakub Ibn Lucifer made people. We have been so completely fooled also deceived by these people until you can't see any way out, of the hell that has engulf us all. Our enemies will not allow anyone to come amongst themselves and changed what they believe in, about themselves; so why should we allow our enemies to come amongst us with their lies trying to influence us my people, in what is best for us black people. Our enemies don't want us to believe in Allah the True and Living Allah our Holy Savior and our enemies don't want us to ever have love for ourselves. This so-called Sunnah Islam is trying to convince black people that the Persians are evil, when history reveals, all this so-called Sunnah Islam evils they have committed, against black people and their own kind. The Persians had absolutely nothing to do with this most evil, diabolical, most deadly Trans- Atlantic Slave Trade; but this so-called Sunnah Islam was extremely involved in the Trans- Atlantic Slave Trade, with their Zionist and Christian brothers, to murder and destroy black people.

History proves beyond a shadow of doubt that we black people must have love for ourselves first and keep the Vicegerent Yakub Ibn Lucifer making from amongst us, always my people. Our enemies come amongst black people in many disguises pretending to love black people, in which they don't. Our enemies come amongst us trying to act like they one of us, but they aren't my people. Our enemies come amongst us for 6 objectives-1-to keep black people from loving themselves-2-to keep black people trusting also believing, in them our 6,000-year-old enemies. 3- To rob black people as they knowingly sell us poisonous foods, drugs alcohol tobacco all sorts poisons-4- to keep us believing in their false interpretation of religions Allah as well as everything else-5- to always be our devious, lying thieving political leaders-6-to keep black people forever locked into this cage of despair, suffering, disenfranchisement and economical slavery. This is the absolute truth my people history will always prove I'm speaking the truth about our enemies. Love for Self- First My People Globally this is one of the keys that we need to defeat our many enemies, given to us by Allah Almighty Himself through His Holy Messenger the Most Honorable Elijah/ Muhammad RasulAllah. This is one of our problems my people that causes more problems, for ourselves. Our many enemies are feasting off our lack of love for ourselves and laughing at us like the hyenas they most certainly are and always will be, when it comes to black people. The importance of we my people having love for ourselves then we will be ready to give our lives protecting ourselves, women, children communities our civilization globally my people. We will stand at the ready to build an economy also protect it from our enemies who only want to destroy, anything that we do for ourselves or attempt to do for ourselves.

Only Through Our Fathers Eyes my people are we able to see the love we had for each other for trillions and trillions of years, until 6,600 years ago, more important approximately 500 years ago. This is when the self-hatred was injected, into our main vain my people. Thus the beginning of self- hatred really began or this next phase of the birth control plan began, this is when the wisdom of the Vicegerent Yakub Ibn Lucifer laws on birth control was implemented again, by the Wizards in charge of their god, the Vicegerent Wisdom or plans on birth control; these wizards are now called the Zionist today my people, in which they don't deny they are the Israelites, children of the Vice gent Yakub Ibn Lucifer whose name was changed, to Israel the enemy of Allah and all of Allah's Creations and that include you my people.

Love for Self-First is something we all should be working on together not listening to our enemies who hope and pray that we black people, never achieve this. Our enemies know this achievement will put an end, to all the devilishment that they our enemies are getting away with and have gotten way with, for the past 500 years. Our enemies my people took this all from us during this Despicable Trans- Atlantic Slave Trade and injected us with their poison of Self Hatred, into all black people globally, especially in the Western Hemisphere. We have more negative sayings towards each other as you praise our enemies that put this poison in us all. Their religions are poison to all black people; their politics are poison to all black people; their practices are poison to all black people; their actions are of those of the snake of the grafted type. We will be complete idiots to follow or believe such people as history points out they all are our enemies. These enemies have always for the past 500 years stood in opposition against black people uniting as well as having sincere love, for ourselves my people. The love for self and their kind my people our enemies practice amongst themselves; yet they our enemies discourage black people from having love amongst ourselves. Therefore, we black people must have Love for Self- First and to hell with everyone else. Imagine my people these interlopers are coming from a different so called righteous countries, come here to America to be

Americans. How righteous can these people be my people they are only pretending to be so-called righteous to trick and fool you my people.

Our enemies are safe due to us not having love for ourselves first they our enemies feel very comfortable cause they believe that they our enemies, can cultivate black people into their way of thinking as well as their practices, also their so-called religions and beliefs, which our enemies have done. None of our enemies ever come to black people aid the ones that do come is only trying to infiltrate whatever, black people may be doing. These infiltrators mission my people is to division also separation amongst black people in America, as well as globally. We must my people recognize the lies, the deceit also the intent, of our enemies; if we black people stay dormant and bend to the will of our enemies, our enemies are happy as well as feel very safe, that black people will do nothing to guard themselves, against the evils that are pretending to be our friends. Look at how we are the ones that are suffering my people not our enemies. Don't you think something is extremely wrong with this I surly do; why are we continuing to allow this to happen to yourselves as you sit back and do absolutely nothing to protect yourselves, from our proven enemies. Interlopers trying to steal our names also our heritage claiming to be one of us my people and they aren't. Coming amongst us spreading untruths and they should be amongst their own people, teaching them; not amongst us trying to teach black people. We don't need these strangers amongst us trying to make their selves, rich from our labor. Thus, preventing us my people; from ever establishing love for ourselves first, before ever loving anyone else that isn't of us my people.

Through Our Fathers Eyes my people we must understand how important this is that we as a people globally as well as individuals and locally, must put into practice immediately. Love for Self-First my people and no one else at all domestically as well as globally. We my people domestically as well as globally must re-establish our language the language of our fathers and not the grafted language, of our father's enemies; we had written language before these enemies were ever grafted out of us by the Vicegerent Yakub Ibn Lucifer 6,600 years ago. America and her partners came up with diabolical plan of gentrification which is nothing but The Vicegerent methods also laws, of killing the black baby at birth, here in America. America isn't the home of the free and the brave; America is the home of the derange cowards, murderers also the depraved; this is the truth of America that America wants to be kept hidden, from the world. These strangers coming to America seeking to become Americans are these deranged, cowards, murderers, also the depraved I don't care what they say their religion might be, my people they are our enemies without any doubt; examine the history my people the truth is there of our enemies' treacheries to our fathers and mothers; by the enemies of our fathers as well as ourselves.

Love for Ourselves My People Domestically as well as Globally we can begin to defeat our enemies, as we take them all off our planet. Our enemies with our forced help made this civilization that we are now living in. Look at this civilization in fact the Vicegerent Yakub Ibn Lucifer civilization is made up of homosexuality. Allah isn't in support of this evil civilization at all my people nor any of his prophets are in support, of this evil civilization either; then explain to me why people are you in support of evil civilization instead of building your own civilization, my people? These are enemies my people always have been always will be to black people domestically as well as globally. The time has come for black people to stand together domestically as well as globally to let our enemies know, their days on our planet are rapidly coming to an end. It doesn't matter what our enemies claim their religion may be history reveals all the evils, they all have committed on black people, as they forced their false religions upon us at gun point or with their unmerciful armies, at the ready to murder in black people, including women and children. Our enemies were also unmercifully raping black women also young black girls; this includes this so-called Sunnah Islam as well.

We my people must re-develop or re-create our language amongst ourselves as we hand back to our enemies their evil language as well as their dialects we have absolutely no use, of any of it at all. For to re-create the love for ourselves we must cast off everything force on us by our enemies. Every 50,000 years the Red and Blue Star appear representing a universal change. The Red Star represents the Disbeliever, The Blue Star Represent the Hypocrite the Red Star is Wallace D. Mohammad and the 90% that went with him helping to destroy the economical foundation, of the Tribe of Shabazz belonging to the Nation of Islam, here in the Western Hemisphere. The Blue Star represents the Hypocrites within the Tribe of Shabazz belonging to Islam, here in the Western Hemisphere; also, the Magicians of America that corrupted the teachings that Allah taught to His Holy Messenger, the Most Honorable Elijah Muhammad and there are many amongst us my people that are guilty of these most horrible crimes, as they try to claim to be, that which they aren't and never will be. Thus, these are more obstacles in our way from achieving the goal of Love for Self-First, my people. These Magicians of Pharaoh/American Government have changed the teachings that Allah Almighty Himself in the person of Master Fard Muhammad to whom all praises, are due forever; taught His last and greatest Messenger the Most Honorable Elijah Muhammad/Muhammad RasulAllah; who in turn taught us all. The Holy Messenger gave us strict instruction not to change a word of the teachings, Allah Himself gave to him. The Red and Blue Stars have done exactly that thus defying Allah Almighty Himself. You will find these members of the Blue also Red Star, claiming to be that which they aren't, or they are allowing others to call them that which they aren't. In fact, you will find my people these Red and Blue Stars advocates have caused a great deal of damage, amongst black people, not only domestically but globally as well.

Thus, complicating our ability; to create love for ourselves first due to their mix instructions or just out right, tampering and changing the teachings, from Allah Himself whom He Allah taught His Holy Messenger face to face, for 3 years and 4 months. So, the damage these Magicians have caused amongst us my people are most devastating, thus aiding the objectives of our enemies to keep black people forever locked into this cage of despair, economical slavery, disenfranchisement, suffering, slavery and death, my people. None of the teachings from any of the Pharaoh/American Government Magicians will ever bring black people, in America any relief at all nor will their teachings bring black people globally any relief. We have suffered enough from false teachings my people that are only causing more self-hatred, amongst ourselves. We must my people domestically as well as globally block out these false teachings from the Magicians of Pharaoh/ America the Accursed Devil; as we return to the pure teachings, in which Allah Almighty Himself taught his last and greatest Messenger the Most Honorable Elijah Muhammad. Absolutely no progress has been achieved by following any of these false teachings, from any of these Magicians my people; only more separation amongst us which strengthens our many enemies and their false teachings.

Thus, my people allowing these want to be magicians to come amongst us spreading their poison when in truth all they want to do, is replace the elder Magicians. One thing you can bet your life on in fact you are my people; if you continue to follow any of these Magicians or want to be magicians only death will be your reward. No relief absolutely no relief will ever come to you from any of these Magicians or want to be magicians. These Magicians and want to be magicians have absolutely no concern for us they are only pretending, to be concern for black people. The only thing these Magicians are concern with is how to rob black people and keep black people believing in their lies also their foolishness, that's all my people. We have my people been exposed to the deadliest toxic poisons than any other people on earth have ever been exposed to, by our enemies. Not only that my people we have been absorbing these toxins by force, for approximately 500 years. Our enemy's religious toxins; our enemy's political toxins; our enemies toxic way of life; our enemies toxic governments; our enemies toxic lies; our enemy's toxic beliefs; our enemy's toxic hatred for ourselves; our enemy's toxic educational system; our enemy's toxic disentrancement of black people; our enemy's toxic gentrification of black communities; our enemy's toxic false teachers; our enemy's toxic love for everyone but ourselves; our enemy's toxic medical system that use black people as lab rats; our enemy's practices; our enemy's toxic holidays; our enemy's toxic jobs; our enemy's toxic movies and television shows; our enemy's most deadly toxic homosexuality; our enemy's toxic wars in which we black people have never gain anything from; our enemy's most deadly toxic integration; our enemy's toxic law enforcement system; our enemy's toxic prison system; our enemy's toxic civilization period my people.

Think about this my people we have absolutely no love for ourselves children, women, parents, or our ancestors. Why are you still allowing these people that aren't of us to come amongst us trying to teach us, about ourselves, this is insane my people; History clearly proves that these interlopers have been nothing but enemies to us all. It is pure insanity to for us to even trust any of these strangers believing they will teach us Love for Self-first, when they are the ones responsible for destroying, the love for self-amongst us. Now we are supposed to trust and love our proven enemies look at what happened to black people 500 years ago, for trusting also allowing these other people to come amongst us. Make no mistake my people these are the descendants of the enemies of our ancestors as well as ourselves; Trust absolutely none of them in fact drive them from amongst us we will be better off without any of them amongst us. Then we can once again begin to build the trust amongst black people all over the world, once again. We can then begin to build our economy globally for and amongst ourselves. We can then begin to build the love also trust amongst ourselves that we had up till 500 years ago after we let our enemies come amongst us. You must understand this, my people we didn't need any of them before our enemies needed us and they still need us today. Here is another thing we all must understand my people none of these outsiders are helping black people to regain the love for self-first and they never will. Consider this my people any person that see themselves as something special, is an enemy to black people worldwide; it's not for one to see themselves at all it is for others to see you, by your work action actions and deeds. Walking around presenting an image with newspapers and bean pies means absolutely nothing at all. Our enemies are doing exactly this believing that they can fool and trick us into believing also take them, as our teachers also leaders.

We must put an end to this foolishness allowing these same strange people who have proven 500 years ago black people, that these strange people can never be trusted amongst black people ever. We must rid ourselves of all these toxins people, their tricks also their deceits, their religions, their false ideologies, their false worshipping, their false practices and all their lives. It doesn't matter what they may call themselves they should go amongst their own people and teach them, if their people will even listen to them; we my people don't need any of them amongst us at all. Once we exile these Vicegerent Yakub Ibn Lucifer makings from amongst us, we can re-build the love also trust amongst black people domestically as well as globally. We my people don't owe any of them anything at all they don't come with any solution to your problems; they come amongst us trying to figure out how they can only rob black people and they have been doing this, for the past 6,000 years. It's Through Our Fathers Eyes my people not through the eyes of our fathers, as well as ourselves enemies my people. We have been foolish to long my people as well as trusting of our enemies we can no longer trust any of them ever, to come amongst and most defiantly, never to live amongst us ever again. We must re-build our world my people we are the people that was create in love for self-cause we are directly from the creator Himself. Therefore no one can find our birth record due to none has ever been recorded. Yet we can find as well as know the birth record of our enemies made 6,600 years ago, on the Island of Pelan. We also know who their maker is by all the names he is called by and none of them are any good at all, my beloved people.

To long my people have we suffered at the hands of others, that aren't of us? Why should we continue this absolutely proven destructive path, that for over 500 years our enemies have been trying, to keep black people; away from the path of Love for Self-First; as every other people are doing for themselves except black people. My people this is what's going on gentrification of black communities is another method of planting our enemies amongst black people; then with the help of this Zionist/Christian/Arab/Asian American Government of murdering, thieving, lying as well supreme deceivers Global Terrorist, help these Interlopers to multiply as well as prosper; while black people are being treated like cattle ushered off to the concentration camps, to die or just to be slaughter.

Through Our Fathers Eyes is so important reason being is that our enemies don't want us to remember, praise or exalt our fathers, only our mothers. In fact, our enemies are trying to convince black male children that they are of their mothers and this is causing black male children to gravitate, to this evil disgusting homosexuality. This is an absolute lie that black men are of our mothers no my brothers we are of our fathers and the work of our fathers, we must do. Our father is the Universal Creator not our mother and this is a mathematical fact that can be proven, at any time. Our father is Allah Almighty my brothers therefore our enemies want you to believe that that you are of your mother, this thought will only weaken your ability to create, a new civilization for ourselves. This may make a lot of colored women very upset, but I don't care if it does, reason being is that this is the absolute truth. This insanity of black men being of their mother comes from one of our many enemies, the Zionist and embraced by the Christians. Black women know I'm speaking the truth and will never oppose what I'm saying because it is the truth. Yet silly colored women will argue scream and fight against this truth because they love the devil, although the devil give them nothing but absolute hell. Colored women teach hatred to their sons of their fathers, even to fight with their father due to her insane ignorance. The Black Woman will never take part in this evil as she is to wise and intelligent to fall victim to the lies, being spread by our enemies. How can you recognize the colored people Saladin? It's very easy my people the colored woman always wants to look, act and sound like the Caucasian Woman; they are very easy to recognize, and they will always oppose Black Nationalism and support White Nationalism, this applies to the colored man as well, my people. They eat poison foods my people physically, spiritually and mentally and inject into their children these most deadly poison, of self-hatred for themselves and love the many enemies of their ancestors as well as themselves.

You won't find any self-respecting black woman making porno movies or having buttocks enhancements, coming out have naked revealing themselves, or anything else as disgraceful as these colored women are doing and this explain why the homosexuality has spread, throughout the black communities, due to these silly ignorant colored women and men, embracing these evils. It is these foolish ignorant colored women also men that spread in fact force black children to embrace this most insane dreadful Christianity, to their children. These colored people make the most disgusting movies on TV or the movies that these Zionist enemies write, produce, direct, also sponsor, are placed on the TV and Films; Depicting that colored woman are running things and are the power, as the colored men, bend to their will; this is total insanity my people and we have absolutely no use for any colored person reason being is that they are made devils and they are all against the rise of the Black Nation domestically as well as globally. This Zionist/ Christian/Arab/Asian American Government of Global Terrorist call these colored people, African Americans what a disgrace. These people are against Black People loving themselves first these cowards believe in loving our enemies first and never having love for ourselves at all.

We can never achieve Love for Self-First my people with these Colored People called African Americans, as our religious, political, spiritual so-called leaders look at what we have achieved under their puppet leadership absolutely nothing but death, poverty, suffering everything we black people received, since boarding these most deadly Slave ships 450 years ago. These Colored people called Africa Americans by their Caucasian master's orders have absolutely no intention of ever, returning to their original selves and this we must accept. The Caucasian Feminist did a great job on corrupting the minds of these colored women also men, until they are happy to have these devils as their so-called friends, no matter how many black children they murder; no matter how many black men they murder or imprison, no matter how many black women they murder or imprison, it doesn't matter to the Colored people at all; as long as it prevent black people from putting into practice Love For Self-First and Looking Through Our Fathers Eyes. Through Our Fathers Eyes we can break this yoke of our enemies and free ourselves from this cage, that we been in for the past 450 plus years to 500 years, my people nothing else will free us at all; we must return to our fathers if not you are all doomed and our enemies know it.

This Zionist control American Government of Global Terrorist will allow other black people coming from other parts of the world, the opportunity at getting and a good education; yet when it comes to the descendants of those who ancestors were there for the Jamestown Landing in 1555 and the second Jamestown Landing in 16i9; this Zionist control American Government of Global Terrorist has done everything in their power to prevent us, from ever escaping out of the cage, they put us in those many centuries ago. These are our enemies my people and they will never be friends to black people; this most wicket, evil also most diabolical American Government, do everything within their power to, to keep black people divided by not telling them the truth, of what they did to their brothers and sisters over 450 years ago. Now this Zionist control American Government of Global Terrorist has as I said in my previous works, partner up with the Christians, Arabs and Asians, to keep black people divided also to prevent black people from uniting and building ourselves a Global Unity thus promoting Love for Self-First. Then we all will be looking Through Our Fathers Eyes together as we all should be doing, instead falling victim to the female enemies of our fathers also mothers, my people; this includes black women falling victim to the male enemies of our fathers also mothers. It doesn't matter where our enemies may come from they are our enemies as well as the enemies, of our fathers and mothers as well.

We must my people stop falling for these tricks of our enemies it is only disgracing to Allah, His Holy Messenger as well as all of our ancestors. Loving our enemies is keeping our enemies in power over black people, so our enemies believe. What loving our enemies is truly doing my people is destroying black people chance, of global unity as well as Love for Self-First. It is Through Our Fathers Eyes my people is where our Liberation from our many enemy's religions, politics, practices, customs, lies also deceit; Lye that will free black people from this oppression we all have enduring, for the past 500 years; some much worse than others but never the less we all have suffered from the same enemies globally. I'm a student also follower of the last and greatest Messenger/Muhammad RasulAllah, the Most Honorable Elijah Muhammad; of Allah Almighty in the person of Master Fard Muhammad to whom all Holy Praises are due forever. Like my leader also teacher I will continue to tell the truth as the Holy Messenger revealed to us all. This is the Judgement we are living in my people and the Judgement is Universal Justice. Love for Self-First my people and Through Our Fathers Eyes not through the eyes of our fathers' enemies as well as our enemies, in the time we are now living in.

CHAPTER 11

PROPER EDUCATION OF SELF AND LOVE FOR OUR SONS IS A MUST BLACK MAN

This chapter my people; is about our black sons that are being murdered also imprisoned all throughout America and absolutely no one cares. Our sons are lacking proper knowledge also love for themselves due to this evil also diabolical American Educational System that discourages black males, from ever reaching the Allah potential that, is in them. We must once again take charge of our sons by any means necessary to preserve our sons, ourselves as well as our ancestors. We can't any longer allow our sons to fall under control of our enemies this includes these colored women; in which you were so in experience that it was a mistake, to have children with. This Zionist/Christian/Arab/Asian American Government of Global Terrorist are murdering our sons all throughout America or they are imprisoning our sons, with ridiculous sentencing if not life sentencing. Our sons are supposed to rebel against this most wicket Government people also; that only want to murder the black baby birth and save the brown baby. The brown baby is the colored people, in which our enemies, are able also have made homosexuals of our sons and these colored people especially colored women, believe it is alright. This is an abomination my people as well as a disgrace to Allah our creator, His Holy Messenger, His Prophets and our ancestors my people.

We my brothers must take control of our sons especially once they reach the age of 12 or even before to begin teaching them to be men, as well as soldiers capable of defending and protecting themselves as well as their people also communities. We must my brothers teach our sons about who they are; who are their creator; their heritage; their history, their ancestors and all about our 6,000-year-old enemies. We must my brothers begin to teach our sons that they are more than just court jesters to entertain our enemies by playing their blood sports, basketball, football, baseball, hockey, tennis, soccer and every other sport, this world has made, for their entertainment and amusement. Boxing and Marital Arts should be taught to our sons as it was years ago taught to us by our fathers. These activities will build up a comradely also brotherhood once again, amongst our sons with the proper teachings of what the goal or objective, is truly about. We must wipe out this false image that our enemies have made for our sons where as our sons are engaged in murdering each other, to the pleasure of our many enemies. We must teach our children that this is one of the many tactics of our enemies' genocidal plan, to destroy; black people nationwide; by giving them our children these images of these drug dealing murderers also for murdering pimps, who only murdered their own people. Destroyed their own communities, made whores of their own children, destroyed black families throughout America without any concerned, that they were murdering their own people, destroying their own communities where their mothers lived, as they helped our enemies finance the war on black people, with the cash these Gestapo Law Enforcement Agencies confiscated from them and used to build their war chest; also justify murdering black men nationwide, or imprisoning them for many years if not for life.

Through TV and movies our Zionist enemies aided by our Christian enemies produced the most disgusting movies and are still doing it, that has ever been made depicting black people as nothing but hyenas preying on themselves, as these fools called themselves also fashioning themselves after our enemies and dared to call themselves the black mafia. We must teach our children these were as well as still are the enemies of black people everywhere. The Gestapo supplied these fools with guns also drugs and confined them into their own communities, where these fools could begin their destructiveness on themselves as well as people, with impunity for a short while in which these fools did. Our sons must be taught the knowledge of themselves since we no longer have Muhammad Universities Of Islam for our children, we must guide our sons to much better schools where they are able to explore their scientific and mathematical minds, where they will be able to contribute to building a nation for themselves; not looking for a job from our enemies. It is a fool to teach his son that he should get a job working for his enemies, rather than create a job for himself after he has received education especially of any science. My brothers we must teach our sons to get education that will allow them to go for themselves and not be dependent on our enemies, for substance. Our sons need to be taught how to properly cultivate black women to his way of creating for himself and not to allow them to cultivate him, into this American nonsense which is a nightmare for black men and always will be a nightmare.

We must let our sons know that we love them enough that we will make every sacrifice for them, to achieve success; regardless of what anyone may say, think or believe, they are of their fathers. We must teach our sons that not to fall into this make believe so-call love that this society has made up, always kissing like dogs but never creating or working together, to build something for self. We must teach our sons not to go out of their selves falling for the deceit, of these Caucasian Women believing that you have found something special, when all you have found is Delilah waiting to cut off your hair and make you a mortal man; when you are a born Allah. Then this Delilah will blind you to the truth of yourself and before you even realize it, she has cultivated you into her filthy evil world where you will die; she will inherit all your assets or divorce you and with the help of her people, just out right rob you of everything you have. This animalistic so-called love of this beast we must teach our sons they must avoid at all cost, if not they will be destroyed as well as humiliated, before the entire world. If any of my sons or daughters marry or have children with these devil women or men, they would no longer be my son or daughter. Mating with our open enemies is never acceptable at all you can't be my son or daughter mating with our 6,000-year-old enemies, this is disgraceful as well as committing treason. Any of my sons also daughters that will denounce Islam to be a Christian will no longer be my, sons or daughters either. Anyone who does this is or except this, is a disbeliever in Allah in the person Master Fard Muhammad to whom all holy praises are due forever also a disbeliever in Allah's last and greatest Messenger the Most Honorable Elijah Muhammad/Muhammad RasulAllah as well as a hypocrite.

Our sons are being gunned in the streets our son being locked away in prison houses all throughout America; our sons are being warehouse in these concentration camps our enemies call shelters all throughout America; our sons have no hope or even a chance at breaking out of this cage of despair, hopelessness, poverty and self-hatred; our sons are dying my brothers as we stand by and do nothing about this. Our sons are receiving the poorest education that America has to offer them which is nothing my brothers. Our sons don't even know how to wear their pants in fact they have absolutely no clue who they are my brothers. Our sons have absolutely no direction about themselves due to them not ever be given any direction. Our sons have picked the worst possible role models, and therefore they end up selling drugs to their own people. Our sons are very misguided due to them following the lies that our enemies have placed them at birth. Our sons know absolutely nothing about love due to them never being loved, so they don't know how to love anyone else, including the black woman. Our sons have targets on their backs as well as their chest walking around this Gestapo Law Enforcement Agencies, throughout America. Our sons my brothers what chance do our sons have under this Zionist/Christian/Arab/Asian American Government of Global Murdering Terrorist. Our sons my brothers don't even have complete knowledge of themselves or a complete knowledge of their 6,000-year-old enemies. Our sons are wondering in this wilderness of sin, iniquities and transgressions and don't even know it as they fall into the traps, our enemies have set for them. Our sons are still being taught to believe in this most deadly, slave making so-called religion. Our sons are so confused with absolutely anyone trying to help them. Our sons are being exterminated and this society is very happy that they are being exterminated. How long are you going to stand by black fathers and allow our sons to be slaughter by our enemies or allow our enemies, to destroy the minds of our sons by injecting their poisons into their minds; this includes this so-called Sunnah Islam.

We black fathers must take control of the raising of our sons well being physically, mentally also spiritually and keep all our enemies away from them. We black fathers must teach our sons the proper foods to eat also the time they should eat depending on their age. We must my black fathers and brothers teach our sons the complete knowledge of themselves as well as their heritage. We black fathers must show our sons that we love them unconditionally as we embrace them and kiss them on their cheeks. We must teach our sons the discipline that they are so much in need of black fathers. Our sons are being murdered left and right all throughout America this insanity must stop, even if it cost us our lives; we must defend our sons with our lives if this is what it takes to save ourselves. Our sons are ourselves black fathers I don't care what their mothers have to say. Their mothers are the nurse that is pricking their brains of our sons with the lies, of their enemies, thus killing them at birth; reason being the nurse is teaching them to hate you and for our sons to hate their fathers, is to hate themselves thus giving power to this most evil filthy Matriarch rule of the Caucasian woman and homosexuality.

Black Fathers are we going to stand by and allow this to happen while we sit around helping other people, as we forget about our sons. Our sons must be educated in doing something for themselves not crawling back on the plantations, of America called jobs. Our sons need to be taught by black fathers how to go into business for their selves, so that they can be free, of the slave masters children and their insanity. Our sons need our undivided attention black fathers to guide them into the right direction including picking the right mate, for their selves' black fathers. Black fathers our sons need you to explain what is really happening also to suck the poisons out of them, that was put into them by our enemies and teach them that they must look Through Our Fathers Eyes and not the eyes of our enemies. This so-called Sunnah Islam will never free our sons it will only transfer ownership of them, to another enemy of black people. The women in this so-called Sunnah Islam is never to be trusted they are liars also deceivers as well and our sons must know this.

Through ignorant colored women our enemies have been able to separate father and son and through silly ignorant colored women, teach the sons lies about their fathers so that the sons hate themselves due to them hating, their fathers. So, the sons grow up without any father image as these silly colored women, claim to be father and mother; this is insane thinking that has and still is destroying black families throughout America. If you examine every successful black man; as in the cases of Floyd Mayweather Jr. and Michael Jordan had the love of their fathers with them at all times on their journeys look at the successes, they both have achieved. The arguments they might had have amongst themselves, the love for their sons were always there. We must understand black fathers that we can't allow anyone to get in our way or between our sons and ourselves, especially some ignorant colored woman. We must black fathers put an end to our sons being forcing to except this slave making most dreadful Christianity, as well as all the lies our enemies spread amongst and to our sons. This so-called Sunnah Islam is just as poisonous to our sons as well due it only leading our sons back into the evil talons, of our enemies and history proves this to be true.

History always will reveal the truth of our enemy's, as well as who are our enemies also what part they all played in the Despicable Trans-Atlantic Slave Trade; in which we must never forget, nor must we never forgive everyone that was involved in this Supreme Treachery. These same enemies have partnered up with the Zionist and Christians this includes this so-called Sunnah Islam. We must keep our sons away from these enemies as well as their ideologies, black fathers. Our enemies all of them black fathers are about White Supremacy and White Nationalism; always have been as they always will be. History will always prove the evils these enemies of black people are doing here in America, to help their other partners in crimes to keep black people trapped in this cage of despair, especially our sons' black fathers. These enemies of our black fathers are extremely treacherous they will lie to us wanting us to commit Federal Crimes so that they can get green cards and then they say Humdlullah; what lying hypocrites my people. They have absolutely no love for black people they only seek to learn how they can use black people as a tool, to help them our enemies, sell beer, cigarettes as well drug paraphernalia throughout every black community in America.

None of these traitors that are working for this so-called Sunnah Islam don't even care about the evils that, that these so-called Sunni Muslims are committing in black communities throughout America. They turn their backs to the evils that they are doing which leads us with one conclusion black fathers, we must take control of what is best for our sons and this isn't any good for our sons, at all. We all have been taught to forgive and forget what our enemies have done, all black people. When you examine the history, there isn't any reason why we black people should forgive any of them. History reveals to us my people the evils that this so-called Sunnah Islam did to black people, so it is useless for us to follow or practice what these open enemies, have to offer which is absolutely nothing for black people. We must enlighten our sons into the knowledge of their selves, ancestors, as well as their true heritage. We had our own language until our enemies stole it from us and force their language upon us; now we have these thieving Arabs trying to force their language on black people. Therefore, Sunni Ali didn't allow this so-called Sunnah Islam into his country of Timbuktu and he denounce the ways also practices of this so-called Sunnah Islam; as he created Islam as a way of life for his people. We must my black fathers teach our sons the Islam that Allah Himself gave to us through the mouth of His last and greatest Messenger and nothing else. Once our sons understand that we have the ancient Islam which has no beginning or ending, and it has been given to us by the Ancient of the Days Himself; they will understand that they need absolutely nothing from the enemies of our ancestors as well as our enemies.

Once get our sons out from the evil grip of our many enemies their religions, practices and politics we will be able to teach our sons and daughters, the love for black self as well as each other domestically and globally. We need to re-build the temples for our children to have a place of their own, where they can learn all about their selves, their Allah the True and Living God also the True Messenger that sacrificed his life, teaching us the truth that Allah Himself taught Him, for 40 years. Our sons must under that they are the lost found members of the Tribe of Shabazz, members of the Nation of Islam that spans 76 Quinn Trillion Square Miles, which is the diameter of the Universal. Only the universal creator could know these things and He taught His Messenger that which wasn't known, by anyone else. Once we make our sons understand who he is and that he doesn't have to turn to these enemies for answers about himself. Our sons don't have to run or join any of our enemy's religions or their practices, as well.

We must remove the poison foods from our sons, mouths, minds, spirits and hearts then replace these poisonous teachings with a complete also, exact teachings of their selves, as well as our enemies. Then we will be able to show them why they must look Through Our Fathers Eyes and not the eyes of our many enemies, that are only out to deceive black people also rob black people. We must begin to make our sons understand the necessity of them going into business for their selves, as we drive these infidels from amongst us. We must educate them in the proper way of doing business so that they will be able to expand the business, into international commerce, amongst their original people. We must teach all our children the necessity of them manufacturing their own clothing as well as foot wear, for ourselves. We must understand black fathers this burden is on you and you must meet this challenge, head on. We must black fathers point out the destructiveness also wrongs of following our many enemies, way of life that was designed to keep them caged up. We must educate our sons how to be the protector and not the destroyer of himself, woman and children. Our sons our children period must learn not only about computers, they must learn how to design computers as well as how to build platforms for streaming. We must teach our sons of learning automotive engineering so that they will be able to apply their Allah science, to create automobiles that are being made today, trucks as well. We must educate our sons the necessity of learning aerodynamics, navigation as well as ship building, for their selves and their nation. Our sons must be educated in heavy duty equipment such as how to operate cranes, earth movers, cement mixing, plumbing, electrical, welding plasma welding, under water welding, carpentry, electronics, Hydroid engineering, Hydraulic engineering, electrical engineering, physics, nuclear physics, architecture once we remove the poison of our many enemies black fathers from our sons, they will once again become the great creators of, great civilizations that will out this present one, to shame.

Black fathers we must re-build Muhammad Universities of Islam so that we can make this happen for our sons as well as all our children. This Zionist control American Educational System has by designed discourage our sons, never to think about things like this and this so-called Sunnah Islam has joined in with the Zionist, in keeping black people trapped in this cage of Abyss. Thus, black fathers and sons have no love for each other, then our enemies present their families, and everything is going well for them. What these enemies of our this is especially directed at this so-called Sunnah Islam; aren't telling you black people how they so-called Sunnah Islam plotted with the Zionist/Christian American Government of Global Terrorist, to destroy everything that black people were building for ourselves and the Islam in which Allah Himself brought also gave us through His Holy Messenger the Most Honorable Elijah Muhammad/Muhammad RasulAllah. J. Edger Hoover head of the F.B I; with the head of the C.I.A. along with the traitors within our ranks, now you must remember my people the so-Sunnah Islam was heavily involved, as these cowards hid in secret; with this evil plot, to destroy everything that we were building under the leadership also guidance of Allah's last and greatest Messenger the Most Honorable Elijah Muhammad/Muhammad RasulAllah. The Christians were also involved with this evil plot against black people as these Negro Traitors hid in secret along with the Zionist, to murder us all, this must be understood my people, here in America as well as globally.

These are enemies my people and they don't serve Allah they all serve the Vicegerent Yakub Ibn Lucifer because he, is their maker, not Allah. These enemies just like the Zionist and Christians had a thousand years or so perfect their lies, to convince you they are righteous, as well as ancient also wise. These are nothing but lies made up by our enemies, my people in which we must abandon at once. This Zionist/Christian/Arab/Asian American Government of Murdering Global Terrorist keep this truth; hidden from you as they were going throughout the world, murdering black leaders with impunity. Now we black people are silly enough to follow these murderers and their slave making religions, for black people. This so-called Sunnah has a great deal of traitors from amongst us just like Christianity have a great deal of traitors from amongst us, as well. We are fools to believe and trust in them or anything they say especially their so-called Sunnah Islam.

My people these criminals must be expose and brought to justice along with these traitors as well. Therefore, we must expose the truth of what every one of our enemies did, to place us all in the positions that we are in today. We must reveal to our sons every so-called religion that was involved heavily into our destruction, my people. Look at how many of our sons ourselves, our women also daughters have been murdered, by this treachery and their false religions. This isn't something I'm making up this is the history black people that can be proven, at any time. This is very important black fathers to teach our sons the absolute truth about what was done to us all and still being done to black people, by our enemies. We must teach our sons who the enemies are and the religions of all our enemies; we must accept that which is, this can never be change. This so-called Sunnah Islam is just as poisonous to black people as Christianity is poisonous to black people and this we black people all must understand how important it is, that all black people must understand. These enemies who call themselves so-call Sunnah Islam who know absolutely nothing about Allah, Muhammad RasulAllah or Islam because they aren't of Allah; they aren't of Muhammad RasulAllah and they aren't of Islam; they are the makings of the Vicegerent Yakub Ibn Lucifer the father and maker of the devil; also, the maker of imperfection.

Black Fathers once we give our sons the proper education of their selves also all our enemies you will then, showing love for our sons as well as ourselves. We must arm our sons with everything that they need to make war with the beast and this beast is a hydra. We must remove from our sons this most poison belief of a mystery god that can't be seen until you die. We must remove from our sons in fact all our children this belief of some mystical heaven, after they die. These are all lies taught to us by our enemies to keep black people mental and spiritual slaves. We black fathers must rally to the cause for us to teach our sons to be soldiers and put an end to them being ignorant thugs; going around their communities killing and selling drugs to themselves. We must guide them back to the true Islam that Allah in the person of Master Fard Muhammad Allah Almighty Himself to whom all holy praises are due forever. We must teach our sons in fact all our children who is the last and greatest Messenger of Allah which is the Most Honorable Elijah Muhammad/Muhammad RasulAllah. We must teach our children to follow all the programs the Holy Messenger gave to us all, that would restore us back to be an independent Black Nation. We must teach our children to honor the Flag that Allah Almighty Himself gave to us all because this Flag Is Sent From Heaven For All Black People here, in the Wilderness of North America. We will then be showing our sons the love of their fathers in which they all so desperately need; in fact, you will be showing the love of a father to all his children, Black Fathers.

If we black fathers allow our sons and children to follow behind strangers and their religions of doom, for black people; our sons and all our children will forever be living this cage of despair, hopelessness, disenfranchisement, self-hate, suffering slavery and death. You can't believe the lies these partners of this American Government of Global Terrorist. None of America's partners are friends to any black people they all have the same objective, in mind and that is to keep black people caged up; forever the economical slave of our enemies. Black fathers we must teach our sons self-discipline so that they are able to resist the temptations, of our many enemies; which is nothing but traps that this evil wicket government with their Gestapo police forces, to imprison our sons. We black fathers must teach our daughters to resist the temptation of our many enemies offering them money, for sexual gratification of the many enemies of our daughters as well as ourselves. We must educate our daughters of the follies by hiding the devil under their skirts. We have a great task black fathers you will never be able to accomplish this supremely important task, by hanging out in the streets doing nothing. You will never be able to accomplish this Supremely Important task by believing and trusting our enemies; their slave making religions, practices also their culture. We must teach our children that they must be enterprising also creative independent of our many enemies, who only want them to be mental, spiritual as well as economical slaves, for our many enemies.

It is a complete fool that believes he has friend ship with the Zionist and the Arabs then feel proud of himself, as he except the crumbs they give him. These are nothing but ignorant fools that will never stand up and help restore our nation, these fools will never join in at all my people. They talk big in truth they aren't going to do anything at all because they really don't care to do anything, to help their people. So, we have absolutely any need of this kind of a person in fact you will find in many cases this kind of a person promotes the life style, of our enemies. If you aren't ready to put your life on the line for real to inform or play an active role in the re-building our nation, then stay the hell away from those who are willing to give a sincere effort in this mighty and righteous task. We black fathers must drop all this blood, crypts absolute nonsense that is doing more harm than good, to black people except playing right into the hands, of the American Gestapo. This is all the love you have for our sons and families which amounts to absolutely nothing at all. Then the American Gestapo arrest you put you in jails for a very long sentence and now you are asking your families to send you commissary. This is insane black fathers that you allow yourselves to fall into these traps that a blind man can see, and you fall for it every time, this is a shame black man and black fathers.

Where black fathers are any love for your sons, or any love for any of your children due to your ignorance also your silly arrogance, is more important to you. Now you are imprisoned for many years and you want your wives to bring to bring your children up to the prisons, to see you. You black fathers are introducing to your sons and children to prison life, this is a shame. Not to mention the strain you put on the mothers due to her having to make financial adjustments to send you money, also pay for the trip to come see you not only for herself; also, the children depending on the children ages.

Yet you still love our enemies no matter what our enemies do to you and your families. Now your sons and daughters are growing up in an un-merciful jungle without your protection and you still love also to trust our enemies and their religions. If you are that silly black fathers you will never be able to show your sons or any of your children love for their selves, cause you to busy loving our enemies and have no love for yourself. You black fathers will never be able to give your sons the proper education of their selves and our enemies, due to your trust also falling for the lies, of our enemies. This is a shame that you allow this to happen, black fathers. This is what you black fathers are ready to sacrifice your sons also daughters for our enemies' religions rather than pursue that which Allah Himself brought for you, these same enemies are laughing at you for the simple reason that you continue to fall for their lives, their religions and their traps. Remember these black fathers; our children are being sacrificed their blood flow in the streets and not anyone from this so-called Sunnah Islam cares, at all. Remember always black fathers it is Through Our Fathers Eyes not through the eyes of our many enemies

CHAPTER 12

THE ENEMIES WITH IN AND AMONGST US

This subject is about the enemies that surround us that mean black people absolutely no good at all and this is something that is extremely important that we all must understand also recognize. Black people have been trained to except any of these strange people coming amongst us and black people pay it no attention at all. In the meantime, these infiltrators are gathering information on everything that is going on in the communities, throughout America. These infiltrators are sending the intelligences they have gather and forward this on to the government as well as their own people. Due to the lack of poor leadership in black communities and this insane integration evil black people aren't even aware of the enemies within the communities as these enemies are planning black people demise. They have been set up and funded by the government their mission to stop any spread of the real Islam and keep them informed of all black activities in the communities. They have the perfect cover with these filthy bodegas selling nothing but poison and molesting young black girls and women and this is known fact these Arabs are doing this as well as have been doing this since coming into America; the same things the Jews use to do in black communities. The Spanish bodegas owners are just as treacherous with these evil actions also and we all know this true. The different is the so-called Spaniards are gunged ho Christians that hate black people and will also have betrayed black people, for many years. The Arabs are supposed to be so-called Muslims yet their actions in the black communities are no different from the Zionist and the Christians.

These are the enemies within and amongst us my people it is time we do something about this evil and the people that are doing it and have done it.

This is very serious my people our enemies control their communities and they don't allow us amongst their women or amongst their social activities, yet they are always coming amongst bringing nothing but evil. What do you call being the distributors of cocaine also crack cocaine throughout black communities these aren't friends my people, that will poison their so-called friends as they rob them of their food money, rent money, bill money valuable possessions; then call you nigger. These aren't friends never have been and never will be these aren't friends and they certainly aren't our brothers, examine their history also you will find out their ancestors were also the enemies of our fathers. They took the money from you and build up their communities. This is Christianity I'm talking about and those practice this slave making Christianity of black people. On jobs they will under mind black people lie on black people to get black people fired so they can then give black people jobs to one of their own. I'm not speaking about the Indians amongst them although they participated in these evil crimes as well. I'm talking about the decedents of the Spaniards from Spain, who are devils also. What I'm saying is the truth the enemies within and the enemies amongst us, my people. The truth is harsh my people, but it remains the truth that can be proven at any time. This is all we black people received from this dreadful slave making Christianity, by all who practice this filthy evil religion.

We must be extremely careful my people about whom we let around and amongst us none of these strange people, care anything about black people. They desire to bustard's black people through black women and have been doing this for the past 450 years. It is up to us black people to put an end to these horrors once and for all. Black people problem is that they love everyone but themselves and this caused black people a great deal of problems simply because anyone or any people can come amongst your black people and mongolite you, without any resistance from you cause you love everybody and this is insane thinking as well as a most dangerous practice. While black people are out loving everybody, and people has open the door for our enemies, to live amongst us as they plot our destruction. What do you call selling drugs to black people these are your people well they aren't my people, I can tell you that? Every people that move amongst us in our black communities plotted and planned on how to get black people out; so, with the help of one of America's Gestapo Agency called the C.I.A. built the cocaine business in Panama, Columbia, Peru, also other places in South America. Establish the Cartels in these places then began importing tons of cocaine into America, where it landed in the Spanish communities for distribution into every black community throughout America, in which these so-called Latinos did. I'm not making any of this up it is a matter of history also record getting black people hooked on another drug where as many, many black people lost their homes, jobs, business, wives and children. In many cases these people hooked on this drug end up homeless or in prison. Who took over their jobs the Latinos did now black people can't get a job this was their plan ever since, they started the heavy your migration in the 1950s, by the Jews for cheap labor and they are still servants to the Jews today. You call these people friends and your brother how insane is this, my people. Our enemies are strong when they have you out number my people in truth they are a bunch of cowards; you see black people we aren't playing on an equal playing field. Our enemies have the backing of the American Government because they are die heart Christians, who were instructed to hate black people, and this goes back to the 1950s when they took jobs from black people in the factories, all throughout the big cities in America.

We must guard ourselves from the enemies within and amongst us my people and if you think a people that will poison your women also children are your friends, then you are hopeless black people because this is exactly what was done. Who planned this diabolical attack on black people it was this Zionist/Christian American Government at the time, the Zionist controlled American Government launch this phase of America's genocidal plan, to destroy black people here in America. Through Our Fathers Eyes my people you will see everyone, of our enemies and what part they all played in our destruction my people and the misery our women and children, are suffering today. The enemies within and amongst us are extremely detrimental to our rise reason being they always bring to black people some drug that will keep us locked, into this cage of despair and hopelessness. The enemy within are these silly fools that agree to sell these poisons to their own people, thus destroying their own people and communities. These silly fools don't even know or care that they are aiding the enemy's diabolical genocidal plan, to further cripple and murder black people; thus, the perpetual cage of despair, hopelessness, suffering, ignorance, disenfranchisement. This is a chemical attack my people launch on black people by this Zionist/Christian/Arab/Asian American Government of Murdering Global Terrorist. The enemy within and the enemy amongst black people are the ones doing the dirty work for this murdering American Government of Global Terrorist.

The religious also political so-called leaders are never going to do anything about this genocidal plan of the American Government, to murder black people and destroy black families. In a lot of cases you will even find many of these religious and so-called political are prospering off this diabolical plan; prospering off the enemies within and the enemies amongst us; as the death toll escalates. The suffering escalates, the conditions are worst, black families destroyed and the enemies within also the enemies amongst black people were helping a greater enemy amongst black people that was operating in secret, amongst black people and this enemy, are the Arabs along with their so-called Sunnah Islam. This enemy now amongst black began opening bodegas all throughout black communities selling nothing but poisons, to black people. The Arabs began buying black people food stamps at least 60 cents on the dollar and was doing heavy business. The Arabs also began buying prescriptions of different medications from sick black people, with addictions for nothing and shipping them back home to their people. Where were these black so-called Imams at and the blacks that betrayed their own people to follow the Arabs and their so-called Sunnah Islam, where were they at black people? I will tell you where they were at they were aiding these treacherous Arabs and they also didn't care about the evil these people were and still are committing amongst and against black people; these are properly greater fools than anyone. The enemies within and the enemies amongst us are extremely dangerous amongst black people always have been, always will be. What have these enemies received for their participation imprisonment and so –called Quran-an, which isn't the Holy Quran at all.

These enemies within many of them are our children also brothers also sisters that fell victim to the devil and they didn't care; as they aligned themselves with the enemies amongst black people due to them rebelling against that which our Holy Savior Allah Himself brought to us all and the enemies within rejected Allah and His Holy Messenger, for the temporary trinkets of the devil. Then the Gestapo Law Enforcement Agencies supplied these ignorant fools with auto and semi-automatic weapons without any training; then the American Gestapo stirred up trouble amongst the enemies within and the enemies amongst us and the killings also wars went off the scales, in black communities throughout America my people. No one wants to speak about what happen, who was involved and the damage they all did, to black people. Everyone want to talk about scriptures but never about the actual truth my people; I'm here to tell the actual truth even if the truth points at me, it is the truth; I'm speaking the truth about what and how this evil was done, also all who was involved in it. Therefore, you see these black men now living like vagabonds hungry, naked, out of doors also being beaten and killed, for their rejection of their Holy Savior who is Allah in person and Allah's last also greatest Messenger. They are all being punished with a divine chastisement for the evils they have committed, against their selves and people.

The enemies within and the enemies amongst us must all be expose as the truth of their evils are revealed, to the world my people. None of them are righteous people they are only pretending to be righteous people, as they all try to keep the truth of their actions hidden because once exposed they won't be able to hold their heads up high; no, you will see the once so-called proud dropping their heads in shame and disgrace, for the treachery they committed against their own people; as they aided the enemies of their people to destroy their people. I'm not teaching hate my people I'm revealing the hidden truth that our enemies, want to keep hidden at all cost and who are black people enemies every one of them, with no exceptions. The enemies within; come from amongst us who betrayed their own people, for the love of the enemy's world. The enemies amongst us are different strange people or interlopers that have infiltrated black communities, bringing with them treachery and hatred for black people. If these silly foolish black people were also being ready to destroy their own people, the enemies amongst us are very happy because now they our enemies can blame black silly fools, for their own destruction. My people the enemies amongst us were working very hard at making sure, they break the unity amongst black people because they are Christians all of them, in nature my people.

We can't ignore this fact my people our enemies like you for the simple reason is that you are very easily led in the wrong direction and help the enemies amongst black people, to murder, rob and mongolite your own people and for what my people; please tell me why you love the many enemies amongst us, over yourself, wives and children. Why my people are you so protective of the enemies amongst black people rather than protect yourself, from these enemies living amongst black people and these enemies all believe they are white, when in truth they are nothing but mutts; reason being they are all made from the Vicegerent Yakub Ibn Lucifer, every one of them my people. All our enemies this so-called Sunnah Islam included has done everything in their power, to lead your black people away from your Holy Savior; from your Holy Deliverer; Allah in the person of Master Fard Muhammad to whom all holy praises are due forever and you bought into it these lies from the enemies amongst us. The Arabs pick up where their Zionist brothers left off or I should say sold to them. In fact, these Arabs are even worst then their Zionist brothers because they are liars, they are deceivers, they are filled with untruth, they are thieves and can never be trusted at all black people and this enemy is robbing black people every day, as they sell black people pork, beer cigarettes even to our children. The Gestapo Police murdered a black man for selling lose cigarettes, yet the Arabs are selling lose cigarettes with impunity, all throughout black communities; I have never seen the Gestapo Police Force come an arrest them, mainly the Arabs, for violating Federal Laws. The enemies within are just stupid also totally ignorant but very dangerous only to himself and his people. The enemies amongst us are very evil, cold calculating with a purpose my people every one of them and that purpose is keep black locked into this cage as a people of despair, suffering, disenfranchisement, economical slaves, religious slaves, political slaves and any other slave we can think of; these are the enemies living amongst us purpose as well as what they are doing my people, and this has been going on for a very long time. This is what the Holy Messenger of Allah meant when He said, "everyone taking a bite out of you", my black people. I'm not saying that I am without sin I'm not coming of like that; I'm just telling you the truth of what happened who it happened to, why it happened and is still happening, the results of these happenings and who are the participants of this happening to black people and only black people, this is globally my people.

Black people check out how the television and the movie making industry [which is owned and controlled by the Zionist] always make colored people movies, never do they ever make any black movies. Colored People [African so- called Americans] are nothing other than the ones trying to be like the enemies of Black People. We must be aware of the enemies within and the enemies amongst us my people you must, you must understand my people the Holy Messenger of Allah the Most Honorable Elijah Muhammad is the Muhammad RasulAllah, written of or about in Quran-an. He is also written in the Book of Revelations in the Bible in the 18h Chapter "the 23 Elders and the four Beasts cast down their crowns and bowed, "saying worthy is the Lamb of God]. This Lamb of God is the Holy Messenger of Allah the Most Honorable Elijah Muhammad and absolutely no one else at all. The one sitting on the Throne is Allah Himself who's wisdom has no end as the 24-scientist said and the 4 Beasts bowed down to, my people. This Supreme One sitting on the throne is Allah in person and Him Himself visited us not the Sunnah so-called Islam; the Almighty visited us in person, the one that Ezekiel talked about or prophesized of His coming as Ezekiel referred to Him, as the Son of Man; this Mighty One as the Holy Messenger taught us all! Is Allah Almighty Himself in the person of Master Fard Muhammad, to whom all holy praises are due forever and ever and ever and ever, which I Saladin Shabazz-Allah will never denounce our Holy Savior and Deliverer, never will I ever do this my people especially for this so-called Sunnah Islam which is just as poisonous to black people, as Christianity and Zionism have been for black people.

He Allah my people visited it us in person and raised up from amongst us His last and greatest Messenger and that is the most Honorable Elijah Muhammad, my people. The teachings also the programs come directly from Allah, to create us too be a productive civilized, righteous nation and people, once again. This Zionist/Christian American Government of Murdering Global Terrorist turned their complete attention on destroying black people and all black leaders. At this time; the Zionist/ Christian American Government of Global Murdering Terrorist did not want real Islam here in America, it was at this time in the early 60s they the Zionist and Christian made the deal with the Arabs to bring in this so-called Sunnah Islam. The enemies within and the enemies amongst us my people we must always be extremely careful of. These Arabs partnered up with the Zionist and the Christian, they the Arabs part of the deal was to bring these black people back into believing in the Vicegerent their maker, Yakub Ibn Lucifer. The enemies within are silly ignorant so-called African

Americans in some cases miss guided black people. Now my people the enemies amongst us have a very evil purpose of being amongst us, as well as a mission to destroy us spiritually and bring black people back under the control of White Supremacy and White Nationalism; which is this now Zionist/Christian/Arab/Asian American Government of Murdering Global Terrorist and this is what Sunnah so-called Islam has done, to black people. These are the enemies amongst black people supported by the American Government and their Gestapo Law Enforcement Agencies that have committed more horrors amongst as well as to, black people in America. This has been going on my people for the past 450 plus years and this is a matter of historical facts, my people. You my people must stop spending your hard-earned money with these enemies amongst us. All these enemies amongst us in their rat-infested stores are selling black people poison foods, that they the enemies amongst us know will cause diseases amongst black people, our children and shorten our life span. This is by designed my people to murder you and these enemies dare call themselves Muslims. No, my people they aren't Muslims at all they are nothing but another branch of Christianity that was made from the same Vicegerent Yakub Ibn Lucifer, 6,600 years ago.

The so-called Holy Bible which we know is really the poison book took King James 150 years with his scribes of 60, to change the original scriptures into what they now call Holy Bible, in truth it is the poison book. Now this so-called Holy Quran verifies the writing of this poison book of King James version, now how is this possible my people when this so-called bible is the poison book. Allah Almighty himself told his Messenger that the Bible or Quran-an is written 25,000 years in advance so how can any of these books, be holy when they are in the hands, of unholy murdering people and this includes this so-called Sunnah Islam my people and history verifies all the evil they all have done and are still doing. Then explain to me why Maulana Ali translations of Quran-an is different from the Yusef Ali translation of this so-called Quran-an and Maulana Ali was a greater scholar than Yusef Ali. The Arabs gravitated to Yusef Ali because he was one of them and Maulana Ali is Pakistani an. Allah Almighty Himself gave to His Holy Messenger the Maulana Ali translation of this book called Quran-an, to help heal the spiritual wounds, that we endured under this most evil and diabolical Christianity also Zionism my people.

The enemies amongst us are very poisonous to black people this so-called Sunnah Islam is one of black people enemies amongst us, robbing black people every day and this is what they came also come, to do my people. There is so much hatred with each other in this so-called Sunnah Islam until you see this isn't any good for black people at all. Therefore, Allah Himself gave to His Holy last and greatest Messenger the Most Honorable Elijah Muhammad/Muhammad RasulAllah in the Sunnah so-called Quran-an; His Supreme Wisdom which transcend any so-called Bible or so-called Quran-an. The Holy Quran-and He Allah Almighty Himself gave to us Black Original People through His Holy Messenger the Theology of Time which takes which takes us all the way back over 78 trillion years ago before these strange people and their maker, were even a thought. I don't care what any of these traitors, this Zionism, this Christianity, this so-called Sunnah Islam and everything else, have to say and I will never follow this nonsense or any of my children to follow. All Praise be to Our Holy Savior Allah Almighty Himself the True and Living God who came in the person of Master Fard Muhammad, to whom all holy praises are due forever. I thank Allah the Highest, the All-knowing, the Most Merciful, the Most Beneficent for fulfilling the promise, he made to Ibrahim and create us my people as Muslims submitting to the Universal Creator Himself. I give my sincere and most Holy Praise To Allah to Him for raising up from us the down trodden, the rejected and the despise, His last and greatest Messenger the Most Honorable Elijah Muhammad and to hell with everyone else, their religions and their politics.

The enemies within and the enemies amongst us is who we must separate ourselves from my people they this so-called Sunnah are partners with the Zionist and Christians my people, how or why should we trust any of them? They all have been proven to be untrustworthy, liars, thieves and advocates in destroying black people and history will prove what I'm saying is true, my betrayed and deceived black people. Zionism, Christianity, So-called Sunnah Islam all have their chants and rituals in their services one claiming to be better than the next. When in truth they all come from the Vicegerent Yakub Ibn Lucifer, the father and maker of the devil. This Sunnah so-called Islam is being destroyed right along with the rest for their participation, in the evils the Vicegerent Yakub Ibn Lucifer makings has been causing and doing for the past 6,000 years, up to this present day and time. These are the enemies my people we are surrounded by and absolutely none of them care about black people at all, other than to keep black people in a sub servant position to our enemies and this is also a fact.

These enemies amongst were planted amongst us many centuries ago in fact five hundred years ago and now have been planted again amongst us 60 years ago and the Arabs were planted amongst us over 40 years ago. What was the purpose for this Saladin? The purpose was to keep black people destabilized also to help us believing in this most dreadful Christianity. Once black people began rejecting this slave making Christianity the Zionist and Christian American Government focused on murdering every black positive movement that were engaged, in uplifting and protecting black people from this American Gestapo. This Zionist Christian American Government of Global Terrorist wiped out every positive black organization except the black people that were members of the Nation Of Islam, which was having a profound effect on black people, under the guidance of the Holy Messenger of Allah the Most Honorable Elijah Muhammad.

We are now speaking about the enemies within my people as well as the enemies amongst us and the ones that were coming amongst black people that were even more treacherous, than our previous enemies, amongst us these enemies are the Arabs and their so-called Sunnah Islam. There were several traitors amongst black people currently but none deadlier than Wallace D. Mohammad he was working with this Zionist/Christian American Government of Global Terrorist to plant these Arabs, into black communities also to destroy the economical foundation of black people that were members, of the Nation of Islam in North America. Thus, re-forming the alliance between the Zionist/Christians in which they established, during the Trans-Atlantic Slave Trade and planting these Arab enemies in black communities along with their poisonous teachings, too black people. The truth must be revealed my people of who all our enemies are and what they all did to aid this now re-formed Zionist/ Christian/ Arab/ Asian/ Hindu American Government of Murdering, Thieving Global Terrorist. All the above mention my people are the enemies of black people; the Zionist/ Christians and Arabs are the 6,000-year-old enemies of black original people. The Hindus are the 35,000-year-old enemy of Islam and Black People. Therefore, the Indians were exile from the Eastern Hemisphere to the Western Hemisphere, 16,000 years ago.

This was a governmental plot my people these enemies of black people and Islam were purposely planted in black communities, for the sole purpose of destroying black people and the Islam that Allah Himself brought to black people, here in the Wilderness of North America. Once black people began rejecting this Christianity we became marked for death by the American Government and the American Gestapo, job was to make sure the plans were carried out, to the letter. While the Zionist, Christians and Asian Hindus were working with to C. I. A. to manufacture and smuggle 100% pure Heroin into America and dropped it off into Harlem; the Arabs were being placed into black communities to destabilize the growth and development of the real also true Islam, growing amongst black people. This diabolical plot involved different governments working collectively to execute this deadly most diabolical plan, of genocide against black people in America. The enemies within were now called to service Martin Luther King Jr. and the Big Six set this treachery up by agreeing to this most diabolical and most evil plans of the American Government which is the evil Civil Rights and most Supremely Evil Integration. The American Government began the next phase of their most diabolical plan and that was the murdering of Malcolm X and Sam Cooke prolifically singer of that time that could rival Bilal himself, thus entered Wallace D. Mohammad. America was now implementing the next phase of their diabolical plan thus enter the Arabs and their dreadful so-called Sunnah Islam along with the Asian Hindus, were heavily involved in this phase of this evil American plan, to destroy and murder black people at the wholesale level. Thus, the enemies within were now activated.

After the death of Malcolm X and Sam Cooke the American Government declared War on Viet Nam which was nothing but a smoke screen, for the American Government Main Objective in that part of the world and that was to import 100% pure heroin into New York, more accurately into Black Harlem. The war in Viet Nam had absolutely nothing to do with Communism at all, it was about importing 100% Grade A Heroin more potent than the French Connection Heroin, to begin the chemical destruction of black people in America, their target was Harlem New York and that chemical is Heroin. Now the Martin Luther king Jr. believers, became the ones the American Gestapo C.I.A. enlisted, to be the distributors of this deadly poison and they all jumped on it without thinking about the consequences of their actions at all as well as the fall out, amongst their people. At the same time the American Government wanted to plant these Arab and their so-called Sunnah Islam into America, but that plan was shut down, by the Holy Messenger of Allah due to the fact America, Wallace D. Mohammad and the Arabs, were counting on the Holy Messenger dying and He didn't; so, this put a wrinkle into these enemies within phase of the equation. At the mean time the faction of the enemies the Martin Luther King Jr. Christian Negro Followers, phase was operating at peak proficiency, these enemies amongst black people were already operating amongst us preparing themselves, for what was to come very soon, and they would benefit from helping, the Zionist/Christian now Arab/Asian Hindu American Government of Global Murdering Terrorist.

The Enemies within were equally as dangerous matter of fact the enemies within were even more dangerous, than the enemies, form amongst black people. The enemies within through their ignorance weaken their black people from putting up any defense, against the enemies amongst black people because black people were now poison by this American Poison Chemical called Heroin, produced by the Asian Hindus., to destroy black people. So, after the Holy Messenger of Allah didn't die this Zionist/Christian/Arab/Asian Hindu American Government of Murdering Global Terrorist and our enemies were at lost as the members belonging to Islam in North America began to increase and everything was growing at a fantastic pace also rate and this caused this newly formed Zionist/Christian/Arab so-called Sunnah Islam/Asian Hinduism American Government of Murdering Global Terrorist, great fear. So, the Arabs with their so-called Sunnah Islam couldn't be planted amongst black people, yet. So, this held up the plans of this most diabolically Evil Zionist/Christian/Arab Sunnah so-called Islam/Asian Hindus American Government of Global Terrorist, from planting these Arab enemies amongst black people, in 1965 after the death of Minister Malcolm X. This Arab so-called Sunnah Islam is more poisonous amongst black people because these Arabs are nothing but liars, thieves also hypocrites and black people can't as well as shouldn't trust any of them at all.

If these infidels don't have respect for the Islam that our Holy Savior who is Allah Almighty in person brought to us, then to hell with them all. If these infidels don't have respect for Allah's last holy and greatest Messenger the Most Honorable Elijah Muhammad, who is the true and only Muhammad

RasulAllah, then to hell with them all, my people. These are truly our enemies and we can prove it at any time that they are. Since this phase of the plan didn't work it wasn't abandon it was only shelved, for the moment. Then in 1975 after the physical death of the Holy Messenger/Muhammad RasulAllah the Most Honorable Elijah Muhammad; Wallace D. Mohammad went right to work into turning everything over to the Zionist/Christian/Arab so-called Sunnah Islam/Asian Hinduism American Government of Murdering Global Terrorist. Along with perhaps 90% of the disbelievers also hypocrites that surrounded the Holy Messenger of Allah and now this newly formed Zionist/Christian/Arab so-called Sunnah Islam/Asian Hinduism American Government of Murdering Thieving Global Terrorist and my people they are nothing, but bunch of hypocrites and pedophiles and every black person know what I'm saying is the truth. These are criminals my people protected by the American Gestapo if they practice their evil on black young girls also women and agree with the American Gestapo to murder black men and black people in America as well as globally.

The enemies amongst us along with their religions are a danger to black people because they are apart, of this diabolical plan to keep black forever in this cage. Our enemies are successful due your own ignorance black people and aid from the enemies within black people. They have absolutely no love for black people at all they lie to black people, our enemies amongst us are always deceiving black people, bringing all types of evil, amongst black to help destroy black people and black people have falling for the tricks also deceit, of everyone of black people enemies. Your black people won't even open your eyes to see what is happening in fact you act like it doesn't even matter. Black people act like this is alright while you are being herded off into these concentration camps, with absolutely no hope of ever getting out. While our enemies are prospering black people are getting poorer and poorer. In fact, our enemies are receiving better housing than black people in better neighborhoods that black people. Our enemies are being given the opportunities to work in the construction fields and pick up trades, that extremely important, in building a nation. While black people with their inferior education are just sitting around smoking, drinking, drugging, going to prison doing absolutely nothing, for themselves.

The enemies within are on the payroll of black people's enemies our political also religious leaders have failed us absolutely, black people. Black people are so fooled by the enemies amongst us so completely fool and tricked, until it is disgusting, Walking around calling the enemies amongst us my man or this is my girls; while our enemies are full deceit mode and black people are oblivious to what's happening to them and around them. All these enemies have only helped black people destroy themselves, families and children, this is a matter of fact my people. You examine the history and you will see what was done and who participated in these evil crimes, committed against black people. Your black people just sit around laughing and joking not taking your condition seriously it's pitiful how black people are so silly, that you would continue to trust the enemies amongst black people. All the black mom and pop stores of black people have been eradicated to make room for our enemies, amongst us; while the enemies within are helping our enemies to gain control of the economy of every black community, throughout America. Tell me why black people are you celebrating these so-called holidays like Thanksgiving, when Thanksgiving is only worshipping the slaughtering of yourselves and the Indian People? Why are you celebrating this so-called holiday Christmas my people when this is another so-called holiday when our enemies rejoice in the slaughtering of Black and Indian People? Why are you celebrating this so-called holiday called Easter when you my people were being slaughtered along with our Indian people; plus, Easter is only worshiping this whore Ester the mother of Nimrod? Why are you my people celebrating the 4th of July as Independence Day, when it was never independence day for Black or Indian People? Why Black people are you celebrating president day when these presidents were slave owners and murderers of Black and Indian People? Why are you celebrating this so-called Veterans day when you are only celebrating global murderers and after you helped America, to become the super power that she has become; then America resumed her murdering you, raping your wives, your daughters and murdering your sons? Why are you my black people still worshipping the religions of our enemies when all our enemy's religions, only mean the death and suffering of black people? Why are you so blind and scared of our enemies that you won't stand up and deal with them all? Why black man you are so eager to murder your black brother and sister helping our enemies, diabolical genocidal plans, to murder all original people? Why my people are you still perpetuating our enemies' ways of life, their religions and their politics; when all our enemies don't give a damn about black people at all except to keep black people, caged up as the lion in the cage, in one of the many 52 state zoos' and the many zoos in the many different various cities, throughout America for our many enemies amusement? When are you going to stop believing in the enemies within black people when they are absolutely working on the side of our many enemies? When are you going to stand up for yourselves and stop letting our enemies keep you locked into this cage, where there isn't any hope coming to you from our enemies' religions and politics? Why black people, why, why, why are you still falling under the spells, of our enemies within and our enemies amongst us?

The Holy Messenger of Allah the Most Honorable Elijah Muhammad told us all that America and the Caucasian People would not have jobs, for you well that day is most certainly here black people. This is a White Supremacy government and a White Nationalist government this includes every religion in America including this so-called Sunnah Islam, my people. None of these religions are ever going to set black people free due to the fact they were all, involved with the Trans-Atlantic Slave Trade and the destruction of the economical foundation, of the Tribe of Shabazz belonging to Islam here in the Wilderness of North America. The enemies within and the enemies amongst us are all working together against your black people and not one of these enemies within care what happens to black people at all. You haven't achieved a thing from all these other American religions except hunger, nakedness, homelessness also beaten and killed, by everyone who practice these religions. All these American religions teach black people to believe in this mystery god that only answers the prayers, of all black people enemies. All these American religions teach black people to believe in these lies of some mystical heaven, that black people will go to after they die, if you follow them. All these American religions are working together black people to make sure, you never are freed from your prison, by anyone or anything, my people. All these American religions are working overtime to make sure black people stay locked up in this cage, in the bottomless pit of this American Hell, my people.

These enemies within have been betraying black people ever since we were held in captivity by our enemies, for hundreds of years and these same enemies within are betraying black people, into days' time as well; for our historically proven enemies and their worthless religions, my people. Every other people in America can worship and build places of worship for themselves, except black people here in America. This Zionist/Christian/ Arab so-called Sunnah Islam/ Asian Hinduism American Government of Thieving Murdering Global Terrorist, with the help from enemies within destroyed your places of worship built by Allah, His Allah's Holy Messenger and ourselves. Every time black people begin to do something for ourselves these enemies within many from these various religions, betray black people every time. Every time black begin to stand up to do something for ourselves we never get any help from these political enemies within.

My people the only thing that worked for black where as black people were on the road of demonstrating, to America and the world, we are being a self-productive independent people; is when we were following the teachings also programs of Allah through His Holy Messenger the Most Honorable Elijah Muhammad/Muhammad RasulAllah. Everything else has failed black people drastically with the most horrible results, that black is suffering from till this very day and this includes this so-called Sunnah Islam especially. We were completely betrayed my people by the enemies for the so-called love and favors, of these Arab enemies, that America was beginning to plant in black communities throughout America. Even the so-called Africans who is following this so-called Sunnah Islam don't care about black people in America, at all either my people and the Arabs don't care about the Africans either. These enemies within religious and political are very poisonous to all black people in America and throughout the world; these enemies within care nothing about their people they only care about the enemies, of their people. These enemies within don't care at all if black people children have decent schools for their children, if the enemies amongst us have decent schools for their children. These enemies within don't care if black people have decent housing for themselves and families, if the enemies have decent housing for themselves and their families. These enemies amongst us have absolutely no concern that black people don't have decent for themselves as our enemies amongst us have decent food, for themselves and families; as they sell black people the worst of foods as well as other American Poisonous products. These enemies within will protect and even kill protecting black people enemies amongst us and will absolutely nothing to protect black people. These enemies within religious and political are nothing more than traitors to their black people, if our enemies amongst us pretend to revere them and this all the enemies within care about. The enemies within have been demonstrating this despicable behavior of theirs for the past 450 plus years and don't care how many black children are being slaughtered by the enemies amongst us, as they shut their eyes and turn their heads, pretending that they don't see the atrocities the enemies amongst black people are doing and I'm speaking about this so-called Sunnah Islam, my people. The enemies within walk around acting very proud religious as well as political, as they do everything for the enemies amongst black people to gain economical wealth, as black people get even more disenfranchised. The enemies within are so tricked and fool themselves they can't even see that these Arab demons and their so-called Sunnah Islam, can never be reformed, because this isn't from Allah and they aren't from Allah; this so-called Sunnah Islam is from the Vicegerent Yakub Ibn Lucifer as well as the Caucasian People, this includes these Arabs also, my people. In fact, everyone who is following this so-called Sunnah are the enemies, amongst black people and the enemies to black people in America as well as black people globally.

These enemies within are so silly no different from the silly Christianity preachers as they support and protect these Arabs who are just as poisonous to black people as these demon Zionist my people were also are poisonous to black people, no different. These Arabs just like the Zionist with their poisonous religions are nothing but smelly serpents, crawling and slithering amongst black people, looking for some unsuspecting black person, whom they can sting with their most deadly poisons. The Holy Messenger of Allah the Most Honorable Elijah Muhammad told us to separate from America into a land we can call our own; or America should give us some of these states, that we can call our own; where we black people could begin to build something for ourselves, with the absent of all these enemies being amongst us. No this is what America dropped into black communities these filthy Arabs and this so-called Sunnah Islam in which these enemies within, couldn't wait to crawl back on the plantation. The religious enemies within not being as wise as they thought they were couldn't wait to crawl on these Arabs plantations and their so-called Sunnah Islam. These enemies within didn't realize that embracing the Arabs and protecting these worthless Arabs and this so-called Sunnah Islam, they were just crawling back on to the plantations of America once again. They the enemies within didn't know that the Arabs with their so-called Sunnah Islam had partner up with the Zionist, Christian and Asian Hindus, to prevent the Lion from escaping from the cage. These new or once again partners of Zionist/Christian America then made some of these enemies within so-called Imams and the Arabs taught the enemies within their language, their ways and this book they called Quran-an. They even help them the enemies within to build out post into black communities throughout America, to inject the teachings of the Vicegerent Yakub Ibn Lucifer amongst black people and the disbelievers joined on as well, thus giving the Arabs their black cyborgs and terminators as these enemies planted themselves amongst black people and began doing the evil devilishment as they always been doing amongst the Original People, since Yakub grafted them out of the Original People 6,600 years ago.

These enemies within denounce Allah and Allah's last also greatest Messenger the Most Honorable Elijah Muhammad who is the true and only Muhammad RasulAllah; not Prophet Muhammad Ibn Abdullah. Therefore, there isn't no recorded death of the of Holy Messenger of Allah the Most Honorable reason being the Holy Messenger is the Elijah of the Bible and the Muhammad of the Quran-an. Prophet Muhammad [may peace and blessings of Allah forever be upon him] was only a sign for the real Muhammad to come approximately 1,400 years later. So, the enemies within denounce the Holy Savior the Holy Deliverer, the Holy Redeemer, The Great Restorer, the Most Merciful, The Most Beneficent Allah Almighty Himself if the person of Master Fard Muhammad to whom all holy praises are due forever. The enemies within aren't going to like exposing the about what these hypocrites did, to their own black people. What did these enemies do Saladin? These enemies within helped to put the black people back into the cage my people, so that these filthy Arabs like the serpents they always have been and always will be, could plant themselves into black communities with this so-called Sunnah Islam, that is useless for black people locked into this cage of despair, poverty, homelessness, disenfranchisement, hopelessness, suffering and death. I'm having a hard time distinguishing this so-called Sunnah Islam from Zionist, from Christianity, from Hinduism, it is all the same results for black people in America as well as globally. These enemies with their false Islam is just as dangerous as well as poisonous as any major drug dealer, that was working for this Zionist/Christian American Government at that time. My people it is written there is a New Jerusalem coming from the Kingdom of heaven and that is the Islam in which our Holy Savior Allah Almighty Himself taught to his last, holy and greatest Messenger the Most Honorable Elijah Muhammad; that would set black people back on the square in which we were created.

Look at what happen to black people since this dreadful so-called Sunnah Islam came amongst black people absolutely nothing of any good, for black people. Black men are walking around with these disgusting beards; dying them red, on top of this now eating with their fingers like savages, in a cave because the enemies of our fathers as well as our selves; told them this is how Prophet Muhammad use to eat, how foolish is this my people. Our fathers didn't eat this way or dyed their beards red, so why the hell are these enemies within, doing this foolishness and teaching other black people to denounce their ancestors and embrace the enemies of our ancestors along with their language, customs and ways. How could we disgrace our ancestors as well as ourselves, my people we didn't ever eat like this nor do anything like this to disgrace our fathers, for the pretended love, from our fathers' enemies and our enemies as well my people; so why are we doing this nonsense in today's time it is because you have no love for our ancestors or yourselves. The enemies within have done so much damage amongst their black people until, it is unforgiveable; in love with the enemies of themselves and we all know that what I'm saying is the absolute truth. While those amongst us want to stay under the radar and say absolutely nothing, about what has taken place, what is taking place and who were involved in these most horrific crimes against black people since 1975. The truth must be revealed my people and Allah Almighty Himself through His Holy Messenger the Most Honorable Elijah Muhammad has given me the tools, to reveal the truth about our enemies within and our many enemies amongst us, pretending to love black people when in truth none of them do, as they never have care and they never will care about black people, the ex-slave of America. Look at how ridiculous this sounds my people because you follow this so-called Sunnah Islam, the enemies of our ancestors as well as ourselves, should be forgiven. This is the same teachings of Martin Luther King Jr. we should love everybody and forgive them for the evilest, the most diabolical, the most wicked, treachery at its highest level have done to black people and this so-called Sunnah was involved heavily, every step of the way of the Trans-Atlantic Slave Trade and the Destruction of The Black

Civilizations, in North Africa this is all historical facts, my people. So now these same enemies of our black ancestors as well as ourselves, in this day and time claim to be so-called want a be Muslims and they read the Arab made Quran-a which didn't come from Allah whatever they are supposedly to have, it came from the Vicegerent Yakub Ibn Lucifer; their maker not black Original People Creator. The Enemies are spreading so much poison amongst black people until most black people can't see how all our many enemies, are working together, this diabolical most evil plan. Just examine what exactly is going on around your black people you are surrounded by enemies even bring them into your homes and you don't even know it, this is a shame my people that you could be so blind, in this modern day and time.

The enemies within have given their full support to the enemies amongst black people no different than what they, when we were all in Chattel Slavery and escaping through the Underground Railroad; where was this so-called Sunnah is at then my people? This so-called Sunnah were murdering black people in Africa they are evil people my people in which we should stay away from and keep them from amongst us my people. I hear quite few brothers saying we must wake our people up; my question to them is how are you going to wake our people up, if you don't tell them the complete truth about who their enemies within are and who are the enemies amongst black people? How can you wake our people if you don't tell them the complete truth about these so-called religions of America? How can you wake our people up if you won't tell them the truth about their treachery? How can you wake our people up by not telling them the truth about what part this so-called Sunnah Islam played in the murdering of Minister Malcolm X and the destruction of the economical foundation of black people, belonging to Islam here in the Wilderness of North? How can you wake our people up if you won't tell our people about the disbelievers and the hypocrites that were amongst black people belonging to Islam here in the Wilderness of North America, or the Western Hemisphere period? How can you wake our people up and not tell them who are the people that benefitted from this Supreme Treachery? These are the questions that our people need answers to brothers then we will be able to teach our people the truth, that our enemies within and our enemies amongst us, have been trying to keep hidden from black people. These are the answers that these disbelievers also hypocrites are also trying to keep hidden from black people also. The truth must be reveal my people it can no longer stay hidden we must make America and all her partners in these unholy crimes, know their sins, every one of them my people.

We must be aware of everyone that is in opposition against black people rising and reclaiming their own. We must be aware of all our enemies that are in opposition to us rebuilding that which Allah Almighty Himself Gave to through His last and greatest Messenger, who in turn taught us all. It's not just having temples we must begin to form a government a national government for ourselves, where we can operate as a people and Nation. We must begin to rebuild Muhammad Universities of Islam in every state, every city, every town, all throughout America. We must have unified governing body where everyone is on the same page, as we rebuild the Temples of Islam across America. We must begin to farm on a mass level were as then we can set up distribution amongst our people; then we will be able to bring to our people the best food, that will give them better health and help to prolong their lives. Thus, giving our people the ability to resist the poisonous food our enemies have been selling to them. We must begin to work together as a self-governing people as we begin to move into textiles then we will be able to supply our people with clothing, at much affordable price as well as superior quality. We must once again rebuild Shabazz Restaurants, Shabazz Steak Houses, the Steak and Takes, so our people can have decent places, to take our families and relax with our own good food. We must raise our cattle as Allah's Holy Messenger taught us that way we can have our own dairy products, for ourselves and people. We must raise our chickens as the Holy Messenger taught us how to raise them above ground, then we can produce eggs for our people, with the absent of the poisons from the foods of our enemies. We must once again rebuild our banking system and bank then institute the not the 3-year program but a 5-year economical program, for ourselves. We must raise our Flag never to be removed, by anyone ever again; then we will be able to engage in international commerce, with our many people throughout the world. We must once again build the Hospitals for ourselves all throughout America for ourselves and people. We must educate our children preparing them to be capable to enter various engineering schools and fields that every nation must have in this modern day and time, in fact in anytime, also medical schools to help staff hospitals, for ourselves to help cure our people of the many diseases, our people have been infected with by our enemies being amongst us and from their poison foods. We must understand that we must begin to build housing for ourselves and people, to put an end to these 6,000-year-old robbers and thieves, who have been unmercifully robbing black people with impunity. We must begin to build our own political system for us to govern ourselves. We must build our own security force to protect and secure the Nation, by the Fruit Of Islam; that will protect the nation from being infiltrated by our many enemies, as well as keeping our enemies from ever coming amongst us ever again and especially our women and children. We must come together so that we aren't ever again poisoned by our many enemy's holidays or religious so-called rituals. We must unite ourselves my people there isn't anyone person in charge of black people who are members of the Nation of Islam, here in the Wilderness of North America. We must form a National, State, City also Town governments, all answering or forming the National Government for ourselves; and this damn Sunnah So-called Islam and people, that aren't members of us, my people; these are the enemies of our fathers always have been, always will be. Whomever; doesn't have respect for our culture then to hell with them all and they will never be allowed amongst us to, to spread their poison ever again amongst black people.

Through Our Fathers Eyes not an enemy of ours can escape our site they all are revealed, and we must accept the truth my people, of our enemies their religions, politics and their business practices. We can no longer stay under the radar or not wanting to join in and be part of that which is greater than whatever any individual, may be doing. What could be greater than building a National Government, a State Government, a City Government and Towns Government; all of us belonging to the whole operating together as we build a Nation Economy; where all black people, can benefit from. We must understand my people then we can build a social network amongst ourselves, thus keeping our enemies from amongst black people. The enemies within as well as the enemies amongst us must forever be driven from amongst us, never ever being allowed amongst us again; in any shape, form or fashion. All who desire to be with their enemies can do so but leave us alone and don't ever come amongst us, we don't need you nor do we want your kind amongst us. The food that Allah Almighty Himself in the person of Master Fard Muhammad to whom all holy praises are due forever, taught His Holy Messenger the proper foods for us even how to prepare these our food, is 100 times better than this so-called Halal food, my people. We my people who are followers and students of the Holy Messenger the Most Honorable Elijah Muhammad the true also only Muhammad RasulAllah, never sold poison food to our people or any of these other poisons, that this so-called Sunnah Islam has been doing and still are doing; nor did we sell any poisons to anyone else. We must form our National Government so that we can bring the message to our people, in the Jungles of East Asia now called Africa thus setting up not only international commerce, but international brotherhood and sister hood as well.

Whomever; wants to love also to trust the devil then go and join unto your devil friends but stay away from us, we don't need you it doesn't matter who you may be. We must always protect ourselves from the enemies within and protect ourselves from the enemies amongst us. If there isn't any good coming from our enemies or the enemies amongst us in which I never seen any good from any of them; then we have absolutely no reasons to be dealing with at all. These enemies within as well as all of enemies amongst us will be totally wipe out of existence along with their religions and evil practices, also all the lies they teach about Allah, being a mystery god that can't be seen until you die. We my people; have absolutely any use for such ignorant and foolish teachings that represent the Vicegerent Yakub Ibn Lucifer; and has absolutely anything to do with Allah Almighty the True and Living Allah. If you know this truth and you believe you can get away with not working towards a National Islamic Government, for black people you are setting yourself up for a serious chastisement from Allah Almighty our Holy Savior in the person of Master Fard Muhammad, to whom all holy praises are due forever. We must understand that there isn't any time for us to be under the radar we must make ourselves known, to the entire world. Narrow minded thinking is very detrimental to us black people rebuilding our Nation. There are many factors to be consider before they are just dismissed my people without a thought and this is totally wrong absolutely. Being narrow minded and short sighted is also not tolerated also especially by someone trying to stay under the radar or those who wouldn't dare to step up and take a stance, against what we all know what's going on; yet scared to speak the truth about our enemies within and the enemies amongst us.

I've had some brothers say to does any good comes from out of New York. These brothers should be asking is what good comes out of this so-called Sunnah Islam. We all know absolutely no good comes from out of Zionism, Christianity and Hinduism but everyone is shutting their eyes to the evil that comes from out of this so-called Sunnah Islam. In fact, these so-called Sunnah Islam practioneers mainly the Arabs, Pakistanis, Yemenites, Bangladeshis, Egyptians, Turkey all of them, have proven to be the enemies of black people as well as the enemies of Allah and Allah's Holy Messenger. If you don't have the courage to tell our people the absolute truth about everything then you aren't, deserving to dare call yourself a minister. If you aren't preparing to speak the truth about the enemies to the lost and found members of the Tribe of Shabazz and black people in general; belonging to the Nation of Islam here in the Wilderness of North America and the Western Hemisphere period; then how could you consider yourself worthy to believe that you are capable of leading or representing black people. If you aren't ready to name all black people enemies along with their so-called religions and expose them all to the world, for the frauds that they are; then you can't be a follower and student of the last also greatest Messenger of Allah, the Most Honorable Elijah Muhammad/Muhammad RasulAllah. The time has come that we speak the truth or die. It's time we stand up and tell the world that Allah Almighty Himself visited us in the person of Master Fard Muhammad, to whom all holy praises are due forever and there is no other Allah besides Him and He has absolutely no associates. He Allah is a true and living Allah that can be seen and heard everywhere. You don't have to look up into the sky searching for this mystery god my people; the mystery god is the Vicegerent Yakub Ibn Lucifer and he is dead, along with his wisdom.

We must expose the enemies within and the enemies amongst us as we let them know that we know who they all are and what they all have done also what they all are still doing. If the Holy Messenger of Allah had not stood up here in America and expose the Caucasian Race as being a race of devils, none of us would have known who the devil is also we would have known the grafted devil and the made devil are. The hypocrites and the disbelievers that were amongst us should never be taken as friends of ours reason being is that they aren't our friends, they are also proven enemies of Allah, Allah's Holy Messenger and ourselves. Black children dyeing and suffering which one of these hypocrites or disbelievers care? The answer is absolutely none my people these enemies only care about the enemy's children; these hypocrites and these disbelievers must all be expose my people. Look at what these disgusting Palestinians members of this so-called Sunnah Islam; during world war 2 were on the side of Mussolini and Hitler when they invaded Ethiopia, as they were trying to colonize Ethiopia and dethrone also over throw the Emperor Haile Selassie and the government of Ethiopia. The Moroccans aid the American Army Tank Core under the leadership, of 3 Star General Patton, a blood thirsty murderer during World War 2, in their war in North Africa against General Rommel, also during World War 2. The Moroccans are also members of this so-called Sunnah Islam. Saudi Arabia is America the Accursed Devil greatest allied in the Mid-East in fact Saudi Arabia asked America for help, to murder the Iranians. There is an obvious pattern about this so-called Sunnah Islam where they are always, involved some evil, with their Zionist/Christian/Asian Hindu Brothers. This is what these hypocrites and disbelievers joined on to what fools, they all are, and this also is a matter of historical fact, my people. It isn't possible such evil, in which this so-called Sunnah Islam has been involved in and are still involved in, can be any type of Muslims at all. There is so much clear proof against this so-called Sunnah Islam being from the Vicegerent Yakub Ibn Lucifer. Then explain to me how this so-called Sunnah Islam could be involved in so much evil my people, then want to come here and pretend that they are righteous people. They are no more Allah's people than the Zionist, Christians and the Hindus are Allah's people. No, my people this is an abomination as well as a most diabolical lie, from the enemies of Allah and Allah's Holy Messenger. In fact, these same above mention people have always been in opposition against Allah's Prophets even murdered also maimed Allah's Prophets in the past, this is a matter of historical facts my people.

We must stand up against these enemies within perpetuating the lies and false teachings from our enemies amongst us, to black people as they rob black people with inferior food and inferior products, with impunity. Here is something else about the enemies within the self-defense they have all learned came from being in Islam here in the Wilderness of North America and then they betrayed Allah, Allah's Holy Messenger and us; to become the watch dogs and protectors for the enemies of Islam. This so-called Sunnah Islam had a habit of castrating black men in North Africa as well as the Mid-East, as they raped the black women and you are silly enough to believe that this so-called Sunnah Islam is representing Allah; no, they aren't my people as the Holy Messenger told us all I wouldn't give you two cents, for this Weak Orthodox Islam. We must let the world know that the true and living Islam is here today from Allah Himself through the mouth of Allah's last and greatest Messenger the Most Honorable Elijah Muhammad/ Muhammad Rasul Allah; and we aren't on the side of this Zionist/Christian/ Arab so-called Islam/Asian Hinduism American Government of Murdering Thieving Deceiving Global Terrorist. Who will make war with the beast the true believers in Allah Almighty Himself, who visited us in the person of Master Fard Muhammad, to whom all holy praises are due forever; how can you fool; denounce the unimaginable gifts Allah Almighty Himself gave to us through His last and greatest Messenger, when history shows and proves the same evils that were committed by the Zionist and Christians against black people; were also committed against black people by this so-called Sunnah Islam.

Through Our Fathers Eyes my people all truth will be revealed to us about everyone, of our enemies my people, in which our enemies are trying to keep hidden from black people and this includes all our enemies my people. We must stand up to our enemies my people as the Holy Messenger stood up in America and revealed to us and the world, who is the true and living God also who is the true and living Devil; we must stand up and reveal all our enemies to our people as well as also what they have done to black people as they are still doing to black people globally. This 6,000 years of treachery must come to a complete end; especially the last 500 years of the most horrific, the most evil, the most diabolical, the most insane treatment, done to black people and these are the partakers in these most horrible of the horrible crimes, in the history of our planet and this accursed so-called Sunnah Islam was and still is in the thick of this most terrifying evil, that could ever be imagine, my people against you and black people globally. To say that I am happy to do this is an understatement my people I was born to make war with the beast and make war with this hydra, I welcome it my people with their iron clad grip on the seven continents, must be broken forever. I can't thank Allah Almighty Himself for sending to me my name Saladin Shabazz-Allah because in the name Saladin Shabazz-Allah is a Supreme Purpose and He Allah has given me the tools to accomplish this and that is to make war, with the multi headed hydra called the beast or dragon, in the Revelations. All I can say is all holy praises are due to

Allah Almighty the True and living Allah that can be seen also heard everywhere in the entire universe; and he visited us in the person of Master Fard Muhammad; I submit also bear witness that the Most Honorable Elijah Muhammad is Allah's last and greatest Messenger, also known as Muhammad RasulAllah. This is a great honor that has been bestowed upon me in this day and time as well as this junction, of my life. Allah U Akbar, Elijah Muhammad RasulAllah.

The mix instructions and the changing of Allah's teachings to whom, He Allah taught His last and greatest Messenger the Most Honorable Elijah Muhammad, has caused and still are causing, nothing but division amongst black people. Thus, allowing our enemies; within and our enemies amongst us to operate with completely impunity. This insanity must come to an end my people none of these self-appointed leaders with their self-appointed titles, are teaching the truth that Allah taught His Holy Messenger and just examine the results of this insanity my people, produced absolutely nothing. You will see we haven't made any accomplishments as a people and as a nation, from these false so-called leaders. We must prepare ourselves to do battle with this hydra and we are engaging ourselves with insane people insanity for leadership. While our real enemies are walking around laughing at us and the best we can do is debate, argue and threaten each other, in these homosexuals made Social Medias. What kind of weak leadership; is this my people, I won't nor, will I have anything to do, with this insane foolishness at all. Instead of fighting against the enemies within and the enemies amongst us, we are ready to go to war with each other. This shows just how weak their leadership is also how in affective their leaderships truly are my people. How can we defeat our multitude of enemies that are prepared under such weak egotistical insane leadership, my people? This is impossible it can't be done we must have a National Government; we must have State Governments; we must have City Governments; we must have Town Governments all throughout America not some insane Despot leadership, that produces nothing for the mass of black people. I know this for an absolute fact none of these people calling themselves the leader of the Nation of Islam, have been chosen or even elected to lead the Nation Of Islam, here in the Wilderness Of North America or any place else in the Western Hemisphere.

We must understand self-appointed leaders who are insane for leadership is only in-powering our enemies and nothing else; this is certainly not helping black people in America at all. With holding the truth of who Allah as well as Allah visiting us certainly isn't helping black people at all in America as well as no other place in the world, my people. Not teaching the truth about who the Most Honorable Elijah Muhammad is and what his title is, isn't helping black people in America and no other black people in the world. Whomever; is not teaching that Allah visited us in the person of Master Fard Muhammad, to whom all holy praises are due forever; whomever isn't teaching that the Most Honorable Elijah Muhammad is the last and greatest Messenger of Allah, is miss leading Allah's people, my people. Whomever; is not teaching what Allah Almighty Himself taught to His Holy Messenger for black people in the Wilderness of North America, is miss-leading black people absolutely. We must get into battle gear which is our FOI uniforms and fall into rank, to make war with this hydra called the Red Dragon or the Beast. This is the same 6,000-year-old enemies my people now if you want to argue, insult and threaten me for telling the proven truth, then to hell with you because the enemies of black people called Goliath, prepared and waiting for us and they aren't going down without a fight. The enemies within and the multitude of enemies that are amongst us, have joined forces to wage war against us my people; against Allah and Allah's Holy Messenger.

I haven't anytime for absolutely anyone nonsense saying nothing but always talking about nonsense that always amount to absolutely nothing, at all. I am making war with the beast if you aren't ready to do this that's fine with me, I will stand as David when he had to face Goliath by himself, with absolutely no fear of Goliath and he slew Goliath with the truth that he received from Allah, before he David was even born. I also know this I will not let any narrow-minded thinking person get in my way get my way of making war with the beast, the enemies within and the enemies amongst us not me, my people. The time to take Jerusalem from the devil is now and if you aren't prepared also ready to make war with the beast then continue to do whatever you are doing and whatever you have been doing I don't care absolutely one bit at all. As my leader and teacher taught me I will stand on the other side of the hedge because the time has come, that you stop hiding behind the hedge and face this unmerciful Dragon which is a Hydra my people. I'm not a Sunday come to meeting Muslim. I'm not a Friday come to meetings so-called Muslim either. In fact, these so-called Friday come to meeting so-called Muslims are the enemies amongst black people throughout America and the time has come that all of them must be reveal, for the real demons that they truly are; they must also be reveal as being one of the heads, of this Hydra called the Dragon; which is none other than this Zionist/Christian/Arab so-called Sunnah Islam/Asian Hinduism American Government of Murdering, Thieving, Deceiving American Government of Global Terrorist.

If you aren't prepared or ready to deal with all our enemies within and the enemies amongst us then how are you ever going to wake our people up, when you aren't giving our people the complete truth, about everything and everyone involved, in the destruction of the economical foundation of black people belong to Islam, here in the Wilderness of North America? The time is now not to come but is here and all our enemies must be revealed. We must stand up for ourselves and present a unify front against all our enemies, if not then get out of the of those who aren't afraid to stand up and face our multiple enemies, trying to keep black people lock up in this cage of ignorance, despair, suffering, disenfranchisement, hopelessness and homelessness. If you aren't ready to name our enemies within and amongst us, to our people also the truth about their so-called religions, you are never going to wake black people up. If you are just going to walk around saying I'm a follower the Honorable Elijah Muhammad and do nothing about all the suffering, your people are enduring at the hands of our multiple enemies and their religions, you are a poor example of a student also follower of the Allah and His Holy Messenger. If you won't stand up and do something about the injustices that our many enemies within along with the enemies amongst us, how dare you think you can be upset with me because you are so narrow minded, you aren't able to see what I am doing. If you believe that you are doing the work of Allah's Holy Messenger then want to stay under the radar and not enter the war against this Hydra, you are only fooling yourself. If this is what you are about then you can keep your so-called brotherhood because it isn't worth having at all anyway. Through Our Fathers Eyes and if you aren't ready to look Through Our Fathers Eyes you are doing me a great favor by not talking to me and I don't need or desire your friendship or so-called brotherhood and my people you should view it the same way. If you aren't prepared and ready to sacrifice your life for black people to gain independence from all of our enemies and their religions, when history clearly proves the evil they all have done, been part of and are still committing, what need do black people need of you, regardless of what your name is or may be; in truth you are nothing but disgraceful cowards to our Holy Savior Allah Almighty Himself who visited us in the person of Master Fard Muhammad, to whom all holy praises are due forever and a total disgrace to our Leader and Teacher the last, Holy and Greatest Messenger of Allah, the Most Honorable Elijah Muhammad/Muhammad RasulAllah.

CHAPTER 13

THE VANGUARDS

Who are these Vanguards being this is what we must examine very closely my people why we must have Vanguards, in every black community throughout America. Black people in America have absolutely no protection at in their communities always at the mercy of the American Gestapo or some other people. Drugs are always being placed in black communities while the government sits back acting like they don't know how they got there, when they are the ones responsible for all these poisons ending up in black communities, throughout America. Guns are also being distributed into black communities throughout America by who my people? By this American Gestapo for the express purpose, for black children to murder each other, for the poisons that this American Government have placed in black communities, throughout America and we all know this is happening, as well as it has been going on for many years. You can sit back and convince yourself that you don't know you are only lying to yourself and aiding this American Gestapo Government, to get away with these evil crimes they have been getting away with, for many years. This is the reason why we must have a Vanguard to police this Gestapo called police department, that has been committing all types of evil crimes in black communities, throughout America. We are at war for our survival my people and we are the only people that don't have any protection, for themselves. This protection comes from our Vanguards my people if we had this in place for real, then the things that are happening in black communities, wouldn't be happening. We all know these Gestapo law enforcement agencies will never do anything to help or protect black people, never have and never will. These so-called

African American Gestapo police officers do absolutely nothing to protect black people, in fact in many cases they are even worst, then the Caucasian Gestapo Agents.

There are many reasons why we black people must have a Vanguard to protect ourselves from our many enemies, that crawling and slithering throughout black communities all throughout America; committing all sorts of evils and getting away with them. The evils our enemies get away with in their stores these Gestapo agencies allow them to do so but if black people retaliate, then the Gestapo law enforcement is there to protect, the enemies of black people always have and always will. Where is black people defense against the many evils being committed against black people it certainly is coming from the American Gestapo and that's for sure. We black people have been victimize all American Gestapo Agencies called police department or law enforcement agencies, ever since the government started them, using the Irish immigrants first to start these Gestapo so-called police forces all throughout America. Yet every other people have a Vanguard except black people we are the only people, that the American Government does everything to prevent black people from protecting themselves against outside insurgents and our enemies. The American Government want black people defenseless against our enemies them included; while our many enemies rob, rape and molest black women and young black girls, with impunity my people. We need a Vanguard to protect ourselves from the evils of our many enemies, are committing on black people and getting away with it, my people.

The Vanguard is needed amongst black people here in America and the best Vanguard is the FOI my people and this American Gestapo knows this to be the truth. You must understand my people the Allah Almighty Himself created the FOI for the Nation we were building and for black people protection period, in black communities throughout America. This is what must be re-introduce amongst black people again; for us to protect and defend ourselves from outside invaders as well as all our enemies. We can't give any of our enemies any advantage with it comes down to our protection, security and defense, of ourselves, wives and children. This Gestapo so-called police have never been about the protection of black people only to Harass, terrify, robbed, beaten even in many case rape black women with impunity. In many cases these Caucasian Gestapo Brutes made black women service them whenever these murdering Gestapo so-called police officers, they desired it. If they didn't the black women were thrown in jail on trump up charges, beaten and in many cases murdered, by these Caucasian Gestapo so-called police officers; then these cowards would pinned these crimes on some unsuspecting black man; here is another part of this injustice is that these Gestapo so-called police officers, brothers and sisters in the court system the judges, district attorneys, bailiffs everyone involved in this wicket, evil Gestapo court system, knew these Gestapo Murdering so-called police officers were the guilty parties and the black man was innocent.

The Gestapo so-called police officers all throughout America would manufacture evidence against these many, many, many innocent black men and in many, many, many cases either lose or destroy evidence, that would have proven these black men innocence; this was and still is an ongoing practice by this American Gestapo, my people. Who need Vanguards other than black people living in America at the mercy of the American Gestapo and this is all what they all are, my people. In fact, every Black Nation, every Black Country, every Black Villages I previously said these so-called African American so-called police officers, aren't going to do anything but aid these many different members now belonging to this American Gestapo, as they murder black men, children also women; and these so-called African American so-called police officers never stand up for their people, at all. Therefore, my people we black people need our own Vanguards to protect and monitor these murdering Gestapo so-called police officers and their multitude of injustices, they commit against black people especially our black male children. Very, very, very rarely are any of these murdering members of the American Gestapo are ever brought to justice especially when it involves black people, one reason being is that they all know these so-called African American police offers aren't going to say or do anything, to help their people; what they will do is help these murdering Devils Caucasian Gestapo Members, to destroy evidence proving their Caucasian Gestapo Murdering brothers, are 100% percent guilty. Who people my need Vanguards more than black people living in this Valley Of Death called America?

In fact, my people domestically and globally we all need the Vanguard in every Black Nation, every Black Country, every Black Village, every Black Town, every Black City, every Black Neighborhood, every Black

Community, not only in America but Globally as well. It only been 500 years since these many different enemies came amongst black people. Ever since this time we were stripped of everything we had and either put in physical slavery or mental slavery, in the case of the ex-slave of America we endured physical and mental slavery; from one race of people this is the Caucasian Race and history proves also verifies the evil this race has done to black people, as they come in many disguises, with their many different religions as they claim to be of some set or another; this is an absolute fact anytime any one of them that comes amongst black people, Hell Follows With Them for Black Original People; it doesn't matter where you maybe on this planet if you black and you aren't practicing Black Nationalism, you are a colonized people and nation.

Throughout America black people are defenseless against their enemies and what the shame is that those who claim to know the truth or is a follower of the Holy Messenger, sit back and do nothing about the wrongs that are taking place against black people. The time has come for every able body brothers and sisters, report for duty and rebuild the Vanguard amongst black people. We are purposely kept out of everything that an independent Nation needs, to provide the medical, dental, eye, ear and throat to meet the needs of every and for black people. There is much work to be done for ourselves and we need a Vanguard to protect ourselves, property and all investments, form our many enemies; who love to come around to sabotage, vandalize and destroy everything black people do for themselves. We can't depend on this Gestapo Law Enforcement Agencies to protect anything that black people do for ourselves, except try help our enemies to destroy whatever we do, for ourselves. The only way we can protect ourselves is to establish a Vanguard to police ourselves and protect every black man, woman and child throughout every black community throughout America, as well as globally. If you embrace any of our enemy's religions black people will never be able to free themselves, from our enemies domestically as well as globally. Our enemies come amongst black people and through murder, deceit, lies, false religions and downright treachery, steal the resources from black people domestically as well as globally. So, the Vanguard must be put back in place for black people to have a mechanism in place, to guard black people against all insurgents, their religions, their evil practices, their lives, their deceit, their conniving and their thievery; in which they [our enemies] have been operating in full gear, for the past 500 years.

Black people domestically and globally you must understand it is time we stop hiding or staying low key under the radar and make ourselves known and we need to rebuild the Vanguard. I hope everyone understand that the FOI is the first organized Vanguard in America, since Marcus Garvey Back to Africa Movement in the early 1920s. You must understand my people these drug dealers or drug kingpins were taught by black people enemies, for destroying black people and reducing black people to nothing, but America's sub-human waste; as America flushed black people into this filthy cesspool of America, at the very bottom of this American Cesspool. These are the traitors or some of the traitors that betrayed their people and aided black people many enemies, to openly destroy black people with our enemies Heroin, Crack Cocaine which was produce and manufactured in the laboratories, of America; and not to forget alcohol either my people. These traitors amongst black people that sat and learned from these Satanic enemies; of black people how to best assist the enemies of black people, to murder black people at the whole sale level. My people these so-called drug kingpins and so-called black gangsters were some of the traitors amongst black people, along with these hypocritical religious also political traitors, destroy their own people as well as destroy their own black people, without any conscious or regret to what they were doing; For the love of and the praise, of the enemies of black people. We need an extremely strong Vanguard my people for us to put an end, to these type of traitors, operating against the rise also unity of black people in America; as well as throughout the world.

The Vanguard that was in place at the time was attacked viciously by the FBI, CIA and every other Gestapo state, local and town Gestapo law enforcement agency, throughout America, including the Nation of Islam here in America. The Zionist/Christian American Government through their American Mafia supplied these black drug kingpins with weapons, as these other factions of the Gestapo Law Enforcement Agencies hunted down the Vanguards to allow these traitors to sell dope throughout America with impunity; thus, making the American Gestapo rich and all black people enemies richer, for years as they destroyed their people and communities throughout America. The Gestapo along with black enemies were able to trick many of these Vanguards to try arm struggle against the Zionist/

Christian American Government, not realizing that two other heads of this Hydra, was kept a secret, from them. All through the Holy Messenger warned them of the great error they were making because they weren't prepared to go to war with America, but these Vanguards wouldn't listen to the Holy Messenger and subsequently were wiped out. Had the Vanguard had concentrated their attention on these black drug kingpins they would have been able prevented the devastation caused by these murderers of their own people and black communities throughout America. So, all the money that people were beginning to put their hands on went right back to our enemies. The Federal Government and every local Gestapo law enforcement agency never returned any of these illegal gains, to be return to black people at all. The Vanguards must be more logically thinking into day time instead of being emotionally thinking and this is what the Holy Messenger was telling them, in which they all ignored. We can't have an intelligent Vanguard then have our enemies joining our Vanguard this is silly thinking also impractical thinking my people.

We must my people be more pragmatic thinkers than what we are being as a people, in the day and time in which we are living in. Our Vanguard is most desperately needed for us to advance ourselves as a people and produce the kind of political also religious leaders, black people need. We must reject all the religions of our enemies no matter what they may call it, it all comes from our enemies we don't need it nor do we black people want it. We my black people domestically and globally are in a life also death struggle; we can't win following the religions of our enemies, we can't win following the corrupt politics of our enemies; we can't win following the corrupt ways of our enemies; we can't win by following the corrupt policies of our enemies and we certainly can't win by trusting our enemies; also we can't win by allowing our enemies to be black people protectors; no black people need their own Vanguard to protect black people as they keep our enemies and all of their poison goods, from amongst black people domestically as well as globally. Examine our enemies 6,000-year-old history then pay very closely to the last 500 years of their history and you will see with conclusive historical evidence, that they are all liars, they are all thieves, they are all deceivers, they are all haters of Original Black People and their religions are nothing but poison, to black people domestically as well as globally.

Our children were so completely tricked and fooled by this Zionist controlled American propaganda machinery instead of being the Vanguards of their people and communities, they became the enemies of their people and communities now that their enemies have flipped on them and they are in prison, they believe they are deserving of financial assistance from their families, in which many cases they did nothing for them. Instead of being the Vanguard for themselves and people they chose to be the enemies of their people, just like the drug kingpins and dealers before them. No, my people the Vanguard is for the protection of black people against these traitors amongst black people as well. We can no longer allow these evils to be practice against and amongst black people. Since the American Gestapo is allowing them to operate with impunity selling drugs also commit murderers in and throughout black communities, they all should be dealt with extreme harshness. If they don't want to get down then they should be put down and this is one of the many responsibilities of the Vanguard, as they stand vigilant over black communities every in America and throughout the world. The Vanguard should operate 24/7 365 days a year, every year. Always on the alert as they walk their post in a perfect manner, taking charge of all Nation Property and allowing absolutely no one, to create a disturbance on or nearby their post; Report all infractions; that they may observe to their superior officers. Always neatly dressed and groom ready to help aid their people anyway they can without deserting their post; the Vanguard will only leave their post after they have been properly relived also after they have given their relief, a proper briefing of everything that happened on their shift. All Vanguards should keep a running log hourly if there is an incident then every member of the Vanguard must be trained to give a detail report minute by minute, in writing to their superior officer. Every member of the Vanguard from the commander, all officers and even private soldiers must keep their logs up to date with extreme accuracy even if you are doing roving patrols; there shouldn't be any less than a five-minute differential in the time, of each member of the Vanguard report of all incidents, to their superior officers so that everything is documented. The Vanguard should be uniformly dressed always while on duty and even off duty, for they may have to be able to take up post, at any given time ready to defend, police and protect their black people and communities al throughout America, as well as globally. This is what the Holy Messenger of Allah taught us all my people.

To stand up for ourselves, protect ourselves, police ourselves and defend ourselves to the death, if necessary protecting our Nation and people in America and globally. Any fool who think they know what's happening and can't see this you are just as dead and lifeless, as you were before the coming of Allah Almighty Himself.

Whomever; doesn't see the necessity of the Vanguard in and throughout black communities in America as well as the world, is an enemy to all black people in America as well as an enemy to all black people throughout the world. The only time our many enemies allow us to defend anything is when we are helping to defend our enemies and this we must stop doing this worldwide. We have never prospered anything from joining our enemy's army, navy, air force or marines, at all. Our enemies are the ones that prosper, and we are still left with absolutely nothing, at all, but more hell, more poverty, more suffering from our enemies and that is all my people. No, my people we need to create our own well trained in the martial arts and extremely well discipline Vanguard, for black people domestically and throughout the world. Through Our Fathers Eyes my people and never through the eyes of our many enemies, our enemies will keep us black people globally locked into this cage of despair and hopelessness; as it has been for the past 500 years, for all black people globally. We must raise the Vanguard my people to protect ourselves from all our enemies, trying to sneak amongst black people with their evil intentions to destroy black people because they are our enemies, my people. Therefore, we need our Vanguard to sort out these trouble makers that have caused trouble and mischief amongst black original people, ever since the Vicegerent Yakub Ibn Lucifer grafted them out of us.

History will reveal that black people always had Vanguards to watch over black civilizations ever since Allah created black people. It wasn't until 6,600 years ago when black people had truly relied on the Vanguard because we didn't have this kind of devilishment amongst us. We never had robbing, lying, fornication, murder, rape amongst us until Yakub's grafted people came amongst us. In six months these devils turned paradise/Heaven into hell and the Government of Arabia which was all black original people commissioned General Muk Muk to round them all up and drive them across the hot Arabian Desert, into the cave sides of West Asia now called Europe. This further proof that we need our Vanguard to round up these trouble makers amongst us spreading lies, stealing, fornicating with black women and producing these bastards; then take off leaving their bastard seeds hidden under black women dresses, we must prevent our enemies from coming amongst us selling drugs amongst while the Gestapo police officers, do absolutely nothing; and the these dirty Arabs with their so-called Sunnah Islam are also doing the same evil deeds amongst t black people; the lies, the deceit from our enemies as they operate with impunity, must be eradicated from amongst black people and all that are involved in these evils must be brought to justice by us black people, not judge by their Zionist/Christian/Arab so-called Sunnah Islam/Asian Hinduism brothers and sisters; when it comes to murdering, stealing, fornicating with black women, destabilizing black communities and worst; these enemies always get off. This is a historical fact my people and we all know it to be true; what is even more disgusting is these ignorant silly foolish African so-called Americans embracing the enemies of their people, then help the enemies of themselves and their people, to destroy themselves and their people. This is concrete proof that we our own Vanguard to wage war against our many enemies and against the ignorant, foolish, silly so-called African Americans, as well.

It doesn't matter if it's your son or my son they are the enemy to rise of black people. It doesn't matter if is your brother or my brother they are the enemies to the rise of black people. It doesn't matter if it is your sister or my sister they are enemies to the rise of black people. It doesn't matter if is your daughter or my daughter they are the enemies to the rise of black people. It doesn't matter if it is your mother or my mother they are the enemies to the rise of black people. It doesn't matter if it is your father or my father they are the enemies to the rise of black people. It doesn't matter who you are if you are involved with helping our enemies, to destroy black people you must also be brought to justice and punish an extreme punishment, without any mercy given to any of you enemies of black people. it doesn't matter who you are or whatever your reason was, and this includes all women that partake in these evils crimes against black people; and they are supposed to be your people, so your crimes are worst, and you will meet with the same punishment as our enemies and that is death, this includes all women involved or reaping the rewards, from these evils. We my people domestically as well as globally know that the Caucasian Gestapo Law enforcement are never going to do anything about any crimes being committed against black people, by any of their brothers and we all know this to be accurately true; we have been watching also experiencing these diabolical horrors by and from our enemies; along with their lackeys for the past 500 years, up to this present day and Time. Through Our Fathers Eyes my people is where all our answers are at and what we must do to secure ourselves, wives and children. The Vanguard must be re-established amongst ourselves with qualified men in charge of the daily operations and of the highest sincerity, commitment and dedication, to cutting out these cancers amongst black people domestically as well as globally.

This is how extremely important having our Vanguard in place at all time under qualified officers that are very skilled in every aspect, of training as well as supervising the daily operations of the Vanguard. Rewarding of these soldiers by promotion must be place into the bylaws of the Vanguard which should be complying of our National Laws, Rules and Regulations also why the Vanguard has been put in place, domestically as well as globally, my people. We can no longer entrust our enemies to protect us any longer one reason being is that our enemies never have, protected black people anywhere on our planet. So, we will be foolish as well as insane to expect our enemies to have a change of heart towards black people, anywhere on our planet. The Vanguard must always be respected also appreciated by everyone they are protecting as well as defend against all insurgents. All insurgents are the enemies of black people and they come amongst us it doesn't matter what they call themselves or what their religions maybe they are all insurgents, thus the enemies of black people everywhere; to keep black people disabled also confused, to prevent black people from ever unifying ourselves, these are the enemies my people absolutely. The Vanguard is to be spoken with respect and this includes the officers, in charge of operations, once the soldiers in the Vanguard are properly trained, they will understand exactly what they must do, as well as will do, once their orders are given to them and explain to them. If the Vanguard must go into action or engage any of our numerous enemies, they are to be supported by every black person in the community whom they are protecting as well as defending, always without any exception.

This is our Vanguard my people and you should encourage your sons to join unto once they come of age. In fact, there should be a junior Vanguard to monitor all the young black children due to the filthy homosexuals and perverts, our enemies have placed amongst black children. There should be a senior member of the Vanguard supervising the operations of the young Vanguard, at all time teaching also training them, to be prepare for also how to deal with all our enemies, at any given time. The Vanguard is fearless, the Vanguard is respectful, a Vanguard is always helpful towards their people, if it doesn't require him, not breaking security protocols. The Vanguard must be intelligent well-read also quickly able to assess all situations especially able to critically analyze, all situations and if necessary if not able to get to a supervisor, make a judgment call base on of the intelligentsia he was able to acquire, at any time rather on duty or off duty; in truth the Vanguard is always on duty, my people for all our protection. The Vanguard should be very astute in investigation techniques while on patrol or on a fix post, to gather all intelligentsia especially against all our enemies and this includes the American Gestapo, the American Gestapo, spies, lap dogs also our enemy's flunkies as well. The Vanguard is our first line of defense against all insurgents sneaking throughout black communities, for starting trouble and causing mayhem amongst as well as for black people. Every other people have a Vanguard in their community black people have been stripped of this basic human right and thus every scavenger, every parasite, every canine, every enemy of black people bringing death and destruction have been sanction by the government, to invade black people communities. Little miss guided black children gravitate to the negativity these enemies display to them and they begin to attack the elderly black people, in the communities throughout America. Since we have fell victim to the lies also deceit of our enemies also treachery of these so-called African American religious traitors, these traitors betrayed their people for another one of America's partners and their worthless so-called Sunnah Islam, for black people. So, these traitors tuned the Vanguard that was in place to protect black people from these deadly Cobra like Rattle Snake Arabs and their worthless Sunnah Islam, for black people; and joined up with these Arabs as they embraced the lies, that is extremely poisonous from this so-called Sunnah Islam; protecting the enemies of black people and history will prove that what I am saying is 100% accurate and right also exact.

These traitors walked around praising these enemies of their black people as they now look down on their people, like they are better than their own suffering people because now they have this so-called Sunnah Islam.

This is the same thing the foolish so-called African American Christians are saying I'm better than you because I'm so-called saved. What they have both done is betrayed their black suffering people, for the love and false admiration of black people enemies and nothing else. Examine the history my people the truth of this so-called Sunnah Islam and those that have embraced it is revealed in the history, the unforgiveable evils, wickedness, diabolically and downright hatred for black people in America as well as globally. My people there are some out there that know what I am saying is the accurate 100% absolute truth; in fact, our enemies who is pushing this poison amongst black people know that what I am saying, is the accurate 100% absolute truth about them and their worthless so-called Sunnah Islam; but they don't want black people in America as well as globally to know this truth about them and their so-called religions. As I said there are some if not many that know this truth but will not stand up against our enemies and reveal our enemies for what history reveal them to be which is as follows Liars, Thieves, Murderers, Rapist and haters of black people everywhere on our planet. What kind of so-called god would protect or forgive these demonic diabolical devils, and this is what our enemies are, and this includes, their made up so-called Sunnah Islam so called religion, which have demonstrated and proven that this so-called Sunnah Islam is just as poisonous also deadly as Zionism, Christianity and Hinduism, my people just examine the history that is all you have to do, to learn the truth about all of black people enemies and their worthless religions. These are enemies my who believed that they could put out the true light of Allah Almighty the True and Living also Only Allah as they our enemies denounce the true Muhammad Rasul Allah the Most Honorable Elijah Muhammad, and this includes this so-called Sunnah Islam. Therefore, we must re-establish our Vanguard to protect black people from all these Vampires, sucking the life energy out of black people in America and throughout the world, ever since Yakub the Vicegerent grafted this evil race of people out of black people.

My black people after you study the history of all our enemies, their religions so-called Sunnah Islam included then asked yourself this question; what god would forgive them and make them caretakers, of God's Holy Words? History proves absolutely and conclusively that they are all demons from of hell because their actions, deeds as well as the lies they spread, amongst the Original Black People every go and everywhere they have been; Why would Allah the all wise, the all-knowing choose such evil people be that may call themselves Zionist, Christian, Arab so-called Islam and Asian Hinduism, why would Allah choose any of these demonic people to represent Him, when history proves conclusively that they are all demons of and from hell? If god did do this then god isn't a just god and preferred the most evil, diabolical and wicked race of people along with their worthless religions, to represent Him. No, my people God would never do something as stupid as this. So here is proof that neither Zionism, Christianity, so-called Sunnah Islam also Hinduism are not from Allah the Universal Creator nor are these so-called religions are from Allah either. No, my people these every one of the above mention are the makings of the Vicegerent Yakub Ibn Lucifer, father and maker of the devil. So, any black people to believe in their enemies and the enemy's religions, is totally insane my people. These aren't noble honest people these peoples and all their religions are nothing but criminals' fugitives, from the chastisement and Judgement of Allah Almighty the Universal Creator as well as the True and Living Allah; who visited Black People in America in the Holeyest person of Master Fard Muhammad to whom all holy praises are due forever, and ever, and ever and ever. He Allah Almighty Himself raised up from amongst us my people His Last and Greatest Messenger the Most Honorable Elijah Muhammad the True and Only Muhammad RasulAllah. This is what Allah Himself brought to you and me my people and taught us through the mouth of His Holy Messenger.

Therefore, we black people need our Vanguard to protect what Allah has given to us from all our enemies and this includes this worthless so-called Sunnah Islam, which is still involved with the Supreme Evils their Zionist, Christian and Hindu brothers, are committing all over the world and this is also a current event fact that is presently happening today, my people. How foolish are we to ever embrace our enemies and their worthless religions it doesn't matter what they may call it my people, these are all poisons to and for black people? If we black people continue to believe also following our enemies' poisonous ideology and religions, we are forever doomed my black people. We must have our Vanguard re-establish in every black community throughout America and throughout the world black people. For us to defend, protect and defeat all enemies, who dare believe that they can encroach on anything that we do for ourselves, in America and throughout the world. We don't need or want any of their books, style of dress in which these dirty so-called Sunnah Islam stole from black people. Remember these Arabs are part of the Caucasian Race which means they were also living in the caves on all fours, when Prophet Musa may peace and blessings of Allah forever be upon him; came to teach them how to conduct themselves as some type of civilize being. This is the history my people of this wretched Caucasian people and the Arabs are part, of this wretched evil, diabolical people, called mankind. This race of people is nothing but thieves, liars, Murderers, rapist, as well as great deceivers, what God will ever bless this evil race, but their maker Yakub the Vicegerent maker of the devil. The truth must be told and revealed my people; we must stand up if you say you believe or a follower and you won't stand up and make war with the dragon in this day and time, ask yourself my brothers what is the purpose, of you living? Reason being you say you believe but you rather criticize your brother as you stand by keeping your mouth close, when it comes down to reveal the truth of black people, many enemies and this worthless so-called Sunnah Islam included, along with all the traitors that lied to Allah and Allah's last and greatest Messenger. If you aren't ready to do this then keep your narrow-minded opinion, to your scare self and don't bother me because I was born, to do what must be done, for black people globally.

Therefore, my people we need our Vanguard to be re-establish amongst black people we must run Yakub and his made devils, from the roots of civilization along with all their evil worthless religions and this includes this so-called worthless Sunnah Islam, form amongst black Original People; never ever to return amongst black people again. We must understand that we are the David going up against this Goliath of pure evil made up of all black people enemies and their African American Cyborgs called Preachers, Reverends, Priest and Imams my people. These are the enemies of black people worldwide and these are the traitors of black people, that our enemies will put on the front line hoping that we will hesitate when it comes to us slaying this evil, wicket, diabolical, unmerciful Goliath and all his religions including this useless so-called Sunnah Islam, for black original people. Our Vanguard must be trained for real in secret because these traitors are training and teaching our enemies, how to protect and defend themselves against black people. We must stop fooling around and prepare ourselves seriously against all our enemies, my people. We will defeat all our enemies including their Cyborgs African American servants all we have to do is keep our faith in our Holy Savior Allah Almighty Himself in the person of Master Fard Muhammad, to whom holy praises are due forever. We must follow the example He Allah gave to us who is Allah's last and greatest Messenger the Most Honorable Elijah Muhammad/the true and only Muhammad RasulAllah. We must follow all the programs Allah's Holy Messenger gave to us all, that will elevate black people towards independence, Freedom, Justice, Equality, Knowledge, Wisdom, Understanding, Food, clothing, Shelter, Love, Peace and Happiness. This is what's being denied to black people by our enemies and all our enemies' religions, it doesn't matter what they call these useless religions, my people; our enemies are always trying to bog black people down with their insane nonsense my people; these are the desire of our enemies to keep us black people believing in their insane lies about religion and politics.

The Vanguard my people is for all our protection against our enemies and we must not ever trust these traitors, that we know are traitors to black people. If you are silly enough to join unto the enemies of black people then you are also the enemy, of yourself and people as well. The Vanguard is in place to protect all black people, from all traitors. We are in Al-Jihad my people we shouldn't trust any outsider at all, when we know what they believe in is against black people rise back to National status and who doesn't believe in this useless so-called Sunnah Islam. Many of the Africans coming out of West Africa have absolutely no love for black people in America; in fact, these West Africans don't even know anything about the lies this useless so-called Sunnah Islam is trying to spread, throughout the world, amongst black people. For what purpose are they doing this Saladin? To keep black people forever locked into the cage of despair, hopelessness, ignorance, suffering and death, my people, this is their purpose; just examine the history of these infidels especially the history of the past 500 years, if you think I'm not telling the truth. In fact, examine the history of these made people ever since Yakub grafted them out of your black people they all have been the enemies, of black people; this is historical and mathematical facts my people. Pay absolutely no attention to their language because they this so-called Sunnah Islam is only reciting in the dialect of Qurush tribe. This isn't the real language or original Arabic my people these so-called lying Sunnah Islam practioneers, are never to be trusted amongst black people because they are proven liars, deceivers, murderers, thieves, rapist as well as enslavers; no better than Zionism and Christianity; and this is why they are all partners in crime today, here in America and who know better than you and I my brothers and sisters in America and throughout the world, how treacherous this useless so-called Sunnah Islam has been for black people in America and throughout the world.

Through Our Fathers Eyes my people and never through the eyes of our proven enemies and this includes this useless also worthless so-called Sunnah Islam, to all black people in America and throughout the world. I'm not speaking hatred my people towards our many enemies I'm speaking about all the people and their filthy religions also ideologies, that have been demonstrating absolute hatred for black people and this so-called worthless Sunnah Islam is the most hypocritical of them all; and our enemies have been doing this for 6,000 years and the last 500 years have been an absolute nightmare, for black people and history will always prove, that what I am saying is accurate and absolutely 100% right and exact. Our enemies believed that they could get away their evils because Wallace D. Mohammad betrayed black people and through murder, deceit, thievery and lies, he along with all these other traitorous, hypocrites and disbelievers that were amongst the Holy Messenger of Allah as well as amongst ourselves and everyone that was there, know I am speaking the truth. In fact this Zionist/Christian/Arab so-called worthless Sunnah Islam/ Asian worthless Hinduism American Government of Murdering, thieving, rapist, lying Government of Global Terrorist and this is the absolute truth; and I'm not afraid to tell the entire world this truth that all of our enemies have been trying to keep hidden for the past 6,000 years and especially the past 500 years, as they profess to be righteous when history proves they are nothing but devils; all of them my people until proven different and this none of them have done, and we all know I'm telling the absolute truth.

The Vanguard my people is seriously important for us to have for our protection in place these cowards could never defeat us in hand to hand combat or with the spear, sword or knives, so these cowards always seek an unfair advantage over us and this ruthless, worthless, useless so-called Sunnah Islam is no different from their Zionist/Christian/Hindu brothers and sisters all one have to do is examine the history the real truth will be reveal to you, if you are looking for truth if you aren't then go read this Yusef

Ali Translation of their Quran-an. I guarantee you this my people; you will be as blind as any Christian when it comes to learning the truth, about the enemies of Allah; Both Bible and Our-an come from the Vicegerent Yakub Ibn Lucifer the father and maker of the Devil; and not from Allah the True and Living Allah my people, that exist everywhere because He Allah exist in every Original Black Person on this planet also in the Universe and the Seven Planets with life on them very similar ours; which the enemies of Allah call the seven heavens. Further proof that they aren't created by Allah the Universal Creator because they aren't created by Allah the True and Living Allah; and this is why they know absolutely nothing about the Seven Planets of Life, like the Original Black People on the Third Planet, names Asia or Asa in which Yakub the Vicegerent made devils are not a part of and this includes all of their made up so-called religions; this includes this worthless, useless so-called Sunnah Islam, which has never been any good for black people anywhere on our planet. The truth must be told my people and I'm just telling the absolute truth that is spoken about in secret, by many brothers. I'm just not afraid to tell the entire world the truth. The reason being is that Allah Almighty the True and Living Allah in the person of Master Fard Muhammad, to whom all holy praises are due forever, is my protector, guide and I will have none other than Him; my enemies can keep their mystery god and mystery heaven, I want absolutely no part of what these fools believe in, at all never have and never will.

Through Our Fathers Eyes and never through the eyes of our fathers' enemies' eyes this is how our enemies can control black people, as they laugh in black people face, then curse you in their grafted language as these dirty, filthy so-called members of this worthless so-called Islam, to black people. Examine the history my people whatever our enemies are trying to pass or represent as a holy book, my people it isn't at all. Our enemies made it up to make you believe they are righteous people, when in truth they are nothing but demons that crawled out of the pits of hell and trying to pass themselves off as righteous people; when they aren't any different than the evil, wicket, diabolical Zionist, Christians and Hindus and they know it themselves my people. Prophet Muhammad [May the peace and blessings of Allah forever be upon him] told the companions that in three days you will forget my revelations, in which we all know that in three generations these so-called filthy, evil, wicket, so-called Sunnah Islam did exactly that. How can you be so silly to believe also trust these worthless people proven enemies of Allah, Allah's Holy Prophets and the enemies of Muhammad RasulAllah which is the Most Honorable Elijah Muhammad?

Therefore, we need our Vanguard my people because our many enemies don't want the truth of themselves being revealed, to black people and the entire world. The truth must be reveal my people and I have absolutely no choice but do what Allah Almighty commands me to do. I am a servant of our Holy Most Merciful, Most Beneficent, Most Gracious, our Great Deliverer Allah Almighty Himself in the person of Master Fard Muhammad to whom all holy praises, are due forever. I consider it a privilege to have born in the time of Allah's last and Greatest Messenger the Most Honorable Elijah Muhammad the true and absolutely the only Muhammad RasulAllah. I also consider it great honor that came into the temples and was able to hear the Holy Messenger of Allah; Allah U Akbar Elijah Muhammad RasulAllah. I don't care if everyone, stay away from me because of the truth I am revealing to the entire world, especially my black brothers and sisters globally. My sacrifice, my life and my death are for Allah and absolutely no associates has He and I Saladin Shabazz-Allah am command and I'm of those who are first to submit. I took this oath over 50 plus years ago as a young boy and I will never turn my back on Allah or His Holy Messenger. I am a FOI to the day I die I am a member of the Vanguard and I say this with absolutely great pride and I consider this at the age of 66 approaching 67 years of age, the greatest honor I could ever achieve in life praise be Allah Almighty, for choosing me to be a scribe, of Allah and His last and greatest Messenger. To the death my people I will die on the square, before I desert my post.

My people This filthy, evil, diabolical Zionist/ Christian/ Arab worthless American Sunnah so-called Islam/Hinduism American Murdering, thieving, rapist American Government of Globally Terrorist have been selling rat meat purchased from China, to you stupid so-called American Citizens; this supremely evil American Government and her partners, have already sold over a couple of million tons, of rat meat into America and where do you think this poison ends up, my people. I even was privileged to hear that the American Government is reporting right now has purchased over 100 million metric tons of Raw Meat, from China; my people you can bet your life if this capitalistic American Government is involved and I don't doubt these devils aren't involved; America has purchased over 200 million metric tons, of rat meat from China and where my people, do you think this poison is as well as has ended up? I will tell you my people where in black communities, all throughout America that's where my people. Now through their America's propaganda machinery the government is trying to deny the evil that they are involved in. My people the American Government and her partners are moving this rat meat poison, faster also greater than Heroin and Crack put together. This is what these cowardly so-called African Americans have sold black people out to and for my people. Who needs a Vanguard more than black people I ask my people? These are some of the crimes that our enemies are involved in to destroy black people as well as their American citizens. Therefore, we need our Vanguard in place our own farms to produce our own food for ourselves our own livestock, as we re-take control of feeding ourselves. My people we need our own restaurants, grocery stores, dairy farms, so that we can prevent this evil that America and her partners are involved in. We had much better food than this so-called Halal food in which I wouldn't give you two cents for either; before the great betrayal of 1975 by Wallace D. Mohammad and all the hypocrites also disbelievers, that sold out everything we had built under the leadership and guidance of the Holy Messenger of Allah Almighty.

These hypocrites and disbelievers are nothing but traitors that cast their people back into the bottom of the well of economics, education, engineering, agriculture, medical as well as all the science that every civilize intelligent independent Nation needs; then turned it all over to our enemies and this includes this worthless so-called Sunnah Islam, which in truth is nothing but another version of Christianity in which black people have absolutely no use of or for. Therefore, we need our Vanguard my people so that we can prevent our enemies from selling us poisons product in their filthy stores in which we all know that our enemies are, and they have been doing so, for over 450 plus years; the Arabs and Asian jumped on board in the last 40 plus years. Now they are selling black people rat meat the question is how long this have been going on, my people, as our enemies grow fatter and fatter. How can we trust such people they aren't righteous people these are demons that crawl out of pits of hell, their religions as well and this includes this worthless so-called Sunnah Islam, for all black people globally? All one must do is examine their wicket history the truth of them is in the history, my people. We are foolish to leave ourselves unprotected at the mercy of these unmerciful, demons and I mean every one of them my people. Nothing good for black people have ever come from any of our enemies and this is an absolute proven fact, my people. Here is a question my people that we all should ask ourselves. King James Version of the Bible took over 150 years to change and tamper with the original writings and this we know; and Allah Our Holy Savior called it the Poison Book; now this book these so-called useless Sunnah Islam verifies the lies that King James and his scribes of 50 to 60, that change the original text; So how righteous is this book in which Prophet Mohammed of Arabia, this is how his name is originally spell; had absolutely nothing to do with this book being in book form, he was dead 23 years before this happen; then who verified the lies of the Bible and why would this book our enemies are calling Quran-an, support the lies of King James and his scribes? Why would this book our enemies called Quran-a support the enemies of black people including the Torah? The reason being is that it all comes from their maker, the Vicegerent Yakub Ibn Lucifer and not from Allah Almighty the True and Living Allah. Examine the history yourself my people stop listening to our enemies and their lackeys of traitors, to their own black people, for the truth. No, my people this is insanity for us to trust our enemies and those who have betrayed their own people, for these filthy Arabs along with their worthless so-called Sunnah Islam, for all black people. When history proves that they all came out of the cave sides of West Asia now called Europe, which they all crawled out the pits of hell of Europe.

This Zionist/Christian/Arab so-called Sunnah Islam/Asian Hinduism American Government of Murdering Thieving Global Terrorist have absolutely no intention of letting black people out of their evil grip. This is something we must put an end to. We can no longer sit back pretending that we are waking our people up, when you aren't telling them the absolute truth about black people enemies and who they are. Also, why aren't you naming the traitors of their people, if you want to raise your people? No, you are living in the past who ever want to use this method, but that was in that day and time and you want them to write a letter, so some ignorant fool can you an X. This is ridicules my people because whomever is asking such a thing has not elevated their thinking up into modern day and time; which means they can't possibility raise or uplift black people, due to them operating in the past. Our ignorant egoistical want to be so-called leaders are thinking only about themselves and in truth not their people. If you claim to be trying to raise your people in this day and time then why aren't you teaching your people about their enemies are, what they have done and the traitors that were involved, in betraying them. Giving them an X is counterproductive in this day in the time in which we are now living in. The Vanguard must be re-established in this day time and time and the methods that were uses 40, 50, 60, 70 or 80 years ago, will not work at all. Therefore, the Holy Messenger of Allah told us that we must be fast moving and fast thinking up to the modern day and time and having young soldiers out on the street selling newspapers isn't up to the modern day and time, in which we are now living; and if you don't know this then you are behind the times and not worthy to call yourself a minister.

Once you understand what must be done then you must understand how it must be done and wasting our youth on selling papers, the youth should be in school requiring the necessary education that black people need, to re-build that which was stolen from us. You are only aiding our enemies to remain in power to continue to rob, lye also steals from black people, domestically as well as globally. Thus, you are the instrument that is more harmful to your people that you are a help to your people and our many enemies are just loving, your foolishness. The Vanguard must at all cost be re-establish for protection of black people and the Nation that must be re-establish, for black people domestically as well as globally. This Zionist/Christian/Arab so-called Sunnah Islam/Asian Hinduism American Government of Murdering Global Terrorist are laughing at you because they our enemies know, that you so-called false leaders are misguiding black people and keeping our enemies in power, thus allowing our enemies to rob, steal, murder even rape my, with impunity due to these so-called foolish self-appointed ministers. The FOI are the Vanguards that created by Allah Almighty Himself for the protection of black people and the New Jerusalem, in which He Allah was creating, for us the seed of Ibrahim, that would be lost from their own people, for 400 years; in a strange land amongst a strange people and made a slave. The mist understanding also self-importance of these so-called ministers are causing more damage than good; always wanting to challenge or debate whit each other, while our enemies are laughing all the way to the bank. I refuse to sit back and be this foolish I will tell the truth and make America know her sins. I will reveal to the world of black people domestically as well as globally, who all our enemies are and worthless as well as all their worthless religions are.

If you aren't preparing to do this then get out of the way for others who are prepare and willing, to make war with the beast. The Vanguard must be re-establishing under qualified leadership and not some idiots with their self-important worthless egos, aiding black people enemies to destroy black people and you think for second that you are doing the work, of the Holy Messenger of Allah you delusional. No, my people a delusional fool is just as dangerous as our many enemies in fact his or her delusional behavior, qualifies them to be consider enemies, of all black people as well. Allah Almighty Himself in the person of Master Fard Muhammad, to whom all holy praises are due forever create this Vanguard name the FOI, for protection of black people that He Allah came to save. Yet every so-called follower speaks and giving credit to His Messenger rather than Allah Himself. Yes, you do in fact you even denigrate Allah's last and Allah's last and greatest Messenger by calling him the Most Honorable Elijah; instead of calling him the Holy Messenger of Allah. I even heard many say these are the teachings of the Most Honorable Elijah Muhammad which in fact is incorrect. These are teaching come from Allah Almighty Himself in which He Allah gave to last, greatest and Holy Messenger the Most Honorable Elijah Muhammad/Muhammad RasulAllah and this is an absolute fact, my people.

This is the reason why you can't raise the Black Nation is due to you having forgotten the Allah that came to save you and credit His Allah Holy Messenger for the teachings that he received from Allah, in person and him the Holy Messenger of Allah told us this over and repeatedly for over 40 years. In fact, it was Minister Malcolm that created the Muhammad Speaks Newspaper; it was Allah in the person to whom all holy praises, are due forever; created THE FINAL CALL TO ISLAM NEWSPAPER long before Muhammad Speaks Newspaper. What I'm saying is an absolute, accurate, undisputed fact; that can't be denied by anyone, my misguided people. We my people and everyone that want to be or call themselves a minister if you aren't praising Allah by His Name Master Fard Muhammad and you aren't praising Him much as well as often, you are disrespecting the only Allah of black people salvation. The Holy Messenger; is not responsible for Our Holy Savior's creation not. Our Holy Savior Allah Almighty is the creator of His Holy Messenger no matter how anyone try to dress this factor up, it is in correct. Allah Almighty sits on the throne alone, with the Lamb standing at his side on the right of the Mighty one and that Mighty One is Allah Almighty Himself in the Holiest person of Master Fard Muhammad, to whom all holy praises are due forever and to hell with the entire world, that disbelieve, and this includes this worthless so-called Sunnah Islam, my people globally as well as domestically.

We must at all cost put the Vanguard back in place my people this is eccentrically critical to our survival my people and this we all must understand. We don't use the Vanguard to peddle newspaper this is a waste of valuable resources, can't you see this, my people? You are the cat on the hot tin roof and those you believe in are most defiantly leading you into the wrong direction, for their own selfish silly egos. Young men going around selling unauthentic so-called Muhammad Speaks Newspapers to please some fool selfish ego, calling themselves minister, when any intelligent person should know; these young people should be in school learning the sciences, of what is needed to build a nation, for their selves. They say they believe in nation building but truth they don't; they are in ego building of their own self-image. While our enemies are getting away with murder also thievery but that isn't important to these self-style so-called ministers. Instead of building the Vanguard for protection as Chairman Mao build the Red Guard to protect also help the Chinese people, to farm also involved in the big step forward, that has propelled China as one of the greatest economies on our planet; while black in America are doing absolutely nothing to aid their people, at the mass level. I tell the truth about our enemies because they won't these so-called ministers do it, no they want to use methods that were used in the past in the day and time in which we are living in today and this is ridicules, my people. Arguing, debating, name calling, also to threaten each other, is not the teaching of Allah our Holy Savior nor is this conduct is what Allah taught His Holy Messenger at all; so, where did it come from my people? How is it possible to have unity and not have a National Vanguard to protect the Nation or whatever we are trying, to build this totally impossible as well as insane my people. All we are doing and have done is slip deeper into the darkness of absolute total ignorance. No unity, no production, no enfranchisement no nothing, but a bunch of foolishness that is only empowering our enemies.

These ignorant fools aren't looking Through Our Fathers Eyes these fools are still looking through the eyes of our enemies and our enemies know this to be an absolute fact, that allow our enemies to do the evil that they are doing in every black community throughout America, laughing at these many fools calling themselves ministers because they; our enemies know that they aren't going to do anything to stop or prevent our enemies and the evil that they commit amongst as well as to black people, as they all operate with impunity. I wouldn't waste my time engaging anyone who is afraid to step up to the plate for real and do something instead of pretending to be do something, when in truth they are only satisfying their own selfish egos. In truth many of these so-called ministers come from out of the camps of these Magicians of Pharaoh or some other misguided person. Therefore, we must have a National Vanguard to stand Vigilant always 24/7 365 days every year, ready to go in action whenever they may be needed and where ever they may be needed, at any given time for the building of our Black Independent Islamic Nation; against all insurgents, interlopers, encroachers and all black people enemies. This Vanguard that spear headed the Original Vanguard is the FOI but there were other Black Organizations that joined unto the Vanguard, to protect black people here in America. It doesn't matter who feelings I hurt or offend it matters not to me at all; the Holy Messenger of Allah Himself taught us all we must tell the truth, even if the truth hurts our own selves. Every black man in America should be a member of the Vanguard and save the antics for the pretenders, I have absolutely any use for any of you at all and neither do the real Vanguard who stands ready, to give their life to protect and defend the re-construction of the Nation that these hypocrites also disbelievers, helped to eradicate to please our 6,000-year-old enemies, are you up for the challenge I most certainly am.

CHAPTER 14

THE FORGOTTEN PEOPLE

The questions my people that must be ask are these; who are The Forgotten People? Why are they The Forgotten People? Let us expand on this subject my people The Forgotten People we must ask ourselves are who? The Answer is you are The Forgotten People my people are you my people, due to this worthless Zionism/this worthless Christianity/ this worthless Arab so-called Islam/ this worthless Hinduism, have absolutely no love, for black people at all especially the ex-slaves of this American Government of Global Murdering Terrorist. Since you my people have denounced our Holy Savior Allah Almighty Himself and Allah's last also greatest Messenger, your enemies have been able to take complete advantage of your ignorance. Thus, you became disenfranchise, homeless, death and absolute destruction by our many enemies, while you The Forgotten People walk around completely oblivious to what is being done to you and who are ones, that are doing it to you. My people you don't even know who your enemies and this are why you my people, are The Forgotten People because you my people are so blind, deaf and dumb to the times, in which you all are living in. People that are out there calling themselves raising the dead my question is how the dead can raise the dead. If you are trying to use the methods that were used 40, 50, 60 even 70 years ago and even better, then the ones who are using these methods are just as dead as the ones, they claim to be raising in which they will never do my people. You we my people are The Forgotten People with a bunch of complete fools, trying to sound like they are intelligent when in truth they are the blind leading the blind, into nothing but their own destruction my people. You my People are The Forgotten People and in this American society of today you are nothing more than lab rats. Once this worthless Zionism/ worthless Christianity/ Worthless Arab so-called Sunnah Islam/worthless Hinduism American Government of Supreme Murdering Thieving Global Terrorist; are done with you they put you back into your cage, until these demons need to test or conduct another experiment and they [these devils] come and get you again your children as well. You are The Forgotten People my people.

These so-called ministers aren't truly trying to help you they all have their own agenda trying to compete with the real Magicians of Pharaoh because their desire is to one day replace the old Magicians and then they can become the new Magicians of Pharaoh which is America the Accursed Devil. Of course, they will agree to keep The Forgotten People, forgotten so that they can now become wealthy, off their people suffering and to hell with you my people. These so-called ministers are nothing in truth but pimps that are too lazy to work so they believe that they can prosper financially off you The Forgotten People because our enemies told or even telling them, that they could if you keep them all being the Forgotten People. Now these new wants to be Magicians have a click amongst themselves I've seen and heard them, and they sound act no different than the Christian preachers and we all know that we can't trust them at all. In fact, my people many of these new wants to be Magicians never served under our Leader and Teacher the Holy Messenger of Allah and they never sold one Original Muhammad Speaks Newspaper either. No, they all come out of the camps of these Magicians and they are trying to make you believe, they have the answers when in truth they have absolutely nothing at all, that will stop also prevent you my people from being The Forgotten People. They aren't ever going to reveal your real also true enemies to you because they are down with the enemies my people in keeping your black people, for ever being The Forgotten People. I will never listen to anyone of these phonies reason being is that I know who and what they all are; which is the enemies to the rise of black people, domestically as well as globally; thus, keeping you my people The Forgotten People.

The Forgotten People are you ex-slaves of America that fore filled the prophecy of Ibrahim when he Ibrahim asked Allah to make them Muslims. Ibrahim wasn't talking about the Zionist, he wasn't talking about Christians, he wasn't talking about the Arabs and their worthless so-called Sunnah

Islam and he Ibrahim wasn't talking about this worthless Hinduism as well; Ibrahim was speaking about us my people and our enemies know this to be the absolute truth. This is a truth that is seriously being kept hidden from you, not only by our many enemies but also by these self-so-called ordained ministers that only fools will dare follow behind, feeding their egos of self-important, as they keep the truth hidden truth hidden, from all black people. Yet if you truly examine what they are talking about you will see these frauds have absolutely nothing to say about any physical progress at all, for The Forgotten People. These so-called self-ordain ministers are only playing on your emotions to get you not to look at building anything at all except a temple because these so-called self-ordain minister are able to work their con game better, inside that way they don't run the risk of being expose if they were outside. We can't have any disbelievers at all amongst black people. Once you find out who the disbeliever maybe we must get rid of them; it doesn't matter if is our sons or daughters even if it is our grandchildren, we must cast them all from amongst us because it is in their hearts to destroy us all; look at what this disbeliever Wallace D. Mohammed did, to his father the Holy Messenger of Allah, once the Holy Messenger expired in 1975.

These disbelieving cowards are the enemies to the rise of black people as they aid our enemies, in keeping black people the ex-slave of America, The Forgotten People. These cowards are aiding black people many enemies to stay in power because they are disbelievers and I have absolutely no love for any of them at all. Even if you show them the correct way these cowards will always reject our Holy Savior Allah in the person of Master Fard Muhammad, to whom all holy praises are due forever and Allah's last and greatest Messenger the Most Honorable Elijah Muhammad/Muhammad RasulAllah. These disbelievers love the devil even though the devil gives them absolutely nothing, but they will and always will sell out their black people; my people none of them can ever be trusted. These fools don't even realize they are The Forgotten People if they can walk around pretending, to be free they are happy participating in American Hypocrisy. Black People you are The Forgotten People and all disbelievers also hypocrites are a serious threat to black people existence as well as black people rise. We must be strong my people one you discover the hypocrite also the disbeliever they must be dealt extremely harshly with absolutely no exceptions at all; or we will forever be The Forgotten People. If your son or daughter are disbelievers or hypocrites how can they be your son or daughter because they certainly aren't mines and I want absolutely nothing to do with them. The Forgotten People are black people and we will not be The Forgotten People ever again and we shouldn't let any disbeliever or hypocrites get in our way, of achieving self-independence for black people and it doesn't matter who they might be, they are our enemies that should never be trusted ever.

If you aren't ready to make the harsh decision on dealing with these disbelievers and hypocrites, then this make you a disbeliever also a hypocrite; I can, and I will make this harsh decision on all disbelievers and hypocrites without any hesitation at all. I will refuse to be forgotten any longer any longer I will give my life before I stand by and do nothing, as I stand around partying with disbelieving people I don't care whom they might be at all. If you say you believe in Allah Our Holy Savior Master Fard Muhammad to whom all holy praises are due forever; if you say that you are a follower in Allah's last and greatest Messenger the Most Honorable Elijah Muhammad/Muhammad RasulAllah; yet you harbor, protect also defend any hypocrite or disbeliever it doesn't matter whom they may be; then you are a disbeliever and hypocrite yourself as well as the enemy of Allah Our Holy Savior and Allah's Holy Messenger. Thus, anyone that house and protect these enemies, are determining to keep black being The Forgotten People and this is not acceptable to me at all. Through Our Fathers Eyes my people we have absolutely no other choice but look their eyes and we must act on what our Fathers reveal to us, so that we will no longer be the Forgotten People, in modern day and times in which we are living in right now. This worthless so-called Sunnah Islam is designed by the Vicegerent Yakub Ibn Lucifer to keep Allah's people, as The Forgotten Black People in America as well as Black People globally.

We are The Forgotten People due to others that won't stand up and do something, yet these do-nothing people or so-called believers sit back and are afraid to do anything at all; except to aid black people enemies to keep Black People as The Forgotten People. These young so-called black men are a disgrace they act as well as talk like colored women and they can't be trusted at all. In fact, they aren't even man enough to deal with the problems they make what these cowards will do is call the police on their fathers as well as their mothers; I personally have experience this from my own so-called son in which I will never trust again in life because he is a disbeliever he said it from his own mouth. I have been holding post ever since I was 12 years old and I'm now approaching 67 years of age. I would have put a gun to my head and pull the trigger before I called the Murdering Gestapo on my father, not these new cowardly colored boys. These cowardly boys will never honor their father no they honor the colored woman and my people who refuse to be The Forgotten People any longer, we must be ready to deal with these young colored boys and girls severely, if they don't want to join on, if they don't want to join on to themselves and grow up to be real men; That will be prepared to defend and protect their own to the death; then we have absolutely no use of them. We can't accept anything less my people our cry to Allah Almighty is that we will no longer be The Forgotten People, in this Worthless Zionist/Worthless Christian/Worthless Arab so-called Sunnah Islam/ Worthless Hinduism American Government of Global Murdering Terrorist, any damn longer we Black Original People refuse to accept this any longer, from any of America's partners any longer this includes Zionism and their brother partners in crime this worthless so-called Sunnah Islam; we aren't The Forgotten People as our enemies want us to believe; no my people We Are Allah Almighty Chosen People. Our enemies will soon be the forgotten people including this worthless so-called Sunnah Islam, my people.

Our enemies have launch every attack upon us for making us The Forgotten People that time has forgotten this is untrue my people; time will forget our enemies my people, never us. Our enemies will be wipe completely out of memory and existence, never will our enemies raise its ugly head ever again, my people. We must prepare our grandchildren to prepare our great grandchildren so that our great grandchildren can prepare our great, great grandchildren, to be prepare to rule the planet as we did before the Vicegerent Yakub Ibn Lucifer grafted the Caucasian race out of us also before the Vicegerent Yakub Ibn Lucifer sent a revelation or inspiration, to Prophet Mohammed of Arabia approximately 1,400 years ago, which was predicted 13 to 14,000 years before either Yakub in which was born in the year 8,400 Prophet Mohammed was born approximately 5,000 years later.

My people the Vicegerent Yakub Ibn Lucifer came in or was born in this vacuum and his [Yakub] wisdom was given 6,000 years to rule. The Quran-an is not going to tell black people this truth because our enemies will be giving up the power to rule black people, once they learn the actual truth.

So in the so-called Sunnah Islam there are many truths that aren't being told because our enemies believed that burying the actual truth of black people, they could make the Original Black People Forgotten People of power and glory; this is why even in so-called Mecca they so-called Sunnah Islam is destroying, removing or covering up, all existence of black people being the Original People of Arabia and Mecca as well, as well as all surrounding countries including Palestine, Iraq, Iran and all the rest. As the Zionist and Christians use their interpretation of the scriptures better yet the changing of the True Quran-an, History or Bible they our enemies had to change the actual truth, to make the Original Black People the Forgotten People and make themselves the chosen people, of Allah which is a complete an absolute lie this includes this worthless so-called Sunnah Islam to black people. If you examine any of our many enemies, so-called history and religions, they are filled with lies and they always make the Prophets of Allah look like themselves as they hide the real actual truth. Our enemies my people; which whom they all are the makings or the experiments; of Yakub Ibn Lucifer, the Vicegerent and not Allah. Our Enemies were instructed on how to conquer also the importance of hiding the truth, about who the Original People truly are. So, implanting the laws, rules and regulations of their make Yakub Ibn Lucifer the Vicegerent, they have been using ever since Muza brought then out of the caves of Europe. One of the greatest weapons to use on the Original People is lies because they are trusting people. To conquer the Original would be obtained with steel and once one examines what our enemies have done, you will see the truth, and this includes this worthless so-called Sunnah Islam; it's in the history my people.

Our enemies know for an absolute fact that I'm speaking the truth but our enemies, desire for you not to know or except, the truth that will set you free, of our enemies as well as all as their worthless slave making religions, ideologies, politics as well as their way of life. In which they stole from us and dare call it theirs; what disgusting liars they all are my people and we should never trust them or turn our backs on any of them ever. My people our enemies made the Original Black People the Forgotten People to present their selves as Allah's chosen people. Our enemies corrupted the true also Original History which they are presenting as being from Allah, when in truth it's from Yakub Ibn Lucifer the Vicegerent, the enemy of Allah and the Original Black People. The truth must be told my people the actual truth and the Hidden Truth, in which all our enemies are all a part of my people and have been for the past 6,000 years ever since Yakub Ibn Lucifer the Vicegerent grafted these other races, out of the Original Black People. My people the people that you are looking at now brown, yellow and red are the grafted people of Yakub Ibn Lucifer the Vicegerent. These so-called brown, red and yellow are not the Original brown, yellow and red people. These are the grafted so-called brown, yellow also red people and they come from Yakub's experiments, of grafting another people, out of the Original People; and these grafted people are a part of keeping the Original Black People the Forgotten People so that they can keep the lives of their maker also god [Yakub Ibn Lucifer the Vicegerent] alive; as they suppress the Original Black people the world over trying to keep us Black Original People, The Forgotten People.

This is the real actual truth my people that our enemies are working on in over drive to keep hidden, from black original people the world over. These enemies of black original people use their so-called religions along with their so-called religious books as well as false writings, my people to keep black original people believing in their 6,000-year-old lies. These enemies have absolutely no love for black original people and every chance these enemies believe they have, they will always as well as have try to hurt the Original Black People; and there are more treacherous or conniving than this so-called Sunnah Islam, to Black Original People. Then want to say As Salaam Alaikum and Humdlullah they are more treacherous, deceiving and conniving than any Zionist, Christian or Hindu, when it comes to Black Original People and trying to keep us The Forgotten People; which they can't do my people their time is up our enemies know this to be the actual truth. It doesn't matter how many so-called African Americans join our enemies ranks, the truth of them all has been revealed, the truth of their religions have been revealed, the truth of their politics have been revealed and their disgraceful, disgusting history has also been revealed; all of them my people they all want the Black Original People, to remain The Forgotten People; in which our enemies cannot do and It doesn't matter how many so-African Americans join our enemies ranks; Allah will as well as is destroying them all including this worthless so-called Sunnah Islam, to Black Original People the world over.

In fact, these immigrants so-called Sunnah Islam are cowards as they all run to America because they are all cowards, they all come to America swear a legion to America /Satan The Accursed Devil as they promise to up hold as well as defend White Supremacy and White Nationalism. Even the stupid Africans that come here to America swear their legion to White Supremacy and White Nationalism; and are a tool for White Supremacy and White Nationalism; to help also aid in every way possible to Keep the Black Original People The Forgotten People; as they are nothing but lap dogs always smiling in Caucasian People faces, without any shame at all. You must Original Black People see what our enemies are doing; why our enemies are doing this evil and how our enemies are doing their evil, with impunity so they believe.

What kind of insanity is this my people? America through her laboratories has made a nation of Colored People that buy into this American devilishment of loving everybody. While the ex-slaves of America are ushered into concentration, prisons and horrible deaths; and not one of these discussing immigrants care about black or Indian people and what we had to suffered through here in America. In fact, my people Black People have suffered the most horrifying in the history of our planet for the past 500 years. This worthless Zionist/worthless Christianity/Arab so-called worthless Islam /Worthless Hinduism, are all totally worthless to the rise of black people. The movie industry has painted black people; as fools also, criminals but are kept disenfranchisement, while other people of different races are embraced into this American Society; and these people are on the side of the extermination of black people being and independent self-sufficient enterprising Nation of People; flying their own flag. This is what is being done to black people if you receive any so-called notoriety by our enemies' black people, are always playing a part as a second-class citizen. No different than being clowns for Caucasian people, as they did when they were in Chattel Slavery. It is totally insane to worship these American Negro Athletics when they never come back to black communities, to inspirer young black youth; yet you will find them all in Caucasian communities inspiring Caucasian children and their partners in unholy crimes against black children, for all our multiply enemies children. This is a disgrace my people; this is the disgraceful dream of Martin Luther King Jr. and every time you look at this filthy BET as well as other Zionist Control TV and movies; they our Zionist/Christian/Arab so-called worthless Sunnah Islam/Asian Hinduism America the Accursed Devil, of Global Murdering Terrorist; sit back as they laugh at you while they make billions of dollars from these simple cowardly Colored People called African Americans, this is absolutely disgusting my people.

Black Original People you are the ones this filthy, evil disgusting society are working in over drive, to make sure, you are my people, The Forgotten People. Look at these American Colored People specifically Colored Men are always dressing up and acting as women also these fools believe this is funny American comedy. Where these big strong colored men; ex-football players and basketball players are putting on dresses, to please their 6,000-year-old enemies as well as the enemies of our ancestors, as they act like complete Court Jesters, for our open enemies. Martin Luther King Jr. is an absolute disgrace to our ancestors and you dare call this coward, a hero; when he [Martin Luther king Jr.} was taking his orders from these evil Zionist to destroy his people; and Martin Luther King Jr. along with the Big Six didn't care one bit about their people, if they got paid from their masters. If you are dumb enough to believe these are heroes it is very easy to understand how the rest of these enemies of black people were able to take control, over the economics in every black community throughout America with impunity. In fact, this worthless so-called Sunnah Islam has absolutely nothing to do with Islam being in the Western Hemisphere at all my people. No, my people they are all nothing but worthless, lying demons who are in total support of White Nationalism and White Supremacy; including this worthless so-called Sunnah Islam, for black people period. How many of these so-called worthless Sunnah Islam practioneers are or have given jobs, to any of the foolish black people who are dumb enough to follow this worthlessness? The answer is none my people and this is an absolute fact in which we all know to be true. None of them are to be trusted my people at all and their women are just as much a liar and a deceiver, as their worthless men.

You sit in prison as well as these concentration camps just wasting away still involving yourselves, in the foolishness that got you there. Instead of trying to escape the cage in which our enemies have you entrapped in, you walk around like petty fools not doing anything to help yourselves. Oh yes you will kill your own black brothers and black sisters, sell drugs to your own black brothers also black sisters, destroying black families and black children aiding our enemies, to keep black people disenfranchised; but the enemies that are stealing from you every day, you consider your enemies to be your man your friends. You are too stupid or just too much of a coward, to stand up and be men then do something positive for yourselves as well as your people. You are a joke a complete worthless fool my brothers also sisters, in the eyes of civilized people and the entire world. No, you would rather be The Forgotten People because in truth you are all nothing but cowards who would rather serve the enemies of our ancestors as well as yourselves, rather than stand up for yourselves as black men and black women; and let our enemies as well as the entire world know we will no longer be The Forgotten People and we are going to take our rightful place, on our planet. We must let our enemies know that we have absolutely no use for any of their phony religions, politics or their useless customs at all, including their worthless so-called holy books, that has been as well as always will be worthless and useless to black people.

If you aren't prepared to stand up for yourselves then get out of the way of those of us that refuse to be, The Forgotten People. Through Our Fathers Eyes I looked as well as every other positive black man, black woman and black children are in search of Freedom, Justice and Equality for black self. Get out of the way you cowards you are all a disgrace to our ancestors; no different from these treacherous traitors back in 1964/1965 and 1975.Get out of the way or suffer the consequences of getting in our way as we march towards our Liberation and Salvation. Get out of our way cowards as we return to our self and people. Get out of our way you scared cowards as we returned to the True also Living Allah Almighty who came to us, in the Holy Persons of Master Fard Muhammad to whom all holy praises are due forever. Get out of our way you scared cowards as we returned to the teachings of Allah through the mouth of Allah's Holy Messenger the Most Honorable Elijah Muhammad/Muhammad RasulAllah and the only Muhammad RasulAllah. Get out of our way you scared insane cowards with your grafted teachings dare calling it Islam that you received, from a traitor also a thief. Get out of our way you scared ignorant cowards as you will not only be The Forgotten People you will also be destroyed, along with all the enemies of Allah, Allah's Holy Messenger, our Ancestors as well as our elves. Just get out of the way you scared despicable cowards crawl back on the plantations of America and serve one of the Heads of this American Hydra and their phony religions; this includes this worthless phony so-called Sunnah Islam, for all black people everywhere on our planet.

CHAPTER 15

THE SINS OF THE WORLD FOR THE PAST 6,600 ATLAS

This chapter my people you must pay very close attention due to the lies that this society of Yakub Ibn Lucifer the Vicegerent, wisdom has made as well as this Vicegerent grafted makings along with their false religions and politics have completely tricked and fool you my people; until you just sit by doing absolutely nothing, to prevent this economical as well self-cultured, educational Holocaust that have black people trap and locked into this ongoing Holocaust of the mass of black people, in this American society, where you aren't wanted or needed. These BET movies aren't about or have anything to do with any of Black People True Unlimited History as well as culture, at all. Explain to me this my misguided people; why a black man in the entertainment world; not all my people but the absolute majority; must dress up like a woman tight skirt, high heels, make up talking and acting like a colored woman, with blond or some other silly color hair, explain to me why my people? We my people are carrying the sins of the world upon your shoulders because we aren't supposed to be caught up, in the madness of the end of Yakub's [the Vicegerent] wisdom and world; everyone that buys into this society, will be destroy along with this society, we have already been told this by the Holy Messenger of Allah the Most Honorable Elijah Muhammad/Muhammad RasulAllah. Yet through the plan of the Zionist control American Government plan was being unfold on how to turn brother against brother. The Zionist controlled American Government constructed this Dreadful Civil Rights and Integration movement. Examine the history of the 50s and 60s my people? Examine my people what was happening around the world amongst black people and Latin People that were shaking off America's Colonization and demanded Independence, for their selves. This is what the Holy Messenger of Allah the Most Honorable Elijah Muhammad Our Leader, Teacher and Guide, was involved with gaining Independence for us Black People, here in America as an Independent Black Nation with our own Flag, our Own Declaration of Independence as well as our Own Constitution, to Govern Our Own Black Selves.

My people you must wake up to the truth because you have rejected the Allah of your Salvation and His Holy Messenger, America has importing a smorgasbord of different immigrants to replace you and they all have embraced the American way of life. While this evil Zionist/Christian controlled Movie also Television media went to work on giving to you the absolute lowest, of this American Society and you my people fell for it hook, line and sinker. This couldn't have worked without the help of Martin Luther King Jr. along with the Big Six supporting our enemy's diabolical plans, of Civil Rights and Integration. At the same time this Zionist/Christian American Government went to work on making their selves a Colored People as they began the systematic destruction of Black People. This assignment was given to the CIA, FBI, NSA and every other Gestapo Law Enforcement Agency throughout America. At this time the Holy Messenger of Allah was Spear Heading the Black Revolution as well as Black Nationalism not only in America but the entire Western Hemisphere; with the new true Islam that was taught to him directly from Allah Almighty Himself, in the Holy Person of Master Fard Muhammad to whom all holy praises are due forever, Our Holy Savior and Deliverer my misguided people.

My misguided people haven't a clue that Martin Luther King Jr. along with the Big Six were enemies, of Black People and did everything in their power to help and aid this Zionist/Christian American Government of Murdering Globally Terrorist and now these devils turned their attention on destroying your black people, with the help of Martin Luther King Jr. along with the Big Six. Now you must examine the history my people of this time; America decided to launch a chemical attack on the ex-slave of America and this chemical was Heroin; being imported by this filthy, evil, diabolical Zionist/Christian American Government and embraced by Martin Luther

King Jr., the Big Six and every other Negro Civil Rights Organization in America. So, the War in Viet Nam was a smoke screen; the propaganda of Communism was a complete deception, for the American Government to go and strike a deal with the Hindus in the Northern Region of Viet Nam to supply America with the purist Heroin that has ever been produce. South Viet Nam was already down with America so was South Korea as America re-connected with the defeated army of Chang Ki Check and began importing this Heroin, into Harlem. It didn't matter how many innocent people men, women and children had to die, for America to accomplish this diabolical plan of theirs, at all. Martin Luther King Jr., the Big Six and every other Civil so-called Rights organization were down with this evil including the NAACP, which was formed as well as founded by these Zionist Devils.

It was Martin Luther King Jr. believers that the American Gestapo CIA and the FBI brought this Heroin into Harlem as they enlisted these Southern as well as these ignorant Negroes living in Harlem, to help our enemies destroy every positive Black Movement in America and Black People Period; while Martin Luther King Jr. along with the Big Six as well as every other so-called Civil Rights Organization profited from as they all closed their eyes to the truth, what disgusting cowards my people. All these traitorous so-called Civil Rights Organizations opposed the Holy Messenger of Allah the Most Honorable Elijah Muhammad. All these traitorous so-called Civil Rights Organization rejected the Holy Savior, the Holy Deliverer that our ancestors prayed for, for hundreds of years to come and deliver us out of this hell. You My People Are the Atlas; Carrying the Sins, Of Yakub's World on Your Shoulders; And This Is How It Was Done my people.

Once you believed in these traitors amongst us then began excepting Caucasian People as your friends, while you rejected Allah the Savior of you and His Holy Messenger, you were now condemned by your own actions my people. Now as this Zionist/Christian American Government of Diabolical Murdering Terrorist plan of spreading this poison amongst as well as in every Black Community throughout America, they hit a very, very huge snag; that snag was the Holy Messenger of Allah the Most Honorable Elijah Muhammad/Muhammad RasulAllah. Black People were beginning to wake up as they began gravitating to these wonderful teachings from Allah, which is the true Islam that would free Black People not only in America, but Black People throughout the world.

This is the sixties now my people this is when this diabolical, evil American Government of Murdering Global Terrorist began looking for the traitors amongst, the Holy Messenger. Thus, Enter the Disbeliever also Traitor to Allah's Holy Messenger and father, Wallace D. Mohammed is as well as was a traitor to also for every Black Person, in America and throughout the world. Since the Original True Islam was revealed to One of Us my people by Allah Almighty Himself In Person, not by or to these other fools who stole the Teachings Of Allah Our Holy Savior and tried to change as well as use the Holy teachings of The Original as well as New Islam, to make their self-appeared to be that which they weren't; and many was on the side of this Zionist/Christian American Government of Global Murdering Diabolical Terrorist, pay role also spies for the enemies of all Black Original People. This Zionist/Christian American Government of Global Murdering Terrorist examine the history my people this is what happened during this time period!!!. Now this evil diabolical Zionist Controlled American Government realized that Christianity was surly losing their control of and over the youth, of Black People, in America. They [our Zionist/Christian Enemies] needed a different approach to put the Lion back into the cage. There were two problems that had to be contended with; the first as well as most powerful of our enemy's problems was the Holy Messenger of Allah the Most Honorable Elijah Muhammad/Muhammad RasulAllah Himself; The second was Minister Malcolm and the Disbelievers also Hypocrites were very hateful of Minister Malcolm because Minister Malcolm had the ear of Black people, not only in America but throughout the world. Yet Minister Malcolm allowed himself to be seduced by the Zionist/Christian American Government of Murdering Global Terrorist; Supreme Spy in the Nation of Islam or Islam Here in the Wilderness of North America; as well as the Western Hemisphere period. The plan examines the history all the history of these time periods when the order was Murder the Black Baby by this Zionist/Christian American Government the Real Also True Global Murdering Terrorist. This means this every black man and woman that stopped believing and they were the mass of black people, had a death wish upon them, physically, educationally, economical, emotionally, spiritually, every way possible my people to murder; the Black Thought of Building an Independent, Self Sufficient, Self-Reliable, Government in Some of These

States or Some Place Else; With Our Own Declaration of Independence and Our Own Constitution, Along with Our Own Flag.

Islam was growing amongst Black People the respect for your brother also sister was on the rise, this New Islam Taught Black People in America Who Allah Is; so we black people began doing things for ourselves as days and years went by, Black People for the first time since 1555 began conducting their selves as a Solve rent people and this Zionist/Christian American Government Supreme Agent which is also was Wallach D Mohammed, the Supreme Agent working with Arabs and The Arab's so-called Sunnah worthless Islam into America, to replace the True and Living Islam which had been given by Allah Almighty Himself through the Mouth of His [Allah] Holy Messenger, The Most Honorable Elijah Muhammad. My people the mass of black people were caught up into the transgressions and inquiries, of this Civil Rights and Integration Plans; Yet my people the real and absolute plan was to Murder the Black Baby At Birth; To Murder any thought of Independence for Black People; to Murder the Thought of Building a Nation and Government for their selves; to Murder all thoughts Of Unity Amongst Their Selves; To Murder all thoughts of rejecting Zionism and Christianity along with their mystery god; To Murder all thoughts of having a self-control educational system; Murder all thoughts of manufacturing and distribution of their own self creation. To murder all thoughts of being an engineer, designers, mathematicians; us less they are controlled by us their open and concealed enemies; To Murder all thoughts of becoming doctors and building hospitals for our Black People; To Murder all thoughts of becoming Independent of our Former Slave Masters and build a Nation, for our Black Selves. To Murder all thoughts about ever farming for their own selves and the absolute necessity of farming yourself; thus, being able to control our own food; as well as produce other products from our own farms and dairies; To Murder the Black Baby at Birth My People. You my Black People are carrying or better yet are being punished by Allah, for Rejecting Allah and His Holy Messenger. This worthless so-called Sunnah Islam is part of your Destruction My Black People because it was designed by the Zionist/Christian American Government to incorporate the Arabs worthless so-called Sunnah Islam, for Black People; as one of the heads of this multi headed Hydra American Government; and therefore, you are carrying The Sins of Yakub's Civilization Upon Your Shoulders My People, You Are the Atlas.

The weight of your Rejection of Allah and His Messenger; both of whom were designed, for you my people and the weight of your rejection has brought you to one knee my people. The reason why you can't rise is because you are accepting also following the religions, practices also customs of the enemies of Allah and His Messenger this includes this worthless so-called Sunnah Islam, for all black people. Yet once you reject the Enemies of Allah and Allah's Holy Messenger, we can; also, will defeat our enemies and all our many enemies, phony religions also ideologies as well. This worthless so-called Sunnah Islam is one of the many conspirators in the Murdering of Minister Malcolm as well as many more followers, of Allah Almighty Himself in the persons of Master Fard Muhammad to whom all holy praises are due forever; also, students and followers of the Holy Messenger of Allah the Most Honorable Elijah Muhammad/ the true and only Muhammad RasulAllah. This worthless so-called Sunnah Islam with Wallace D. Mohammed as the Arab League Ambassador, entered into agreement with this Zionist/ Christian American Government of Murdering Global Terrorist; this unholy alliance objective was as well as always will be is to Murder The Black Baby at Birth; one of the many weapons the Leader of the pack is the Zionist; so they enemies [Zionist/ Christianity] knew that it was absolutely Paramount to keep Black Original People believing in the Vicegerent Yakub Ibn Lucifer, the unseen god my people. Islam that was given to Original Black People in the Western Hemisphere, no longer believed in this mystery god teachings; yet we were young very young at this time up against an unmerciful set of enemies and there were plenty of Treacherous Traitors amongst us Black People who were beginning to exit the cage of ignorance, were helping our enemies Zionist/Christians American Government. While the Zionist/Christian American Government were planning on importing this worthless so-called Sunnah Islam, to re-poison also condition Black People, to believe in the enemies of Allah, Allah's Holy Messenger, Our Ancestors as well as ourselves.

This Zionist/Christian American Government of Murdering Global Terrorist then used their propaganda machinery, to present to black people the worst of their society to black people and this was these murdering low life American Gangsters, in which event the Christian Churches bought into it and projected to the mass of black people. My people you are responsible for your own destruction, by believing also practicing, the life style of our open enemies. Examine the history my people these traitors calling themselves building a so-called Black Mafia, were the greatest danger amongst as well as for, the rise of Black People; as they began selling drugs to murder their own people in their fathers and mothers communities also neighborhoods; these traitors were even selling drugs into their Grand Parents neighborhoods as well committing murders, prostitution of young black women and they didn't care one bit; these complete absolute fools were supported by Martin Luther King Jr., the Big Six and every other so-called Civil Rights Organization including the NAACP. These fools only helped black people enemies to destroy as well as break whatever unity, we were building amongst ourselves. None of these traitors cared one bit about helping their people to overcome the 400 years, of oppression their people have been suffering from. Sins of The World for The Past 6,600 years has been placed on your shoulders because you believe, trusted and followed, your 6,000-year-old enemies and the traitors that were amongst us, my people and the traitors of Allah Our Holy Savior and Allah's Holy Messenger.

As this heroin was being distributed throughout every black community in as well as throughout America by the Christian factor amongst black people; Wallace D. Mohammed was working with the Zionist/Christian American Government, with importing these disgusting Arabs and their worthless so-called Sunnah Islam, to replace the Islam that Allah Himself brought to us, my people. So after these Enemies had murdered Minister Malcolm which was headed by this dis-believer Wallace D, Mohammed; they believed that they could insert this worthless so-called Sunnah Islam, amongst black people in America thus dragging the mass of black people, back into worshipping the falsehood of our enemies; but it failed my people this was in 1965 my people; while the Christians were the stupid silly puppets selling our enemies poisons, amongst their own people, believing they were untouchable. All these stupid Fools were doing was only killing and destroying their own people also these fools believed that they were loved also respected by our enemies. These drugs dealing simple minded fools aren't heroes my people they are all the enemies of their people and if you love any of them, then you are an ignorant, stupid fool also; that should never be trusted by black people that are working on rising out of these ashes, from the hell fire of these traitors Betrayal and Treachery to their own people. Thus, placing the Sins of Past 6,600 years on you my people and these traitors didn't care one bit my people. The only fools that will glorify and praise these traitors are stupid, ignorant, silly want to be Traitors their selves. In other society or people that encountered these traitors amongst them, these traitors would have been executed without hesitation publicly and their names erased from the history books; except you ignorant, horribly miss-guided black people, praising the enemies of the rise of black people and all the evils, they all did to their own people. Praising the enemies of Allah and His Holy Messenger look at yourself now you ignorant fools, still a slave of a mental death and power; first to these evil Zionist and Christians and now to this worthless so-called Sunnah Islam; that was imported by this Zionist/Christian American Government of Global Murdering Terrorist; to destroy black people as these cowards [worthless Sunnah Islam] keep White Supremacy and White Nationalism alive, not only in America but throughout the world.

Through Our Fathers Eyes my people which we all must examine everything through and never through the eyes of our enemies and this worthless so-called Sunnah Islam is the secret enemy of Black People not only in America, but throughout the world. Yet my people these enemies can no longer hide in the dark or behind made up rituals, these grafted devils have made over a short period of time for themselves; yet in their heart they held as well as still hold, hatred for Allah's Holy People which is us my people and not this worthless so-called Zionism or this worthless so-called Christianity, or this worthless so-called Sunnah Islam, or this worthless so-called Hinduism; they are all the enemies of Allah the True and Living Allah, the open enemies of Allah's last and Greatest Messenger the Most Honorable Elijah Muhammad/Muhammad RasulAllah, our Ancestors as well as our enemies; everyone one of them my people are the enemies to every black person on our planet and the history will verify everything I am saying is the absolute truth.

So my people due to your profound ignorance as well as your undeliverable refusal to submit to the Holy Savior also Deliverer that our Ancestors, prayed for, for hundreds of hellish years, that even these water down movies, made by the Zionist will never capture and these enemies of ours will never tell you the real truth about the real evils, they have done to us; and remember my people this worthless so-called Sunnah Islam was also is apart, of Murdering The Black Baby At Birth My People. How can you my people sit back and believe in these lies that our enemies are telling you, every one of them my people are our enemies especially this worthless make believe so-called Sunnah Islam, when in truth this is nothing, but advance Christianity and they are all liars my people. Casting their wicked, evil, diabolical sins against Allah and His Holy Messenger, on you black people for you to endure and carry the burdens of their Maker Yakub [the Vicegerent] the maker of this grafted devil and this worthless so-called Sunnah Islam; You My People Are The Atlas that is subsuming this indescribable burden so our enemies can live comfortable, while black people suffer unimaginable sufferings under this worthless Zionist/ this worthless so-called Christianity/this Arab worthless so-called worthless Islam/ this worthless so-called Hinduism American Government of Murdering Global Terrorist and these are the Four Heads of the Dreaded American Dragon; that are keeping you locked in your cage Black People, for the past 450/500 years and you are still locked into this cage that this Four Headed Dragon called the America Government, to keep black people imprisoned in.

I heard this silly ignorant so-called Sunnah Islam practioneers say to me I'm not buying coffee from Star Bucks because they detonate to the murdering of Muslims. Yet this same cowardly ignorant hypocrite is working for the same machinery that is also contributing, to the murdering of Muslims and this same cowardly hypocrite, loves these Zionist Devils. Why do these cowardly worthless so-called Sunnah Islam practioneers, are supporting this worthless, evil, diabolical Zionism Saladin? This is the reason my Black people; they are all grafted out of the Original People By Their God Also Maker Yakub Ibn Lucifer the Vicegerent; maker and father of this Devil, which is Supreme Evil and this worthless so-called Islam is a part of this Supreme Evil due to them all, coming from the same maker Yakub Ibn Lucifer the Evil, diabolical also lying Vicegerent; whom he Yakub the Vicegerent, left complete instructions, diagrams and plans, for all of the top administrators and this was to be kept secret from all others, of their own kind. Therefore, the Zionist seized control over all the writings of their maker, all the future of their maker, how they were to accomplish these plans and how to use religion as a weapon, against the mass of people. Yakub even left for them where to locate the minerals, elements, where these resources were at and who were the owners of these resources; also that they must murder Black Men, Women and Children by the hundreds of millions; and set their maker Yakub the Vicegerent Wisdom as God, Allah, Jehovah and anything else these fools choose to call him and the Zionist Knows Best above all of the others of Yakub Makings; much better than this worthless so-called Sunnah Islam and this is why here in America Saudi Arabia as well in fact throughout the Mid-East and North Africa also, are under the control of the Zionist and have been for the past 4,000 years.

You my people are carrying the sins of these worthless enemies of the Universal Creator, who rules all life on the seven planets of life on them very similar to ours and the entire universe including the Sun; so that all of our enemies can live the lives also build the world, their maker Yakub had designed for them 6,600 years ago and you should be able to see what they [Yakub the Vicegerent Makings] have made, it is written in the 18th Chapter of the Revelations by Yakub the Vicegerent, under the name of John the Revelator; this is a name that was kept hidden, from you my Black people; even from the mass of Yakub's makings yet, held also kept in secret by the Zionist. A thirdly third-degree Mason is not privilege to the true Plans, of their maker Yakub Ibn Lucifer the Vicegerent, only in certain degrees and this worthless so-called Sunnah Islam is absolutely a part of this thirty-third-degree Masonry my people; and therefore, Allah the Universal Creator, can't be seen by any of Yakub's makings; so why put any trust or belief in any of Yakub's Grafted Makings, My Black People in America As Well As Black People Throughout the World. History will always prove that none of these Yakub's makings are worthy or worth that we Black People should be, carrying the sins of these devils on our shoulders any longer.

We my people must cast down the life styles, religions, beliefs, customs and practices of our enemies and re-create our own way of life, our own beliefs, our own customs, our own practices, then you my people will be able to cast off your shoulders the Sins of Yakub's Civilizations for The Past 6,600 years. We all must return to the Holy Savior also Deliverer that our Ancestors prayed for those many ungodly centuries, at the murdering clutches of these Caucasian Devils. My people in America as well as throughout the world this Mighty One Came to Us in the Holy Person of Master Fard Muhammad, Allah Almighty in person to whom all Holy Praises are due forever. We all must follow the teachings also programs given to us all, by Allah through

His Last also Greatest Messenger the Most Honorable Elijah Muhammad the True and only Muhammad RasulAllah; no matter what our enemies are trying to claim, we must all remember that our enemies are all complete and absolute Liars, and this includes this worthless so-called Sunnah Islam; in which absolutely no black people should give two cents for. When you hear that our enemies are killing their selves, women as well as their children, we should praise our Holy Savior Allah Almighty the Lord Of Retribution and feel what our enemies felt for our Ancestors as well as our selves, when they were murdering us and are still murdering black people with all of the poisons also false lies that they spread amongst black people; as they care absolutely nothing about the evil they all have done to black people and this includes this worthless so-called Sunnah Islam.

We must stand up against this evil my people in America and throughout the world and let all our enemies know, that we are no longer carrying the sins of their maker and god Yakub Ibn Lucifer the Vicegerent. Once we do this as we focus on looking Through Our Fathers Eyes you see our enemies are nothing but scared rodents, trying to hide from their ultimate faith in which they can't my Black People. All their phony religions, religious books, paintings, drawings, customs, politics, practices and everything else about them, will be as well as are being destroyed, as I write these words. I'm standing on the Square of Truth My Black People and I'm not afraid the reason why I'm not afraid is due to Allah Almighty Himself is behind me in the person of Master Fard Muhammad, to whom all holy praises are due forever. I submit, follow as well as a student of Allah's last and greatest Messenger the Most Honorable Elijah Muhammad the True and Only Muhammad RasulAllah. Though I walked through this Valley of Death which is America I fear not the evils, the lies, the threats, and the deceit of our enemies because Allah Himself is my Sheppard and I will have no other Allah than Him. So let our enemies gather in secret council together, as they have been doing for the past 6,000 years plotting the Murder of the Truth Bearer, I fear Allah Almighty Himself and not a one of our enemies, So let these Worthless Zionism/so let these worthless Christians/ so let these worthless So-called Sunnah Islam practioneers/so let these worthless so-called Hinduism practioneers bring it; I Stand On The Square Of Truth Given to Us By Allah Almighty Himself Through the Mouth of His Allah's Holy Messenger; I Challenge this Four Headed Hydra called the American

Government because it is the time, to make War With the Beast My Black People Globally.

This isn't a war for the fearful or the doubt full this is the war for the faithful my people because our enemies will absolutely be wipe out of the memory, of our History also our minds. Their phony religions will be completely wipe out of History as well as memory; their wicked customs will be wiped out of History and memory; their phony religious books will be wipe out of History and memory; their grafted languages will be wiped out of History and memory; everything about all our enemies will be completely wiped out of History and memory, So Saith Allah Almighty Himself. If you are dumb enough to support or side up with Allah's enemies you also will be wiped out of History and memory, so make your choice my people because the Devine Destruction Is Hear; it's not coming my people it is here right now as we live and breathe. This is the War of Armageddon my Black People; this is Al-Jihad My Black People not this absolute nonsense our enemies are lying about including this worthless so-called Sunnah Islam. The War of Armageddon; Al-Jihad is Black Original People verses the grafting also makings of Yakub Ibn Lucifer the Vicegerent; all of their filthy, evil, phony and deceit religions; their filthy, evil, deceitful politics, their filthy evil customs that they stole from Black People and perverted them, their filthy, evil practices, their filthy, evil lies, their filthy evil, evil, deceitful way of life, their filthy, evil lying History, My Black People Domestically as well as Globally and this includes this worthless so-called Sunnah Islam, the enemies of Allah and Allah's Holy Messenger/Muhammad RasulAllah.

Black People in America and throughout the world we are the Atlas carrying Yakub Ibn Lucifer the Vicegerent grafted people sins on our shoulders, for the past 6,600 years, it has reached it Supreme Evil Heights, in the 500 years; and now is the time for Black People to quake and erupt, so that we can shake these demons off of us, every one of them along with their worthless religions as well as their worthless religious books, worthless politics, worthless practices, worthless customs, worthless grafted languages also worthless dialects and everything else about all of them My Black People. Our enemies do not remember Allah since Allah the True and Living Allah, never made His Holy Presence Known to any of them because none of them worthy, they will know only Allah's Devine Raft. Allah the All Knowing as well as the All Wise is not fooled by these demons or what these demons have done as well as are still continually doing. So, all Black People Enemies also Allah as well as Allah's Holy Messenger enemies; so-called prayers they are always asking Allah to guide them or protect them or something else, as they continue to commit evils as well as practice evils every day, here in America and throughout the world. My Black People you must realize that these are Historical Facts of History My Black People that can examine see this is the absolute truth.

Look at your condition from worshipping some mystery god or some dead prophet; when I say dead, I don't mean this in a derogatory manner, my people. What I'm saying is that the wisdom of these Prophets is non-applicable, in this day and time in which we are living in my people. This is why Allah Himself came and raised up from amongst us the ex-slave of this Zionist/Christian American Government of Domestic Murders with absolute Impunity, the First Born Of Allah Himself; In The Land Where No Holy Man, Has Ever Came Before Which Is The Western Hemisphere, in search of Ibrahim's lost seed and that lost seed of Ibrahim's is us My People the Ex-slave of America and absolutely no other people, this is why Allah Manifested Himself to the Lost Seed Of Ibrahim to fore full His Promise To Ibrahim; this was in the year of 6,400, 2,000 years before the birth of Yakub Ibn Lucifer who would become the Vicegerent and the Maker also Father of the Devil, Yakub's grafted people.

You my people are carrying the sins of every immigrant in America on your shoulders and have been for the past 500 years. None of these immigrants or strange people; don't care anything about you because you don't care about yourself, women or children. Black men women also standing on corners or riding the trains, begging for money before you stand up and do something for yourself. You would rather wallow in the mud like pigs rather than stand up and do something for yourself. You Black People have allowed our enemies to reduce you to nothing and you haven't the courage to stand up and do something for yourself. Your rather buddy up with your enemies as they sell drugs to your people, killing women and children, before you do something to stop these enemies from destroying your people, with their poisons cocaine, heroin, crystal meth; pills and other poisons. You are so stupid to learn, a trade, a skill something that you could use, to aid yourself and people. These so called black women have only one desire and that is to look, dress and act like Caucasian Women how disgusting my people. When History clearly reveals these religions all of them are the death for black people always have been the death for black people and they always will be the death for black people not only in America but throughout the world; and you silly ignorant foolish black men women especially are still following also believing the lies, taught to you by our enemies and the enemies, of our ancestors this is absolutely disgraceful Black People; this worthless so-called Sunnah Islam is one of the heads of Four Headed Dragon/Hydra.

Black People in the prisons of America; Black People in the concentration camps of America stop listening to these false teachings, that offers you no direction, no solutions, no progress and no change in your behavior; then you dare call yourself god when you are doing absolutely nothing to change your conditions, this is also disgraceful my black people. Our enemies are elated that you follow these false teachings because the authors of these false teachings, when our enemies know that they were agents of the American Government; working with the government to stop the rise of black people and turn black people away from our Holy Savior Allah in person and Allah's Holy Messenger. In truth they were nothing but thieves and robbers in which I wouldn't give any of them no more consideration than I give this worthless Zionism, this worthless Christianity, this worthless so-called Sunnah Islam and this worthless Hinduism. Thieves also Liars my people for the purpose to mislead black people away from our salivation, in which they have all done every one of them. You believe in the agents working for the Zionist/Christian American Government of Global Murdering Terrorist, as they grafted and changed the teachings of Allah Almighty the True and Living Allah and His Last Holy also Greatest Messenger.

Since many of these government agents were now supported by this Zionist/Christian American Government of Global Murdering Terrorist, the FBI, CIA, NYPD, CPD, PPD, DTP, and every other member of this American Gestapo called Law Enforcement Agencies were able to move among black people and spy on black people and report back to their Precincts, or FBI Headquarters, CIA Headquarters and NSA Headquarters then were able to construct the plan to murder or imprisoned many black men even some women and get away these murders with impunity. As this Zionist/Christian American Government of Murdering Global Murdering

Terrorist, were negotiating with the Arabs through the Arab's Ambassador Wallace D. Mohammed, to begin importing these Arab enemies into America along with their worthless Sunnah Islam. Our Zionist and Christian enemies knew these fools most them so caught up into the drugs as well as being completely fooled by their enemies, couldn't see what was happening as well as who was responsible as well as who was helping our enemies, to accomplish their ultimate goals of Murdering the Black Baby at Birth and placing Black People back into the cage, in which they had built for us all, over 500 years ago.

These are absolute facts of History my people that can be proven at any given time if you could read and understand. When these young men come out of prison many of them will end up in the concentration camps throughout America, with absolutely no hope, training or even skills to provide for their selves let alone their women and children. Instead of following the teachings and programs of Allah's Last and Greatest Messenger, they decided to follow the enemies of Black People. So, what did these young ignorant fools invested in? They chose to invest in corruption and the destruction of their people because many them didn't want to work, or go to school, or learn a trade, or some skill, so most of the youth became crack dealers and murderers of their own people. Picking up where the Heroin Dealers that preceded them, left off at; as many of the black youth nationwide, ended up in prisons with long prison terms; in many cases even gunned down by themselves in the streets in fact these youths became nothing more but hyenas against their own people and communities throughout America. Now when these youth who won't be youth any longer get out of prison they will be late 40s or early 50s, with absolutely nothing to offer their selves, people or communities. What have you received or gained by following the life style of our enemies, my young brothers and sisters? What have any of you contributed positively to yourself, your people, your women and children, by following the life style that our enemies laid out for you? When you are release from prisons then return to the neighborhoods that helped destroy; and find out that you have absolute no control in the community at all? How are you going to feel when you see our enemies have gained complete control over the economy, the housings, the education and everything else in the community? How will you feel when all you have left is to Carry The Sins of The World For The Past 6,600 years, on your shoulders and you are down on one knee because these sins are very heavy; especially the sins you have committed against your own people as you Denounce Allah Our Holy Savior and His Allah's Holy Messenger, for the love also life style of our many enemies, their religions, their politics, their customs and just plain nonsense, my young brothers and sisters.

CHAPTER 16

THE STRUGGLE WITHIN

The Struggle Within my people is what you are all face with right now as you try and fool yourself it doesn't matter. Well it does matter, and it matters greatly after you sit back and examine what you are responsible for doing, then what you must answer to yourself, is what can I do to help improve the conditions of my and people. It will be a shame to come out of prison and you didn't learn a damn thing about the errors of your ways also your actions and how destructive your actions were, against your own people. It will be a shame that you spent all this time in prison and didn't re-evaluate the ideologies that you ascribe to, that did absolutely nothing to change your attitude towards yourself also your people. It will be a shame that after spending years and years in prison and you didn't re-evaluate the results that you were a part of destroying yourself, women and children; by following the worst that this American society gave you, when you had a defendant choice to reject this way of life; after all you had concrete proof that this life style would only bring down death also destruction on yourself and people. It would be a shame to know that you spent many years in prison and didn't re-evaluate who are the enemies of yourself and people; then change your course of actions to help black people rather than destroy black people. It would be a crying shame that after all of years you spent in prison you are just as ignorant as you were, when you arrived in prison and change anything to improve your thought pattern. Now you are face to face with your own destructive behavior in your community and amongst your own people. This is the Struggle Within that you must face or are you going to come out of prison and embrace our many enemies' way of life, our enemies' religions, our enemies' politics, our enemies' customs and are afraid to stand up to do something for ourselves, with you people to better ourselves.

We are all face with this Struggle Within my people it is more difficult to continue keeping the blinders on pretend, that nothing has ever happened while black people are still disenfranchised, are still economically at the mercy of our enemies, are still at the mercy of the poorest educational system, in the world; are still blind to the reality of who are our enemies as our enemies laugh at you, in your face. The Struggle Within is the truth that we all must face and you my people must face up to the fact these are, the enemies of black people throughout America as well as throughout the world. If you aren't strong enough or have the courage to acknowledge that our enemies are running the economy, in black communities throughout America. My people; there is no doubt that this worthless Zionism/this worthless Christianity/this worthless so-called Sunnah Islam/this worthless Hinduism are all the enemies of black people and history verifies this is the absolute truth my people. In fact, all these grafted ideologies are useless because none of them offer black people any economical relief, none of them offer black people any educational relief, none of these grafted ideologies offer black people any religious relief and none of these false ideologies also religions will ever free black people, from their cage of absolute despair, suffering, always at the mercy of our enemies. Through Our Fathers Eyes is the only true way to deal with the Struggle Within my people and not through the eyes of our enemies.

All these strange people with their false religions are all the enemies of black people and history proves that they always have been, and they always will be. If our enemies can keep you an economical slave for them our enemies will as well as are safe, as they nave black people in the same position as their brothers the Zionist and Christians; to rob also take advantage of, by our enemies. Our enemies are happy as they praise their Maker Yakub Ibn Lucifer the Vicegerent and some even dare call him Allah; Yakub Ibn Lucifer is the Vicegerent is the Father also Maker of Satan The Accused Devil. Allah Almighty Himself; through the mouth of His Allah last also Greatest Messenger the Most Honorable Elijah Muhammad/is the True also Only Muhammad RasulAllah. All these people are our enemies as they are doing everything within their power, to keep you locked in this cage and they have absolutely no thought of setting black people free from this cage.

The Struggle Within my people must be dealt with in one self as well as a body of people; then and only then can you enter my people Into The Battle In The Sky my people. The Battle of Armageddon; is also referred to also as Al Jihad. Following the path of our enemies, have gotten black people deeper into hell then they ever have been because now you believe your enemies are your friends. Before this Most Evil Civil Rights and Integration you knew who, your enemies were; now today's time you can't, even recognize your enemies; nor can you recognize how dangerous our enemies truly are to black people. It's unbelievable that you can believe that you are an American when all the mass of black people has only received is the worst, from what America gave black people and you must be able to see this, my people, its right in front of your face. What's the matter now you don't have any heart to stand up for yourself, but you have the heart to help and aid our enemies to destroy, your own people. You don't have any heart to unite as we honor the prayers of our ancestors and separate ourselves, from whatever, crawled out of the Pits of Hell as our great grandfather said back in the late 1700s after the Revolutionary War and they never saw any worthless so-called Sunnah Islam, nor did they know anything about Islam, until the late 1700s brought by the Honorable Prince Hall and then later in the early 1900s by the Honorable Prophet Noble Drew Ali. May the Peace Also Blessings of Allah, Be Upon Them All.

This is the Struggle Within my people that you must step up and face up to the truth, to whom all our enemies are. If you can't then at least we know, that you want to be a colored person and nothing else; but a cowardly Negro waiting to do the bidding of one of the Four Heads of this Four Headed Hydra, that call their selves this American Government of Murdering, Thieving Global Terrorist. My people we must make a stand to do something for ourselves rather than play games like write your letter and I will give you an X. This is nonsense my people Allah already gave us the ninety-nine names all one must do, is choose the name that fit your personality. Stay away from everyone that is saying write your letter to me this is nonsense and it shows absolutely no growth or development at all, by trying to replicate things that were done many decades ago; this isn't being fast moving and fast thinking into the modern day and time at all, my people. We must elevate our thinking my people all you have to do is reclaim your own and live according to the teachings that our only also true leader as well as our only teacher the Most Honorable Elijah Muhammad; the last also greatest Messenger of Allah; the True and Only Muhammad RasulAllah. It is time that we stand up my people so that we can begin to do something for ourselves, besides laying down begging our enemies, for subsistence because you are too much of a coward to do something for yourself.

Through Our Fathers Eyes is the only way we can free ourselves my people, from this multi headed dragon or serpent, of our open enemies and bring them to a most deserving an unmerciful destruction, to them all. Look at these commercials that is being produce by the American Marketing also media are projecting these Caucasian Arab women, and this is more evidence proves that this worthless so-called Sunnah Islam, is one of the partners, of this Hydra called the American Government. This isn't Islam at all my people these are the lies being produce by the enemies of Allah, Allah's Holy Messenger, our ancestors as well as ourselves; ever since they came out of the test tubes of Yakub Ibn Lucifer the Vicegerent, on the Island of Pelan 6,600 years ago. This same worthless so-called Sunnah Islam is a part of the Most Evil, Diabolical, Despicable Trans-Atlantic Slave Trade; this is a matter of actual Historical Facts. America my people is nothing, but Satan's Pit filled with every foul, evil and hateful bird [meaning people] that have come care to die, by the waft of Allah because these are all part of this evil Mankind. The Struggle Within my people are you too much of a coward that you will stand by and let your enemies, get away with the evils they all have done as well as they continue to do. Yet when it comes down to murdering your own self, women and children you cowardly so-called gangsters none of you cowards will hesitate, to murder yourself. Rather than Honor Our Ancestors you cowards would rather honor and praise, the enemies of our Ancestors what a disgrace you coward are. In fact, you cowards are nothing but Negro Colored People Disgraceful to Your Selves and useless to any intelligent being on our planet; and you call yourself gangsters I call you all cowardly Negro Worthless Fools and you all deserve to suffer more than what you all, suffer in your master's prisons.

This is the Struggle Within my people where the time has come that you Black Man Stand Up for Yourself and to you Black Woman Stand Up for Yourself and Do Something for Yourself or die right along with our enemies a very horrible and unmerciful death; never ever to be mention again, in history or memory. The Struggle Within in my people must be face straight on if you believe that you matter in this Hydra, called America, you are delusional my people; absolutely and totally delusional which is disgraceful of you my people; not to stand up for yourself, unify yourself and stand as one, as an Independent Nation of Black People; ready, willing and able to make every sacrifice to re-establish ourselves as Civilize, Cultured, Intelligent, Innovative, with self-creativity, self-reliability, with an understanding and responsibility to Honor Our Flag and no other Flag. The Flag Of Islam Given To Us By Allah Almighty Himself, In The Person Of Master Fard Muhammad To Whom All Holy Praises Are Due Forever; In Which Allah Almighty Himself Prepared the Last and Greatest Messenger From Amongst Us; the Most Honorable Elijah Muhammad/the True Also Only Muhammad RasulAllah; Taught Us All what He Received From Allah, For Us Allah.

Nothing else on this planet will save black people from the Unimaginable and Absolute Hell that we Black People, the World; Over Have Been Suffering Under For The Past 500 years. The reason being is that nothing else, gives black people independency, from our enemies; you if you want to disgrace yourself before the world for the recognition, for the make-believe conception that our enemies, are our friends and this Most Dreadful Also Deadly Integration, That Has Brought Every Kind of Filthy, Evil Spirit Amongst Ourselves. That Isn't Of Any Good For Black People In America, Or Any Place Else For Black People On Our Planet. How Great Your love For Our Enemies The Devil; Over The Love Of Our Ancestors; The Love Of Our Ancestry, the Love Of Our Unlimited Heritage, The Love Of Our Women And Children, The Love Of Our Culture, The Love For Our Self; The Love Of Allah Himself And The Love Also Labor, Of Allah's Last And Greatest Messenger. There is nothing my people worth having for black people other than what Allah Himself Brought And Gave To Black People, Through His Holy Messenger; Absolutely Nothing My People And This Includes This Worthless So- Called Sunnah Islam And Every Other Phony Made Up Worthless Religions, Of The Makings Of Yakub Ibn Lucifer/Vicegerent On The Island Of Pelan 6,600; Whom The Vicegerent Makings Are Trying To Convince Black People He Is Allah. Yet My People Allah The true And Living Allah Has Revealed the True Identity of This Mystery God, My People I Already Told You Who He Is And What His Name Is Also What His Position Was For The Past 6,600 Years And Now It Is Over.

The Struggle Within My People; What Are You Afraid Of? That you will have to stand up and be a man or be a woman and take responsibility for yourself, then do something to change your condition? That you have may have to lay your life down for Freedom and Independence? What are you afraid of is it that you are just a disbeliever in the Allah our Holy Most Merciful Savior and Allah's Last, Holy also Greatest Messenger and our Ancestors? You rather believe in this so-called mystery god also enemies of our ancestors as well as yourselves, rather than believe in yourself. What are you afraid my people when we are in the Most Critical time, the Day Of Decision; and now you don't have any heart; now the true cowardice emerges in you, so this make you worthless as well as useless to the rise of black people Globally, as well as domestically. Through Our Fathers Eyes My People we should be looking through and not through the eyes of our enemies, whose absolute destruction is happening right now. These are our Fathers Enemies in the past and they are our enemies today; they will be the enemies of our grandchildren and our great grandchildren; this is the Plan of this Hydra the American Government, of Global Murdering Terrorist.

We are living in the day of decision my people and you are all afraid to stand up for yourself and do something for yourself, independent of your slave masters. Our enemies are revealing the truth of what lies in their hearts and their minds and you silly Negroes walk around believing you are an American and you are the only people that can't feed or house, your own families; because you some filthy Caucasian Women is ready to lie down with you. There are plenty of historical facts that this same beast will lie down and procreate with anything, as she did in the caves of West Asia now called Europe. All these Negro/colored women in America it doesn't matter where they come from, when they get here to America they submit to America the Accursed Devil and turn the male children into nothing but a bunch of worthless homosexuals. Any man that believe that a house/ houses or fine car/cars define you as being a man, is a sorry excuse of a black man and a perfect example of an enemy of their own ancestors; and lovers of the devil himself. These cowards are afraid to stand up and be men they only want to be servants of the enemies of Allah, Allah's Holy Messenger as well as their own Ancestors. Even these silly so-called Africans that called themselves following this worthless so-called Sunnah Islam, are nothing but servants, of this Four Headed Hydra America the Accursed Devil. If they these fools believe in the eyes of Caucasian People, that they are better than the so-called American Negro, these so-called Africans are extremely happy. They don't even speak their own language their language is either French or English, when they communicate with other so-called Africans that aren't of their tribe. When these so-called Africans speak to members of their tribe, they speak in dialects understood only by members of their tribes and the devil.

Through Our Fathers Eyes My People and never through the eyes of our father's enemies, as you receive the crumbs from our enemies table. You may call it business, but it isn't business it just you are selling out like every other immigrant, that has come to America and are still coming to America. You are nothing but an absolute disgrace to our Ancestors as well As a disgrace to Allah and Allah's Last and Greatest Messenger. This is the Struggle Within My People in which we all must face and there is absolutely no chance of any of us, getting around this truth at all. Our enemies are revealing to you that this Christianity is nothing but absolute lies. The history reveals that this worthless so-called Sunnah Islam is the enemy of Black People domestically, as well as globally. It wasn't until Yakub Ibn Lucifer [in the Quran-a Yakub is refer to as the Vicegerent]; makings came amongst us. In the Revelations Yakub's makings, is called the Pale Rider; and Hell Followed With Him. Who have more proof than us Black People And the so-called American Indian; in fact, the entire world of Original People have 6,600 years of physical proof, that the Caucasian Race Is the Pale Rider Absolutely and Hell as Followed with, for every Original Being on our planet.

The last 500 years have been an absolute, complete, horrible and most diabolical nightmare, that any Original Being Could Ever Imagine; Up to This Very Day and Time of these writing; and no one can deny what I'm saying isn't the truth. You may not like what I'm saying; you may not like the way I'm saying it; never the less it Remains The Absolute and Sure Truth. I Received These Teachings From He Who Walked With Allah Himself Our Holy Savior; I Received These Wonderful Teachings From He Who Was Taught By Allah, The Most High, The All Knowing, The Most Merciful, The most Beneficent; Refer To As Rebill Ala Mien; The Lord Of All The World, In the Quran-an; Face To Face For 3 Years and 4 months and absolutely no one could prove that he didn't, including the scholars of this so-called Orthodox which has proven to be worthless to Black People, ever since they started their heavy migration into America after 1975. I am a student also follower of this Holy Messenger Of Allah the Most Honorable Elijah Muhammad/Muhammad RasulAllah. I submit to the Allah of Elijah and never will I submit to any mystery god by whatever names, these foolish people and their foolish religions may call him. I submit to the Allah of Elijah The True and Living Allah; He Almighty Allah Himself His Wisdom Is Seen, Heard also Felt Every Where, on our planet and throughout the Entire Universe; This Is Universal Justice my people; This Mighty One Came and Visited Us My People; This Supremely Powerful One Where There Is None His Equal Nor Is There Any Liken Un To Him, Came To Us Fools of The Planet as Allah's Holy Messenger taught us all; In the Person Of Master Fard Muhammad To whom All Holy Praises Are Due For Ever.

The Struggle Within my people not only in America but throughout the world it is time we shake off every version of Yakub's plans of deceiving Black People or Original People everywhere, on our planet. One of Yakub's Regulations; and this Regulation [will later become a law]; has been perhaps the most effective way, to control a mass of people, is to take their language away, take their beliefs away, take their way of life from them, place fear in their hearts by using the most unimaginable, the most horrible; by the most unmerciful, un moral people ever to walk our planet; then give these colonized Original People Your Way Of Life, Your Concept Of Religion, Your Dilution Of The True Scriptures And History And Your Language, which is their way of life, lying, deceiving, murdering, stealing, rape, enslavement every kind of atrocity, only a devil could imagine and carry out; and this is the language of Yakub Ibn Lucifer the Vicegerent, whose Wisdom would stand in the place of the True and Living Allah's Wisdom for 6,000 years; my people those 6,000 years are up and now only destruction is what Yakub's making is receiving as I write these words, my deceived Black People.

I know that our enemies are going to try and discredit what I'm saying even the American Gestapo will even attack me, my people and I know this; yet I fear them not I fear Allah in the person of Master Fard Muhammad, to whom all holy praises are due forever. I was born and raised in supreme Iniquity; I was born and raised in supreme Transgressions; I was born and raised in supreme Sin, for the past 450 years and I'm still living amongst the sinful, as I write these words. So, I expect our enemies come and attack me I have no doubt; nevertheless, my faith, my trust, belief and protection are in the Hands of Allah Almighty, the Great Mahdi, and the Great Christ, Our Holy Savior to whom all holy praises are due forever. I am a student and follower of the Holy Messenger as well as a follower of teachings of the Holy Messenger, in which he received from Allah Face to Face.

The Struggle Within my people will separate you from all the falsehood that has over taken America like a great plague, is also affecting you as well as keeping you deaf, dumb and blind; which means keeping you confined in the cage, as the trapped Lion., my people. Walking Back and forth between the Hatred of George Washington and The Hatred of Dishonest Abraham Lincoln; now you have a statue of Martin Luther King between both devils, as his insane dream has led to the slaughter of millions and millions of Black People in America and aided in the making of this American Hydra Him and Wallace D. Mohammed. I hear on TV and movies young black men saying I got to get out of these streets; yet they don't even consider who made this hell for them. The majority; of black youths in black communities throughout America are trying to get a scholarship, in some sport or the other and in many cases ends up in hell much worst, then the hell they come from. Every one of these youths or young black men young black women included, should be thinking how the help can improve on the conditions of the community in which they come from, where their parents come from, where their grandparents come from and in many cases where their great grandparents come from and in some cases a hundred years or even better. Black People and all Black Children should cast off this insanity of American Pride and the American Flag; and embrace the greatest Flag In The Universe known; given to us by Allah Almighty Himself, through His Holy Messenger the Most Honorable Elijah Muhammad.

How can you can sit by and ignore this most wonderful truth about our most Horrible Enemies; as if the truth doesn't matter and it is the truth that will set us all free. Our Dear Holy Apostle whom I love second to only Master Fard Muhammad Allah Almighty Himself; in person, to whom all Holy Praises Are Due Forever; as the Holy Apostle Taught Us All To Do. Only Colored People believe that they have arrived; only believers in this insane dream, of Martin Luther King Jr. along with the Big Six I mention this before in America's Indictment and named the Big Six; and the evil that Martin Luther King Jr. and his Cahoots sold their people, their brothers and sisters the ex-slaves of America out to; examine the history for real my people.

BET is owned by the Zionist, Death Jam Records is owned by the Zionist nothing belongs to those the young black men and woman, that created it all. My people you are Super Talented and all these interlopers; know this; all these makings of Yakub Ibn Lucifer the Vicegerent, are stealing your ideas my people, from you and these demons give black people absolutely nothing, except Mental Slavery Always At the mercy Of Our Open Enemies; Always at the Mercy of This Four Headed Hydra, the American Government of Global, Murdering Devils.

Trying to avoid or evade the Struggle Within is only driving black people deeper and deeper into this cage of total ignorance and despair, with absolutely no relief on the horizon at all. The reason being is that you my people have denounce and rejected the relief that came to you. If you are such cowards that you would rather prey on your selves like savage canines, then you deserve all the misery you are receiving from your masters. Things that are happening around the world my people are not just by chance? No, my people this is the destruction of Yakub Ibn Lucifer the Vicegerent, world, makings and his Yakub's Wisdom. It doesn't matter how powerful this Insane Giant called Goliath may present itself to be, my people; Goliath will be destroyed by the wisdom and unmatchable power of Allah Almighty Himself; the True and Only Living Allah; in The Persons of Master Fard Muhammad; to Whom All Holy Praises Are Due Forever. Allah's Last and Greatest Messenger is the Most Honorable Elijah Muhammad; in which as Allah open my eyes wider, I soon learned that the Most Honorable Elijah Muhammad is the Muhammad RasulAllah, written in the Quran-an. These Arabs or so-called Sunnah worshipers are purposely misleading black people, away from the truth of whom, the True Muhammad RasulAllah is. My people I and there are many others spread about, are the True Believers also the True Followers as well as Students; Of Muhammad RasulAllah; My People as well as the Entire World the Most Honorable Elijah Muhammad is the True Muhammad RasulAllah; anything else or anyone else is a complete lie and total fabrication, by the enemies of Allah Himself; the enemies of Allah's Last Holy and Greatest Messenger; and Our Ancestors who have been traveling our Planet Asa/ Asia/Earth, ever since the Universal Creator created His personnel Home; although He is the Creator Of The Entire Universe, He Allah Chose to Rule His Unlimited Universal Kingdom, From the Planet Asa/Asia; Many,

many, many Trillions of years; before Yakub was even a thought or Yakub's Wisdom ever came into existence.

The Struggle Within my people is a matter of life and death for us all as a black people. Other people on our planet is allowed, to practice also develop their own customs and way of life, except black people. All our enemies are superimposing their way of life, their religions, their customs and their way of life. None of these enemies mean black people any good at all and they our enemies have never meant black People any good, for the past 6,000 years. Death and destruction are all these makings of Yakub Have, gave to our planet. This is a matter of historical facts my people that can be proven at any given time. Instead of standing and fighting for your black self you would rather stand up for the freedom of our Enemies, as our enemies are heavily engaged in black people genocidal liquidation; every one of us our Enemies my people with their worthless religions, customs, practices, their politics; are all working together my people; is the destruction of black people in America and throughout the world. Through Our Fathers Eyes my people is where we must begin looking through. By looking through the eyes of Our Multiple Enemies are keeping black people, in the role of servant and this is all you will achieve by following our enemies and history will verify that what I'm saying is the truth.

The Struggle Within my people is you standing up to the truth that history clearly proves that Allah Almighty Himself visited us in person of Master Fard Muhammad, to whom all holy praises are due Forever; the Most Honorable Elijah Muhammad is Allah's last and Greatest Messenger also the true Muhammad RasulAllah; and we are that seed of Ibrahim the chosen people that would be in a strange land under the ruler ship of a strange people; held in bondage for 400 years. Everything else including all religions, practices, customs and politics, are an absolute and total lie including this worthless so-called Sunnah Islam and everything else; that was brought here to America to further mislead black people and Keep, as our enemies keep us at the bottom of the well of society. You must my people wake up to this awesome truth you can run in fact you my people are cornered, and you must face up to the truth; either you stand up and deal with the truth, or laid down like cowards begging our enemies for help and compassion. I would rather die fighting for our freedom and I will, rather than serve our cowardly enemies; or any of our enemy's worthless religions, practices, stolen customs or politics. Death Before Dishonor my people I choose death. Through Our Fathers Eye I Look through and absolutely no one else; I know who my creator is, and it isn't Yakub Ibn Lucifer the Vicegerent. I also know that Yakub Ibn Lucifer [the Vicegerent] makings are nothing to me except the enemies of black people.

CHAPTER 17

THE ABSOLUTE HORRORS THAT WERE PREDICTED TO COME AND ARE NOW HERE

When I was a child being raised under the poison book [Bible Kings James Version} as a young boy, I had absolutely no understanding or knowledge, of what any of this meant. Yet what I knew instantly this was something, that was absolutely and morally wrong and this upset me, to my vey being. I have seen so much horrors in my life and our enemies get away with genocide and have been getting away with it for close to five hundred years. Now we are living in the days of complete insanity and the decedents of the first slaves brought to America, are living no better than our ancestors four hundred years ago. We are suffering so much horrors until it is unbelievable, and these immigrants don't care one bit. They have sworn an oath to up hold America's evil and they all participate in America's evils. What happens to us my people aren't any of these interlopers, concern in fact they are happy, that they can be an American. They just ignore what America has done to black people that are the decedents of those who came here, on the slave ships Jesus and Amazon Grace and there are many more. Yet these cowardly immigrants want us black people to be concern about them and their plight and their people. To hell with them all my people they are the horrors for black people. None of them and I mean all these immigrants, my people have absolutely nothing to do with, helping America become the rich super power she claims to be, except we my people and these interlopers and immigrants, aren't my people and they aren't your people either, or your friends; this is extremely critically my people that you must understand.

If one study the horrors that we the decendents of the first slaves that arrived in the Northern part of the Western Hemisphere, in 1555 aboard the Slave Ship Jesus have been enduring for the past four hundred and fifty years is criminal. Look at the conditions of black men, women and children in this day and time. The mass of black people is relying on the government to pay their rent, to buy food for their selves and families. Getting high doing nothing all day every day without a clue as to what do. Many black men are relying on untrustworthy women that believe and love our enemies, more than she will ever love them. Then these young fools believe that I should trust these enemies because they can't see that they are dependent on these enemies, well I'm not dependent on them nor do I trust any of them. These are extreme horrors that black men are living under until they can't even recognize their enemies, until it's too late; by the time these ignorant foolish black men figure it out, they are either put out of doors, going back to jail, murdered or allowing some ignorant colored woman to rule them and this is a faith worse than death. As our enemies are sitting back laughing at us and admiring their handy work, as they walked to the bank with your money and you are to blind to see what's happening, nor are you capable of doing anything about it.

Why aren't you capable of doing anything about these horrors is due to you eating poison mental food and you don't even know that you are being poison, by these colored women. This horror my people is at the highest level, as you sleep and have children with your enemy and you don't even know that this is the enemy. This is a physiological horror and prison that black men are suffering under to this present day and black men must be completely aware of all, of their enemies in which they aren't aware of. Instead of black men coming together with other black men to begin doing something positive for themselves, without the interference and input of these colored women. Keep women out of men business and she doesn't need to know what goes on in meetings. Any woman that wants to know what is going on in men business, is an enemy to and for black men uniting. In most cases she is a spy, for our enemies and these are just some of the horrors we as black men must live with and overcome. We must denounce all phases of our enemy's thoughts and ideas that only lead to our destruction and the preservation of our enemies. This is very hard to except my people but never the less it remains the truth and these are great horrors we all must deal with.

We black people must put an end to this Caucasian Feminist Matriarch Garbage that have poison the minds and hearts of black women, not only in America but throughout the world; where this poison mentality of this Caucasian Feminist Matriarch Evil excepted by these colored women, are producing homosexual children and destroying the image of a strong black man. A strong black man ready to take responsibility and stand up for himself as he demonstrates to the world, that he is the Original Man and he will no longer except this evil as his way of life. Any colored man or woman that wants to believe and remain under this un-godly evil, then let them remain. We who choose to look Through Our Fathers Eyes and reject this evil let us all, stand together we have absolutely any use of these colored people male or female.

These ignorant colored women are producing more bastards amongst black people because she is having sex with anyone and this is a fact. These strangers aren't claiming these bastards as their own no they aren't as these same ignorant colored woman, are still hiding the devil under her skirt, as she did six thousand years ago and are doing it today; this is not only a crime, this is pure evil my people. My people that have intelligent you can see this evil by this Zionist/Christian/Arab/Asian American Government of Global Murdering Terrorist; look at how they all partner up to fortify their Global Evil and the Destruction of Black People World Wide. Look at how young black men are wearing tight homosexual clothing believing this is fashion as well as hair dos; this is some of the 21st century horrors that we are dealing with. This is all part of this Filthy Evil Feminist Matriarch System that these silly colored people {African American} bought into; which is nothing more than KILL THE BLACK BABY AT BIRTH.

You ignorant colored men are equally as bad you love the very female beast that have been having black men unmercifully murdered for the past four hundred and fifty plus years. She isn't worthy of forgiveness, compassion and mercy black men. The horrors that black men suffered from her over heighten sexual activities and demands and when caught, she claimed that she was raped. Knowing that she was the aggressor and instigator by threating the black men with a death more horrible than anyone one could imagine;

yet black men knew oh so well. Also, my brothers their male counterpart knew that she was nothing, but a lying whore. So, the male counter who was raping, sodomizing black women and girls and in many cases little boys as well. Used these lies of his female counterpart to instill fear not only in the black woman and children, but also in the hearts of many of black men. You see the black man was not ever given an illusion of a chance the Caucasian population from the head of government, to the local peasant devils, thirst for our blood as they all vented their insanity of supreme evil, upon the black man without any merciful. This is still happening today my brother you just can't recognize how it's being done because you have been seduced, by the very enemies of our fathers and our ancestors' brothers.

We must understand that regardless of the many overwhelming illusions that are presented at black people through sports mainly, none of this wealth never aid your black people. Entertainment as well your wealth never aids black people and black children. Those that are in business and have achieved a degree of success, your wealth never aids black people and black children. You only operate in the guide lines, that your Caucasian Master allows you. Helping to aid and inspirer black children is the main thing that you must never do, or you will be stripped of your fortune, your reputations will be destroy as in the case of Bill Cosby. Once Mr. Cosby decided to put together a black organization to purchase satellite capabilities, the American government came after him like the angry hungry wolves and hyaenas that they are. This isn't something that shouldn't be expected of them; the travesty is that you Negro Cowards deserted your brother Mr. Cosby and left him on the battle field by himself. In fact, it was plenty of you ignorant Negroes that believed the lies that these devil women began launching at and against him, with absolutely no proof or evidence to support their lies; this include all of them. So once again the positive image of a successful black man is destroyed and replace by some Caucasian or Colored homosexual, as black children heroes or some silly weak kneed Colored person, as their heroes. This Zionist/Christian/Arab/Asian American Government of Global Terrorist are all hands in, when it comes to destroying black people not only in America, but throughout the world. This is these are the horrors that have been for told and are most certainly here right now. This isn't 21st century horror my people? Young black men coming out of prison and they aren't so young any longer, have absolutely no prospect at all. In most cases they are or will end up with an ignorant colored woman. The results he will either end up dead, back in prison or one of the many concentration camps this government has install for them all.

The Horrors My people are happening in this present day and time and they are not to come, they are here. Black people shutting their eyes to the truth at this crucial time in life is nothing more than suicide and you have absolutely no one to blame but yourself. These atrocities are haunting every black man woman and child that are the decendents, of our ancestors that boarded that Dreadful Slave Ship Jesus in 1555. This is the reason why we have been enduring these horrors and atrocities for the past four hundred and fifty plus years, that left the ex-slave of America politically, socially, educationally, economically, religiously and culturally, completely castrated as a people and even as an individual. Believe me my people every other people in America are permitted by the American government to pursue these basic, human rights except black people. This is the reason why there aren't any black parades on Firth Ave, Six Avenue and Madison Avenue, so the world doesn't have to recognize black people as a nation and the world doesn't recognize us as a Black Nation of People. These horrors you are living everyday of your lives and you would rather live the illusion, made by our enemies; than stand up and change these extremely horrible conditions. Your fancy car, your fine home, your back account, your job and your illusionary so-called social position, your church as well; means absolutely nothing because you are still living under the rule of our enemies and the enemies of our ancestors.

The Horrors my people are looking at young black women and men trying to design their bodies to look like Caucasian women and they don't even realize this body that has been designed by our enemies, are for seduction and not for reproduction. This is the body of the serpent that seduced Samson and this body type is still being used to seduce Samson of the 21st century; by Caucasian and Colored people this include these homosexuals. When you look throughout America the male factor is acting more feline than masculine, due to these ales being raised by their mothers and the mothers are teaching the males to be more feline; while these same mothers teach their daughters to be more masculine, tell me this isn't horror. The language these young women and girls are using is disgraceful and they believe that they can get in men face and mouth off, then when the male retaliates against them this evil, wicked society call the male a coward and seek to put him in jail. While the instigator the aggressor these disrespectful young women get away with their evil and men are supposed to sit back like cowards and take this abuse; this is absolutely horror my people that we must put an end to immediately.

My people we are living in some very terrible and dangerous times and this society is doing everything possible, to make sure black people have absolutely no defense to protect ourselves. This Caucasian Matriarch Rule System is the evil that is turning young black men into homosexuals and these colored women have embraced this evil and think this is cute, treating young men like little girls. If this isn't horror my brothers than what is? Black young men being taught by their mothers to hate their fathers, don't be like your father, thus they grow up hating themselves and are now acting like their mothers and this is an abdominal shame as well as a disgrace. Instead of young men taking the head and lead, they have been taught by these ignorant colored women to be soft and passive, nothing but a bunch of emotional cowards. Afraid of their own shadows and not capable of defending anything as a man this is absolute horrors my people. If this is being an American I say to hell with America and everyone that loves America. Then you have young women walking around thinking and believing they are men what insanity my people and these disgraces of Yakub's makings bring nothing but horrors, for real straight black men willing to be men. Black men catch more hell from these colored women and their homosexual children that any other people, on our planet. Who is living in horror my people other than you and me here in American and throughout the world. How could you possibly believe in this American Government of Global Murdering Terrorist that are still holding you in fear, with their Gestapo Law Enforcement Agencies, spreading fear amongst black people throughout America and throughout the world.

This Gestapo so-called Law Enforcement Agencies make sure that they protect these colored women and their homosexual children. There is no protection for black men under this evil, filthy Zionist/Christian/Arab/Asian American Government of Global Murdering Terrorist. Believing that a car, a house, a pair of sneakers and clothes make you an American, or part of this homosexual society, or this matriarch wickedness; there is a faith worse than death and that faith is living under the most evil, wicked, diabolical American Government of Murdering Global Terrorist, the world has ever known. Through Our Fathers Eyes black people is the direction in which we must all look through and absolutely no one else; it doesn't matter who they are, what their religion may be, their politics may be or the lies that they all tell, to keep you locked up in this cage of ignorance and economical oppression. This is nothing but Tranny my people and black as well as Indian people, have been living under for the past 500 years. This is the reason why black people, we all must examine the true undistorted history and the lies these devils are trying or have been ramming down black people throats, for the last 500 years.

These are the horrors that we have been living under for the past five centuries and it's only getting much worst for black people, here in America. Yet in the meantime black people have bought into the illusions that this American government of Supreme Evil, has made and the traders amongst us have lured black people, into this snare of pure evil of America and the American people. Never to know what it is to be a free and independent people; never again to be a creative and self-governing people ever again, to always be at the feet of our enemies begging them for exception, begging our enemy's food, begging for shelter, begging for clothing, begging for everything from our enemies. Just like a dog that's hated by his master, kicked around by its master, beaten by its master, locked or changed up by its master and still loves his master as well as still always ready to defend and serve its master. This is a shame my people to live in horror and tranny is a disgrace to our ancestors and you dare call yourself a black man. I will always see things through Our Fathers Eyes and never through the eyes of our many enemies. We are men my brothers and we must stand up against these American Murdering Tyrants as others are doing around the world.

These horrors and nightmares must come to an end my people. This Caucasian Feminist Matriarch American completely evil System mentality and ways must come to an end. It will only come to an end when we my brothers, stand up and put it to an end. We can only put this filthy evil to rest when we Look Through Our Fathers Eyes and be our original black self. Nothing else will change our conditions, nothing else will relieve us of the hell, that we have been enduring for the last five hundred years. Nothing else will put things back into the natural mathematical order, in which we are created. We weren't the experiment of Yakub on the Island of Pelan; the Caucasian Race is the Experiment of Yakub on the Island of Pelan when he {Mr. Yakub Ibn Lucifer, the Vicegerent} grafted this race of people out of us the Original Black people. We must stand up in unity and organize ourselves in order, for us to deal with this multi headed dragon American Government of Global, Murdering, Rapist, Thieving Terrorist. This matriarch nonsense of using the word love is completely deceiving as well as an absolute lie manufactured, by this evil matriarch control society and government. How can such a people especially this wicket matriarch of them knowing anything about love, when they were made, out of hate to be nothing more than the hateful unmerciful murderers, that they are and always will be. Our Way of Life Must Prevail Rather Than Exist Under These Present Conditions; imposed upon us by our 6,600-year-old enemies and the enemies of the Universal Creator.

These great historians I have mention in America's Indictment; the greatest Messenger {the Most Honorable Elijah Muhammad} of the Universal Creator Allah Almighty Himself, who visited us in the person of Master Fard Muhammad to whom all praises are due forever; I talked about in America's Indictment, are our fathers. To end the horrors that are still and have been haunting black people for the past 500 years, it's Through Our Fathers Eyes; Our Fathers Conviction; Our Fathers Work action and deeds, is our path to heaven while we live and to hell with this heaven after death. It doesn't matter what so-called religion that is telling us these lies my black people, they are nothing but lies and should be ignored by all black people in America and throughout the world. Then and only then are we able to put an end, to these horrors and traumas of the past five hundred years.

CHAPTER 18

ECONOMICAL AND
FINANCIAL TYRANNY

We my people have been living under financial Tyranny since the Reconstruction Period 0f 1866 instituted by this devil Andrew Johnson, the 17th or 18th president of America. This gave the Southern Caucasian devils to do whatever they wanted to black people, physically, mentally, financially, educationally, medically and socially. With the Jim Crow Law in full effect these American devils were able to legally deprive black people of a decent existence supported by the American government. This meant that what cost Caucasian people a penny at local store, would cost black people a dollar and even more in many cases. With the support of the American government and its military these Southern devils were able to black ball black people from having a quality life. This was also happening in the North as well. Where inferior meats, produce, education, medicines and the poorest of housing, were denied to us black people. If any black person was caught planting crops to feed his family he was either out right murdered or cast on to the chain gang, for life. Now his wife and children were at the total mercy of our enemies and these Caucasian devils had a fields day raping his wife and daughters with impunity. This was being enforced by the American Gestapo during this time tying black men, to a wagon wheel and beat them unmercifully. This was after the Civil War and this carried on for another hundred years my period. Denying the mass of black people education and protection they the Caucasian race and their evil government, were able to keep black people held in captivity with impunity. Every black man that stood up to speak out against this evil was quickly murdered by the American Gestapo or imprisoned for life of hard free labor.

This gave our enemies; it didn't matter if these devils were nothing but poor white trash, they were able to rob black people, murder black people, kidnapped black people and rape black women; the Caucasian women were equally involved in these atrocities in fact urging their male counterpart along. During this time and this carried all the way into the twentieth century, where they our enemies sold us poison foods at an astronomical price, while their people were able to buy better food and a lot cheaper rate than black people. The fact that Jim Crow Law was still in affect the American government headed up by the Zionist and Christians, all the immigrants coming from all over Europe in the early twentieth century and late 19th century, jumped on the Jim Crow Band Wagon and were just as evil and wicket to black people; so black men couldn't get jobs when all this building was happening or a decent place to live. Many black people in fact the majority, of black people were catching absolute hell, from every Caucasian person in America. We weren't even allowed to produce clothes for ourselves or anything else for ourselves. Everything was controlled by our enemies and our enemies are still in control of our food, clothing and shelter to this very day. Still making us pay insane prices for everything up too this present day and time. This is economical and Financial Tyranny my people in which we have been subjected to for the past 500 years. When black people wanted to buy some land, a house or set up a business that would help black people, the Caucasian people made the interest rate extremely high for them. This is the same practice that they are using today against black people in every phase of our lives, Economical and Financial Tyranny.

The harder black people try to be friendly with our many enemies we come up on short end of the deal, while our enemies grow richer and richer and black people become more disenfranchised. While the atrocities amongst black people continue escalate and our many enemies sit back and get richer and richer off, of our miseries. Our enemies through their propaganda machinery are in over drive keeping black people divided against ourselves, as these Zionist/Christian/Arab/Asian American Government of Global, Murdering, Thieving American Terrorist get away with Economical and Financial Tyranny. Thirty Year mortgages high very high interest rates where black people are concerned, are being held in

Economical and Financial Slavery. Whereas you work all your lives at a lower pay scale that Caucasian people. This isn't anything new my people this has been going on for more than a hundred years and is still happening into this day and time. Our enemies and all, of their corrupted religions are nothing but vampires sucking the very life energy, out of every black person in America and throughout the world, keeping us all in Economical and Financial Tyranny. The worst part my people you sit back and take it with a smile, on your face and participate in our multiple enemy's evil way of life believing if there is a change in the president or if there is a change in the parties, things will get better and never it will. The Democrats are just as evil as the Republicans, the so-called Liberals, the Conservatives are all just as evil and there will never be any peace amongst us ever. As long, as we black people, allow any of these devilish political parties to control us or control our vote, black people will remain in and under Economical and Financial Tyranny of our enemies.

The homes that black people are buying and have bought cost absolutely pennies to have them built yet these devils charge black people an arm and a leg, for these houses. Since the majority, of black people buying these homes and cars work for our enemies, you are nothing but an economical slave living in and under Financial Tyranny and if you open your mouth or make the enemies up set, you won't have a job nor home or fine car; so now you live in fear of our cowardly enemies. Tyranny is Tyranny my people and we have been living under Tyranny for the past 500 years and our enemies aren't about to stop or let up, on exploiting black people until we stop it. You my people have embraced our enemy's style of dress and behavior, towards yourself and kind; while our people and kind throughout world are rising, against this Zionist/Christian/Arab/Asian American government of Globally Tyrants. Your Agreement with Hell Will Not Stand my people supporting our multiple enemies' way of evil living their religions, their politics and everything else they do. You and I are living under Economical and Financial Tyranny, social Tyranny, educational Tyranny, medical Tyranny Political Tyranny every type of Tyranny there is, we black people are living under and our enemies made up religions are keeping us all prisoners.

Through Our Fathers Eyes my people I have looked I advise you to do the same then and only then will you be able to understand the Economical and Financial Tyranny that we are living under and what we must do, to put an end to this evil. Laughing acting like everything is alright and except their way of life where the matriarch and their homosexual children, are the rulers; such a society cannot ever stand for long and this society is falling rapidly they are at war with themselves within. The government of America is monitoring every move or thought on Facebook, Instagram and twitter there are even companies working secretly for this Federal government of international criminals; to keep these international criminals and government in power, by collecting all this data and manipulating this data to control the outcome of a major election such as Donald Trump presidency and the Republican Party, seizing control of every aspect of the American Government including all branches of the military. This is the Goliath my people written in scriptures both Bible and Our-a mention in their writings. This Legalized Government of international Gangsters made, supported and funded by America; in which America gave the military close to eight hundred million dollars is more deadly, treacherous, wicket and diabolical that any, of Yakub's makings since he began his {Yakub the Vicegerent} experiment 6,600 years ago.

These devils and their helpers are the instrument that is holding black people in Economic, Political, Educational, Medical, Manufacturing, Financial, Industrial and Religious Tyranny and have been doing this for the past 500 years. It doesn't matter which party wins the next whatever election, black people will continue to live under Economical, Financial, Political, Educational, Medical, Manufacturing, Industrial and Religious Tyranny and this is an absolute fact, my people. I know many of you my people believe that these other political parties are better than the present one, believe me my people believing in nonsense is much worse than believing that Reindeers can fly. None of these other political parties or religious organizations are going to bring black people any relief, at all. Only fools and those who have doubt in Allah and His Holy Messenger believe in the lies, of our made enemies. We will never gain any independence following or believing in any of Yakub's making lies and deceit. I have absolutely no faith or belief in any of these American political parties and neither did Allah's Holy Messenger had any belief in them. We must stand up and create our own civilization for ourselves once again. Quoting the Holy Messenger means absolutely nothing if you aren't prepared to make America know her sins and do something about it. Going on social media and arguing with your people is ludicrous believing that your knowledge or wisdom, are greater. This is a great waste of time as well as energy and does absolutely nothing but keep black people divided and this is only giving our enemies reasons, to continue their plan course of depriving black people of Economical Freedom, Financial Freedom, Educational Freedom, Medical Freedom, Industrial Freedom, Manufacturing Freedom and Social Freedom; that has been keeping black people being ruled under Tyranny, by our 6,000-year-old enemies.

Other people coming into America and being prosperous is due to them all jumping on the American band wagon. The American government give them financial support through grants and loans, to startup businesses in black neighborhoods to begin robbing black people. These people that are really filtering into the American society have their own language, own culture and people. Black people have none of these things going for us due to our enemies, have stolen these essentials from us and given black people absolutely nothing for us to build a world for ourselves. Through Our Fathers Eyes my people I beg of you to look there are no other eyes we can trust but our fathers. Integration and this Clandestine Civil Rights for Negro people; is in truth Civil Rights for the Caucasian Feminist and the Homosexuals my people and these cowardly immigrants, not for you. These people are all one people and they are all the enemies that are keeping black people, under the rule of Economical, Financial, Educational, Medical, Social, Industrial, Manufacturing, Political and Religious TYRANTS; and this Tyrant are these that make up the American Hydra Government Zionist/Christian/Arab/Asian, that are robbing black people globally; this is the Goliath my people we are up against and these devils are robbing you every day, of your hard earn money. This is nothing but Financial Tyranny my people it doesn't matter how much an individual make playing sports, acting, singing and dancing, they are not allowed by this American government to truly aid and help black people because they are ruled, by these American Tyrants.

Financial and Economical Tyranny is what we have been living under for the past 500 years without any help from anyone, in fact everyone that came to America has done nothing more than show absolute content, for us the decendents of those who came aboard the Slave Ship Jesus in 1555 and have suffered un-imaginable suffering than anyone care to acknowledge because they are all the enemies of our fathers and mothers, thus making them our enemy as well. What is happening is by design my people to keep black people globally living under Economical and Financial Tyranny and none of these immigrants in America and that are coming to America, are ever going to help black people the decendents of the ex-slaves of America. In fact; these immigrants agree, with keeping black people in the bottom of the well and do everything to make sure we stay there, for al all eternity if they can help it. It is a damn shame that we have absolutely nothing in place to help our brothers and sisters who are in desperate need, of our help and you want to sit back believing and following the lies and trickery of these foolish magicians. Still you are living under Economical and Financial Tyranny but these magicians, have convinced you believe in and trust in them, and abandon the love and trust in the Allah of our Salvation Master Fard Muhammad to whom praises are due forever. You believe and trust these foolish magicians who have completely led you away from the teachings that Allah's last and greatest Messenger the Most Honorable Elijah Muhammad the true and only Muhammad RasulAllah. We must stand up for ourselves my people there is no other way for us, to overcome this Economical and Financial Tyrants and Tyranny. These magicians my people are working for our enemies it doesn't matter what the nonsense they are saying it may sound good, but all of them are spreading nothing but lies. I don't believe in absolutely none of these so-called ministers no matter what they call themselves my people, they are all liars and they are misleading you to and with our enemy's absolute destruction. They are all living a very good life with your hard earn money as they feed you nothing but lies. These magicians know that you are my people very easy to be led into the wrong direction and rob you of your hard earn money. This is Financial and Economical Tyranny my people by these magicians that you are silly enough to love and believe in, as they turn you away from the Allah of your Salvation and His Holy Messenger.

Through Our Fathers Eyes and not through the deceitful eyes of these magicians disguised to look and sound like our Fathers, but truth be told they are disciples of Yakub Ibn Lucifer {the Vicegerent} and they are leading you to destruction my people because they all are disbelievers in Allah and Allah's Holy Messenger. These magicians keep you living under Economical, Financial, Social, Political, Religious and Educational Tyranny, in the bottom of the well my people. If you want to be free of this Tyranny my people you must return to the teachings that Allah in the person of Master Fard Muhammad taught to His Holy Messenger the Most Honorable Elijah Muhammad and everyone else are nothing but liars and thieves and they still leading you to this mystery god, whose name is Yakub Ibn Lucifer the Vicegerent while billions of black people suffer globally. As long you, my people believe in these magicians billions and billions of black people, will remain in and under Economic, Financial, Social, Political, Educational, Medical, Industrial, Manufacturing Tyranny. The reason why is that these magicians don't have the Master Grip because they changed the Master Teachings, present themselves, as something that they aren't and will never be; this includes every one of them my people. Yes! my people they may sound good my people, but you must look beyond their bag of tricks and then you will see these magicians for what they truly are and who they truly are.

We must free ourselves from this Economical and Financial Tyranny my people globally as we build a black or Original Global Economy, for original people and to hell with our enemies. Following the teachings of Allah given and taught to us by His last and greatest Messenger the Most Honorable Elijah Muhammad, we can and will make this happen again, for all original people globally. Through Our Fathers Eyes my people we must always look through you will discover that we always have created civilizations, greater than what we are living in today. Where we didn't at any time ever experience Economical, Financial, Educational, Medical, Industrial, Manufacturing, Political and Religious Tyranny, as we have been suffering under for the past Five Hundred Years. Young black men and boys have absolutely no idea of what it is to be an independent, self-productive black man and they will never achieve this mandatory goal living under this Evil Matriarch American System; where this system is designed to make young black men and boys Homosexuals. There is absolutely no god present under this evil wicked Matriarch American System, for Black people and especially for Black men. Absolutely no black people and especially black men should embrace this evil system, we have no future in this evil Matriarch system at all; only suffering and death is our reward my people.

Even if you enter into a legal binding contract with our enemies their hatred for black people telling the truth about them and the situation, breeds only hatred for the truth teller as I now have been experiencing. The lies, the deceits are always present when dealing with our enemies and if you pay attention and you must always pay attention to what our enemies attentions truly are about. We are hated by them my people especially if you are one of the truth tellers, as I am. The Holy Messenger said to us make America Know Her Sins and this is what I am doing, and I have been experiencing hatred from our enemies, for upholding our Lord and Savior Allah in the person of Master Fard Muhammad to whom all holy praises, are due forever. I'm hated by our enemies because I am a follower and student of Allah's last and greatest Messenger the Most Honorable Elijah Muhammad. We are living under Economical and Financial Tyranny and our enemies believe that we will give up our march, to Freedom, Justice and Equality. Our enemies believe that under their Economical and Financial Tyranny we will give up our struggle to become an independent nation of Black People. Our enemies using their methods of Economical and Financial Tyranny will make and force us to turn our backs on Allah our Holy and Most Merciful Savior Master Fard Muhammad, to whom all holy praises are due forever. I will never denounce Allah's last and greatest Messenger the Most Honorable Elijah Muhammad; the true and only Muhammad Rasul Allah and to hell with America's Arab partners in crime.

This is how our many enemies are trying to intimidate black people and keep us living under Economical and Financial Tyranny, by them. If you haven't learned who our enemies are once again I will tell the world again; it is this Zionist/Christian/Arab/Asian American Government of Global, Murdering, Lying, Deceiving, Thieving Terrorist. We must stand up and face this Goliath and this legion of absolute devils that are on this Goliath side; along with their religions and politics. We must understand my people in America and throughout the world, the time has come to live or die. The time has come that we make the enemies of our fathers and mothers pay, for the evil crimes they have committed against them as well as ourselves. I refuse to live under these evil, wicket and diabolical conditions by this filthy Zionist/Christian/Arab/Asian American Government of Global Murdering Thieving Terrorist; and not tell my enemies the absolute truth about themselves. I fear Allah Original People throughout the world our Holy, Most Merciful Savior in the person of Master Fard Muhammad, to whom all holy praises are due forever. I am a follower and student of Allah's last and holy Messenger to us all my people, the Most Honorable Elijah

Muhammad. To Hell with any; and all whom may disagree with what I am saying and don't like what I am saying. We my people globally must stand up and build our own Globally Economy for black people globally to put an end, of this Economical and Financial Tyranny designed by our enemies, to keep original people in the bottom of the well; subjected by our many enemies, evil, wicket and diabolical wishes and desires. Through Our Fathers Eyes my people and not through this devil's ancestry evil, they the enemies of all original people are advertising on television and the websites; Through Our Fathers Eyes my original people let us all look through them together. Then we will together as a unified Original People will be able to put and end of this evil by our six thousand-year, old enemies. Then and only then will be able to put an end to this Economical, Financial, Educational, Medical, Political, Religious, Manufacturing, Industrial hell that we all have been living under, for the past five hundred years. We deserve my original people to have Freedom, Justice and Equality while we live and to hell with all their make-believe heavens from these make-believe religions and enemies of original people, the world over.

CHAPTER 19

THE DECEIT WITHIN

What is the meaning of The Deceit Within? What is The Deceit Within my people? This chapter will try to illuminate exactly what this is, my people. What we my people must truly understand how devastating the past five hundred years, have left us totally ignorant and dependent on our enemies to teach us the truth, in which they didn't and never will. The many false leaders calling themselves representing black people in the past fifty plus years, up to this present day and time my people, have deceived all black people and are still deceiving black people. We must understand my people that we have been completely mis-led by our enemies and their Negro Political and Religious helpers, to keep black people believing in the lies and deceit that they have been feeding us and are still feeding us up till this very day. During the time when the Zionist/Christian/Arab/Asian American Government murdered Malcolm X they also murdered our brother in Kenya on the same day. This government of America has committed the most hideous crimes and financed these hideous crimes, where black brothers and black sisters murder each other, for the love of our enemies the devil. Now when you look around today in America and throughout the world, black people are living a life of absolute lies and black people have grown up physically believing in the lies and deceit of our enemies. This is one of the many reasons why black people have no love for themselves because our enemies make sure we have no love for ourselves; yet black people have love for our many enemy's false religions, politics and way of life. This is all boiling down to The Deceit Within our very selves, placed in us by our enemies.

We my people are haunted by us believing and trusting our enemies, believing in their false religions and trusting them, to also be our political leaders and you never question how did or were these enemies, able to achieve their goals. They all were able to achieve their goals by deceiving black people into believing and trusting them, who are our enemies and are a part of this absolute five hundred years nightmare we are still living. This American government and society are re-enforcing the self-deceit in black people through these false religions and this so-called Sunnah Islam is one of the main false religions, being used to keep black people held in the prisons made by our enemies today. The Deceit Within my people is do you believing and trusting our enemies and believing this evil Matriarch society that believes and do everything in its power, to murder the black baby at birth. All these filthy disgusting tv programs and movies are designed to keep The Deceit Within black people, thus keeping you caged in the bottom of the well of Economical, Financial, Educational, Medical, Industrial, Manufacturing, Engineering, forever if our enemies have their way. You know my people, or you should know that what I am saying is right and that you should change your course of actions, that will produce a more positive and constructive course for black people. This will begin the process of self-healing from The Deceit Within that we have been suffering from and under the last five hundred years.

I look around us my people and I see all the dis-enfranchised black men and black people throughout America as well as throughout the world, it is a horrible site my people. White Supremacy and White Nationalism is on the rise is on the rise and this so-called Sunnah Islam has embrace this whole heartily and this why we must reject this evil. When it comes down to evil this so-called Sunnah Islam has always been part of it all one has to do is examine the history. Once you denounce our enemies stop believing in them, their religions and their lies also deceits, you will be able to combat The Deceit Within my people that haunts us all. Our enemies lie to us constantly without any hesitation no matter how much good faith we show, our enemies are always out to rob us of everything we have, and this has killed many black artist and people, in the day and time we are now living in. The Deceit Within my people along with the poison foods are causing many ailments amongst black people and there isn't any cure, following our enemies' recommendations. We must reject our many enemies' religions and politics then turn to ourselves, for us to deal with this poison of The Deceit Within ourselves.

The Deceit Within my people you can no longer run from or hide from this must be dealt with face on and within yourself. I look around America and for the mass of black people there isn't any hope at all for us, living under these present conditions, religions and politics of our open enemies. We must my people combat The Deceit Within which is caused by you believing and trusting our enemies you may believe or think that they aren't our enemies, history teach us all that this isn't true they are our enemies. Whoever want you to sell drugs to your people, or present to your people a false religion and politics, poison foods, alcohol are the enemies of black people and these are the things in which all our enemies, are asking you black people to do to yourself and kind. Through Our Fathers Eyes my people not through our multiply enemies' eyes we must look through. Our multiply enemies have the same objective and that is keeping the mass of black people, living a life of lies which keep the mass of black people in Economical, Financial, Medical, Educational, Industrial, manufacturing, Engineering, Social, political and religious slavery; where by following and believing in our enemies will only keep us in mental and physiological slavery and feed The Deceit Within ourselves; a life of an eternal prisoner for our enemies; believing in whatever lies our enemies can, will and do conjure up.

The Deceit Within one self keeps you off balance and haunted by yourself because within yourself, you know that Yakub's civilization and Yakub's making, are completely wrong and this evil and must come to an end. This Deceit Within my people have been implanted in black people heavily over the past five hundred years and over the past fifty plus years, it has gone into complete over drive. Therefore, the drugs have been introduced into every black community throughout America and these laboratories made diseases have been introduce into every black civilization throughout the world, as well as amongst black people in America. The truth must be told to you my people in America and throughout the world. The truth of our enemies must be made known to you my people and to black people throughout the world. The truth of our enemies' false religions, politics and society must be told to black people, in America and throughout the world. These enemies are liars all of them my people their false religions are designed to keep you locked into the cages, in their human zoos called society, for black people and this Sunnah so-called Islam, is one of the many partners in this evil most horrific crimes, being committed against black people today and have been for the past five hundred years. Our enemies have stolen Rock and Roll from us which was created by Mr. Chuck Berry and now it's Homosexual Role. Our enemies have stolen from us the Gospel which goes back hundreds of years before the Reconstructive Period and now it's Homosexual Gospel. Our Enemies have stolen Blues from us which was created after the reconstructive period of 1866 and now it's Homosexual Blues. Our enemies have stolen from us Rhythm and Blues and now it's Homosexual Rhythm and Blues and this was created in the twentieth century. Now our enemies have stolen Hip Hop from us and now it's Homosexual Hop my people. This is nothing but White Supremacy and White Nationalism my people. By you allowing this to happen is causing the demons of The Deceit Within to grow with in you with impunity, my people.

Everything I am saying is hard because this is the absolute truth my people and all these different immigrants and their false religions, are designed to keep black people in the bottom of the well, as our enemies steal your hard earn money as they all sell you nothing but poison foods and inferior products; as they laugh all the way to the bank my people, on how easy it is to rob black people. You deceive yourself my people by believing and trusting our enemies. Our enemies are in many disguises and they pretend and sound very sincere; truth be told my people this is nothing but deceit from our enemies. The Deceit Within my people is do you trusting and believing our enemies, while they are building and protecting their families and to hell with black families. These traitors that look something like black people but in truth, they are the Colored People; those who have been made weak and wicket like their Caucasian Masters. This is the Nightmare that Martin Luther King Jr. insane Dream has rewarded black people in America and throughout the world with. The results are plain to see if you aren't afraid to open your eyes and see the truth. This is The Deceit Within that is haunting every black man, woman and child here in America and throughout the world. You Love the Devil because the Devil Gives you absolutely nothing and never has given black people anything and never will give black people anything except, absolute hell. This we can always expect from our enemies my people and we do have many.

They make movies projection these Arabs as noble people, trusting people, people who are worthy of being treated as human beings and they deserve human rights. Their plight to be recognize as a Nation of People with their own culture, with their own language, with their own interpretation of religion, with their own Economical System, with their own Financial System, with their own Educational System, with their own Doctors, with their own Importing and Exporting System, with their own Manufacturing System, with their own Industrial System, able to participate in the sciences that every people on this earth, have the right to have and be given the chance to obtain these human necessities; everyone but the black man, woman and child in America and throughout the world. These very people I am speaking about and all immigrants period, have taken an oath to America to help keep black people from obtaining our human rights and freeing ourselves from this Economical and Financial Tyranny, we have living under for the past five hundred years; to be a Free Nation of Black People and the right to Look Through Our Fathers Eyes, for guidance; to pray to our creator for guidance, for mercy, for forgiveness, for protection, for his blessings, for our own culture and not the ways and beliefs of our enemies, all of them my people.

The Deceit Within is paralyzing my people because it truly must be dealt with for us, to enter the planetary scale, as a civilize independent black people. By avoiding The Deceit Within is causing us more problems and is only causing black people more problems; on top of what we are already faced with and we have a mountain of problems that we must deal with, my people. It doesn't matter how much money you make as an individual it never serves or use to elevate your people; the money that you are making or have made is only helping the enemies of your people. Since the Destruction of Muhammad's University black people in America don't have any schools, that we can educate our children properly and this is causing mental retardation amongst black people. We have no Educational System for our children teaching them mathematics, shop classes teaching them trade, biology, business classes to prepare them for dealing with the world, marketing classes teaching our children on how to market their inventions and their ideas, to the world and society at large. Muhammad's University Of Islam did exactly this for all black children and all black children were invited to attend. Our enemies have schools independent of the local so-called educational system that the government provide, for black children which teach them absolutely nothing. Hand a black man a ball it doesn't matter what kind of a ball just give them a ball and watch how they will amaze and entertain our enemies. Now they have expanded this to black women where as black women are being seduce into these same blood sports and to hell with producing and raising black families. While our enemy's children are going to schools to learn how to become doctors, engineers, scientist, builders of civilizations and our children are still the court jesters, wearing funny colors to entertain the wizards of Yakub's Civilization and Yakub the Vicegerent Makings; as they did since we crossed the Atlantic approximately five hundred years ago. This is all cause by The Deceit Within in which black people believe they can run from and hide from, until it affects them. Then they realize that they are no different from their suffering people in which they come from.

The time has come for us to face up to this Deceit Within and do something about it other than worship the very emissary of black people enemies to embracing this insanity and Abomination called Integration; put to black people whom he knew were and are our enemies'; that were and still are deceiving black people, in which he was paid to do by our enemies. This is the History my people that can't be ignored, changed nor forgotten by all black people. Our enemies' religions are false, and this includes this phony so-called Sunnah Islam, who have replaced the Zionist in black communities throughout America to sell black people poison foods, inferior products, molest and proposition black women and young black girls; their obvious false religion is no different from the Zionist and Christians which are their partners in these horrific crimes, to further implant this diabolical web of The Deceit Within in black people. What I am saying is the absolute truth my people taught to us all by Allah Almighty Himself through the mouth of His Holy Messenger the Most Honorable Elijah Muhammad. The Deceit Within my people are the demons that haunts us all and we can't run nor hide from this fact.

The mass of black people in America are completely lost and don't know how to find their way back home, to sanity. The Magicians of this Pharaoh American Government or I should say Yakub the Vicegerent civilization, which is surly crumbling; are these so-called religious and so-called political leaders working extra hard to keep you, black people in prisoned and trapped in The Deceit Within, with absolutely no exit leading black people to Freedom, Justice and Equality; that will propel black people toward being and independent, self-creative and self-sufficient people, once again. Through Our Fathers Eyes my people we have absolutely no other way to look we can no longer trust our lying, deceitful, most treacherous enemies. We can no longer trust any of our enemies' religions, politics and their practices, you will know the truth when you study and embrace the Truly Holy Apostle, the True Muhammad RasulAllah and the Supreme Wisdom that Almighty Allah Himself taught His Holy Messenger the Most Honorable Elijah Muhammad and absolutely no one else.

Why should we want to be friends with anyone who don't want or have any love for us, my people? Why should we trust people where history and time, have proven beyond a shadow of doubt, that they are the enemies of our ancestors and ourselves to this very day? How can we sit back and allow these Colored People to dare called themselves the representatives, of black people when we know that they are all the servants of our enemies? Look at these extremely ridiculous, stupid Negro TV shows produce by this evil Propaganda machinery and Media controlled by the Zionist; depicting black people and black men as nothing but complete weak-kneed fools, Homosexuals, buffoons and black women as absolute ignorant sluts and absolutely nothing else; who aren't worthy or qualify to be an independent people because they can't govern themselves. We must stand up my people and face the music my people we have no other choice, or we are going to become extinct my people. We must take a pro-active approach towards our circumstances, that affects every part of the mass of black people, survival in America. Whereas we black people have our own needs and wants separated from all other people and our needs and wants are different, from all immigrants coming into America and has come to America.

It doesn't matter how this society paints this most ugly picture of we are all getting along together, this is an absolute lie. The mass of black people is getting nothing but absolute hell from this society and government my people. Examine the history my people there is nothing being given or allocated for black people, to improve themselves which is feeding The Deceit Within black people. Black women wearing false hair and nails are making our enemies richer, when black women should be taking care of their own needs, as they always did before this most Dreadful Integration. This

Homosexual style of dressing and clothing are making the enemies of black people richer and black people poorer and this is a fact. Young black men wearing these Homosexual hair styles and colors are absolutely disgusting and a disgrace to our ancestors; projecting to the world that black men and women are worthless on the planetary scale of civilize, productive intelligent people. The Deceit Within my people cannot be over look by any of us whom you think are your friends aren't your friends; they are only gathering information on how well, their diabolical plan of genocide projected at the mass of black people. Calling yourself an African American is a great disgrace when history proves that a Caucasian Homosexual Alexander named the entire continent of East Asia, after his Homosexual Lover Afrikaner. We are Original people and when you examine history beyond six thousand six hundred years and you will never find such a word as Africa; this is the name given to this continent by our open enemies. As our enemies stole, looted and destroyed our libraries, our schools and universities, medical facilities, universities of engineering, architectural, mining engineering everything was stolen, from us the original people, including mathematics and astrology. The Deceit Within my people is you believing that these demons, could ever be our friends absolutely none of them can ever be the friend or friends black people.

Our enemies' lies concerning religion is an abomination it doesn't matter what name our enemies call their false religions, they are all an abomination of made up lies and deceit. Our enemies' politics are also nothing but made up lies and deceit that benefits, our enemies my people and never black people. Having the Skunk of our Planet as you women or husband is a great sign of how ignorant you have become black people, and therefore black people especially in America, aren't welcome by original civilize people throughout the world. Why aren't black people recognized by original civilized people throughout the world Saladin? The is very simple my people we aren't Looking Through Our Fathers Eyes we are looking at life through the eyes of our enemies; and this is The Deceit Within that is producing diseases, illness and retardation amongst black people, including the many cancers that have over taken black people, as well as many other diseases that are shorting the life span of black people not only in America, but throughout the world. The poison foods this society feeds to black people with absolutely no nutritional value at all. The extremely poison fast food eateries are designed to produce cancers and other diseases amongst black people, whereas these foods produce aliments amongst black people and black children; that are making the medical industrial and our enemies filthy rich while black people are suffering horrifically, without any recourse. Now you have the legal world getting in on this action making money off black people horrific medial conditions this includes the pharmaceutical aspect of the medical field, selling black people medicines and drugs that only shorten the lives of black people.

While black people are living the illusion of the American Dream our enemies are living the American Dream, as they rob black people every way possible. Since our people blinded by all the false religions of our enemies are nothing but sitting ducks, on a pond or a river; being picked off by unmerciful murderers, as the murderers get richer and richer while we black people are dying horribly, believing in the false lies of them going to some make believed heaven that doesn't exist and has never existed. The Deceit Within my people is keeping black people anchored into the insanity that our enemies have made to keep black people, forever locked in this caged of absolute despair with absolutely no help or relief, from our enemies. Through our enemies' false religions and this includes all of these made up religions that only came into existence, in the past four thousand years. Before this none of these false religions ever existed and this includes this so-called Sunnah Islam. All our enemies are doing their absolute best trying to instill and keep fear in the hearts and minds of black people; if their phony religions can't do it than threats and another Mafioso technique, are being used to planet fear or used to keep fear of our enemies' in the hearts and minds of black people and our enemies even have the support and backing, of the American Gestapo and their American Government. Our enemies are working overtime to make sure black people in America never unified ourselves. This Zionist/Christian/Arab/ Asian American government of Global Terrorist are all working against black people, throughout America. You can deceive yourself all you want my people; you can believe that our enemies are cool and your friends, you my people are playing right into these deceitful devil's hands. The enemies' have mounted their offensive against black people; they our enemies have fortified themselves and have their defense in place, which give them an advantage against black people. We black people have absolutely no defense because our enemies don't want black people to have any defense against them. Once we put up any defense against our enemies, we are label as criminals and enemies of this Zionist/ Christian/Arab/Asian American Government of Global Terrorist.

All of this is cause by The Deceit Within black people in America that black people believe they can ignore and not look at the damage, this has cause us all. Why are you so concern about Arabs killing each other in the Mid-East? When these infidels get to America they will jump right on the band wagon to begin suppressing and oppressing black people, throughout America. If not for a so-called American Black man name Mr. Andrew Young, the Palestinians would have never gotten their case in the United Nations and look at how these ungrateful Arabs repay black people, who helped them at the expense of their lives, families and their careers. This is The Deceit Within my people that we must overcome within ourselves, to combat this over whelming evil of our enemies. Living under these present conditions and do nothing to change them is ludicrous, while our enemies are enjoying Economical, Financial, Educational, Social, Religious, Medical, Industrial, Manufacturing, Engineering, Sciences, Politics and everything else, that make an independent people independent. Black people you are so concern with pleasing our enemies before you even begin think about your own survival and how do black people, profit and benefit from what is going on. I Look Through Our Fathers Eyes and never through our enemies' eyes and our enemies made up phony religions. Our enemies steal from us our language and now want to give black people their dialect and lie about it being the original language or Arabic; when Ibrahim, Isaiah, Ismaeel and every original person before them, never spoke this dialect and this is a matter of historical facts. This proves these Arabs that are piling into America like the locust they are, do not speak the original language because they aren't from the original people or original family; this is further proof they our enemies aren't created by the Universal Creator, so it is impossible, for us to be brothers and sisters, with our enemies.

The Deceit Within is all around you my people everyone that is controlling the economics in black communities, are our enemies and they are armed to kill any black person that voice their disagreement. Our enemies already know that the Gestapo is going to support them in murdering black men and the Colored People employed by the Gestapo aren't ever going to do anything at all, they never do. Our enemies are armed while this government make or are making sure black people have no defense against, these enemies of ours. So black people are left defenseless and the Gestapo called Law Enforcement, are on the side of black people's enemies and history supports what I am saying. This Zionist/Christian/Arab/Asian American Government of Global Terrorist has designed this wicket, evil society, to keep black people in prisons and a non-productive people. Black people don't want anything from or of our enemies and this includes their false religions, politics cultures; take all of this to hell with their complete destruction. I heard this fool say to did I read Quran I answered you don't even what the Holy Quran truly is. It is a historical fact that Prophet Mohammed of Arabia had absolutely nothing to do, with these Arabs writing a book and rituals and they called it Quran, twenty-three years after Prophet Mohammed had died. Twenty-three years later these same unworthy companions wrote a book and called it Quran and twenty-three after this, these same unworthy companions wrote another book and called it Hadith. Prophet Mohammed was dead may peace and blessings be upon him and absolutely nothing to do with any of this nor did he authorize anyone to do this, my people. Stop listing to our enemies or our enemies Negro servants and examine the history yourself, then you will learn the truth of this so-called Sunnah Islam. This so-called Sunnah Islam is just as hateful toward black people as Zionism and Christianity and we black people all see this hatred every day of, our lives, since this evil was imported into America by the Zionist and Christians; to keep black people believing in a mystery god and a dead prophet; and help prevent black people from believing in themselves and the Allah/God of our Ancestors.

My people we shouldn't put any stock in anything our enemies have to say at all or any of their false religions, that our Ancestors were against. Tell me in this so-called Sunnah is where they give any credit to black people? The answer is never this so-called Sunnah Islam has as much hatred for original people as Zionism/Christianity and Hinduism, with Hinduism being the oldest of the enemies, of our Ancestors and these are the people that are robbing black people and black communities in America and throughout the world. How can any of these people be your friends black people? Our enemies are keeping you so distracted until you don't have time to examine who these demons are and all these wicket, evil colored people programs, are part of the plan to keep black people distracted, while our enemies rob black people blindly. While black children are in enrolled in inferior schools that produce retardation and more cases than often, end up in prisons; while black people enemies children end up in private and better schools with a chance of superior education, than black people and they didn't do a damn thing to earned any of this, or than support the Zionist/Christians and Hindus to destroy black people and keep black people, forever locked in this cage of despair made by our enemies.

We must stand up my people against this evil and everyone who is part of this evil then and only then can we defeat The Deceit Within my people because then you will be able to recognize our enemies and defeat our enemies; this includes all our enemies' religions, politics and their worthless customs in which they all stole from black people and trying to claim them to be theirs. We are the creators of civilizations not one of our enemies can say or prove that they have created anything because they didn't create anything, they only stole from us black people as they are all stealing from us today. All our enemies are doing everything they can to prevent black people from Looking Through Our Fathers Eyes; Through Our Fathers Eyes our enemies will all be reveal that they have been our enemies, since Yakub the Vicegerent grafted them out of us six thousand six hundred years ago. Through Our Fathers Eyes will also reveal all the false religions of our enemies and their mystery god. Through Our Fathers Eyes will reveal the evils that we are caught up in and all who are responsible, for us being subjective and over whelm by these evils, for the past five hundred years.

If we black men are interested in saving our sons and saving our daughters then we must take a stance against all, of our enemies, their religions, their politics and their customs and create our own once again; with the absent of all our enemies' interference and evil input, we my people don't anything from our enemies. To stand up for ourselves in unity will such a powerful weapon that will drive our enemies scaring away from black people. Of course, our enemies will sit in conference with their evil brothers on how best to, bring black people into subjugation again. If we stand my people together unified as one people, we will be able to defeat all our enemies. The most important truth my people we all must remember is that the Allah/ God of our ancestors prayers, since they fell into grasp of the devil the makings of Yakub Caucasian race Arabs included; and being betrayed by the Arabs and their so-called Sunnah Islam five hundred years ago; has come to us and made himself known to us through the mouth of His Holy Messenger, the Most Honorable Elijah Muhammad; whom these Arabs and their phony so-called Sunnah Islam, are trying to steal from Allah's Holy Messenger the real and only Muhammad RasulAllah, the Most Honorable Elijah Muhammad and not Prophet Mohammed of Arabia, birth right.

Through Our Fathers Eyes my people is where the truth lye and the Universal Creator, The Great Mahdi, Christ the Crusher, the Son of Man visited us in the Holy Persons of Master Fard Muhammad, to whom praises are due for forever; whose proper name is Allah Almighty and there is none greater than He; nor is there any liken unto Him. He Master Fard Muhammad is or I should say Allah U Akbar there is none worthy to be serve, besides Thee. No matter what our enemies may say or bring against us they will not prevail against us my people. All their wealth, all their seemingly mighty weapons and their armies, navies, air force and marines and satellites, my people, will be and are being destroyed; by the Great and Magnificent Deliverer our Ancestors prayed to and for. Through Our Fathers Eyes my people we can walk in Supreme Confidence, that the true and living Allah will never be defeated by Yakub's the Vicegerent Makings, on the Island of Pelan six thousand six hundred years ago; so, saithe Allah Almighty Himself through the mouth of His Holy Messenger the Most Honorable Elijah Muhammad.

Our enemies and their false religions are condemned by their own transgressions due to their hatred of black people and their hatred of Allah and Allah's Holy Messenger the Most Honorable Elijah or Elijah Muhammad RasulAllah, take your pick it all means the same. We were given my people the Supreme Wisdom from Allah my people Himself but due to the many traitors amongst us, have mis-les black people from the path that Allah Himself chose for us and the teachings Allah Himself taught to His Holy Messenger and this includes Malcolm X and many others; and who knew or know better than Allah and His Holy Messenger. So, these believers in Yakub, were working with Yakub's makings to take us away from looking Through Our Fathers Eyes and began teaching black people to look through the eyes, of Yakub Ibn Lucifer the Vicegerent and maker of the physical devil on the Island of Pelan, in the Agent Sea six thousand six hundred years ago. This is how you combat the Deceit Within my people by excepting the Allah the Great Deliverer our Ancestors prayed for and not the phony religions of our enemies and our enemies' mystery god. It doesn't matter what name they call their mystery god it is all a lie from and by our enemies and the enemies of our Ancestors. This mystery god that can't be seen and these phony heavens after you die are only speaking about Yakub Ibn Lucifer the Vicegerent who never saw his experiment completed because Yakub died at one hundred and fifty years old; four hundred and fifty years before his Yakub experiment was completed.

The Deceit Within was an orchestration not only by the enemies amongst us but by the enemies that were looking on, the Zionist, Christians, Arabs and Asian Hindus. The Arabs and Asian Hindus who at that time were finalizing their partnership with the Zionist and Christians, to form this new American Government of Global Terrorist. Thus, enlisting into their ranks those that would mis-lead and betrayed their people, for and to this newly formed American Regine and didn't care one bit about black people except to help murder off the real black people seeking independence, from our enemies; and deliver black people back on to the plantations of America and back into the cage of despair, which they were able to complete in 1975; after the physical death of the Holy Messenger of Allah the Most Honorable Elijah Muhammad. There are many people that won't like this statement, but it doesn't matter because this is the truth, the teachings that Allah Almighty Himself taught the Holy Messenger, is what will live forever and Allah's Teachings through His Holy Messenger, live forever in all the believers.

We must my people understand the importance of us all Looking Through Our Fathers Eyes because as it stands, you aren't looking Through Our Fathers Eyes; you are all looking Through the eyes of our enemies the devil. You love the devil because the devil gives you absolutely nothing. You fear the devil because the devil put fear in your heart when you were little boys. You fear the devil now that you are big man is because the devil taught you how to the wrong foods. The wrong foods are not just physical food my people; the mental foods of lies and deceit were just as poisonous, as the physical food that many of you are still eating. The Hypocrite of 1964 who stole the teachings from Temple # 7 that did more corruption and damage to black children and people, was on Mayor Lindsay payroll; thus, his assignment was to lead black children and people away from the True and Living Allah, of their Salvation and Allah's Holy Messenger the Most Honorable Elijah. This Hypocrite stole from Temple # 7 the examination of

Kareem and lied to all the black youth, that he was Allah when in truth he was Yakub. He led all black youth to their destruction as he set up an out post, for all the Gestapo Law Enforcement Agencies to easily infiltrate every black organization not only in New York, but throughout America; as he led the black youth and people into nothing but corrupting and self-destruction. He never taught any of the black youths or people to do something for themselves. He never taught any of the black youth and people to once again become a thriving black independent people, who are able, to govern themselves. He never taught black people to reformed themselves from the poisons of our former slave masters. He never taught the black youth about pooling their resources for them to build something for themselves. In fact, he never taught black youths or people the absolute truth because he didn't know the truth; he was envious of Allah's Holy Messenger and he fed the black youth to the cremator. This is the truth all one must do is examine the history the answers are all there, if one open their eyes and look. Through Our Fathers Eyes my people and through the eyes of liars, thieves, hypocrites and the devil himself. We must have absolute Discipline, we must have unity, we must have an economical system that works, for black people, we must have love and respect for ourselves and woman. We can only achieve this is by Looking Through Our Fathers Eyes my people then and only will be able, to keep our many enemies from infiltrating our ranks. How can you call yourself god when you have a beginning and thus you have an ending? This is the truth my people Taught to us by Almighty Allah Himself in the Holy persons of Master Fard Muhammad, to whom all holy praises are due forever; through the mouth of Allah's Holy Messenger the Most Honorable Elijah Muhammad. Through Our Fathers Eyes my people is the only way we can destroy the Deceit Within.

CHAPTER 20

THE ABBES

I heard it say that when you stare into the Abbes the Abbes the Abbes will be staring at you. We my people have been staring into the Abbes for the pass five hundred years and we never realized it. The suffering and misery we have endured is unconceivable by anyone, on our planet ever. I have travel to many states, cities and towns throughout America and the suffering of black people is all the same. The decendents of the first slaves brought to the auction blocks in Jamestown Virginia and other places in the approximately 500 years ago, have absolutely no love for their ancestors or themselves. All through they black people have been suffering unmercifully for almost five hundred, continue to believe in our enemies and our enemies most dreadful religions that have invaded black communities throughout America; which represent nothing more than White Nationalism and White Supremacy. It doesn't matter what religion our enemies are using to keep black people under their spell, as they all rape every black community throughout America of black people finances. The foreigners and immigrants that have come to America and are coming to America, have absolutely no love for the ex-slaves and the decendents of the slaves of America that helped make America become, the so-called super power she claims to be. These colored people are very disgusting to look at and be amongst because all they are doing, is imitating Caucasian people and helping Caucasian people to implant their sick disgusting homosexuality, in every black community throughout America.

This colored woman and man are cowards that like to run off with their mouths especially these colored women and then when it comes time to back up what they are saying up, then they want to call the American Gestapo called police and lie to the Gestapo Police Officers. These colored people are more dangerous to black people than Caucasian People. This is the Abbes my people and this what you are and have been living under for the pass approximately five hundred years. Anything our enemies want to steal from black people they feel that they can just do it and these colored people are always on the side of our enemies, with their Kool aid smiles. We can never rise with such enemies amongst us my people, we must separate ourselves from all our enemies and our enemies colored flunkies as well. The truth my people is that you don't know the truth at all and you believe in the lies and illusions, of our enemies and the magicians of our enemies. My people we all have been staring into the Abbes for the past five hundred years and what lies in the Abbes are the monsters and these monsters' religions, that enslaved our ancestors and kept black people disenfranchise for the past five hundred years.

We my people are all looking into the Abbes and the name of this Abbes is America the Accursed Devil. You my people are trying to fit into a society that has made you the outcast and you don't fit in. The foreigners and immigrants that have been brought here are against the decendents of the ex-slaves of America and this Zionist/Christian/Arab so-called Sunnah Islam/Asian Hinduism American Government of Global Terrorist; promotes this hatred towards us all. If this society, can use us as they choose they keep a token of us amongst them and the rest locked up in some prison, all throughout America. Yet this Zionist/Christian/Arab/Asian American Government of Global Terrorist keep you my people in a state of confusion and helplessness; hated and despise as our enemies rob us blind and give us nothing. Our enemies won't even allow us to have unity amongst ourselves so that we may have a chance, do something for ourselves. Our enemies with the help of these colored people are doing everything to keep the decendents of the slaves and ex-slaves of America, from ever becoming an independent people once again. Our enemies my people steal from us everything that we have created for ourselves and commercialized on it, leaving us with nothing for ourselves. Our enemies have stolen our language, our history, our heritage, our way of life and our culture. These foreigners and immigrants have a language in which they can communicate amongst themselves, except us my people. Making sure that we can never galvanize ourselves as a people.

Our enemies are working extra hard at keeping us from turning to our Savior who is Allah Almighty Himself Master Fard Muhammad; to whom all holy praises are due forever and Allah's last and greatest Messenger the Most Honorable Elijah Muhammad. By you my people rejecting Allah and His Holy Messenger is keeping you in the Abbes haunted by the monsters that inhabit this Abbes.

I was recently down in New Orleans Louisiana for the New Orleans Jazz Heritage Fest and I was also down in Layfette Louisiana for the International Music Fest. I learned some very interesting things, about our people during these travels. I also came through the Bayou and the Katrina disaster area and it is a pitiful site, I must say. Everywhere I have been throughout America I have observed that the decendents of the slaves that were brought here in 1555 in the first Jamestown landing, are disenfranchised and are suffering miserably. These colored cowardly Negro politicians and religious leaders don't even care, about the suffering of their supposedly people. These colored people are only concerned about the enemies of the suffering black people, throughout America. Everywhere where you go throughout America Homosexuality is on the rise in every black community and neighborhood. This is due to this Supremely Evil Matriarch system of the Caucasian Women, that these colored women have embraced. Since these colored women have embraced this evil they are only producing homosexuals and weak little boys. This is the Abbes my people that we are staring into and the monsters that we are looking at, are looking at us and have been looking at us for the past five hundred years; enjoying their evil work and deeds they all have done to us and the conditions that we as a people have been suffering under and are still suffering from.

This Zionist/Christian American Government and people of pure Terrorist and evil mind set have terrorized us black people, since 1555. These lying so-called founding fathers and mothers have stolen and kidnapped our children then sold them all throughout the Western Hemisphere, with impunity. We must make America know her sins and this is what the Holy Messenger of Allah the Most Honorable Elijah instructed us to do. I learned while in New Orleans the truth about our people in New Orleans, who are also the decendents of slaves that landed on the auction blocks in Jamestown Virginia and other places throughout the South. These devils called the founding fathers are nothing more than murderers, thieves and kidnappers their women included. France at this same time colonized Louisiana and it was Napoleon Bonaparte who sold Louisiana to Thomas Jefferson; who was the president at this time and he himself was a slave master and sold his own half breed children, into slavery. How foolish can you be my people to too praise this wicked and supremely evil American Government and all of America's filthy evil religions. America my people is the Abbes and all that you see today is nothing but an illusion and there is no truth in her at all.

I leaned while in New Orleans some of the truth of this so-called Mardi Grad our people have been fed lies, by our enemies. The Truth as I have learned by our people and not by homosexual Caucasian enemies, the masks and costumes are about when the Indians were smuggling the slaves off the plantations the Indians dressed these slaves in these costumes and painted their faces black, so that they looked like birds and the slave masters in New Orleans couldn't recognized the slaves as they escaped the plantations of New Orleans. Once the south lost the war these escaped slaves would come back and celebrate their freedom, by parading through downtown New Orleans on Bourbon Street and throughout the communities. This is a spiritual event to remind black people of their suffering and how they escaped the plantations of New Orleans and there is more to this history, that has been kept hidden from black people. The Caucasian French Homosexuals are the ones that capitalize and turned it into a spectacle called Mardi Grad and destroyed the spiritual meanings, of this magnificent event by black people; as our enemies made and are still making much money from. These black people and there are many are called the Black Mask Indians and I have spoken with many, at the New Orleans Jazz Heritage Fest; my people it is extremely beautiful. This is another fact my people Al Jolson and George M. Cohen stole from the Black Mask Indians and started Vanderbilt and Broadway as well as all, of American entertainment as we know it today, including Hollywood; is stolen from black people. This is where Al Jolson a Zionist devil came up with the black face and the song mammy, due to black women raising also breast feeding these Caucasians devils, little devil children for hundreds of years. Al Jolson is nothing but a thief him and George M. Cohen, an Irish devil, stole it all from you my people. Here is another fact my people I have learned when it comes to music and performances New Orleans will blow everyone in the world out of the water and this include New York as well. This is the Abbes my people that we all have been staring into for the last five hundred years and these monsters have been staring at us. Many of us have fallen victim to the illusion of these Caucasian beast remember my people Delilah was able to trick and fool Samson the black man, as she worked her evil plane do destroy him and this is happening today.

My people here are another fact our people in New Orleans and Louisiana period are our people; and they would farm and the men before they could afford any type of transportation, they would load up their wheel barrels of vegetables and fruits then carry them amongst and to our people. Bringing them good food at affordable prices as they chanted in a cadence that our people could and do understand, in the city letting everyone know that they are here, and they have what everyone needed. The dances are spiritual and very powerful once one understands the true meaning is all about. This is the Abbes my people and these demons are looking and enjoying their evil handy work, at keeping us separated amongst ourselves. We aren't Americans my people we are the victims of America's hatred for black people. America allows these foreigners to own homes, certain type of stores and fancy cars; yet they don't allow them to penetrate the real deal that powers America and that is the science my people. They are all in agreement with being the servants of America as America allows them to fly their meaningless colors, if all these immigrants don't forget that Old Evil Glory is the main deal.

This is the Abbes my people in which Allah Himself in the persons of Master Fard Muhammad to whom all holy praises, are due forever; raised up from amongst us my people his last holy and greatest Messenger, the Most Honorable Elijah Muhammad; and taught His Holy Messenger what we must do for ourselves. We have been betrayed my people by the Colored People you can't miss them because they are all around us. They are all written in scriptures including these immigrants as they serve this Destroying Mountain called America. The only way we can overcome this Abbes is to look Through Our Fathers Eyes and denounce this evil Matriarch American Evil Society. We are of our Father and this must never allow this to be forgotten, over looked and down played, my brothers. We must denounce everything else that is not from our fathers, our ancestors and come back to ourselves, names, religion, practices, culture, language and even style of dress. By us rejecting the ultimate truth that Allah taught His Holy Messenger the Most Honorable Elijah Muhammad, in which Allah's Holy

Messenger taught and instructed us what we should be doing as a people; black people all throughout are suffering greatly. Yet my people you still continue to believe in the enemies of our fathers; you still believe and trust in the enemies of our ancestors; you still worship the enemies of our ancestors, religions and their god; you still are believing and trusting in Satan the Accursed Devil and Satan the Accursed devil comes in many disguises also many of his false religions, all designed to keep you my people locked in this cage of despair, disenfranchisement at the bottom of the well, because you won't unite and do something for yourself. This is the Abbes my people and the demons who made this Abbes have poisoned you and by you refusing to look at our enemies Through Our Fathers Eyes, the enemies of our fathers; the enemies of our ancestors; the enemies of ourselves are getting away with keeping you in the Abbes. Your refusal of Honoring the prayers of our fathers and mothers; our ancestors for the Deliverer; for the Savior to come for them and us and bring us home; That Mighty One Has come my people and He is Allah Almighty in Person; Master Fard Muhammad to whom all holy praises are due forever. His knowledge, His wisdom, His understanding has absolutely no end my people it transcends every so-called religious book; every so-called religion and all the prophets, my people. This Mighty One isn't the Son of Allah; He is Allah the true and living God in Person; The Knower of all things and is why the Quran refer to Him as the Best Knower and His Wisdom is Supreme there is absolutely none, that can compare with him. This is the one that Yakub feared because this one the true One, Wisdom will Live Forever.

The Abbes my people are filled with the evil of our enemies and the enemies of our fathers the demons that all these churches and monuments, that conceal the truth of America, the Caucasian race and all Yakub's makings have been kept hidden from you, by our enemies my people. We have been instructed by Allah to abandon this Zionist/Christian/Arab so-called Sunnah Islam/Asian Hinduism American Government of murdering, thieving, rapist Terrorist. The fact that you are completely wrapped up in these American blood sports and entertainment, you can't see that you are keeping yourself confined in hell. You are confused my people by the illusion of this wicked society and what you believe is cool is a living hell. By you accepting this condemned society and all this society partners religions and politics leave you in the Abbes because you aren't included, in their society and government and none of them have any love for you, at all. You my people should be turning to yourself so that you can do something for yourself. Your refusal and buying into the Supremely evil and wicket Matriarch society has taken you deeper into the Abbes and the only returned is that you look Through Our Fathers Eyes because Our Father is the creator of the heavens and all the stars and planets, and the scientist can't find an end to our creator wisdom.

I can't thank our Most Wonderful Savior Allah Almighty Himself from raising up from amongst us the rejected and the despised, His last and greatest Messenger the Most Honorable Elijah Muhammad; and taught his Holy Messenger that which none of the prophets of old, ever knew and this includes Mohammed of Arabia, Esa Ibn Yusef and Muza. In fact, Ibrahim himself wasn't taught the Supreme Wisdom of Allah Almighty Himself. My people you are suffering because you are and have rejected the Great Deliverer that is the only one who came in person, to show us mercy, love, compassion, forgiveness; then bestowed upon us through His Holy Messenger, His Supreme Wisdom that absolute no one can refute; even this so-called Sunnah Islam and their so-called Holy Quran, which in truth isn't the Holy Quran because it's just a piece of the history written in the Original Holy Quran and Holy Bible, that was written over 8,000 years before our enemies were grafted out of us, the original people. The reason why this so-called Sunnah so-called Islam and this so-called Shite so-called version of Islam is in America, is to try and suppress the true Islam and the true Muhammad Rasul Allah. These frauds have partner up with America the Accursed Devil; now my people what does that make these frauds and their fraudulent so-called religions, beliefs, customs and politics, my people? Why and how are these frauds able to operate in all black communities throughout America, with impunity? If you don't know the answers here are the reasons my people. These frauds are here to help their Zionist, Christian and Hindu Brothers and Sisters, to keep the decendents of first Slaves that arrived here in 1555 and have served America for over 400 years, forever trapped into the Abbes; as they rob you my people and their children integrate into this condemned American society, as all the other foreigners and immigrants have done that have came to America. Each one bringing their own brand of dope to keep us my people deaf, dumb and blind. The Arabs and Shiites dope are their false religion so-called religion they call Islam which is no different than the Christianity, we have, and our ancestors have been enslaved under for over 400 years. These enemies no matter how they present themselves were and are the enemies of our fathers, our ancestors my people and ourselves.

Through Our Fathers Eyes my people is our only hope to escape the Abbes that we have been trapped in, for the past 500 years; caged up like an animal or as the problem book states, the Lion in the Cage walking back and forth searching for a way out of this enemy's cage that they made for us. All these magicians and false ministers are leading and keeping black people in this unholy Abbes because they aren't following the blue print, that Allah's last and greatest Messenger left for us to do. These magicians and false self- made ministers are using the teachings of Allah that He taught His Holy, for their own self- interest and self- praise. We all must return to what Allah taught His Holy Messenger and Allah's Holy Messenger taught us all and stop listing to all, of these frauds. Study and follow what Allah's Holy Messenger taught us all and follow the Blue Print that Allah gave to His Holy Messenger and build an independence Islamic Nation for ourselves. We are supposed to be building a government not this Johnny come later so-called temple where they get nothing done at all, except arguing and debating amongst themselves. None of them are fast moving nor are they fast moving in the modern day and time, my people. This is the Abbes my people because none of these charlatans can nor do they care about seeing you escape, from the Abbes my people.

Through Our Fathers Eyes my people lies the knowledge, wisdom and understanding that will and can free us all, that desire to be free overnight. We must reject this society that have been made only to be destroy at this present time in which we are now living in. When you speak to other people about their history they can only go back a few thousand years this is proof that these people are the makings of Yakub Ibn Lucifer the Vicegerent. Our history has no beginning or ending, and no one can find our beginning because our beginning could not be recorded. Therefore, we are Alfa and the Omega my people these past 6,600 years will be erased from memory as the bad nightmare, in which they have been for black people globally. We are taught by this society to hate our fathers and ourselves my brothers and we can't allow this to continue. We can't allow our enemies in Hollywood and TV land to continue to present black men, as useless and worthless people. Where women are being projected by our enemies in Hollywood and TV land, as protectors and defenders of black people; this is a total lie my people. This is this worthless Matriarch devilishment that is destroying little black males and young black men. This same evil Matriarch rule society is permitting young black girls no older than 14 and 15 years old to be sexually active and getting pregnant and who knows who the fathers may or may not be.

This is the Abbes my people this is you my people the Lion trapped in the cage walking back and forth searching for a way out and all the Lion runs into, is his enemies determined to keep the Lion trapped into the cage that his enemies, have prepared for black people; thus, keeping us starring into the Abbes forever. Through Our Fathers Eyes my people we have no other way to look. We must avoid our enemies' religions this is nothing but religious dope that is designed to keep black people forever caged up staring into the Abbes. There is no hope following the religions of our enemies my people because our enemies are getting richer, their children are getting better education, better housing, better medical care and better financial rewards, as they integrate themselves into this wicket American Society and government; you my people the direct decendents of the first slaves that were brought here in 1555 and cleared also helped build this country, are the ones that are being denied the rewards of our ancestors as well as ourselves for more than 400 years and better, of free labor. The question my people we should be asking ourselves is this; why we should as black Asiatic people should be less than any other people, that has come to America? We should ask ourselves this question also; why aren't we allow to be an independent, self-productive people? We should also ask ourselves is why anytime this American government wants to test some new drug they have made; why are we the decendents of the first black slaves that came here in 1555 are the people that the American government place in our black communities? We must ask ourselves my people if this isn't terrorism then what is?

By us my people looking through the eyes of our many enemies we can never free ourselves from the Abbes. By us excepting the made religions of our enemies we can never free ourselves from the Abbes, that we have been trapped in, for over four hundred years. By us my people allowing our many enemies to be our political leaders, we can never free ourselves from the Abbes. By us believing and trusting our many enemies and their false religions, is keeping us trapped in the Abbes made by our enemies and their god whose proper name is Yakub Ibn Lucifer, the Vicegerent. My people as much as you don't want to except and believe that Allah Almighty Himself has visited us and raised up from amongst us His last and greatest Messenger the Most Honorable Elijah Muhammad; the true and only Muhammad RasulAllah; doesn't matter at all because this remains the absolute truth. The time has come in fact it is over due that we must wake up, unified/ galvanize ourselves as one people and stand up for ourselves and build a nation and world for ourselves, women and children. Our many enemies' lye in our faces as they try to get you to believe in their maker and god Yakub Ibn Lucifer the Vicegerent; the enemy of Allah the Universal Creator, Allah's last and greatest Messenger, all of Allah's prophets, the twenty-three scientist, our ancestors and ourselves my people.

We my people have been held captive in the western hemisphere for close to five hundred years born, breaded and raised in this wilderness of sin, iniquity and transgressions. There are no other people than ourselves that needed the god of mercy; the god of forgiveness; the great Deliver; the Holy Savior; the great Redeemer and the great Restorer, which is Allah Almighty in person; whose name is Master Fard Muhammad to whom all holy praises, are due forever. You can disbelieve in Him; you can reject Him; you can speak evil against Him and His holy Messenger, the Most Honorable Elijah Muhammad. The only thing you have done my people is condemned yourself to hell with the enemies of Allah, Allah's last and greatest Messenger, Allah's prophets and the scientist; and this is an absolute shame my people; this is what's giving our many enemies' the ammunition to project to the civilize world, that you are nothing but ignorant fools because you are looking through the eyes of all of our enemies'; before you even consider looking Through Our Fathers Eyes.

The Abbess my people is where you are barely existing and dying daily or living horrible lives, especially the elders. Our people are riddle with sickness, diseases and poor health and still you believe in our enemies who are the author, of diseases, poverty, ignorance, trapped into this cage of despair name Abbes. My brothers check out these new TV shows and movies see how our many enemies are projecting these colored women as heroes, smart and daring; while they our enemies' project you their made colored man as stupid, passive and cowardly Negroes. As these colored women love and respect these homosexual Caucasian devils. This is being projected at our male children my brothers as our enemies' project our daughters as nothing but whores; The many shames my brothers are that you except these many disgraces being projected by our many enemies through TV, Hollywood and social media, of you and I my people. How they, our multiple enemies project you and us as their made colored people and colored man and woman, If you only knew your history my brothers and sisters you would know, that I am telling you the truth as Almighty Allah in person taught His last and greatest Holy Messenger and Allah's Holy Messenger taught us all; and everything he taught to us from Allah, is the absolute truth my people and everyone else on our planet; their religions, their politics, their customs and their languages. I should say their many dialects that came from the Original Language that all original people spoke at this time. It wasn't until Yakub Ibn Lucifer the Viceregent wisdom was given six thousand years to rule; thus, Yakub was only able to make a world of many imperfections. Reason being is that Yakub went outside of reality because Yakub had eight ounces of brains; thus, he was only able to produce hell. Murders, rapes everything of total and complete evil also my people, false religions, starvation, diseases a complete hell for all original people; and Yakub's wisdom and world was given the next 6,600 years to rule and Yakub's world is over and is now falling to pieces right before our eyes.

The Abbes my is and what you are living in everyone is taking bites out of you and they don't care about you one bit. These so-called West African Sunni Muslims have as much hatred for us the decendents of the slaves, that arrived here in 1555 at Jamestown Virginia and other slave auctions blocks in the south as well as the north; As these cut throat so-called Sunnah Arab Moslems and Shiite Moslem. None of them have any love for us and this is the truth; these black immigrants, yellow immigrants and red immigrants didn't endure or survived the hell that we have gone through and we are still going through, my people. Since the so-called Africans have demonstrated their hatred and disconcert for us my people who are the decendents, of those who came on board the Slave Ship Jesus, in 1555; Why are we so concerned about so-called Africa? The so-called Africans don't even know that a Homosexual named Alexander name the continent, after his homosexual lover Africana and have been ruled by the Caucasian Race, for the past five hundred years.

This is the Abbes my people no one absolutely no one loves us but Master Fard Muhammad Allah Almighty in Person; no other teachings or religions can save us my people. You my people have absolutely no clue how bless you are and we are hated because Allah Almighty Him Self raised up from amongst us my people, His last and greatest Messenger the Most Honorable Elijah Muhammad and the Supreme Wisdom which he received from Allah Almighty in the person of Master Fard Muhammad; to whom all holy praises are due forever; and the Dear Holy Apostle taught us all this Supreme Wisdom. I have received so much disrespect from West So-called Africans until it is a shame and they dare call themselves Muslims, what a disgrace my people of these so-called Africans behavior. Through Our Fathers Eyes my people we must look through because our creator is the Lord of all the Worlds and Universal creator; who has no recorded beginning and no ending. Believing in the True and Living Allah and following the teachings he Allah taught His last and greatest Messenger, we will free ourselves from the Abbes overnight.

CHAPTER 21

THE TRAITORS WE ALL MUST BE AWARE OF THAT LIVES AMONGST US

This subject my people is going to reveal the traitors amongst us and it is going to be very painful because it is going to point the finger, at people that are close to you and you may even love nevertheless they are all traitors to our people. My people these people coming from Africa and West Africa also have absolutely no love for us black people, who are the decendents of the slaves that were brought here in 1555 aboard the Slave Ship Jesus. They have come here to America and many have found success with this so-called African art in which they cater to Caucasian people. These same people also do very well with this so-called African hair braiding and yet they just like the Arabs, do nothing to aid or help black people in America. I understand why the Holy Messenger told us not to dress like them or marry them because they these so-called Africans, hate black people in America. My experience with them has shown me that they want to steal our information and use us like black people in America are their slaves. They believe that we black people who are the decendents of the first black slaves that came here in 1555, are nothing and they treat us this way. They don't believe as we believe they believe as the Arabs believes, or some other Christian Caucasian person believes. The fools that are married to them have been tricked by them in helping these so-called Africans, to exploit their own people. What is extremely disappointing is that these silly decendents of the first black slaves that came here in 1555, are helping them to exploit their people as they walk around feeling and believing they are important, while they are being treated the same way. These fools are blinded by the money and shut their eyes to the actual truth, of what is really going on and they don't care at all.

If what I am saying offends you then you must be guilty of these crimes against your own people. I had a West African Woman a so-called Sunni Muslim, say to me that in West Africa, we call you a white man. She made me aware of the hatred that these so-called African Sunni Muslims, have and think of me. How can I call these my people when they hate me and us, my people? What should I think about those who are helping them to exploit me and treat me and us, with such distain? What kind of fool can shut their eyes and ears to such hatred being spoken about their own people, by the very people they are involved with? These Traitors We Must Be Aware Of my people they use deceit, lies, cunning and sometimes even kindness, to accomplish the mission of our enemies, to exploit our people? We my people were rounded up in the Jungles of East Asia put in chains then brought to the slave departure ports in Ghana and Senegal, in West Africa where our ancestors boarded through the Doors of No Return, aboard the Slave ships heading to the new world, in the western hemisphere. Here is something else my people these so-called Africans have tribal dialects that each tribe communicate with each other, yet when they speak to other Africans not of their tribe, they communicate in French because French is the major language in West so-called Africa; not these tribal dialects, my people. In East Africa English is the major language spoken and English trumps, their tribal dialects. North East Africa speak the dialect of the Arabs so-called Arabic this you must understand, my people.

If you can help and support these open enemies of your people and yourself, how much of a true believer you claim to be, in Allah in the person of Master Fard Muhammad, to whom all holy praises are due forever? How much of a true believer you are in Allah's last and greatest Messenger the Most Honorable Elijah Muhammad? Through your works, actions and deeds you are only showing that you are a disbeliever and even a hypocrite and Allah cares nothing for the disbeliever or the hypocrite, neither does Allah's last and greatest Messenger the Most Honorable Elijah Muhammad; and not the true believers either, once our enemies are revealed. The Traitors We Must Be Aware Of are not so carefully hidden but they are very deceitful, always with a secret and hidden agenda my people. They aren't looking Through Our Fathers Eyes they are now looking through the eyes of those who hate us my people. These people also are part of the foul, evil and hateful birds, written in the 18th chapter of Revelations, that came and begged to come, to Babylon which is America. These aren't friends of ours my people they are friends of our enemies and this you must remember. All these so-called black immigrants that have come to America have absolutely any love for us, my people. They have come to America to be entertainment and please, the enemies of Allah, Allah's Holy Messenger our ancestors and ourselves. America the Accursed Devil allowed them to scrape the crumbs off their table and these cowards are grateful. There is a condition or a provision in them coming here and being allowed to be successful by America the Accursed Devil and that condition and provision is this, never aid the decendents of the first slaves that were brought here, in 1555; and never except the true and living Allah; whose proper name is Master Fard Muhammad to whom all holy praises are due forever; and never follow the true Muhammad RasulAllah the Most Honorable Elijah Muhammad and the real Islam that Allah taught to His last and greatest Messenger. I ask myself, how could a so-called believer of Allah and a so-called follower of Allah's last and greatest Messenger, be involve with so much plain evil by our enemies towards Our Holy Savior Allah Almighty Himself, Allah's Holy Messenger the Rasul, our ancestors and ourselves? What kind of hidden coward these people truly are and how much longer do they believe that they can hide, their evil?

I know this is painful my people, but it is the truth that can always be proven and the ones that are the agents of our enemies, will always be reveal and I have absolutely no problem in showing you my people this truth, that the agents of our enemies want to be kept hidden. I am a decedent of the of the tribe of Shabazz that was deceived and brought here to the western hemisphere in 1555, by our Caucasian enemies; receive absolutely any help or encouragement from these so-called believers, in the work that I am doing; in fact, these so-called believers would rather I crawl back on the plantation, rather than I prove I can do something that they can't do and they don't know how to do and I will do. What fool would want to endanger my life health and well-being, for the enemies of Allah in the person of Master Fard Muhammad to whom all holy praises are due forever and Allah's last

265

and greatest Messenger the Most Honorable Elijah Muhammad? If you think I am wrong and not telling you the truth ask these enemies what they actual think and you will learn the absolute truth, of all of Allah enemies; you will learn the absolute truth about what our enemies think about the Holy Messenger of Allah; you will learn the absolute truth what our enemies think about our ancestors and ourselves. None of them have any love for us my people and they never will, my people. What Kind of Fool Would Fall Victim To This Evil and then defend this evil, my people?

None of these so-called black immigrants that came and are still coming to America have any love or concern for us my people and we shouldn't have any concern or love for them. They are all either Christians or part of this advance Christianity called Sunnah Islam' One thing that is a surety is that they all have hatred in their hearts, for us my people. We must begin to have love for ourselves; we must begin to have unity amongst ourselves and we must keep all these infidels and their agents from amongst us. These infidels are offering black men and women who the decendents of the first black slaves who were kidnapped and brought here, to the western hemisphere in 1555; money to do phony marriages so that these infidels can get a green card and citizenship. After these infidels get what they want then it's to hell with you my people and the brokers of these evil deals care absolutely nothing about you my people because you pay these brokers and these infidels pay them as well. You must remember this my people these refugees or immigrants are our enemies', and everything is an act, to deceive the American government, for a green card and citizenship. When the black woman is involved with this evil deal these male enemies' in many cases get them pregnant; but when it comes to their women they our enemies do everything they can, to prevent their women from becoming pregnant by us black men and they have their agents working very hard on making sure this doesn't happen. I'm warning you my people these people are our enemies and these brokers are their agents and once these enemies get what they want, it's to hell with you. These are the Traitors We All Must Be Aware Of my people and beware of the lies and deceit that they come with.

This is a very painful subject my people because I have experience this evil from one who I believed was close to me and yet this person has tried, to let these so-called Africans exploit me; you can imagine how disappointed I was and am, in this person. I would rather die than allow anyone to exploit my people and these so-called Africans don't consider us my people, their people and only a fool believe that these disbelievers are our people. We must begin to protect ourselves from these interlopers who call themselves Africans because they all love the devil, more than they love us my people. These silly agents of theirs believe that we my people should stand by and let these so-called Africans enemies exploit us and we should do nothing about it, except suffer peacefully. These so-called Africans and their disgraceful agents don't ever want us the decendents of the first black slaves that arrived at the Jamestown Virginia Auction Blocks in1555, aboard the Slave Ship Jesus as well as Amazing Grace; to ever do anything for ourselves and they don't do anything to help their people, to do anything for themselves. I am only telling you the truth about what is happening and when you look pass the illusion of these traitors, you will see that their close friends are the enemies of their own people. How can you deceive your people for your own personal gain and then say that you believe in Allah and Allah's Holy Messenger? It's totally impossible my people. These persons are the Traitors We All Must Be Aware Of That Lives Amongst Us and through deceit, they move amongst us as they allow our enemies to prosper and our people continue to suffer. If I had to do anything like this to help and aid the enemies of our people for a few pieces of silver, death would be much more honorable than living. If I could Betray our Holy Savior Allah Almighty in the person of Master Fard Muhammad to whom all holy praises, are due forever; if I could betray Allah's last and greatest Messenger the Most Honorable Elijah Muhammad, for a few pieces of silver from the enemies of our Holy Savior Allah Almighty Himself, Allah's last and greatest Messenger and our ancestors; death would be more rewarding than this despicable way of life, that only disbelievers appreciated and admire.

Through Our Fathers Eyes we must stay forever diligent because these traitors amongst us care nothing about ancestors at all. These persons that are the Traitors We All Must Be Aware Of That Lives Amongst Us are very dangerous to all of us and they have completely fooled many of us. Many of us refuse to except the truth even through the evidence is over whelming against them, these who have been deceived for many years can't except the truth about these Traitors We All Must Be Aware Of and they Live Amongst Us; you my people deal with them daily and you don't have any clue whom they are because the truth of them, is extremely painful I know from personal experience. When these Traitors are amongst us they believe or act like they believe, as we believe and when they are amongst our enemies they believe as and in our enemies. What kind of fool would think or believe that my writings aren't important and the garbage that our enemies are doing is more important and benefit only themselves? We my people are not Africans and we aren't African Americans Allah Almighty Himself told us through the mouth of His Holy Messenger, the Most Honorable Elijah Muhammad that we are Asiatic Black People. Malcolm X was in complete error calling us Afro-Americans he was in complete defiance and rebellion of Allah and Allah's Holy Messenger; thus, Malcolm X caused more damage than he did good for his people.

All our enemies' love Malcolm X especially when denounce Allah and Allah's Holy Messenger and turned to Wallace D. Mohammed and began following this worthless Sunnah so-called Islam; until he discovered that these Arabs and their worthless so-called Sunnah Islam, was the enemy of his people. He Malcolm X wrote a letter to the Holy Messenger the Most Honorable Elijah Muhammad apologizing and begged for givenness and allow him to come back, amongst him and us. I was then the American government, the Arabs and their other partners, murdered our brother Malcolm X and tried to blame his murder of the Holy Messenger and his followers.

Now here is my question my people, how can anyone that calls him or herself a believer can through in with the enemies of our Holy Savior and Allah's Holy Messenger the Most Honorable Elijah Muhammad, when they know what the practioneers of this so-called Sunnah Islam, has done and continue to do for a few pieces of silver? For a few pieces of silver, they sell out their people to the enemies of Allah, Allah's Holy Messenger, our Ancestors and ourselves. The Traitors We Must Be Aware Of That Live Amongst Us my people are dangerous when you know these so-called Africans have showed black people in and of America, complete discontent and hatred. I know there are many who may not like what I am saying nevertheless I can prove what I am saying, is the truth.

My blind confused and mis-led people you must open your eyes and see what is going on around you and how much danger, you and your children are in. These immigrants are nothing more than interlopers and they aren't our people also they aren't to be trusted. These silly foolish agents that have sold us all out for a few pieces of silver, rather they realize it or not have denounce our Holy Savior Allah in the person of Master Fard Muhammad to whom all holy praises are due forever; they have denounced Allah's last and greatest Messenger the Most Honorable and they have denounced all of us. Forget what they say examine their work action and deeds, in which they work very hard on concealing. These are the Traitors We Must Be Aware Of That Live Amongst Us and through deceit and lies, they are able to disguise themselves and hide amongst us. The Holy Messenger of Allah taught us that the truth only hurts the guilty and the truth must be made known even if the truth, condemns ourselves, the truth must be made known.

What is also very disappointing is that how many believers in Allah and Allah's last and greatest Messenger is that they are easily fooled by these traitors and they can't recognize them. We are living in the judgement and many who said they believe no longer believe, they are pretending to believe. To cast false images and saying what others want to hear are the weapons these Traitors Amongst Us, use to conceal the truth about themselves. You my people supply these traitors with the ammunition that they need, to use on their own people. Many of the followers turned hypocrite or were just disbeliever from the beginning and many have just turned their back to what we should be doing, for ourselves. In fact, my people most of these traitors may make a token effort to keep their disguise in place; nevertheless, they will only make a token effort to help any of their people, to go for themselves, they are more concerned about your and my enemies.

Through Our Fathers Eyes my people we must always examine all things and never through the eyes of our open and proven enemies. There are many enemies around and amongst us that care nothing about nor for us and we must be aware of them all. We black people who are the direct decendents of the first slaves that arrived at the auctions blocks in Jamestown Virginia, in 1555 aboard the Dreadful Slave Ship Jesus and Amazing Grace must come together for us to defeat, our many enemies and their sell out agents that live amongst us. I refuse to allow our enemies to use or even think they can manipulate me in any shape, form or fashion, so that they can make money off my labor; these enemies who call themselves so-called Africans and Sunnah Muslims have more hatred for us decendents of our ancestors as this Zionist/Christian/Arab/Asian American government of global murdering terrorist. We my people need to run them also from amongst us as well, along with their treacherous traitors' agents. Don't be fool any longer my people these agents are crafty and very dangerous, to us all.

My people now we must unify ourselves because our enemies are unified unilaterally, against us. These traitor amongst us are helping them our enemies to attack us and keep us my people economically, educationally, socially, religiously, politically deprived and outcast, in this country that our ancestors and ourselves have built and defended also protected, for approximately five hundred years. These traitors are not concern about our people at all one must do is check out their names and you will find that they are afraid, to claim their true name to the government. When they are amongst us they are this and that but asked them to show you their drivers licenses, social security card, birth certificate, passport and other official document; you will see they still carry the name of the devil and they are afraid to claim their name because they don't want to offend the devil, whom they now claim the devil to be their friends.

We must not be so weak to let our enemies exploit us and we stand by as silly beggars, begging those who have hatred for, to give us a job and thus give them power over us. I would rather die than put any faith in our enemies, to something for me that I can do for myself. If you stop believing in yourself my people then you deserve to be used, under paid and miss treated by our enemies and these disgusting Traitors from amongst us. It is written and we were taught by the Holy Messenger that we will suffer in his name sake; I have discovered that many of you disbelieve in suffering in the name of our Holy Savior Allah Almighty and Allah's Holy Messenger and do something for yourself; no you cowardly in truth disbelievers have decided to throw in with the enemies of our Holy Savior Allah Almighty and Allah's Holy Messenger; no you cowards talk the talk but are truly afraid to walk the walk; you cowards are more Americans than you are believers in our Holy Savior and Deliverer Master Fard Muhammad to whom all holy praises are due forever, Allah Almighty in Person. You cowards who have sold out their people are dis-believers in Allah's last and greatest Messenger the Most Honorable Elijah Muhammad. You are all just pretenders when you are amongst those who are striving to be upright and are working towards be upright to Allah and Allah's Holy Messenger.

CHAPTER 22

THE ORIGINAL ASIATIC BLACK PATRIARCH MENTALITY AND OUR SUPERIOR PHYSICAL STRENGTH

My brothers and sisters that care to listen this is a very important chapter because it will reveal how our enemies, were able to destroy or so they believe the Patriarch rule amongst ourselves and our people, in the western hemisphere. During the fifties and sixties when the Lost Found Members of the Nation of Islam were beginning to flourish under the leadership, of the Holy Messenger of Allah the Most Honorable Elijah Muhammad; the American government devised this feminist movement to destroy the black families. The Federal Beau of Investigations was being led by a homosexual name J. Edgar Hoover who had an absolute hatred, for black people and especially black men. The Federal or American government shared this hatred for black people and black men especially, as well. The American government were complete agreement to keep black men completely suppress and dis-enfranchised as well as keeping them believing in their enemies. This was done by the American government and enforced by every law enforcement agencies and all Caucasian people, in and outside America embraced and agreed to the enforcement of the Jim Crow Law. My people this was re-enforced by the American government and every gestapo law enforcement agency in America, including the arm forces, to destroy the Black Patriarch Rule Mentality.

The Buffalo Soldiers 9th, 10th Calvary, 24th and 25th infantry was either re-named or broken up during World 2, by this devil president Franklin

D. Roosevelt and the war department. The Tuskegee Air Men aren't even mention in America's white supremacy military history, when history proves that they have the greatest escort history when they were escort American bombers, into Europe and Germany; then every other escort so-called Caucasian Companies or Airmen. The Tuskegee Air Men were called the Red Tails and never lost one bomber in the many escort missions, they had been commissioned for. These Tuskegee Air Men were educated at Tuskegee Institute which was founded by our ancestor, the Honorable Booker T. Washington after the Civil War.

Many of the Buffalo Soldiers had joined on to the Nation of Islam and many served under our Savior Master Fard Muhammad, to whom all holy praises are due forever. Then after World War 2 many of these Buffalo Soldiers served under the Holy Messenger of Allah, the Most Honorable and were very instrumental in training the FOI. In fact, my brothers many of the Buffalo Soldiers were with Prophet Noble Drew Ali and the Honorable Marcus Garvey as well. Many of the children and grandchildren of the Buffalo Soldiers served in Korea and their grandchildren and great grandchildren, served in Viet Nam. We must forget the black soldiers that made up the fighting 54th and 55th infantry either all these fighting men divisions, regiments and companies came into existence by our ancestor, the Honorable Fedrick Douglass. Our ancestor the Honorable Fedrick Douglass had the for sight to see and understand what his people, would need in the future and this is how all these fighting units came into existence; that would one day would serve the Allah and Allah's Holy Messenger the Most Honorable Elijah Muhammad. This my people are the Asiatic Black Patriarch Mentality and Physical Strength and this ancestor of ours, was the for runner predicted by the 23 Scientist to come, after the physical three hundred years of Chattel Slavery.

There were many black Asiatic women involved at this time but the difference in these women and these colored women, is that they knew and understood that the Asiatic Patriarch Mentality and Physical Strength, was and is the natural order of the universe; these colored women don't have a clue and reject the nature of such a high order, for the evil of this filthy Caucasian Matriarch devilishment. There were several Asiatic Black Queens that have ruled nations and armies such as Queen Hasphut, Zenobia, Sheba, Cleopatra but they all knew and understood the Asiatic Black Patriarch

Mentality and Physical Strength could never be deny or replace. There were over five hundred female Zulus Warriors and they knew the mental and physical strength of the Male Zulu Warriors and Kings. These Original Women are not the same as these colored women of today's time. These colored women of today's time conspired with our enemies to try and destroy the Asiatic Patriarch Mentality and our Physical Strength; all one must do is look at our male children they have no clue, on who they are or their heritage.

Although the American government and her military changed their name and renamed them, they couldn't destroy the fighting spirit and courage of the Buffalo Soldiers, 54th and 55th Infantry and the Tuskegee Air Men in them, that was birth in many of us and are still in some of us. There were many of our ancestors that served in America's navy that seen many battles and were mis-used by the American navy going back to the American Revolutionary War. Although, many of them had received medals and purple hearts, when they returned home they were deny meaningful employment as the American government and the private sector, were still instituting the Jim Crow Law and the Dredd Scott Decision, against them, their wives and children. Many foreigners were able to join the police department, but our fathers and grandfathers weren't allowed to join, NYPD or any other PD department, FBI, CIA, National Security or Homeland Security. Those whose had joined the police department were mostly immigrants from the Caribbean Island and were very eager to spy on all black organizations, in and throughout America, for our open enemies. There were a few of them who had refused this traitors detail, but the majority couldn't and didn't blink, when our enemies asked them to spy on, the Nation of Islam, the Hebrew Israelites, Black Panthers and every other black organization in America, including the black Baptist Christian.

We must stand up for ourselves my brothers and let the world know who we are my brothers and we will not let our, multiple enemies murder us any longer and get away with it. My Black Israelite brothers and sisters, my Black Nationalist brothers and sisters, my Black Panther brothers and sisters; if our open enemies continue to murder anyone of us and get away with it, our open enemies will be coming to murder the rest of, as they did in the sixties and seventies. We must all unite with each other to prevent these murdering and imprisonment of our young black men and soldiers, by all our open enemies. Our enemies aren't secret any longer my brothers they are all operating in the open because they are all in league with this Zionist/Christian/Arab/Asian American government, of global murdering terrorist. What is the plan of these American global terrorist my brothers and people? To Destroy the Asiatic Black Patriarch Mentality our superior Strength and superior abilities, my brothers and people. In today's time the Matriarch system has been employed against us my brothers and this Matriarch system is in over drive and is having great success, amongst the immigrants that are now coming and have came to America, in the last thirty years to this present day and time. None of us are so-called African Americans we are all Asiatic Black People and we shouldn't let our enemies call us by disgusting title of African American; it would be better if they just called us Negroes or better yet Niggers because that is all our enemies are calling us, think of us and treat us all any way.

None of these immigrants that have come to America and seeking to come to America have any love or concern, what America has done to us. As a matter of fact, my people the American government set up these drug cartels, for murdering black people and then steal the communities away from black people. If you think I am wrong how did all these Dominicans get into West Harlem and Washington Heights? Where did they get their funding and political protection from? Also, in Brooklyn my people this same machinery is in and has been in progress, for at least thirty years as well as Queens and the Bronx. While one set of enemies were poisoning us the other set of enemies were stealing control of the food and housing I should say the economics, in black communities in New York and every other black community, throughout America with impunity. These so-called Africans are no different from the rest of our enemies because they have no love for the decendents, of the first black slaves that arrived in Jamestown Virginia aboard the Slave Ship Jesus, in 1555. They love the devil my people and when they greet their own they are all smiles and laughter; when they speak to us they are all frowns and distain. If not for us my people none of this cowardly devil loving immigrants, would be here and prospered as they have. None of these immigrants cared about us black people if they did they wouldn't have agreed with the American government, to distribute and sell these poisons amongst us black people and in black people's community throughout America. Are you that foolish my people to believe that these are friends and that these are our people? My people these immigrants all of them have sided with our enemies to destroy us black people, everyone of them. Immigrants just coming to America have EBT Cards, Medicaid, Food Stamps and help paying their rent and they haven done a damn thing to earn these benefits at all. Yet when it comes to us my people these same immigrants do everything to either make it difficult for you or just out right deny black people and this can be proven at any time. These immigrants are even taking advantage of the Wick Program while their people, deny or make it extremely hard for black mothers to get them.

What does this tell us my people? It tells us to stand up for ourselves and to hell with everyone else. It tells us that we can't trust any of these immigrants no matter how dark they maybe, they all only have hatred in their hearts for us, my people. Why am I saying these things one may question? The reason why I am saying these this truth because it is a truth that we all must know, understand and recognize who all our enemies are; to prevent our destruction, the destruction of our families and the destruction of our heritage for these disbelieving, devil loving immigrants; this includes these so-called Africans. Through Our Fathers Eyes my people we will find no lies or deceit because our fathers loves' us and we are their children and they want the best, for us my brother. What is best for the descendants of the first black slaves who were kidnapped and brought to the western hemisphere; to the auction blocks in Jamestown Virginia in the year 1555? The best thing for us my brothers, my people is for us to return, to the to the teachings of Allah who visited us in the persons of Master Fard Muhammad, to whom all holy praises are due forever; taught His Allah last and greatest Messenger the Most Honorable Elijah Muhammad; who taught us all. These are the only teachings that will produce the Original Asiatic Black Patriarch Mentality and our Superior Physical Strength.

I'm not speaking hatred my people I am only speaking the truth as Allah's last and greatest Messenger the Most Honorable Elijah Muhammad, our leader and teacher taught us all. The time has arrived that we speak the truth and make America know her sins or die. The time has arrived that we stand up as the original man and people or lay down and die as worthless cowards also a disgrace to our Most Holy Savior Allah Almighty Himself in the person of Master Fard Muhammad and Allah's Holy Messenger the Most Honorable Elijah Muhammad. There is no amount of money that will get me to side with the enemies of our Holy Savior or Allah's last and greatest Messenger. I know this for an absolute fact that the truth that Allah revealed to His Holy Messenger which the Holy Messenger revealed to us all, will restore the Original Asiatic Black Patriarch Mentality and our Superior Physical Strength, in everyone of us that submit to the Allah who has no equal in power, or wisdom; and follow the example of His Allah last and greatest Messenger and the true Muhammad RasulAllah, the Most Honorable Elijah Muhammad. We must understand my people that we all must embrace the truth our fathers left for us to read and study, for us to reform ourselves. Following our enemies will only take us deeper and deeper into the Abbas which is nothing but a living hell, for us all. We must stand up for ourselves my brothers there is no one else, that will stand up for us my brothers and people. The more you resist the truth my people are the deeper and deeper you will sink, into this hell and the shorter the chain that is keeping you bound into the cage of despair, will continue to become and has become a strangle hold upon you and will not stop until your very life is choked out of you, your women and children my brothers.

All over the world they are stealing our heritage and are trying to lay claim to what we brought into existence, here in America. In every blood sport in America we my brothers took it to a level that the Caucasian people couldn't reach and no other people on the planet could reach. So, the American and European Medical Society instituted steroids to their Caucasian people and other people throughout the world, to compete with and against us my brothers. This is American Justice my people that all these immigrants, have embrace and that is to murder us all off by any means necessary. Through Our Fathers Eyes my brothers and people we don't have time to be debating and arguing amongst ourselves because this only produce self-hatred amongst ourselves; therefore, giving our enemies a clear avenue to pick us off one by one. Therefore, keeping us confined in this cage of absolute despair, educational despair, financial despair, social despair religious despair; this is the cage in which the Lion is lock up in and the Lion is you my people.

The arguing amongst ourselves and we are believing that we are superior to each other is a serious mistake because we have no respect or love, for each other. This is the poison that have been injected into us by our enemies and this poison is keeping us separated from each other. Together we stand my people all of us united; divided we all will fall and have been falling as our enemies prosper, of our serious mistake. Others have come and are coming into America and the American government are supporting them and have and are giving them every opportunity to improve and advance themselves, while this very government deprive us my people of these opportunities. While we my brothers are living in these concentration camps called shelters or enemies are living in houses and apartments, that rightly should be ours, if America believed in justice and equality in which America doesn't.

Through Our Fathers Eyes my brothers and people we must always look through because look what looking through the eyes of our enemies, have gotten us; absolutely nothing my people but hell, hell and more hell for the past approximately five hundred years, up to this present day and time. The Original Asiatic Black Patriarch Mentality and Our Superior Strength is what we my brothers, must return to. The only way we can accomplish this is by submitting to Allah our Holy Savior, our Holy Deliverer, our Great Redeemer and our Great Holy Restorer; in the person of Master Fard Muhammad to whom all holy praises are due forever. We must follow Allah's last and greatest Messenger the Most Honorable Elijah Muhammad our leader and teacher; and the true and only Muhammad RasulAllah. My brothers and my people our ancestors prayed for hundred of years for Him to come to do what my brothers and people? To take us away from the evil that we have fell into and the evil people and government that we were and many of us are still are serving, going on five hundred years. He Allah Almighty Himself in the person of Master Fard Muhammad to whom praise be due forever said to us all, through the mouth of His Holy Messenger the Most Honorable Elijah Muhammad; He said through the mouth of His Holy Messenger, "I am your God if thou Bear witness". Allah Almighty also said through the mouth of His Holy Servant the Most Honorable Elijah Muhammad, "I will save them all and I can save them all, if they would only believe" Through the mouth of His Holy Messenger the Most Honorable Elijah Muhammad Allah said, "I will make them the rulers of self, kind and others". He Allah said through the mouth of His Holy Messenger the Most Honorable Elijah Muhammad said, "I will remove fear and trembling from them and put it upon those, who put it upon them". Through the mouth of His Holy Messenger the Most Honorable Elijah Muhammad Allah our Holy Savior said, "I am God and besides me there is no other God". The Holy Qur-a referrers to Him Allah the true and living God which is our Holy Savior Master Fard Muhammad, as the Most Merciful and the Most Beneficent. Where is there any other than Him that have shown us the decendents of the first Black Asiatic Original people that were kidnapped, not from Africa but from East Asia; and brought here to the western hemisphere to the slave auction blocks in Jamestown Virginia; aboard the Slave Ship Jesus in 1555. Who but Allah in the person of Master Fard Muhammad to whom all holy praises are due forever, have shown us my people mercy, kindness, love and forgiveness, other than Him Allah Almighty Himself in Person?

He and only He Allah in the person of Master Fard Muhammad to whom all holy praises are due forever came to restore too us my brothers, our Original Black Asiatic Mentality and our Superior Physical Strength. He Allah Almighty Himself in Person took one of us off to the side and taught this one the Most Honorable Elijah Muhammad, His Supreme Wisdom and missioned this one to teach us all His Allah Supreme wisdom. He Allah Himself my brothers and people raised up from amongst us His last and greatest Messenger the Most Honorable Elijah Muhammad/the true and only Muhammad RasulAllah. There isn't a woman on this planet worth having if I had to denounce our Holy Savior and His last and greatest Messenger in any shape, form or fashion. Either you believe as I believe or leave me alone, if you want to be my wife and I your husband. This my brothers and people we all must understand and live also die by and nothing else. It's Through Our Fathers Eyes my brothers and people in which life everlasting exist and no where else. I will never comprise myself to help other than my own to gain wealth and these same people, do or don't give anything to help my people, just so that I can gain a few pieces of silver. The Holy Messenger of Allah didn't do it when the kings of East so-called Africa offered to build him a palace, he the Holy Apostle the Most Honorable Elijah Muhammad refused their offer. He the Holy Messenger said I must first get my people out of the fire, so there isn't any excuse for such disgraceful behavior.

The Original Black Asiatic Mentality and our Superior Physical Strength must be taught to our male children and the only way to teach our male children, is by teaching them Through Our Fathers Eyes, my brothers and no longer through the eyes of our enemies. Who are our enemies Saladin? Our enemies my brothers are everyone doing everything to lead us away from Allah Almighty who visited us in the person of Master Fard Muhammad, to whom all holy praises are due forever. Who are our enemies Saladin? Our enemies my brothers and people are everyone trying to lead us away from our leader, teacher and guide the Holy Messenger of Allah the Most Honorable Elijah Muhammad. Who are our enemies Saladin? Our enemies my brother and people are everyone trying to lead us away from our ancestors. Who are our enemies Saladin? Our enemies my brothers and people are everyone in our communities throughout America, that have sieged control over the economics, the educational, the politics, the religious and the social activities in our communities and we have nothing that belong to us or that we belong to. Who are our main enemy Saladin? Our main enemy my brother and sisters are ourselves for believing and trusting our enemies. Our main enemies my brothers and people are ourselves for believing that our enemies are our friends. Our main enemy are ourselves my brother and people for believing in all the religions of our enemies and rejecting what Allah in person brought and gave us all; through the mouth of His Holy Messenger the Most Honorable Elijah Muhammad.

If you call yourself a believer in Allah Almighty who visited us in the person of Master Fard Muhammad, to whom all holy praises are due forever. If you call yourself a follower and student of Allah's last and greatest Messenger, the Most Honorable Elijah Muhammad and you won't stand up for our Holy Savior and His Holy Messenger what good are you I ask? What can be more important than sacrificing your life and all that you own, for Allah in, the Holy person of Master Fard Muhammad and His Allah last and greatest Messenger, the Most Honorable Elijah Muhammad/Muhammad RasulAllah, that you refuse to stand up live or die for, my so-called believers this is our sworn oath. Yet many of you have sold out for a few pieces of silver; I Saladin Shabazz-Allah would rather die than disgrace our Holy Savior Allah Almighty to whom all holy praises are due forever and Allah's last and greatest Messenger the Most Honorable Elijah Muhammad and myself for a few pieces of silver. I can't do this, and I will never do this for any amount of silver from anyone especially our enemies. Who are these enemies Saladin? All these silly immigrants that have hatred and distain for us my people and these enemies believe with the help of the traitors amongst us, can use us as their tool and give us nothing my people and these traitors of Allah and

Allah's Holy Messenger and their sworn oath, are doing just that my people, for a few pieces of silver.

Understand my people we can't allow any of our enemies and their agents to use or take advantage of us never my people. Our enemies have all joined together to keep us trapped in this cage of despair their paid agents are working for our enemies, to prevent us from ascending to our Original Black Asiatic Mentality and our Superior Physical Strength, my people. None of these enemies of ours and these traitors have the right to think or believe, that they can control our time to best suit them without even asking us, if we have anything that we must do, for ourselves. To our enemies calling themselves Africans here in America have more hatred for us my people, than the Zionist/Christian/Arab/Asian American government, of global murdering terrorist. These silly ignorant traitors are so blinded by the few pieces of silver that these enemies wave in their face, until they have abandon their oath to Allah, Allah's Holy Messenger and their people; for the love of Allah, Allah's Holy Messenger and our enemies my people. This can be proven my people at anytime because our enemies aren't that smart and the traitors from amongst us that have joined up with our enemies, are even dumber than the enemies they have sold their souls to, for that few pieces of silver.

Through Our Fathers Eyes my people is what we must fully understand, and we must also understand that we aren't Africans. We are the Original Asiatic Black People who have no recorded of birth recorded and we have no recorded ending, Africa and Africans do. When you examine these so-called Africans most them are the servants of the French, English, Dutch and now America. They are here my people to entertain the Caucasian tourist that come to America every year and these so-called Africans are here to entertain them, with their trinkets, as they do in Africa. If black people in America stop going to these useless so-called African hair braiding shops, these shops will be out of business over night, in which they all should be. These so-called Africans are dependent on the ignorance of these silly colored women trying to imitate the Caucasian women, that are keeping these shops in business and truth they hate you; these so-called Africans want to rob these colored people, of their money as they talk amongst themselves in their tribal dialect, how much they can't stand the so-called American black people. These enemies smile in your face yet in their heart they have nothing but hatred for you, my people. Every African braiding shop is set but by some oriental person and shop selling fake hair, wigs, nails of all colors and styles and most of their business is being supported by these ignorant colored women. I don't understand how any so-called follower or believer could fall into the traps laid by our enemies, just for a few pieces of silver. What is even equally disgraceful as how these so-called believers turn their backs, on the truth of what is really happening and act like they don't see the evil these traitors have sold out to and this is the truth.

These traitors and they are traitors my people have abandon the true course for a few pieces of silver and are aiding our enemies to prevent us my people, from achieving our Original Black Asiatic Mentality and our Superior Physical Strength and try and replace it with a grafted mentality of lessor strength, named so-called African the Europeans Servants and Slaves, who have no love for us my people and this can be proven at any time. This truth my people must be told no matter who this truth points to and no matter who it may hurt and reveal, as the traitors amongst us; this truth must be told. Why must this truth be known Saladin? For us to defend and protect ourselves from all our enemies, my people. Anyone that have betrayed the teachings of Allah through the mouth of Allah's last and greatest Messenger, for a few pieces of silver while they deceive many of you are, on the side of our enemies and it doesn't matter who these people maybe, they are the enemies to us all. If you call yourself a believer and you are afraid to come out of the devil name in this day and time, then who and what are you I asked? We are living in a time when we must make America know her sins. We are living in the time that the Original Black Asiatic Mentally and our Superior Physical Strength, must be deployed for ourselves and not for those that are other than ourselves. It is very hard to believe that for a few pieces of silver you will and have betrayed our wonderful, most merciful Savior Allah Almighty and Allah's Holy Messenger; what a shame there is nothing else to say but what a shame.

Through Our Fathers Eyes my people not anyone else eyes and we shouldn't care whom they maybe, they are only out to deceive us all my people. You must remember my people we are not Africans and we aren't the decendents of Africans at all. We are the decendents of the Original Asiatic Black People that have no beginning, nor do we have an ending. Calling ourselves Africans is still calling ourselves the property of the

Caucasian race and I am not any Caucasian person property in any shape, form or fashion. These so-called Africans do not and cannot demonstrate the Original Black Asiatic Mentality because they aren't original people; they are also the makings of Yakub's experiment better known as Yakub's graftation, from the Original Black Asiatic Mentality and People. They believe they are original people, but they aren't my people they do not have the original mentality, they only have the original complexion and that is all. If they were of the Original Mentality they wouldn't be calling themselves Africans; after a European Caucasian Homosexual. Through Our Fathers Eyes my people and not through the eyes of our enemies and you show me where these so-called Africans that squirmed their way into America, through us my people Arabs and every other immigrant included and after they lie also deceive the immigration department, by your help my people; these so-called Africans, Arabs and every other immigrant tell you, to hell with you my people. This is an absolute fact that they all are doing if their so-called homelands are so beautiful then I asked this question; What the hell are you coming here for? If you say your country is so beautiful what the hell are doing are you all doing here? If you believe that you have a creative mind in which none of you interlopers have, then what are you all doing here? If we my people had our own land we wouldn't be here.

We must not allow these enemies of ours to continue their deceit upon us my people. We must stop doing slave work and long hours for our enemies in which they pay you below the minimum wage, set by the government and this includes these so-called Africans, Arabs and everyone else and their worthless religions, my people. No, the time has come that we should be using our creative minds for ourselves to benefit ourselves and to hell with these foreign interlopers everyone of them my people. Only Through Our Fathers Eyes we will be able to obtain our Original Black Asiatic Mentality and our Superior Physical Strength. This can only be achieved my people is by submitting to our Holy Savior Allah Almighty Himself who visited us in the person of Master Fard Muhammad, to whom all holy praises are due forever. We must follow the Allah's last and greatest Messenger the Most Honorable Elijah Muhammad; he the Holy Apostle is the only perfect example raised and taught, by Allah Himself. All we must do is follow the teachings given by Allah to His Holy Messenger and all the programs and the blue print, which has been created by Allah for us my people.

Things are very critical for us my people and we can't hesitate at all don't be fool by the language our enemies use when they call you brother or sister, there isn't any truth or sincerity in what they are saying my people they are all deceiving us with the help of these disgusting traitors, that are working for our enemies to destroy us all. To keep the mass of black people as the Lion in the cage mention in the Problem Book. You must recognize these are the Hidden Symbols that Allah Almighty Himself taught us through the mouth of His, Holy Messenger the Most Honorable Elijah Muhammad; whose writings will and has surpassed All of the so- called recognize Scholars of Immensity, exceling every one of them in wisdom that they couldn't allow Black Original Asiatic Mentality People, these are our enemies thoughts and actions: One: In Congress my people: we have shut off every means of light to the Negro this is us my people and the light is nothing more my people than us having some understanding or clue, of how the Monetary System and the importance, of understanding the Monetary System, is very important. There are many people in this society that some have much greater than others; with the knowledge and privilege to this information, can extract more money and everything else in this society than you are able to, my people. This means my people it is incumbent that we understand all monetary banking systems and how to make it work for you and us all. This requires a great deal of discipline and the controlling the non-essential expenders, on absolute nonsense and foolishness my people. To compete in the modern day and time we must make this adjustment to; getting out of dept is the key because dept, is a not so new designed plan of slavery, for the entire mass, it's been told to me there are approximately seven billion people on our planet. So, ten percent of the seven billion people are controlling the lives of perhaps six billion people, monetary futures, before they are even born.

As a people we must have a better more matured serious understanding of this Yakub's made world and especially their monetary system, which includes the banking system greatly because these two systems are keeping most of the world population, living slaves to the Monetary systems that are in opposition to Allah Almighty and Allah's last and greatest Messenger the Most Honorable Elijah Muhammad. I Saladin Shabazz-Allah am a believer in Allah in the person of Master Fard Muhammad, to Whom all holy praises are due forever; the finder and life giver to us my people who were completely dead, to the knowledge of ourselves and others. I Saladin Shabazz-Allah am a true follower of Allah's last and greatest Messenger the Most Honorable Elijah Muhammad the true and only, Muhammad RasulAllah; his wisdom that he received, the Holy Messenger received directly from Allah Almighty. His name in Qur-an is Mahdi; in the Bible he is referred by many names such as the Son of Man, the Christ, the Holy One, the Father and this person is God/Allah Almighty in person to whom praises are dur forever and this is no one else, but Master Fard Muhammad Our Lord, Savior, Our Deliverer my people, our Restore and Our Redeemer my forgotten people.

We can no longer stand by acting like none of this has happen and have continue to happen to us my people, for the past near five hundred years. Liars, thieves, murderers, rapist and every other kind of evil, are standing judgement over you my people. Only Through Our Fathers Eyes will we able to see and pilot ourselves through this, mankind made of Supreme Evil. My brothers and people we are being judge by murderers, thieves, kidnappers, rapist and liars, there isn't any justice for you and me under this American system and government; and there has never been any justice for us under this present American system and government, my people. We must stand up and do something for ourselves and get away from this evil system of America, the American people and most treacherous government. We must my brothers return to our Original Black Asiatic Mentality and our Superior Physical Strength, this is the only way for us to overcome, the many enemies that are lying and waiting to murder us all.

Remember the prayers of our ancestors as they were being smuggle from East Asia by enemies and brought here to the western hemisphere, in chains. Remember the prayers of our ancestors when they were on the auction blocks not only in the South but the North as well. Remember the prayers of our ancestors when they labored for our enemies and were treated by our enemies, less than the beast of the field and every other creature. Remember the prayers of our ancestors when they were forced to eat the worst possible food, that was never meant for any human being consumption and many of you are still eating this food. Remember the many raping's of our foremothers and young boys for hundreds of years by our enemies and nothing has ever been done about it. Remember my people the inhumane treatment by these devils towards our ancestors cutting the babies out of the mother's wombs, then smashing the baby's heads against rocks or under their boots, as the Caucasian women sat back and laugh; as they our enemies had orgies as they enjoyed this supreme devilishment, along with their children. Remember the tortures, the burnings, the hot tar and feathering of our ancestor's men, women and children. Remember the many unjustified lynching's of our ancestor's men, women and children, by our enemies and our enemies expect us my people to forget and forgive them for these un-godly acts, they have done to us my people. Our enemies are supremely devious when it come to us my people.

Don't ever forget that America started a war in South Asia for the CIA to smuggle in one hundred percent pure Heroin, for the express purpose of murdering black people, by the millions. Remember how this American government and their law enforcement agencies pump that crack into black communities throughout America, in which the American government made up in their laboratories to murder us my people, therefore murdering millions black people again. All of this was done my people to prevent us my brothers from excepting our Original Black Asiatic Mentality and regaining our Superior Physical Strength. This was all done by this Zionist/Christian/Arab/Asian American government of Global Terrorist, to prevent us from submitting to the Savior who is Allah that our Ancestors prayed for, the Great Deliverer in the person of Master Fard Muhammad, to whom all holy praises are due forever. This my people were done to us, by this Zionist/Christian/Arab/Asian American government of Global American Terrorist, to turn us away from Allah's last and greatest Messenger the Most Honorable Elijah Muhammad. This was designed by this Zionist/Christian//Arab/Asian Hindu American government of Global Terrorist, to prevent us from excepting the Islam that Allah Almighty taught to His Holy Messenger the Most Honorable Elijah Muhammad; whose mission was to teach us all and build a protype for us a government, for ourselves. This was designed by our enemies my people by supremely evil Zionist/Christian/Arab Sunnah/Asian Hindu American government of Global Murdering Terrorist; to prevent us from ever becoming, an independent self-sufficient government; capable of governing ourselves and reclaim all the stolen treasures from black people, that can be found in every museum in every Caucasian government, banking system, diamond market and society, throughout the world.

All this supreme evil my people was done to us by designed by our 6,600-year-old enemies up to this present day and time, to prevent us my brothers and people from returning to our Original Black Asiatic Mentality and regaining our Superior Physical Strength and this is a fact my people. Yakub's world which is the Caucasian world that we are now living in, is now falling to pieces and it is time that we my people organize ourselves and build a new Jerusalem for ourselves. We must come out of her my people because there is no other way for us, to save ourselves. There isn't any reason for us not turn to the only teachings that led us all, to freedom, justice and equality. There aren't any other teachings that will lead us to total self-independence. There aren't any other teachings that will put us back on the road of being, a sovereign nation; as we were before these dreadful slave ships and our most dreadful enemies. We are living in the day in which we my people must make the hard decision and choose what is best for all of us and not a few of us. We must leave this world practices and beliefs behind and strive for the world that Allah's Holy Messenger the Most Honorable Elijah Muhammad, taught us all to work and strive for; with every fiber in our being.

Through Our Fathers Eyes is the only way my brothers and people will be able to regain our Original Black Asiatic Mentality and our Superior Physical Strength. There is nothing to fear my people from doing for ourselves we must understand this, we have plenty to fear by following and believing in our enemies; their religions, politics, their way of life and their practices. We must return to ourselves my people and leave others to themselves. We must learn how to unify ourselves into a productive machinery that the world will marvel at, forever my people. We must remember that for the past approximately five hundred years we were brainwashed, spiritually washed, socially washed, educationally washed politically washed, economically washed, into believing in our enemies; our enemies have been successful while we have been suffering in hell day and night year after year, century after century. How much longer are you willing to suffer at the hands of our enemies my people? I'm not willing to suffer any longer my people. We must raise our Flag the Sun, Moon and Star that Allah Himself, gave to us through His Holy Messenger the Most Honorable Elijah Muhammad; declaring us to be a sovereign and independent nation of righteous people. Through Our Fathers Eyes is the only way we will my brothers achieve our Original Black Asiatic Mentality and our Superior Strength. Remember the name of our Most

Holy Savior and Deliverer Allah Almighty Himself in the person of Master Fard Muhammad, to whom all holy praises are due forever. Obey and follow the teachings and programs that Allah taught His last and greatest Messenger the Most Honorable Elijah Muhammad and the Holy Apostle taught us all; Our cry is Freedom, Justice and Equality for us all.

CHAPTER 23

THE MOST WONDERFUL AND MOST MERCIFUL STRANGE AND HIS DEFENDER OF TRUTH

This chapter is about The Defender Of Truth and who the Defender Of Truth truly is many of us haven't a clue who this Mighty Warrior is because the truth about him, is kept hidden from you. The Defender Of Truth was born in Sandersville Georgia in 1897 a seventh son of a seventh son. His grandfather knew he was a special child and he held him at heart. As a child growing up in Georgia he personally seen many horrors being done to his people and there was never any justice, for his people. The lynching's, the rapes, the many false charges imposed upon black men and young black boys who were completely innocent, of these false charges and then given another life sentence of Chattel Slavery, now called the Chain Gang. As shear croppers our people couldn't afford to barely keep food on the table in the decrypted shacks, they all lived in on top of each other. Education was non-existence for the mass of black people every able body and male, was sent off into the fields, without hesitation and in many cases, women included with new born babies on their backs, or in baskets. From here my people The Defender Of Truth would rise and has been raised and his people didn't know it would be him.

The Defender Of Truth to be grew up took on a wife and together they started their family and within a few years he, his wife and children move to Detroit Michigan in a section known as The Bottom. They were totally shock at the conditions in the North-West, were equal to the hell in the South, perhaps even worst. Arriving in Detroit Michigan around the mid,1920s or so they began setting up house hold conditions were horrific and extremely dangerous, for all black people in America. Hard ships and the Jim Crow Law in Full Effect you must remember this my people the American Government just murdered Noble Drew a few years ago and our beautiful brother Prophet Noble Drew Ali gave his life, in the Defense Of Truth. The American Government just destroyed Marcus Garvey and his movement and deported him back to the Island of Jamaica, as a criminal and un-wanted in America. The American Government had our brother Paul Roberson on the run and the Caucasian Governments tract him Mr. Paul Roberson around the world, relentlessly and there were many others captured and either lynched, burned, tarred and feather I'm speaking more horrible than any movie you have ever seen because it is real, for The Defender Of Truth To Be in living color everyday of his life and people lives as well.

Through the most un-imaginable conditions being inflicted upon them by man-kind appeared a Stranger, to The Defender Of Truth To Be, this happened in 1930/1931. This Stranger had been here since 1914 a matter of fact, this stranger arrived in Detroit Michigan in the section called the Bottom July 4th, 1914, and began teaching Islam, as a way of life. The Stranger Started the First Publication of The Final Call To Islam in the twenties, along with the first 25,000 followers in which the Stranger named Himself. The conditions my people our people and ancestors had to exist under, can never be forgiven and we my people should never forget. So, in 1930 The Defender Of Truth met face to face with the Stranger and he knew who the Stranger was. In the old Gospel Original Gospel of our ancestors Jesus Gave Me Water and it Was Not From the well; I first heard this being sang by our beautiful brother Sam Cooke and The Soul Stirrers, who was also murdered in 1965 and the murderers went free as usual. In this beautiful Gospel The Woman From Samira that went to the well, to get some water is not a female. That woman that met the Stranger is The Defender Of Truth. That woman started shouting as her drinking became richer and from the water He gave her, and it was not from the well. This woman started shouting because his drinking became richer. It was The Defender Of Truth who began telling everyone that Allah/God is here in person and He is a man like ourselves; this is in 1930/1931 my people and the world. So, The Defender Of Truth was no longer to be; The Defender Of Truth had now began his private Toer ridge, by The Stranger Himself for the next three years and four months.

The Defender Of Truth began his mission in 1934 and he never falter at all in faith, belief or physically and this Defender Of Truth would eclipse, all those before him and he certainly did my people. The Defender Of Truth Mission ended physically for him in 1974; there are many who will say 1975 but this is incorrect. The Defender Of Truth Mission ended after Saviour's Day 1974 the Farewell Address Of The Defender Of Truth, to you and me my people. My people I am a student and follower of The Defender Of Truth and if not for him and the God of him, I wouldn't be able to do the work I am doing now. Many have sat at the Defender Of Truth table or in his living room, as he lectured them all. Many of them thought that they knew better and rejected The Defender Of Truth, believing they were The Defender Of Truth and they all have failed and responsible for a lot of black people being killed or imprisoned, for life as well as themselves because they thought they were The Defender Of Truth, when in fact they weren't and never could be, The Defender Of Truth.

I can tell you my people and the world none of them were The Defender Of Truth it doesn't matter whom their names might be, none of them were The Defender Of Truth and they did more harm than good. The Defender Of Truth received his teachings and instructions and was appointed to his mission by This Most Wonderful Stranger; that none of these other so-called leaders and teachers didn't even know, who this Stranger was or is and they weren't anointed by The Stranger. None of these so-called leaders of the past and none of these so-called leaders of the present, were ever appointed or anointed, by this Most Wonderful Stranger. The Defender Of Truth had taught many and many people through the course of his forty -year mission and without a doubt ninety to ninety-five percent turned hypocrites' and these hypocrites screamed the loudest, "Teach Us Dare Holy Apostle We Don't Know". The Defender Of Truth burden was so great none around him could begin to understand, what really was happening with him and what is the real goal and how too, obtain the objective.

Many different organizations started popping up in the early and mid-sixties and the seventies, calling themselves this and that but none of these so-called leaders of these organizations had a clue, as to what the real objective was and is. The Defender Of Truth had to deal with the enemies within and had to deal with the enemies, that were on the hunt seeking to slay him; and those who followed him. Yet this Chosen Defender Of Truth By The Stranger kept his faith in The Stranger and The Defender Of Truth kept his word to The Stranger. So, beginning from 1934 the Defender Of Truth began his mission and he was now, the Leader and Teacher of the new Jerusalem and the builder of a new government, nation and people. There were many false leaders trying to project themselves as the Defender Of Truth and they all have failed us; their constructed ideologies that they believed would avail them, ended up failing them and all those that believed in them.

During all this confusion The Defender Of Truth continued his mission and began making greater strides, for his people and nation. Then these silly foolish so-called leaders without any preparations or organization jumped on this Arm Struggle Approach and the results were disastrous, for you and me my people. These so-called leaders of this arm struggle approach didn't have a clue on what must be done first, before there could ever be such a thing, as arm struggle in America and this includes Malcolm X as well. Instead of truly gravitating to what the Wonderful Stranger brought and taught His Prized Student, The Defender Of Truth; who intern taught all these hypocrite so-called leaders that caused more harm than good; and this also includes Malcolm X and all the rest. In fact, my people this is our problem today everybody wants to be a minister, for the self-praise. Yet very few have the conviction in their hearts as The True Defender Of Truth thus can only mis-lead you my people and rob you my people, of your hard earned, money.

The Defender Of Truth mission was and is the greatest mission that Allah had ever placed upon any of His prophets, before because the Defender Of Truth would be the fore-filler in a land that hated him; from a people that hated him; and our enemies despised him. I heard many of these charlatans calling themselves many things including Allah, as they spread poisonous teachings amongst the youth mis-leading and condemning them to a life, of prisons and misery. What made their teachings poisonous Saladin? What made their teachings poisonous is because they were not appointed by The Stranger and the Stranger never taught them anything and they only stole, the teachings of The Most Wonderful Stranger, from The Defender Of Truth. Those that were around The Stranger during the twenties and early thirties, didn't know who this Strangers was. So, when The Stranger appointed His Student to be the Defender Of Truth the click of Iblis was formed and there were a few of them as they plotted the death, of The Defender Of Truth and cursed The Wonderful Stranger.

The Defender Of Truth was also given the task of reading and studying a certain one hundred and four books in the Library of Congress and else where's and the Defender Of Truth began his mission. In the mean time the enemies of The Defender Of Truth began setting up their own organization as they began telling lies and robbing black people without mercy and keeping them in hell. Judge Rutherford is an enemy of the Defender Of Truth and he was a member of the Iblis Crew as well, that sought to murder The Defender Of Truth as he and the click, cursed The Most Wonderful Stranger. This so-called scientology is the enemy of the Most Wonderful Stranger and The Defender Of Truth. Anyone that teaches you my people to trust and believe with anyone or their untruth ideology that conspired to murder, The Defender Of Truth is our enemy my people; I don't care what their names might be, he or she they are our enemies and they mean us no good at all. The Defender Of Truth forged on with all the obstacles that were in his path, The Defender Of Truth stayed faithful and diligent to his mission and if not for The Defender Of Truth I wouldn't be doing what I am doing today.

The Defender Of Truth was imprisoned by the American Government during the early 1940s to prevent him, from teaching his people not to join the American Armed Forces because they had nothing to gain from joining and they never gained anything ever, from joining the American Armed Forces, starting from the Continental Army led by George Washington and the founding fathers. So, the Defender Of Truth was taken of to prison, for the next five years. Nevertheless, The Defender Of Truth spread Islam throughout the prison system, in America and very, very strong soldiers, ministers, captains, first officers and many more joined with The Defender Of Truth when they were release from prison. The Defender Of Truth was release from prison in 1946 and The Defender Of Truth got right back on business of building a nation and teaching his people the truth as Allah taught him.

The Defender Of Truth never once doubted The Stranger that taught him everything that had been hidden, for the last sixty- six trillions of years.

The truth was fire pure energy re-shaping the minds and the way black people thought of themselves also what was and has been going on around them; and now it is time we stand up and do something for ourselves. My people from the thirties, the forties, the fifties, the sixties all the way to 1974/1975. The Defender Of Truth remained on post as he searched out better opportunities for his people that would set us all up with being able to go, to the market of inter-national trade, as a sovereign nation and people. It was The Defender Of Truth that taught us why we must leave our enemies names behind and re-claim our own name. It was the Defender Of Truth that taught us the necessity of us, uniting amongst and with ourselves. It is the Defender Of Truth that awaken millions of his people and set them back on the road, of being a nation and self-reliant. It is the Defender Of Truth that all of these want to be leaders stole their information, to propel themselves as a so-called leader. All these so-called rebellious students met with extreme failure death and long prison terms, including Malcolm X. Their egos caused the death of many young black man and women because they were all envious, of The Defender Of Truth and they sought to over throw him and they all partnered up with his and our enemies.

The enemies love Malcolm because Malcolm fell under their spell and he Malcolm was fascinated by this, he was receiving recognition and praise from our enemies. The wizards of this American society new he Malcolm and the rest of these so-called want to be leaders, were not capable of leading us out of the mental slavery, we were all in-caged in; then we start receiving mix instructions, from them all. This only caused more confusion amongst a people that were already confused and slowed down all forward progress, for million of black people in America. Not only intellectually but spiritually, educationally and economically. They were all failures my people and they only lead us back into the grave, that we are in right now. This society have you my people believing and praising the rebellious students of The Defender Of Truth and the enemies of The Defender Of Truth and they themselves became the enemies, of The Defender Of Truth and we as well. One thing is clear, and history verifies this, that all have failed and caused the un-necessary death and imprisonment, of many young black men, women, children and families; that still affects us all till this present day.

Through all the scorn from his own people and enemies The Defender Of Truth forged on for you and I although there were many enemies and disbelievers, around him plotting with our enemies to over through The Defender Of Truth and kill off all his followers; that believed in him and the true and living Allah, The Defender Of Truth represented. There has been much self- hatred produce by these false teachers amongst ourselves mainly due to these false teachers not knowing what the truth really was and is, so they cause division amongst us my people, rather than unity. These false teachers and leaders have taken all those that believed in them deeper and deeper into the Abbas with no solution, in us redeemer ourselves and all these false teachers are gone and you my people don't know what to do. All these false teachers have failed us miserably with their lies and false teachings, trying to present themselves as something they know they aren't. None of these false teachers are The Defender Of Truth many of them are the rebellious students of The Defender Of Truth and were part of trying to over through The Defender Of Truth and they don't teach you my people, who is the real Defender Of Truth. This I can say with absolute surety none of these rebellious so-called students are The Defender Of Truth nor are any of them, are a sincere student, of The Defender Of Truth.

The Defender Of Truth said to the American government if they believe in truth and are fair. The Defender of Truth said give us the ex-slaves three to four states, for ourselves. Give us everything that we will need to set up civilization for ourselves and twenty to twenty-five years of aid, until we are able to go for ourselves. My people this is what our ancestors did for their maker and god Yakub and our enemies know this, to be the truth. Everything that we need means engineers of construction, aero dynamics, mechanical engineers, chemical engineers, ship construction engineers and Noematic science, heavy duty equipment engineers and builders, of this earth moving equipment, electrical engineers and technicians, Hydronic engineering which plumbing is a major part of this science, when developing states, cities and towns, Agronomy engineering and algaculture engineering so we can learn once again, to grow food for ourselves so none us no hunger ever again; We must have experts in carpeting and experts carpenters, Plumbers, electricians, concrete engineers, brick masons, roofing engineers, foundation engineers, Doctors of all fields of medicine, nurses and everything which maintains and daily operations, of all hospitals clinics and we need the mangers and staff as well; we automotive engineers technicians and mechanics; every thing that every other people have, we want it also my people. This is the real and true Reformation my people anything else is a joke and all intelligent wise civilization know this to be the truth, that can't be challenged by anyone, people or government.

My people and the people of the world, all that I have learned in my life came from The Defender Of Truth and not from any, of these, Pharaoh Magicians. I made sure I didn't confused falsehood with the truth; you have only received false teachings from Pharaoh's Magicians and their false concept of religion and most defiantly Islam. What these Magicians of Pharaoh/America has helped our enemies designed a stronger cage my people, to keep us trapped in; while they collect their few pieces of worthless silver. This is being carried out on levels my people and by people that are close to you; I can tell you this if you closely examine these frauds, you will see that they aren't the students of The Defender Of Truth and they have in truth abandoned The Defender Of Truth and The Most Wonderful Stranger. I've had some of these people say to me I should write a book I said go ahead and do it and none of them could do it, or wouldn't make the sacrifice it takes, to do it.

I place no one on the same level or above The Most Wonderful Stranger to whom praises are due forever and I am a student and follower, of The Defender Of Truth and the teachings he received, from Allah, The Most Wonderful Stranger, to my grave. All the atrocities that happened to us my people in the sixties, seventies and eighties, were a direct result of these false teachers and their false teachings, that threwus backwards and allowed more of our enemies to migrate into America and infiltrate our communities, under false pretense. This is due to the false teachings and false leaders like Yakub thinking they could make a better so-called Negro, than The Most Wonderful Stranger and His Defender Of Truth; and each and everyone of them have failed; miserably couldn't even equate with the unilateral Carnage, they made for their own people; by those that are physically dead; by those that have insane years in prison; and by those who still walking around us, disguising themselves as a high society type; when in truth they are the members of the Pharaoh's not so secret society of Magicians.

The Defender Of Truth taught us about the big and little snake in the Theology Time so how is it possible that you can't recognized them, when they are in your mist. The Magicians of Pharaoh are very in fact they down right masterful, at painting a self- portrait, of themselves and with skill language, choice words and statements, these magicians have cast their spells down for Pharaoh and these magicians have cast you all away from The Most Wonderful Stranger and His Defender Of Truth; and into the clutches of our six-six hundred years enemies and these magicians don't care that you are being destroyed because they consider themselves to be high society. Pay close attention to the words of the magicians because they lead you away from The Most Wonderful Stranger and His Defender Of Truth and tried to implant themselves, as The Defender Of Truth in which they know they aren't and will never be.

They all sat in the ranks as The Defender Of Truth educated them and taught them how to eat to live, fasting and so much, much, much, much, more it's truly hurtful to see how much these little boys, hated The Defender Of Truth and The Most Wonderful Stranger that visited us, my people to whom all holy praises, are due forever. Then how is it possible that so many false descriptions and statements that these Magicians of Pharaoh have been making and are making, can be proven lies because none of them are The Defender Of Truth, my people? None of these magicians of Pharaoh are appointed or anointed by higher intelligence or power, which immolates from this Most Wonderful Stranger to whom praises are due forever and most surly not from The Defender Of Truth, the Holy Servant Of The Most Wonderful Stranger Himself; none of these other magicians can make this claim, so the magicians of Pharaoh use hocus and pocus, fancy words and antics, not only to bring you my people under their spells, but to keep you away from asking and studying the teachings of the Holy Defender Of Truth in which The Holy Defender received from The Most Wonderful Stranger to whom all holy praises, are due forever.

We can no longer believe in this hocus pocus devilishment coming from Pharaoh's Paid Magicians and we must keep our eyes on these little snakes also because they are always around you, seeking a way, how they can increase their few pieces of nothing silver dust, into the few pieces of silver, that Pharaoh is handing out, to his best workers. So being deceitful and a liar and they teach this to others knowing that this path, is the path of death it doesn't matter if they get paid. Anyone that can teach this devilishment and they believe they are doing it in secret, so no one knows it is coming from them, this is a most despicable person and you will know this or these persons, by the lies they are constantly telling and the false image that they have made for themselves.

The Defender Of Truth taught us all for over forty years revealing to us the hidden truth of America's history and all our enemies. We didn't even know that our enemies look like us or something like us and they were all working on the side, of the American government to keep us locked up in their cage. Every accomplishment The Defender Of Truth had achieved he achieved it by pooling the resources of his people and invested these resources, on building an independent nation, for his people and himself. The Defender Of Truth under his guidance, built Muhammad University Islam across the country. He purchased thousand and thousand acres of farm land, throughout the country, so that we can begin growing our own food, for ourselves and people. The many bakeries steak houses, stake and takes all throughout the country. The Guarantee Bank, the many housing projects and developments and factories that we could begin producing, our own clothing. The three hundred bed hospital for our sick and wounded and much, much more; that none of these Magicians of Pharaoh could ever produce. The Defender Of Truth had struct up deals with governments in south America Peru is one of these countries, where as we were importing thousand and thousand of metric tons fish to help feed all of us, at a price we all could afford. Muhammad Temples Of Islam in every state and city, throughout America where our people could come and learn the truth, about Allah and the devil. None of these false leaders I don't care what their names maybe, have done anything on this magnitude and they never will be able to this because they aren't The Defender Of Truth; they are the hateful and rebellious students of The Defender Of Truth.

I have heard the false teachings from these rebellious students and they all have mixed falsehood into the teachings that The Most Wonderful Stranger taught and gave to His Defender Of Truth, so that The Defender Of Truth could teach us all. These false teachings have only poison all of those that fell under their spells. As they accomplished absolutely nothing for the mass of black people and everything for themselves. These rebellious don't even teach the truth about The Most Wonderful Stranger that visited us; no, they teach lies about The Wonderful Stranger to mis-lead you my people and set themselves up as though they are high society type, as they aid our enemies in keeping the mass of black people trapped in this cage of despair. Instead of these rebellious students of The Defender Of Truth setting up together a National, State, City and local government, they all chose to set themselves up as some make believe, king that has done nothing for their people at all. You can believe in these magicians all you want but I can tell you this my people, they are all mis-leading you so that may live a life of luxury and to hell with us all. We all must stand up and demand that these so-called self-appointed leaders and so-called ministers, teach you the truth about The Most Wonderful Stranger and His Mighty Defender Of Truth. If these so-called self-appointed leaders and so-called ministers can't do this then you should run away from, as fast as you can and stay as far away from them as possible and this is the truth my people. I am not telling anyone that they should follow me or that I am special and put me on a false pedestal because I'm not; I am a student and follower of The Defender Of Truth and I submit to the Most Wonderful Stranger, that chose His Defender Of Truth. I can also tell you this none of these so-called leaders or ministers have been chosen, by The Most Wonderful Stranger and they have all corrupted the teachings that The Most Wonderful Stranger taught His Mighty Defender Of Truth; and the Mighty Defender Of Truth taught us all. Anyone no matter how sweet their words may sound, and they are trying to claim the position of The Defender Of Truth is nothing but a liar. Anyone that is trying to claim the identity of The Most Wonderful Stranger is also a liar and all these false leaders are keeping us divided my people; so that they can feel important and special. I can't see how any of them believe they are important or special, be one of the Magicians Of Pharaoh. In fact, these false self-appointed leaders are supporting this evil matriarch mentality and helping to suppress the Original Asiatic Black Mentality and our Superior Physical Strength.

We my people cannot allow ourselves to be fooled and mis-led by anyone any longer while these parasites live a life of luxury, in which they don't deserve; while the mass of black people suffer and suffer this includes women and our children, my people. These false so-called self-appointed leaders have not done anything to produce one tenth, of what the Defender Of Truth had accomplished and they never will. This our problem today my people these so-called self-appointed leaders are spreading false teachings, all of them and this is only helping to keep us all confused. That Wonderful Stranger is the Lord Of The Dawn and He has no associates and there is none like Him. That Wonderful Stranger demonstrated to us my people, His and only His mercy and no one else He gave to us, a people that didn't know any mercy at all, for four hundred years. I don't see anyone of these so-called self-appointed leaders equal to Him. It is due to The Wonderful Stranger that you now have an idea of who you truly are and what we must do for ourselves. Therefore, we my brothers and sisters must form a National Government For Ourselves. It's upon our shoulders to Re-Build The National Government for the Lost and Found Members of the Tribe of Shabazz, belonging to Islam here in North America.

Many may have doubt but if we don't sit down across the board we aren't never going to get anything done, on the National and International level. Our enemies don't want us to operate on this level they our enemies want to keep us local and divided, therefor we are contained. We are a Sovereign Nation our problem is that we don't have a National body of government; we don't have any State body of government; we don't have any City or Local body of government. There is no chosen leader my people and don't fall victim to the manipulation of words, go directly to The Defender Of Truth and the teachings that he received, from The Most Wonderful and Most Merciful Stranger; and The Mighty Defender Of Truth taught us all, about The Most Wonderful and Most Merciful Stranger and what His name is; where He came from and why He was here, at his time; The Mighty Defender Of Truth oh yes he is because the teachings The Mighty Defender Of Truth received from The Most Wonderful and Most Merciful Stranger, whom the scientist can't find an end to His Wisdom.

This truth must be known not only to us my people but to every being on our planet and that is the reality, on who Allah is. He Almighty Allah visited us not as a spook or invisible, He Allah appeared to us as He is which is a man. None of these so-called religious factions in which they control at least three-fourth of the earth population and what they think and believe in; want this to be known because this ten percent click are keeping three-fourth of the world population, believing that Allah is a spirit and can't be seen until one dies; and there this make believe, heaven that you are going to, after you die. We aren't living in the of Allah's prophets, we are living in the days of Allah Himself. All the destruction that's happening in America and throughout the world, This Most Wonderful and Merciful Stranger taught His Defender Of Truth would come and there is no stopping it and this Mighty Defender Of Truth, taught us all what The Most Wonderful and Most Kind Stranger taught him. This Mighty Defender Of Truth stood on the square if he didn't, we wouldn't my brothers and people as well as these false so-called leaders, would be as deaf. Dumb and blind today, as we were hundreds, of years ago. If not for this Wonderful, Most Kind, Most merciful all wise Stranger we will be still eating the guts of the pig and hog, believing that this was a delicacy. If not for what this Mighty Defender Of Truth brought to us all, which are teachings and Message From Allah, all of us would be nothing. Yet all of you false so-called leaders and so-called ministers, denounce The Holy Most Wonderful and Merciful Stranger and His Mighty Defender Of Truth and believe that you are greater; how insane you all sound and are, to believe this insanity.

You couldn't save yourselves so-called self-appointed leaders and so-called ministers so why are you teaching our people, these dis-graceful lies; trying to make our people believe that you are something that everyone should know, that you aren't. Trying to integrate this devilish Scientology with Islam is an abomination and a dis-grace, to The Most Wonderful, Most Wise, Most Kind and The Most Merciful Holy Stranger and His Holy Servant The Defender Of Truth. It is most mind boggling that all these so-called self-appointed leaders and ministers, came to The Mighty Defender Of Truth hungry, naked and out of doors completely deaf, dumb and blind and now you rebellious little boys, believe you all know better than him and The Most Wonderful Stranger, who brought you wisdom, from heaven in which He is the Soul Master and His Holy Servant The Defender Of Truth, is His right arm. While The Holy Defender Of Truth was making inter-national contacts with our people in different parts, of the eastern hemisphere and South America setting up inter-national trader that would benefit the mass, of his people; these same jealous and envious little boys were going behind The Defender Of Truth, trying to cut their own deals for themselves; and you my, people are that foolish to choose these jealous and envious little rebellious boys, as your leaders when they all defied The Defender Truth and The Most Wonderful and Most Merciful Stranger.

Can't you see the extreme necessity of building a National, State, City and local government because we don't have any at all. Where are our National Contracts with other governments and people, throughout the world? Where are our farms, dairy plants, tanning plants so that we can make clothes and shoes, for ourselves, my people? We have absolutely nothing as a people living under the rebellious students of The Defender Truth, rulership and so-called leadership. What was torn down by the rebellious students and there were many hypocrites and disbelievers amongst them and ninety percent if not better, jumped ship and said they didn't believe in The Defender Of Truth nor do they believe in the Most Wonderful Savior, this was said by them all. Then they jumped on the Sunnah band wagon and integrated themselves back into arms, of America the Accursed Devil; still second now third class so-called American citizens. These traitors believed that submitting to the Arabs so-called Sunnah Islam; that Allah can't be seen until you die; believe in prophet you will go to a glorious heaven/Jeda. My people this is the same thing that we were taught when we were under the religion of Christianity, which many of you still are. My point is this; what is the difference my suffering and misery will never end and hasn't end, now we have demoted to third and fourth class, so-called American Citizens. Which only amounts to being, the ex-slave of America and her partners.

Ninety-five percent of the earth's population has no clue on the reality of Allah and they also have no clue, on who Muhammad RasulAllah is, this is the Islamic world my. Ninety-five percent of the Christian world has no clue who Jesus or the Son of Man is, my people. Both worlds my people have rejected the Most Wonderful Stranger and His Defender Of Truth/ Muhammad RasulAllah. If you choose to play games and believe that you can deceive Allah go head and try; I know you only deceive yourself, so I'm not bother by these traitors because a traitor is a traitor, no matter what level these traitors are operating on; they are still nothing, but traitors and they can never be trusted. The Most Wonderful, Most Merciful, Most Wise and Most Kind Stranger, to whom praises are due forever. I consider it an honor to be the follower and student of The Defender Of Truth and the teachings that he received, from The Most Wonderful Stranger. I'm not making any of this up it is a matter of history that can be examine by anyone, at any given time.

By works, actions and their deeds spotting the traitors of The Most Wonderful and Most Merciful Stranger and His Defender Of Truth. When you pay attention on how secretive and clandestine they are my people these are the traitors cloak of invisibility; false image, smooth whispered lies and deceit are the weapons that these traitors use, to control your mind and your purse my people. This is happening at all levels of society my people and it's being performed on and against you. Every slick talking traitor who don't want to take charge of his/her destiny, are also out to pick your bones clean and none of them care my people. By operating in a fine mist that the naked eye cannot detect theses traitors feel they are operating with impunity because they now have so-called friendship with our Zionist and Arabs enemies. The truth is my people our enemies are using these traitors and with the help of these traitors, our enemies can gain a stronger grip, of the economics in black communities throughout America. This is what is happening my people if these little snakes can get a crumb or two, from their twenty first century masters, they will continue to help and aid our enemies to rob their people and this is going on at the local level my people, as well as the so-called higher echelon. Then these traitors dear believe that that they can fool the true at heart, mind and spirt of The Most Wonderful and Most Merciful Stranger and His Mighty Defender Of Truth; and in many cases these traitors have done just that.

I have heard many of our people say that they are righteous because they follow so-called Sunnah Islam and I have personally witness evil and dis-grace, from the authors of this so-called Sunnah Islam; so how can you achieve righteousness from people that have proven, they aren't righteous and killed the last prophet, that was sent to them Esa Ibn Yusef. How do you make your salat and then go out and commit evil and we all see this every day, here in America? You are a fool my people to accept any of these people as our friends because they all have partnered up with America the Accurses Devil. This partner has the so-called Torah, This one has the so-called Holy Qur'an and this one has the so-called Holy Bible and this one has the ancient scrolls of Buddha in which has also been corrupted by our enemies, now and for a very long time has been called Hinduism. This is as least thirty-five thousand years before the birth, of prophet Muhammad and thousands of years before the birth of Ibrahim and many others; Islam as a way of life has been working for us my people and has always been amongst us my people, every since Allah created Himself and the entire universe, un-told trillions of years ago.

The Defender Of Truth was and is one hundred percent sincere to The Most Wonderful Stranger that had the True History Of Time, what happened during certain points, in time and when will be the end of the present time, in which we are living in and taught this knowledge to The Defender Of Truth. The Defender Of Truth never once thought or believed that he was greater than his teacher, The Most Wonderful and Most Merciful Stranger; that the world has been waiting for, since the birth of Yakub; this Most Wonderful and Merciful Stranger is our friend my people and our creator. The Defender Of Truth wasn't rebellious, jealous and envious of his teacher and leader, The Most Wonderful Stranger as the rebellious, jealous and envious little boys that were only pretending to be followers and believers and soon as the opportunity presented itself; these rebellious, jealous and envious little boys, betrayed The Defender Of Truth and The Most Wonderful and Most Merciful Stranger and even denied them both, to the enemies of The Defender Of Truth and The Most Wonderful and Most Kind Stranger.

The Defender Of Truth never in his entire mission ever changed a word of what the Most Wonderful and Most Merciful Stranger taught him, for three years and four months. Even after the Most Wonderful and the Most Supremely Wise Stranger placed The Defender Of Truth in charge, of the lost and found members, of the Tribe of Shabazz and Islam in the western hemisphere; he The Defender Of Truth never became rebellious and began changing the teachings of his leader and teacher The Most Wonderful, The Most Merciful, The Wisest and The Most Kind Stranger, who was so Beneficent to teach him so that The Defender Of Truth could teach us all. Yet more than ninety percent of these rebellious, jealous little boys did just the opposite to The Defender Of Truth and The Most Wonderful Stranger, for the love and praise of our enemies and their grafted teachings have produce nothing but grafted twenty-first century American slaves, living in a false past therefore rendering them useless my people, on ever building a future filled with independence, glory, honor and praise amongst the civilize people of the world. Never being able to take or re-claim our original origin, on our planet in which we come from and were created to be and created on; in which no one can find a beginning of us my people.

Saying that you are a so-called African or African decent is only saying that I have birth record, I have a beginning and I have an ending. Africa is the name given to those who eventually submitted to many different Europeans, that was murdering off men, women and children at a whole sell level, enslaving the population, stealing from the whole the original and natural language and super-imposing one of the different European languages. Many has kept or developed their tribal languages but on the mass scale these Africans communicate with each other, through French. So, these so-called Africans only have history of themselves that our enemies, allow them to have. West Africa follow this so-called Sunnah Islam so, they pray and believe, as the Arabs do, and they believe in that, which does not exist my people. So, these rebellious, jealous and envious students of The Defender Of Truth have only led you my people deeper into error, because they are rebellious of The Defender Of Truth and The Most Wonderful Stranger. In fact, my people you will find out these rebellious, jealous and envious students are on the pay-role of Pharaoh and their titles are, the Magicians of Pharaoh. Their duty and purpose my people is to keep you my people forever trapped in this cage of despair, without any hope of ever being free.

We were given specific instructions by The Defender Of Truth that we must honor, obey and follow and none of these rebellious, jealous envious little bays as The Defender Of Truth referred to them as being; have the right or the wisdom to changes these instructions and teachings, my people. These rebellious, jealous and envious little boys have all mis-led us my people and they continue to mis-lead us because their wisdom is very weak and grafted from the original teachings that The Defender Of Truth, taught us all; and therefore, The Defender Of Truth called them all little boys and these are the ones you my people, have chosen for your leaders. I am very proud that I haven't never taken any of them as my leader, teacher and I certainly don't follow any of them and I don't waste my time reading their weak grafted teachings.

Why would I a student and follower of The Defender Of Truth waste my time listening to any of the rebellious, jealous and envious students of The Defender Of Truth, when I know who and what they are? Why would I waste my time on these traitors of The Defender Of Truth when I know what these traitors crimes are? How intelligent could I be knowing who these magicians of Pharaoh are and know what they are doing? How can I Saladin Shabazz-Allah ever trust any of these traitors when I heard and read how they denounce The Defender Of Truth and The Most Wonderful and Most Merciful Stranger and the Teachings that This Most Wonderful, Most Merciful, Most Kind, Most Wise, Most Beneficent Stranger, taught His Defender Of Truth? These rebellious fools my people can never be trusted because they only lead you my people, into error because their wisdom is so weak until it can't produce freedom, justice, equality and independence, for

304

you my people as a Sovereign Independent Nation of, Original People. How silly would I be if I allow myself to fall under the spells of these rebellious, jealous and envious little boys and their weak insane wisdom? My people this is the truth that can be proven at any given time, if you want to know the truth, or the lies of the rebellious, jealous and envious little boys and their weak wisdom and fake teachings.

The only one person that has more knowledge, wisdom and understanding than The Defender Of Truth is his leader and teacher, The Most Wonderful and Most Merciful Stranger to whom all holy praises are due forever; and not these rebellious, jealous and envious little boys, who know nothing in comparison to The Defender Of Truth. Since these rebellious, jealous and envious little boys have rejected the Most Wonderful and Most Merciful Stranger and His Defender Of Truth, we my people have only suffered greatly because the rebellious little boys, haven't a clue as to what they are doing and have led you all in the wrong direction and don't have the intelligence to stop their foolishness submit and follow the teachings that the Defender Of Truth, had taught them in person; then and only then will they able to lead our people in the right direction but they are rebellious, jealous, and envious little boys; that want things according to how they want, even if we all must die due to their errors of them being rebellious little boys.

We must understand my people Allah did not send the Great Mahdi this a complete lye my people; this is one of many lies made up by the rebellious, ungrateful, jealous and envious so-called students, of The Defender Of Truth and The Defender Truth never taught us these lies at all. The Great Mahdi is Allah in person as The Defender Of Truth taught us all but these rebellious, jealous, envious and ungrateful students, chose to concoct these abdominal lies against The Most Wonderful and Most Merciful Stranger and His Defender Of Truth; so that they all could remain in the favor, of America the Accursed Devil. What is being taught by these rebellious, jealous, envious and ungrateful students are nothing but lies, designed by Pharaoh and his Magicians to keep us my people, forever trapped into cage of despair, that we have been caged in for the past approximately five hundred years.

This is the reason my people why we all must understand why it is such a great necessity that we study the teachings, given and taught to The Defender Of Truth, by The Most Wonderful, The Most Merciful, The All

Wise, The most Forgiven Stranger; to whom all holy praise are due forever taught to The Defender Of Truth in person face to face. I am so grateful that the Most Wonderful Stranger raised up from amongst us my people, His Holy and Mighty Defender of Truth the last and greatest Messenger Of Allah the Most Honorable Elijah Muhammad/Muhammad RasulAllah. It is more important that we my brothers and sisters must keep the pure and true teachings of Allah intact and not include the false teachings of these rebellious, jealous, envious and ungrateful so-called students, teachings who are nothing more than disbelieving hypocrites and traitors.

There are many who know who these rebellious, jealous, envious and ungrateful so-called students are, but they only speak about this in secret and amongst those they believe, won't reveal this truth of them. I don't care my people The Defender Of Truth did not teach me to be a coward and sell my people out, for anything. The Defender Of Truth didn't teach me to be a coward and not stand up for the truth, even at the risk of my own life. The Defender Of Truth didn't teach me to throw in with the enemies of The Most Wonderful Stranger and His Mighty Defender Of Truth and our people, for some maybe silver dust/crumbs. The Defender Of Truth taught me as well as us all, to stand on the square and not pretend too be standing on the square; as many of them are doing today. The Defender Of Truth taught me and us all that we must reveal the truth even if the truth, condemns our own selves. The Defender Of Truth taught us that we must speak the truth or die; he didn't teach us to mix falsehood with truth and The Defender Of Truth never told us to trust, believe or follow any of these rebellious, jealous, envious and ungrateful disbelieving and hypocrite so-called students; that claim to be believers and jumped ship faster than the rats, jumping ship off the Mayflower, at Plymouth Rock. Denying The Defender Of Truth and our Most Wonderful, Most Kind, Most Merciful, All wise and Most Forgiven Stranger who is Allah the True and Living Allah, in the person of Master Fard Muhammad; to whom all holy praises are due forever.

February 26,1975 they all revealed themselves and their true natures my people, I was There. It was the most disgusting time for our people in the twentieth century, twenty-five years before the twenty-first century/ sixteenth thousand year of history from our present twenty-five-thousand-year cycle, of history that we my people, recorded in advance. Our enemies wish that the mass of us never learn this truth because this truth will destroy our enemies, everyone of them, their false religions and filthy politics. So the Zionist/Christian, Arab so-called Sunnah Islam/Asian Hinduism Wizards came up a very useful way how to best utilize these rebellious, jealous, envious, ungrateful students AKA little boys; so in order to keep the chosen people of Allah, from obtaining freedom, justice and equality; to keep the chosen people of Allah from ever becoming a Sovereign Nation, with Allah at the helm and the Defender Of Truth, as His second in command. I'm not making any of this up just examine the facts and be-able to coordinate the time frame, when all of this took place and all who have prospered off this Betrayal, up till this present day and time. The rebellious, jealous, envious and ungrateful little boys are living great; while the rest of the mass must struggle believing in the lies, of this ten percent, with in our nation my people, disguised as one of us; but in truth they are the Magicians of Pharaoh/America the Accursed Devil.

The betrayal my people by our own people was an is catastrophic leaving us all in a very compromised position, up till this very day. Many of our young men are wondering in this concrete and steel jungle not knowing what to do or how to do because these rebellious, jealous, envious and ungrateful so-called students, robbed us of our atmosphere and sold it to our enemies with out any concern, for any of us. Then as time progress our enemies began arriving in America like locust getting help and housing from the government including medical and food. With help and aid our enemies were able slip into our communities and began setting up out post, all over America. Therefore, forcing us my people out of the communities where we had been, for generations. With the great betrayal of 1975 by these rebellious, jealous, envious and ungrateful little boys, we had no first line defense against our enemies second wave attack of chemical destruction, called crack.

My people, these rebellious, jealous, envious and ungrateful students of The Defender Of Truth caused all this destruction, amongst us. You don't look around yourself my people and access the damage that was done and the pitiful condition, it left us all in. Not one of these so-called practioneers of this so-called Sunnah Islam, rather they be Arabs, West Africans, Pakistanis, Palestinians, Egyptians, Chinses and everyone else; give employment to black people. What they will do with the help of these traitors from amongst us, is use us my people, for cheap labor lower than the minimum wage set by the federal government. They will never and none of them has tried to educate black people on how business is conducted, and this includes what the market is about, due to our atmosphere being stolen from us, by these rebellious, jealous, envious and ungrateful little boys and given to the rest of the above mention people.

My people there isn't any justification for such despicable behavior, actions and deeds, by these rebellious, jealous, envy and ungrateful little boys; that they would, and they did destroy everything The Defender Of Truth built, for us all my people; to put us on the road of another chemical holocaust; as our enemies plotted the liquidation of millions of their people; these rebellious, jealous, envious and ungrateful little boys helped and aided our enemies, in the disenfranchisement of their people; help the enemies to lock us up there people; in these cages, which was nothing more than chemical sterilization of us my people, The Most Wonderful Stranger to whom praises are due forever, and His Mighty Defender Of Truth and the teachings from the Wonderful and Most Merciful Stranger that He taught His Mighty Defender Of Truth; as these criminals, sat and split up the money that we all contributed to, for many years were stolen from us my people and sold off everything that would make us my people, a sovereign, independent nation; that has earned the right to sit amongst every other sovereign independent nation of people, on our planet. My people there is much that is being kept secret from you of the Great Betrayal Of 1975 that you all should know about and the players that were involve, in this most Diabolical Treachery from amongst ourselves, since we been in the western hemisphere my people, from 1555 to the present day.

The Defender Of Truth is greater than any of his rebellious, jealous, envious and ungrateful so-called students, will ever be because none of them were chosen by The Most Wonderful and Merciful Stranger and The Defender Of Truth never appointed any of them, to the position of leader and teacher. As Yakub came in a vacuum these rebellious, jealous, envious and ungrateful little boys also came in a vacuum; if you understand that this vacuum is produce from the dissatisfied and produces nothing but chaos and destruction, as we have witness. Yakub was working with only thirty percent dissatisfaction amongst the people. Ninety percent of The Defender Of Truth followers were dissatisfied because they either wanted The Defender

Of Truth position, or a position that they felt offer them power and respect or in many cases it was both position of power and money.

We my people have nothing to atone for unless you were foolish enough to put your trust in the rebellious, jealous, envious and ungrateful little boys and allow them to mis-lead you away, from The Defender Of Truth and the Most Wonderful and Merciful Stranger and the Mighty Supreme Wisdom, which are the teachings, The Most Wonderful And Most Merciful Stranger taught to His Mighty Defender Of Truth; in which This Mighty Defender Of Truth taught us all; ninety percent of these rebellious, jealous, envious and ungrateful little boys, threw the teachings that The Most Wonderful, Supremely Wise and Most Merciful Stranger, behind their backs and didn't care as they began making up their own so-called teachings, from their own weak wisdom. These rebellious, jealous, envious and ungrateful little boys are the ones that need to atone, for their crimes. The progress of our nation has been stagnated by these rebellious, jealous, envious, ungrateful and foolish little boys and their very weak wisdom. All of them are trying and have been trying to incorporate the Nation Of Islam as their personal business and this is truly evil and wrong, my people. We the lost and found members of the Tribe of Shabazz belonging to the Nation Of Islam in the western hemisphere, do not agree or support this foolishness, of these rebellious, jealous, envious, ungrateful and foolishness of these little boys.

The Nation Of Islam in the western hemisphere is not a corporation to be use by these dis-believing hypocrites, to make themselves rich of our labor and money. No, my people we are a nation swallowed up by another nation because of the treacheries of a bunch of disbelieving hypocrites and they do not represent any of us my people, they only represent themselves and how well they can live by keeping you, deaf, dumb and blind my people. These false so-called leaders do not represent Allah that visited us in person to whom all holy praises are due forever; The Most Wonderful, The Most Merciful Stranger. These false so-called leaders are the ones that rebelled against Allah's Defender Of Truth and then threw in with the enemies of The Most Wonderful and Merciful Stranger, His Mighty Defender Of Truth and you my people; for their own selfish personal gain. Through lies, deceit and trickery these false leaders have convinced you my people, to believe in them and not The Most Wonderful and All Wise Stranger and His Mighty Defender Of Truth. Since 1975 to this present day we haven't made any progress at all especially under the false leadership, of these disbelieving hypocrites. This isn't something I made up what I am saying is a matter of history that these rebellious, jealous, envious, ungrateful and foolish little boys, want to keep conceal of their part, they played in this diabolical treachery against The Most Wonderful and Merciful Stranger, His Mighty Defender Of Truth and their own people, for a few pieces of silver and to recognize as a person of status, from our enemies and amongst our enemies.

The Most Wonderful, The Most Merciful, The All Wise, The Finder and Life To Us My People is Master Fard Muhammad Allah Almighty Himself, in Person; to whom all holy praises are due forever. He Allah Almighty himself raised up one from amongst us my people, who had been suffering in this strange land; in a strange hemisphere; amongst a stranger people since 1555 and absolutely no relief ever came our way, until the coming of This Most Wonderful, Most Majestic, All Knowing and Wise and The Most Merciful Stranger and this is a fact. History proves that the American government and people have murdered, tried to murder or made them go into hiding in different parts of the world, that tried to stand up for us my people our ancestors. The list of murdered of our ancestors is endless because the American government and people, have been doing this to us my people; every since we boarded the Dreadful Slave-Ship Jesus and landed in Jamestown Virginia in 1555.

Justice my people has two scales and Justice isn't blind my people; Justice can see the truth because Justice can weight which is truth and which is the lie, by weighting the true and absolute facts, of all situations. The Truth of this Zionist/Christian/Arab so-called Sunnah Islam/Asian Hinduism American government, Of global terrorist has been made known. The Truth of every rebellious, jealous, envious, ungrateful and foolish little boy, that rebelled from the teachings of the Most Wonderful Stranger and His Defender Of Truth, are also known my people. This is the reason none of them have been able to galvanize us as a people with a National, State, City and local bodies of government. This would show the world that we are a true Sovereign Independent Nation with our own Flag, belonging to Islam every where we go. None of them are our leader and teacher because they don't qualify, to be our leader and teacher and history and Justice, will always back me up with absolute, true facts, about what I am saying.

I my people am a follower, believer and student of The Mighty Defender Of Truth the Holy Messenger of Allah, the Most Honorable Elijah Muhammad/Muhammad RasulAllah and absolutely no one else and most certainly not any of these rebellious, jealous, envious, ungrateful and foolish little boys. I submit to The Most Wonderful, The Most Merciful, The All Knowing and Most Wise Stranger who is Allah Himself, in the person of Master Fard Muhammad to whom all holy praises are due forever. My people these rebellious, jealous, envious, ungrateful and foolish little boys are nothing in comparison, to the chosen Defender Of Truth and everyone should be studying the teachings that The Defender Of Truth received from Our Most Wonderful and Most Merciful Visitor; rather than read and study the trick knowledge, these rebellious, jealous, envious, ungrateful foolish little boys, that betrayed Allah and Allah's last and greatest Messenger and robbed us my people, of our atmosphere, for a few pieces of silver that was stolen from us my people and so-called prestige.

The Defender Of Truth is as I previously stated the Most Honorable Elijah Muhammad/Muhammad RasulAllah and absolutely no one else and most certainly none of these rebellious, jealous, envious, ungrateful and foolish little boys, dis-guised as so-called leaders and teachers. This is why we must form our National, State, City and Local Governments, for ourselves and elect the most qualified, to represent us all at all levels of government; and do away with this self -appointed monarch rulership, which has led us all into nothing but hell especially since 1975, when through trickery and manipulation of true facts and with-holding these true important facts from you my people; these hypocrites and dis-believers were able to gain control and set themselves up as our leaders and teachers; when they all were and are the enemies of Allah Almighty Himself and His Mighty Defender Of Truth the Most Honorable Elijah Muhammad. Everything I am saying my people is the truth and a matter of our history that we can't ignore, no matter how it may hurt the truth remains the truth. Through Our Fathers Eyes my people we much search through and not through these false leaders eyes, who set themselves up as our leaders and teachers thus beginning their weak and no progress, monarchial rulership and this started on a grand scale in 1975, The Great Betrayal by these rebellious, jealous, envious, ungrateful and foolish little boys, now dare themselves our leader and teachers, when in truth they are nothing more than traitors, hypocrites and dis-believers to Allah The

Most Wonderful, The Most Merciful, The All Wise and Knowing, The Most Kind and The Most Merciful Stranger and His last and greatest Messenger the Most Honorable Elijah Muhammad, The Mighty Defender Of Truth.

I submit to the true and living Allah and due to the Mighty Defender Of Truth I know who He is, and I am truly grateful to the Mighty Defender Of Truth or I would be defiantly still blind, deaf and dumb, to the reality of Allah and Satan the Accursed Devil as well as all, of our enemies. So, I have no use of our enemies' interpretation of religion and especially Islam because our enemies have no clue, on what is the real and true Islam. Islam was perfected as a ritualist form of Islam, for the enemies my people and their maker Yakub the Vicegerent, who was given the power to act as Allah for the next six-thousand years wisdom, last act to and for his makings was to make or perfect this ritualist version of his, the Vicegerent Islam, for his children and makings not us my people; in which his the Vicegerent children and makings, had only for approximately one thousand four hundred years. This is also an absolute fact my people these so-called practioneers of this so-called Sunnah Islam, will never tell the truth of their part in the International Slave-Trade and their partnership with this Zionist/ Christian/ Asian Hinduism American government, of Global Terrorist. We are complete fools to follow, trust or believe in any of our enemies, at all. These are the co-conspirators along with the rebellious, jealous, envious, ungrateful and foolish little boys that betrayed us and turned over everything that we our parents and grandparents, had worked so hard for, under such hellish conditions, to our enemies; what a dis-grace my people. How could you trust any of these dis-believing and hypocrite little boys and their so-called Sunnah friends? This Diabolical Betrayal that our enemies collectively launch on February 26,1975 was implemented against us all; should be remember by us all as the Birth Of Our Most Wonderful and Most Merciful Saviour; and not of what these traitors, disbelieving, hypocrites, rebellious, jealous, envious, ungrateful and foolish little boys, Diabolical Treachery, in which they all participated and did willingly, to us all; for the stolen pieces of silver that is rightly ours my people.

As they tried to and did dis-graced themselves and their dis-belief towards the Most Wonderful Stranger and His Mighty Defender Of Truth and us my people. Nothing I am saying isn't the truth my people and to the world this is a matter of history, that can be proven at any given time.

I love my people that have the courage to stay at home and fight our six-six-hundred -year old enemies. I have absolutely no respect for these many cowards that are in America killing themselves, to prove to America they are true African-Americans; this is an absolute dis-grace my people and they aren't our people. The fools who have joined on to them and believe you can walk both sides of this fence, to hell with you to. None of these West so-called Africans or any so-called Africans period don't want anything to do with us, my people only when they believe that they can prosper, off our labor when in truth they have no love in their hearts, for any of us my people. When it comes to being deceitful and conniving to us my people, these so-called Africans wouldn't hesitate to deceive us all, my people; they are true African-Americans and damn proud of it.

This is Universal Justice and the truth must be told about everyone my people including ourselves. The picture isn't pretty at all my people nevertheless, we my people have the power to make everything beautiful for ourselves, once again. All we must do is return back to the teachings that the Most Wonderful and Most Merciful Stranger taught His Mighty Defender Of Truth and which The Mighty Defender Of Truth taught us all and don't shut your eyes to the truth and never shut your eyes on who our enemies are and whom our enemies are working for.

CHAPTER 24

THE CONCLUSION

In my conclusion my people and everyone that has taken the time to read this book I want everyone to understand that I'm not angry with anyone. It isn't my intentions to start any kind of race riots or what America calls hate crimes; although we my people have been the victim of hate crimes for approximately the past five hundred years, up till this present day and time. No other people other than us my people have any right, to be upset than us. We don't want to try and change this present government and society because they are already condemned for destruction. No, my people my writings are to call us all back on our post so that we can build a world, for ourselves with the absent of the evils from this world and this world people. We have absolutely no use for any other peoples' religions, politics, practices, customs, religious books, language and everything else about them because they all have proven to be our enemies. The only thing we want from our enemies is too stay away from us and leave us alone. Every time we allow any of our enemies amongst us or around us, hell follows behind and with them and this has proven to be by designed. So, I say my people we are behind the times and we must work extra hard to place ourselves heaven, at once and as we live. This society and government my people are absolutely doomed and if you continue to follow and believe in this government and people, you, your wives and children are doomed also.

We have suffered enough my people our children have suffered enough these programs of America will never bring you my people, any permeant solution or an end to your suffering. You must remember my people this Caucasian Matriarch System was and is designed to turn the black male soldiers, into nothing more than homosexuals and the females are laying with each other as well. This is hell my people that all the scriptures are speaking about. All these immigrants that have come here to America and are killing themselves to get here, have all embraced this evil and wicket American sub-culture because they can be anti-black there for showing America that they are in complete agreement, in keeping the American so-called Negro forever lock up in their cage, of despair and misery. Thieves, murderers, liars, kidnappers, rapist, are nothing more than global terrorist and these are the ones judging you and myself. These aren't people or a government of honest people these people and government have no more love for us my people, than they did for our ancestors. These American people along with their filthy, evil American government are trying to force feed black people, into embracing this satanic homosexuality and teach our black children that it is okay. Well my people it isn't okay with and they should keep their filth, amongst themselves and their colored people; and all the immigrants that love and believe in them and our enemies' way of life.

Religion is used as a weapon against us my people to not only control us to keep us my people trapped into their prepared cage, of misery for us all my people. This so-called Sunnah Islam is not a friend to us my people no more than Zionism, Christianity and Hinduism have been a friend; no, it's just another weapon that our enemies are able, to use against us my people, that will forever keep us, the decendents of the first Asiatic black slaves that were kidnapped and brought here to the western hemisphere, aboard the Slave Ship Jesus, in 1555. Trapped into this cage of despair, educational despair, financial despair, social despair, medical despair, political despair, religious despair; trapped in this prison walking where you aren't even allowed, to fish or plant crops for the mass of our people. Entrapped in this un-merciful prison where we are being led away from the sciences to provide, for ourselves, as a civilize intelligent people. We can no longer afford to allow ourselves to continue to fall into these enemies, of ours made traps my people for the soul purpose of Destroying the Original Black Asiatic Mentality and Our Superior Physical Strength. To turn us away my people from Allah and Allah's true Holy Messenger, the most Honorable Elijah Muhammad and the Islam Allah gave to us all, through the mouth of His Holy Messenger. None of these other so called- Africans, Arabs, Hindus, Christian, Pakistan, Palestine none from the east hemisphere, came looking for us because they knew that we my people, are the stolen people and that we were kept hidden, in the Far North; in a land they didn't understand and amongst a people not of their own, my people and the world included, The Mighty One would come from East in fact from the mountains of Paran or Mount Paran, with horns of power in His Hands driving nations asunder. This Mighty One is none other than Allah Almighty Himself in the person of Master Fard Muhammad to whom all holy praises are due forever. The Finder and life giver to us all if you just believe and Follow the teachings in which He taught His Holy Messenger the Most Honorable Elijah Muhammad and all the programs the Holy Messenger taught and built the porotype of our being one of the many members belonging to Islam, in the Wilderness of North America, that we are my people a Sovereign Nation; the lost and now found members of the Nation of Islam.

We must execute all the programs and progress reports during the time the Holy Messenger, was physically amongst us my people. We must act and conduct ourselves in a more broader scope my people. A governing body must be elected or approved by most of our people, we have been doing business or commerce, for trillions of years and we always had elected or chosen officials, or appointed officials that represented the Kings, Sultans, Emperors and Queens at times; in the last six thousand years and all their people, that were under their leadership. My point my people and the world, is this! There have always been government and laws and people entrusted to carry out and monitor, that everything operated perfectly, for trillions and trillions of years. This was a fundamental procedure and way of life for us so having a governing body, for ourselves is perfect sense and logical thinking, my people. Us having laws, rules and regulations is what keep the government, the culture, harmony, the prosperity, the people and the wonderful enjoyments, flowing forever. There for we all must understand that Yakub's making stole this all from us and did everything in their power to deny and prevent us my people, from returning to our Original selves.

The fools amongst us that have gravitated to this mystery god teachings and through you may pretend that you didn't know, nevertheless you through in with the enemies' of our ancestors our proven and open enemies and history prove that what I am saying, is the truth they were our ancestors enemies and they are our enemies today, as it escalated in 1492 and our ancestors were brought here to the Far North in 1555 and this is a matter of history. Our Holy Deliverer has restored in us that which He Is. So, we may forgive our brothers and sisters and give them a chance to repent their mistakes and come home off cloud nine, where you belong because our Holy Savior Allah Almighty in the person of Master Fard Muhammad to whom, all holy praises are due forever; is Allah the Universal Master and Lord of all the Worlds. He is the Most Merciful, Most Forgiving, Most Wise, the Best Knower and the Most Kind. He is my people the Great Mahdi, Christ the Crusher the One that all scriptures speak about, the Son of Man, is Allah in the Holiest Person of Master Fard Muhammad, to whom all holy praises are due forever. The Most Honorable Elijah Muhammad is the last and greatest Messenger of Allah and the First Born From Amongst the Slain.

There are many issues amongst us my people we must iron out but there are millions of colored people that we are surrounded by, makes us the thirty percent dissatisfy. Therefore, we must have a more realistic approach that can and will impact us all my people and leaders, our duty is to make sure, it will be a one hundred percent positive impact, for us all my people. We must my people and ministers have a clear understanding of, what is meant by this statement by the Holy Messenger; "we must be fast moving and fast thinking, up to the modern day and time". What is most important is that we set up a governing body in every state, city and town, for us my people. Then we must set up a National Government all representatives must be qualify and agreed upon by the masses of their state, city or town, to be best qualified to represent, their people at the national level.

Implementing the three- year program or five -year program would be even better for us to invest, in ourselves and place ourselves back on the right path; that Allah has chosen for and what Allah's Holy Apostle taught us all. This should be in every state, city and town and then we will be able to create our own banking system because we are a Sovereign Nation with our own flag, so saith Allah Himself through the mouth of His Allah, last and greatest Messenger the Most Honorable Elijah Muhammad. We must my people take control over our own destiny so that we may never dishonor, our ancestors ever again. Our Ancestors weren't Americans they were the held captives of America and so are we my people are held captives, of American propaganda, advertisement, marketing and enforced by the American Gestapo called Law Enforcement Agencies and their military. We have my people been subjected to terrorism for the past five approximately five hundred years, by the greatest terrorist our planet has ever seen. This matriarchal society must be destroyed and never rise its evil and wicket head amongst us my people, ever again. It is Through Our Fathers Eyes my people in which we must search through. We don't need any approval from any of our enemies; we don't need any approval from any of our enemies' religions, politics customs, practices and their educational system. All we have received from our many enemies' religions and this include this so-called Sunnah Islam, is suffering, slavery and death. While our enemies are living well, their children are receiving better education than our children, eating better than us and our children because they have partnered up with the Zionist, Christian and Hindus; and agreed to keep us my people locked up in their made cage/prison of total despair and some make believe heaven after we die; this is all an absolute lie my people always have been and always will be, for us my people.

The only way my people we can free ourselves from these monsters is our swift return to our fathers and leave these other demons alone and their made up religious practices and their politics completely alone. If we continue to believe in our enemies made up religions and practice as they do, we will forever remain a slave waiting for some make believe heaven, after you die; with no chance, of escaping from out of their made cage for us my people, so we can enjoy heaven while we live. Look around you my people and see how your children are the ones dying and suffering; are you so silly and scared to stand up for your children to provide for them, a better life and conditions. Are you to much of a coward to stand up and demand to the world that our women are to be respected and protected? You are all concerned about our enemies' women and children being respected and protected and to hell with your own. Such cowards and that's exactly what they are should be put to death, for the cowardly traitors that they all are, to their people.

We my people forming a National, State, City and Town governing body is essential to the growth and development, of our people and our Sovereign Nation. We must choose the most qualify amongst us to represent us at the national level, as we set up the three to five years economical program, for us all. We must have vision my people and not egos and this is greater than any one person because we can project and forecast, our future; the future of our women and children. We will then begin to give our children purpose because they will be doing this for themselves. We all will be investing in ourselves and not other than ourselves. We will then be able my people to regain control of the educational system that will breath life, into our children and not death as this American educational system, has been breathing into our children for the past 100 years or so. We then will control our way of life with the absent, of interference from any of our enemies input. The knowledge, wisdom and understanding of our ancestors, will live again amongst us, our women and children and the world will know that we who were once dead, have been restored to life by Allah Almighty Himself, through the mouth of His Allah last and greatest Messenger. We have no use for any of our enemies' customs, religions, practices and their filthy politics, or their women. This supremely evil Integration has been the death of us my people. This fairy tale of Civil Rights is another supreme evil because we my people haven't received any Civil Rights, from our enemies. All our enemies have received this so-called Civil Rights, but we haven't received any of this American fairy tale, when it comes to us my people. If you aren't ready to stand up for ourselves seriously and do the proper things to organize for ourselves a National, a State, a City and Town governing body, this is a sign of dis grace and disbelief to Allah and Allah's Holy Messenger. Let he or she who has wisdom take heed to my words because these words come from Allah through the mouth, of Allah's Holy Messenger. It is Through Our Fathers Eyes is where our escape from the cage, our enemies have kept us all imprisoned in, for the last approximately five hundred years.

I point out several Caucasian People such as Alexander Hamilton. The Krupp and others are for purpose my people our ancestors knew how much of a demon these so-called, men of Honorable truly were and are. These writers that have written nothing but lies about them all, projecting them as noble men and women, when in truth they were all the vermin that crawl out the dungeons of England and Europe period. These TV shows and movies projecting them in such a manner of being noble and kind are nothing but lies, my people; especially these slave movies or pre-Civil War Era and during the Civil War Era, is as silly as Popeye, Mighty Mouse and the rest of this insanity, as my generation was subjected to this white washing and brain washing into believing; which was and still is White Supremacy and White Nationalism.

My people we must prepare ourselves to step up to the National Level, the State Level, the City Level and the Town Level and declare ourselves, to be a Sovereign Nation and people. The time has arrived my people that we must stand up for ourselves and stop this nonsense going on, in social media; which is getting us nothing at all except creating enemies, amongst ourselves. There is so much work for us to and we don't need anymore false teachers with egos, of self- importance. These egotistical false leaders and want to be false leaders, don't even have the capacity to bring anything of good, into a reality. They just believe in their own-selves that they can produce but their tract record will show something totally different. The time has come that we hold council amongst ourselves and we elect the best qualified to represent us my people at all levels and anyone that believes they are better qualified and should have such a post, without any tract record because of what their father did, we must get rid these and this mentality immediately, we have no use for them at all. It's Up You Mighty Nation You can Accomplish What you will As Salaam Alaikum.

ABOUT THE AUTHOR

I Saladin Shabazz-Allah was born in North Brooklyn by the water front and the Naval Yard in a section called Vinegar Hill. It was an illusion of my parents that they thought that life would be better in the North, rather than the South; they soon found out that these conditions only seem to appear different when in fact, they were even much worst. Now they had to deal with all different members of the Caucasian race and they all were happy to embrace America's Jim Crow Law and were happy to deprive our grandparents, our parents to be able to provide, for their families properly. None of the horrors of the South had gone away but they all still exist and when these monsters reveal themselves. They were completely shocked to find out that the conditions, were even much worst. My people you are acting like complete fools as you are walking, into death chambers of American society and don't know it.

No one from so-called Africa or the Arab League ever reached out to help us at all and none of them cared and they still don't care. We my people needed The Defender Of Truth teachings the teachings he, received from the most Wonderful Stranger; more than anyone else or more than anything else, in the world. We my people needed a Holy Saviour and Deliverer also a Great Redeemer because no one else cared about us at all. The Defender Of Truth was on his way before many of us were even born and he will be a Mighty Defender, in which we all needed. The suffering had no end; the torturing had no end; the misery had no end; the lies and deceit had no end, for us my people. We had labored in this Death Camp called America for hundreds of years and received nothing but hungriness, nakedness, out of doors and beaten and killed, by the ones who advocate this mystery god and their false religions.

I have experience first hand the unmerciful treatment from all our enemies; I have first hand experience the lies and deceit from our enemies; I have experience the hatred from our enemies; I have experience the falsehood of our enemies many religions and their politics. When you examine these false religions of our enemies, they all have the same basic principle of a mystery god that you can't see until we die; and this insanity of life and heaven after we die and us my people, believing and trusting in them. I have seen the many traitors that have jumped ship and joined on to and with our enemies, for very few pieces of silver. These traitors aren't never going to stand up for The Defender Of Truth and the Most Wonderful stranger, if they continue to collect their few pieces of silver. There are some whom call themselves so-called believers and believe they can tell me what I should do or shouldn't do, like they know what is happening and I know that they don't because they have taken these traitors into their mist and don't know the truth about these traitors, but I do know some of them and who they are.

I once again confess by total subsistence to The Defender Of Truth the Holy Messenger Of Allah, the Most Honorable Elijah Muhammad and to the Most Wonderful Stranger Allah in the person of Master Fard Muhammad to whom all holy praises are due forever. In Allah's Holy name and His Holy servant, The Defender Of Truth, I will continue to fight even if death, be my reward. The conditions were another set of murderous and treacherous conditions my parents and all black parents coming from the South, had to adjust to. Drive by shootings bombings, gangland slaying in which many times NYPD were the hitmen and were getting paid. We aren't talking about the beat cops we are talking about Captains Lieutenants, Sergeants and even up to the Commissioner office and City Hall, were all against our parents, grandparents and great grandparents, as they all were so thrilled to enforce this Dreadful Jim Crow Law. The low life filthy Europeans who was consider nothing but disgusting scum, was so happy and ready to jump on the American band wagon, of hating, depriving, rubbering, murdering black people and raping black women with impunity. There is no forgiveness for these crimes my people that the Caucasian race did to our people, in our very life time and this evil filthy Zionism and Christianity were the most brutal and hateful in fact these devils were either Zionist devils or Christian devils and they were ecstatic that they could vent their hatred on us my and

Federal, State, City and Local governments would support them and their evil towards our people and not one of these devils hesitate to join in with this unlawful law as they vented their hatred towards our grandparents, parents and even great grandparents, with impunity.

The educational system was filled with our lying enemies from the school principal on down to the custodians, all had nothing but hatred and content for us all and we were all children at this time. The educational system was completely under the control of the Zionist devils and the Irish devils ran the most corrupt police department on earth. The chances of us my people mounting to anything was dead in the waters because all these Zionist so-called educators were doing nothing but lying to us and feeding us nothing but false information and false facts. The physical abuse by these Caucasian devils was nothing but barbarism to black children, with impunity; this is the educational system I and my entire generation who were first generations born in New York after World War II. We were taught by the American that we didn't play any part, in the building and physical input in America reaching the heights that she has become; these are the lies we were taught in the educational system controlled and operated by the Zionist and Christians. It was either you bow down to our will or we will cast you down to a less, intelligent breed, of your people.

The most hurtful thing about it at that time I could fill this was all and completely wrong and rebelled against this evil, how much evil I would surely learn in very a short while. If not for The Mighty Defender Of Truth I wouldn't write about this today. How important all the programs, developments and growth in all fields of science and recognize by other and all societies and governments, as a Sovereign Nation of Black People belonging to Islam, through out the world and thrown away by rebellious, jealous, envious, ungrateful little boys; gave it all away to our enemies. So, the truth must be known to everyone my people, so I take great pride in what I am doing and forever grateful to The Most Wonderful and Most Merciful Stranger Allah in person of Master Fard Muhammad to whom all praises are due forever, that visited us. I am forever grateful of His Wonderful Gift to us all His Mighty Defender the Most Honorable Elijah Muhammad and I will never denounce either one of them.

BIBLIOGRAPHY

The Holy Messenger of Allah the Most Honorable Elijah Muhammad-Saviour's Day 1954, 1964, 1965, 1967. The Historic Buzz Anderson Interview, The History of the Nation Of Islam Documentary 1930-1970 Black Muslims At The Crossroads A 1964 Vintage Documentary. Saviors Day 1974 When The Sun Rises In The West. Saviour's Day 1973 A Saviour Is Born. Saviour's Day 1972 The Birth of a Redeemer. Saviour's Day 1971. 1965 Saviour's Day and 1964 At The 369th Armory. The Accomplishments of The Muslims and the NOI Parade. Lectures from 1959-1961 Muhammad Speaks Uline Arena Address At Washington D.C, At The Mosque Theatre Newark, New Jersey, At The Pittsburg Syria Mosque, The 369th Armory Harlem, New York, Messenger Muhammad Defends The Muslims. The Theology of Time Part I, 2, 3, 4 and 5 Message To The Black Man In America, How To Eat To Live Book One and Book Two, The Fall of America, Our Saviour has Arrived, The Genesis Years, The Theology Of Time, Muhammad Speaks Newspaper Original and the Pittsburg Carrier, The God Tribe of Shabazz The True History, Yakub The Father of Man-Kind, The Secrets of Freemasonry, Salaam Elijah Muhammad's Trip To Mecca, 100 Answers To The Most Uncommand 100 Questions, The Supreme Wisdom Solution to the so-called Negroes' Problem Part one and Part Two, The Time and The Judgement the Day When Self Tells The Truth On Self, Christianity VS Islam.

The Holy Qur'an by Maulana Muhammad Ali
The Meanings Of The Holy Qur'an By Maulana Abdullah Yusuf Ali
The Muslim Prayer Book By Maulana Muhammad Ali
The So-Called Holy Bible The King James Version
The Black Book By Harris/Levitt/ Furman/Smith

Black Justice In a White World By Judge Bruce Wright

The Destruction of Black Civilization Great Issues Of A Race From 4500 B.C. To 2000 A.D. By Dr. Professor Chancellor Williams

Before The Mayflower A history of Black America By Lerone Bennett JR.

They Came Before Columbus The African Presence In Ancient America By Ivan Van Sertima

Sex and Races Negro-Caucasian Mixing in All ages and All Lands Volume One, Two and Three By J.A. Rogers

World's Great Men Of Color Volume one and Volume two By J.A. Rogers

New Dimensions In African History By Dr. Yosef Ben-Jochannan and Dr. John Henrik Clarke

Christopher Columbus and the Afrikan Holocaust Slavery and the Rise of European Capitalism By Dr. John Henrik Clarke

The Myth Of Genesis And Exodus and the exclusion of their African Origins By Dr. Yosef A.A. ben-Jochannan

Cultural Genocide In The Black And African Studies Curriculum By Dr. Yosef ben-Jochannan

Black Man Of The Nile And His Family By Dr. Yosef A.A. ben-Jochannan

Feeling The Spirit Searching the World for the People of Africa By Chester Higgins JR.

The Creature from Jekyll Island By G. Edward Griffin

None Dare Call It Conspiracy By Gary Allen and Larry Abraham

The Arms of Krupp The Rise and Fall of the Industrial Dynasty That Armed Germany at War By William Manchester

Alexander Hamilton By Ron Chernow the Author of Titan and The House of Morgan

The Secrets of The Federal Reserve By Eustace Mullins

The Secret Relationship Between Blacks and Jews By The Nation Of Islam

One Nation Underprivileged Why American Poverty Affects Us All By Mark Robert Rank

The Synagogue of Satan 1878 to 2006 By Hitch Andrew Carrington

The Money Masters is a film produce in Documentary Fashion

2014 3rd Edition of Loose Change is another film produce in Documentary Fashion

ABOUT THE AUTHOR
MR. SALADIN SHABAZZ-ALLAH

Born September 27, 1951 in Brooklyn New York. I have lived through very violent and evil times, but todays times are purely diabolical. Raised under the Jim Crow Act where dark people were deprived of owner ship, education, inspiration and self-importance. This is clearly seen today where black lives, mean absolutely nothing amongst themselves.

The truth of this melt down is never address by religion, politics or any other means. The entire world population or at least ninety percent, is kept deft dumb and blind. Living according to some religious document that keeps the mass of people, suffering, slavery and eventually death. I have chosen to tell the truth and name the culprits behind this and how religions ae use as weapon against the world population.

I am not out to please any one group, organization or religion I am speaking and telling the truth. If anyone is offended by what I am saying I don't care because this truth must and will be told.

Printed in the United States
By Bookmasters